Current Controversies in Philosophy of Memory

The surge of philosophical interest in episodic memory has brought to light a number of controversial questions about this form of memory that have only recently begun to be addressed in detail. This book organises discussion around six such questions, offering two new chapters per question, from experts in the field. The questions are:

I. What is the relationship between memory and imagination?
II. Do memory traces have content?
III. What is the nature of mnemonic confabulation?
IV. What is the function of episodic memory?
V. Do non-human animals have episodic memory?
VI. Does episodic memory give us knowledge of the past?

The book constitutes a valuable resource for researchers, teachers, and students alike. For researchers, it provides an up-to-date discussion of some of the main theories, arguments, and problems in the area. For teachers, the book can supply the readings for an entire course, or particular sections can provide the readings for specific units within a broader philosophy of memory course. For students, the book offers accessible discussions of some of the most recent topics in the philosophy of memory, which, when taken together, serve as a well-rounded introduction to the area.

André Sant'Anna is a McDonnell Postdoctoral Fellow in the Department of Philosophy and the Philosophy-Neuroscience-Psychology Program at Washington University in St. Louis.

Christopher Jude McCarroll is Assistant Professor of Philosophy at the Institute of Philosophy of Mind and Cognition, National Yang Ming Chiao Tung University.

Kourken Michaelian is Professor of Philosophy at the Université Grenoble Alpes, where he directs the Centre for Philosophy of Memory, and is a senior member of the Institut Universitaire de France.

Current Controversies in Philosophy
Series Editor: John Turri
University of Waterloo

In venerable Socratic fashion, philosophy proceeds best through reasoned conversation. Current Controversies in Philosophy provides short, accessible volumes that cast a spotlight on ongoing central philosophical conversations. In each book, pairs of experts debate four or five key issues of contemporary concern, setting the stage for students, teachers and researchers to join the discussion. Short chapter descriptions precede each chapter, and an annotated bibliography and suggestions for further reading conclude each controversy. In addition, each volume includes both a general introduction and a supplemental guide to further controversies. Combining timely debates with useful pedagogical aids allows the volumes to serve as clear and detailed snapshots, for all levels of readers, of some the most exciting work happening in philosophy today.

Published Volumes in the Series:

Current Controversies in Values and Science
Edited by Kevin C. Elliott and Daniel Steel

Current Controversies in Philosophy of Religion
Edited by Paul Draper

Current Controversies in Philosophy of Cognitive Science
Edited by Adam J. Lerner, Simon Cullen, and Sarah-Jane Leslie

Current Controversies in Philosophy of Science
Edited by Shamik Dasgupta, Ravit Dotan, and Brad Weslake

Current Controversies in Philosophy of Memory
Edited by André Sant'Anna, Christopher Jude McCarroll, and Kourken Michaelian

For more information about this series, please visit: https://www.routledge.com/Current-Controversies-in-Philosophy/book-series/CCIP

Current Controversies in Philosophy of Memory

Edited by André Sant'Anna,
Christopher Jude McCarroll, and
Kourken Michaelian

Routledge
Taylor & Francis Group

NEW YORK AND LONDON

First published 2023
by Routledge
605 Third Avenue, New York, NY 10158

and by Routledge
4 Park Square, Milton Park, Abingdon, Oxon, OX14 4RN

Routledge is an imprint of the Taylor & Francis Group, an informa business

Library of Congress Cataloging-in-Publication Data
A catalog record for this title has been requested

ISBN: 978-0-367-43275-1 (hbk)
ISBN: 978-0-367-43279-9 (pbk)
ISBN: 978-1-003-00227-7 (ebk)

DOI: 10.4324/9781003002277

Typeset in Bembo
by SPi Technologies India Pvt Ltd (Straive)

CV 09.21.2022 0122

Contents

Notes on Contributors   viii

**Current controversies in philosophy of memory: Editors'
introduction**   1
ANDRÉ SANT'ANNA, CHRISTOPHER JUDE MCCARROLL, AND
KOURKEN MICHAELIAN

PART I
**What is the relationship between memory
and imagination?**   17

1 **Remembering, imagining, and memory traces: Toward a
   continuist causal theory**   19
   PETER LANGLAND-HASSAN

2 **The relation between memory and imagination: A debate
   about the right concepts**   38
   CÉSAR SCHIRMER DOS SANTOS, CHRISTOPHER JUDE
   MCCARROLL, AND ANDRÉ SANT'ANNA

   Further Readings for Part I 57
   Study Questions for Part I 58

PART II
Do memory traces have content?   59

3 **Remembering without a trace? Moving beyond trace
   minimalism**   61
   DANIEL D. HUTTO

4 **Distributed traces and the causal theory of constructive memory**   82
   JOHN SUTTON AND GERARD O'BRIEN

   Further Readings for Part II 105
   Study Questions for Part II 106

PART III
What is the nature of mnemonic confabulation?   **107**

5 **An explanationist model of (false) memory**   109
   SVEN BERNECKER

6 **Towards a virtue-theoretic account of confabulation**   127
   KOURKEN MICHAELIAN

   Further Readings for Part III 145
   Study Questions for Part III 146

PART IV
What is the function of episodic memory?   **147**

7 **Episodic memory: And what is it for?**   149
   JOHANNES B. MAHR

8 **Episodic memory is not for the future**   166
   SARAH K. ROBINS

   Further Readings for Part IV 185
   Study Questions for Part IV 186

PART V
Do non-human animals have episodic memory?   **187**

9 **Episodic memory in animals: Optimism, kind scepticism and pluralism**   189
   ALEXANDRIA BOYLE

10 **What does it take to remember episodically?**   206
    NAZIM KEVEN

    Further Readings for Part V 223
    Study Questions for Part V 224

PART VI
Does episodic memory give us knowledge of the past? 225

11 **The epistemology of episodic memory** 227
THOMAS D. SENOR

12 **You don't know what happened** 244
MATTHEW FRISE

Further Readings for Part VI 259
Study Questions for Part VI 260

Index 261

Contributors

Sven Bernecker is Humboldt Professor of Philosophy at the University of Cologne and Professor of Philosophy at the University of California, Irvine. His main areas of research are epistemology, metaphysics, and philosophy of mind, and he has published numerous articles in these areas. He is the author of *Reading Epistemology* (2006), *The Metaphysics of Memory* (2008), and *Memory* (2010). He is co-editor of *Knowledge* (2000), *The Routledge Companion to Epistemology* (2011), *Handbook of Philosophy of Memory* (2017), "Medical Knowledge in a Social World" (*Synthese* 196, 2019), and *Kant and Contemporary Epistemology* (History of Philosophy & Logical Analysis, special issue).

Alexandria Boyle is Research Fellow in Kinds of Intelligence at the University of Cambridge and the University of Bonn. She specialises in the philosophy of mind and cognitive science, looking in particular at questions about non-human minds and the methods used to study them. Her current research focusses on episodic memory in nonhuman animals and artificial agents. She has also written on self-awareness, self-recognition and mindreading in non-humans, and more general methodological issues in the study of animal minds.

Matthew Frise is a lecturer at Santa Clara University. His work draws from cognitive psychology to help us understand better the normative significance of reconstruction in human memory. His research has appeared in such journals as *Philosophy and Phenomenological Research*, *Philosophical Studies*, *The Philosophical Quarterly*, *Synthese*, *American Philosophical Quarterly*, *Pacific Philosophical Quarterly*, and *Erkenntnis*. He is writing a book on the epistemology of memory with Cambridge University Press.

Daniel D. Hutto is Senior Professor of Philosophical Psychology and Head of the School of Liberal Arts at the University of Wollongong. He is co-author of the award-winning *Radicalizing Enactivism* (2013) and its sequel, *Evolving Enactivism* (2017). His other books include: *Folk Psychological Narratives* (2008) and *Wittgenstein and the End of Philosophy* (2006). He is editor of *Narrative and Understanding Persons* (2007) and *Narrative and Folk Psychology*

(2009). A special yearbook, *Radical Enactivism*, focusing on his philosophy of intentionality, phenomenology and narrative, was published in 2006.

Nazım Keven is Assistant Professor of Philosophy at Bilkent University in Turkey. He received the Science Academy, Turkey's Young Scientist Award BAGEP in 2020. His main area of research is in philosophy of cognitive science, with a particular focus on memory, narratives, and human sociality. His work is published in *Behavioral and Brain Sciences*, *Synthese*, *Neuropsychologia* and *Hippocampus*.

Peter Langland-Hassan is Associate Professor of Philosophy at the University of Cincinnati. He is the author of *Explaining Imagination* (2020) and of numerous articles on topics including inner speech, memory, imagination, pretense, delusions, and the relation between language and abstract thought.

Johannes B. Mahr is a postdoctoral fellow in the Department of Psychology at Harvard University funded by a Walter Benjamin Fellowship from the German Research Foundation. Before that, he was a mind, brain, and behaviour fellow with a joint appointment in the Departments of Philosophy and Psychology at Harvard. His work combines philosophical and empirical approaches to study episodic memory, imagination, and human communication.

Christopher Jude McCarroll is Assistant Professor of Philosophy at the Institute of Philosophy of Mind and Cognition, National Yang Ming Chiao Tung University. He is also an affiliated member of the Centre for Philosophy of Memory at the Université Grenoble Alpes. His research interests are in philosophy of mind, especially philosophy of memory. He has a particular interest in visual perspective in the imagery of episodic memory and imagination, with which he investigates issues such as the reconstructive nature of episodic memory, the relation between memory and identity, and the relation between episodic prospection and self-control.

Kourken Michaelian is a professor of philosophy at the Université Grenoble Alpes, where he directs the Centre for Philosophy of Memory, and a senior member of the Institut Universitaire de France. He is the author of *Mental Time Travel: Episodic Memory and Our Knowledge of the Personal Past* (2016) and many articles on the simulation theory of memory and coeditor of volumes, including *Seeing the Future: Theoretical Perspectives on Future-Oriented Mental Time Travel* (2016), *The Routledge Handbook of Philosophy of Memory* (2017) and *New Directions in the Philosophy of Memory* (2018).

Gerard O'Brien is Professor in the Department of Philosophy at the University of Adelaide, Australia. He specialises in neurocomputational models of cognition, consciousness and mental representation. He also has a subsidiary interest in naturalised approaches to ethics and values.

Sarah K. Robins is Associate Professor of Philosophy at the University of Kansas. Her research is centred on memory, with a focus on the role of memory traces in philosophical, psychological, and neuroscientific approaches to remembering.

André Sant'Anna is a McDonnell Postdoctoral Fellow in the Department of Philosophy and the Philosophy-Neuroscience-Psychology Program at Washington University in St. Louis. He is also an affiliated member of the Centre for Philosophy of Memory at the Université Grenoble Alpes. His research interests are in philosophy of mind and philosophy of psychology, with a particular focus on the nature of episodic memory and its relationship to perception and imagination.

Thomas D. Senor is Professor of Philosophy at the University of Arkansas and editor of the journal *Faith and Philosophy*. He is the author of *Critical Introduction to the Epistemology of Memory* (2019) and numerous papers in epistemology and philosophy of religion. Professor Senor taught in St. Petersburg, Russia, in 2003 on as a Fulbright Senior Scholar and was the Alvin Plantinga Fellow at the Center for Philosophy of Religion at the University of Notre Dame in 2014–15.

César Schirmer dos Santos is Associate Professor at the Federal University of Santa Maria, where he directs the Philosophy of Memory Lab (MemLab-UFSM). His research focuses on the metaphysics of memory, studying the relationship between memory, imagination, and the past.

John Sutton is Emeritus Professor of Philosophy and Cognitive Science at Macquarie University, Sydney, Australia. His research addresses distributed cognition, memory, skill, and cognitive history. A volume co-edited with Kath Bicknell, *Collaborative Embodied Performance: Ecologies of Skill*, will appear in 2022. Sutton's recent papers address cognitive archaeology, expert performance in live music and dance, collaborative recall, and embodied cognition in the Māori haka.

Current controversies in philosophy of memory

Editors' introduction

André Sant'Anna, Christopher Jude McCarroll, and Kourken Michaelian

I.1 Introduction

'If philosophy begins with wonder', Edward Furlong tells us, 'then the philosophy of memory should have made a good beginning'. The reason, he continues, is that memory 'offers many topics to draw our attention and whet our curiosity' (1951: 1). Given the range of topics of philosophical interest that fall under the heading of memory, it should perhaps come as no surprise that memory has been an increasingly prominent theme over the last few years in philosophy, a period during which the philosophy of memory has established itself as a distinct field of research (Bernecker & Michaelian 2017; Michaelian, Debus, & Perrin 2018). Memory is a theme that a growing community of philosophers has been wondering over and puzzling about.

The philosophy of memory deals both with questions that were already discussed in older historical works and, driven in part by the influence of neighbouring disciplines—including the psychology and neuroscience of memory—with a range of newer questions. Some of these are ethical or political in character. Do we have a duty to remember the past? How do the ways in which we remember past historical events shape our conception of the world today? But most questions are metaphysical or epistemological in character. How many types of memory are there? What is the nature of the conscious experience of remembering? How does memory give us knowledge of the past? These and related questions are the focus of ongoing controversy among philosophers of memory.

A distinctive feature of recent philosophy of memory has been its close engagement with empirical disciplines, such as psychology and neuroscience, which have memory among their objects of study. Results from these fields have been put to work in addressing various issues pertaining to the metaphysics and epistemology of memory, and, perhaps in consequence, *episodic memory*—memory for the events of the personal past (Tulving 1985)—has come to be the focus of most research in philosophy of memory. When one remembers the first time that one visited Grenoble, or when one remembers one's college graduation ceremony, one remembers episodically. Such memories come with a rich phenomenology, involving both quasi-sensory features, such as 'seeing' the mountain

DOI: 10.4324/9781003002277-1

ranges that surround Grenoble 'in the mind's eye', and self-involving and temporal features, such as one's awareness of one's graduation ceremony as something that one *oneself* experienced in *the past*. Understood along these lines,
episodic memory contrasts with semantic memory, which refers to memory for
facts (Tulving 1972, 1985). When one remembers that Wellington is the capital
of New Zealand or that Pedro Álvares Cabral was the first European to reach
Brazil, one remembers semantically. Because semantic memory is solely concerned with facts, it lacks the rich phenomenology characteristic of episodic
memory.[1]

Another consequence of the close interaction between philosophy and the
empirical sciences of memory has been the widespread recognition, in philosophy, of the constructive nature of episodic memory (Bartlett, 1932; Sutton
1998; Schacter et al. 2012), as well as the tight connection between remembering and other imaginative processes (Michaelian 2016b; Addis 2020). Empirical
evidence has demonstrated that remembering is an active process that draws on
various sources of information to construct representations of the past. What
one now knows or feels, for example, can affect how one remembers a past
event. Due to its constructive character, memory is prone to systematic errors.
Yet what may seem like a negative or problematic aspect of memory—its prone-
ness to error—has, in a distinct but related line of research, been construed in a
different way: though construction in remembering often results in mistakes or
misrepresentations of past events, its role may nevertheless be positive on the
whole, in the sense that it allows information to be flexibly recombined so as to
enable simulations of counterfactual past events and possible future events (De
Brigard 2014). The constructive nature of remembering is thought to be a result
of the tight connection between different forms of episodic imagination. The
philosophy of memory today takes constructive remembering as an accepted
starting point and the relationship between remembering and other imaginative
processes as an issue for debate.

The surge of philosophical interest in episodic memory has brought to light
a number of controversial questions about that form of memory that have only
recently begun to be addressed in detail. Taking recent research as its starting
point, this book brings together discussions of six such questions by experts in
the field. The book's focus on episodic memory is justified by two factors. First
and foremost, it reflects the focus of most current work in the philosophy of
memory on episodic memory. Second, given that recent volumes, such as *The
Routledge Handbook of Philosophy of Memory* (Bernecker & Michaelian 2017) and
New Directions in the Philosophy of Memory (Michaelian, Debus, & Perrin 2018),
discuss questions concerning other types of memory, there was a need for a
volume focussing exclusively on episodic memory.

The relationship between this and other recent volumes also played a role in
our selection of particular controversies for inclusion in the book. Given that
other volumes do discuss episodic memory, we have avoided overlap where
possible, giving priority to controversies not discussed elsewhere. While we
believe that our selection reflects some of the main topics driving research in

contemporary philosophy of memory, we emphatically do not intend it to be an exhaustive list of topics that figure in the rich work currently being done by philosophers of memory. Rather, we hope that, by highlighting particular controversies, the book will help to promote and consolidate research on some of the most exciting topics in the field.

I.2 The book

The book is divided into six parts, each including two contributions responding to the same controversial question about episodic memory. The two contributions in each part offer different perspectives on the question, providing the reader with the means to come to a balanced assessment of the controversy. We expect the book to constitute a valuable resource for researchers, teachers, and students alike. For researchers, it provides an up-to-date discussion of some of the main theories, arguments, and problems in the area. For teachers, the book can provide the readings for an entire course, or particular sections can provide the readings for specific units within a broader philosophy of memory course. For students, the book offers accessible discussions of some of the most recent topics in the philosophy of memory, which, when taken together, serve as a well-rounded introduction to the area. Moreover, each part contains a list of further readings and a list of questions for further study designed to supplement the chapters.

I.3 The controversies

The six controversies discussed in the book are the following.

Part I: What is the relationship between memory and imagination?
Part II: Do memory traces have content?
Part III: What is the nature of mnemonic confabulation?
Part IV: What is the function of episodic memory?
Part V: Do non-human animals have episodic memory?
Part VI: Does episodic memory give us knowledge of the past?

In this section, we briefly introduce these controversies and provide a summary of each part of the book.

I.3.1 Part I: What is the relationship between memory and imagination?

The ongoing controversy between the causal theory of memory (Martin & Deutscher 1966; Bernecker 2010), on which remembering necessarily involves an appropriate causal connection to the remembered event, and the simulation theory of memory (Michaelian 2016b, 2021), on which remembering is a kind of imagining and therefore does not necessarily involve a causal connection to the remembered event, has triggered a controversy between discontinuists and continuists about the relationship between episodic memory and forms of imagination such as episodic future thought (Perrin & Michaelian 2017; Michaelian, Perrin & Sant'Anna 2020). On the one hand, discontinuists (e.g., Debus 2014; Perrin 2016; Robins 2020) maintain that, while there may be important similarities between remembering the past and imagining the future—such as the fact that both processes depend on a common brain system—there are fundamental metaphysical or epistemological differences between them. On the other hand, continuists (e.g., Addis 2020; Michaelian 2016a) maintain that, while there may be interesting differences between remembering the past and imagining the future—such as the fact that certain parts of the brain system on which they both depend may be more or less active in one or the other process—there is no fundamental metaphysical or epistemological difference between them.

Discontinuism, at least at first glance, would seem to align with the causal theory. Because causalism treats remembering as necessarily involving an appropriate causal connection to the remembered event, whereas imagination does not necessarily involve a causal connection to the imagined event, and because the presence or absence of a causal connection might naturally be thought to have important metaphysical and epistemological consequences, it is natural to suppose that causalists must be committed to discontinuism. By the same token, continuism would seem to align naturally with the simulation theory. Recent work, however, has tended to call these alignments into question, with some authors arguing that the continuism–discontinuism debate ought, strictly speaking, to be treated as distinct from the causalism–simulationism debate (e.g., Langland-Hassan 2021; Sant'Anna 2021). Both Langland-Hassan's chapter and Schirmer dos Santos, McCarroll, and Sant'Anna's chapter in this volume exemplify this tendency.

Beginning by pointing out that both continuists and discontinuists have failed to give an adequate description of the particular form of imagination with which episodic memory might or might not be continuous, **Langland-Hassan** argues that the form of imagination in question is best understood as what philosophers of imagination have referred to as 'constructive imagination'. He then suggests that the continuism–discontinuism debate can be resolved by determining whether the traces that are involved in remembering impose constraints on remembering in virtue of which it cannot qualify as a kind of constructive imagination. After setting out two incompatible conceptions of traces, the 'prop theory' and the 'replay theory', he argues that the prop theory tends to support continuism and the replay theory to support discontinuism. While he does not think that the available empirical evidence settles things in favour of one or the other of these conceptions—and so in favour of either continuism or discontinuism—he goes on to suggest that it may be possible to formulate a continuist version of the causal theory that combines the prop theorist's conception of traces with the causalist's understanding of remembering as necessarily involving appropriate causation.[2]

Taking a different tack, **Schirmer dos Santos, McCarroll, and Sant'Anna** argue that causalists and simulationists may simply be working with different concepts of memory, so that they end up talking past each other. They do not, however, mean to suggest that the causalist–simulationist debate is merely verbal, for we are entitled to ask which concept of memory we ought to employ. They thus suggest that the causalist–simulationist debate be reinterpreted as a debate about which concept of memory we should employ—that it be understood, in other words, as concerning a normative question, rather than a descriptive question: causalists, they claim, prescribe a concept of memory on which it necessarily involves appropriate causation, whereas simulationists prescribe a concept of memory on which it does not necessarily involve causation. They go on to argue that if this understanding of the causalist–simulationist debate is right, then the continuist–discontinuist debate need not be understood as concerning the necessity of appropriate causation: it can, instead, be understood as concerning the attitudes that characterise remembering and imagining.

I.3.2 Part II: Do memory traces have content?

Memory traces figure centrally in most current philosophical theories of remembering.[3] The causal theory of memory (Bernecker 2010), which treats appropriate causation as the defining feature of genuine remembering, sees them as making the difference between an appropriate and an inappropriate causal connection between an apparent memory and the corresponding apparently remembered event. Only if the causal connection between the apparent memory and the apparently remembered event is sustained by a memory trace is the apparent memory a genuine memory—otherwise, the apparent memory is merely apparent. Consider, for example, a case of relearning in which the subject experiences an event, tells a friend about it, completely forgets about it, is told about the event by his friend, completely forgets being told about it, and then apparently remembers it on the basis of what his friend told him (Martin & Deutscher 1966). There is, in this case, a causal connection between the apparent memory and the event, but, according to the causal theory, the subject does not—given that the trace of his experience of the event is lost and therefore does not contribute to his apparent memory of it—genuinely remember the event. The simulation theory of memory (Michaelian 2016b), which holds that remembering is a matter of reliably imagining the past, disagrees with the causal theory in that it denies that appropriate causation is necessary for genuine remembering but agrees with the causal theory in that it accepts that remembering centrally involves traces. On the one hand, simulationists maintain that relearning can, if the process that produces the apparent memory is reliable, amount to remembering. On the other hand, they assume that the kind of imagination that is at work when we remember itself draws on traces: there is no requirement, according to simulationism, that a genuine memory derive from a trace originating in the subject's experience of the remembered event, but traces nevertheless provide the raw materials for our imaginings, both when we are imagining the future and when we are imagining (that is, remembering) the past.

There is thus a broad consensus on the importance of traces to a philosophical account of memory. Despite this consensus, traces have been and continue to be controversial. Whereas older controversies tended to concern the very existence of traces (Sutton 1998), current controversies tend to focus on their nature. One current controversy concerns the format of traces, with some treating traces as local entities, while others conceive of them as being distributed (Robins 2016a). Another current controversy concerns the content of traces: there is increasing tendency, among both causalists (Perrin 2018; Werning 2020) and simulationists (Michaelian & Sant'Anna 2021), to see traces as being contentless in character. It is in this controversy that Hutto's and Sutton and O'Brien's chapters intervene.

Noting that there is an increasing tendency to treat traces as contentless, **Hutto**, building on the radical enactivist approach to cognition that he has defended elsewhere (Hutto & Myin 2012, 2017), argues that, rather than seeing traces as contentless, we should go one step further, abandoning any reference to traces in our theories of remembering. The basic strategy of Hutto's argument is straightforward. He begins by pointing out that any account of the nature of traces on which they have representational content faces the 'hard problem of content', the challenge of providing a naturalistically respectable theory of content, a challenge that, he argues, likely cannot be overcome. He then singles out Werning's (2020) trace minimalism, a causalist approach that he sees as the most detailed effort to date to provide an account of traces on which they involve only noncontentful information, and argues that even this account does not avoid the hard problem of content. He therefore concludes that we should leave traces behind entirely, focussing instead on developing an enactivist approach on which remembering does not involve even minimal traces, an approach that, he suggests, aligns naturally with simulationism.

Though **Sutton and O'Brien** are sensitive to the kinds of considerations that drive Hutto's argument, they are more optimistic about the prospects of both the causal theory and the idea of contentful memory traces. In earlier work inspired by the connectionist approach to cognition, Sutton and O'Brien argued for a distributed conception of memory traces. Here, they respond to recent charges that the distributed conception of traces is incompatible with the causal theory (e.g., Robins 2016a) and leads inevitably to a contentless conception (see Michaelian & Sant'Anna 2021), seeking to combine an account of traces as distributed but contentful with an updated version of the causal theory designed to take research on the reconstructive character of remembering into account. They begin by setting out a general account of content for distributed representations and applying it to the particular case of memory. They then argue that the resulting account of traces as distributed but contentful is compatible with the causal theory of constructive memory, responding to worries that distributed traces are ill-suited to account for the transmission of content from experience to retrieval and that distributed traces are unable to underwrite the sort of unique causal history that is required by the notion of appropriate causation. While they are confident that their account of traces can overcome the former worry, they acknowledge that more work needs to be done in order to show that causalists who employ a distributed conception of traces can provide a satisfactory account of appropriate causation. Providing such an account will be an important challenge for causalists going forward.

I.3.3   Part III: What is the nature of mnemonic confabulation?

Questions about the relation between memory and imagination, and whether remembering necessarily involves contentful memory traces, speak to the issue of what is at stake in successful remembering. They tell us about the conditions that must be satisfied for genuine memory. Yet a different way of approaching and enriching the debate is to focus on the ways in which remembering can go wrong (Robins 2016b). Accounting for errors in memory may shine a light on the nature of remembering and guide our theorising about episodic memory more generally. In this sense, the question of the nature of mnemonic confabulation is a crucial one (Bernecker 2017; Michaelian 2020).

In his contribution, **Bernecker** suggests that the current debate about the nature of mnemonic confabulation has reached an impasse. Mirroring the debate about the nature of the relation between memory and imagination, theorising about mnemonic confabulation is primarily articulated in terms of the causal theory of memory (causalism) or the simulation theory of memory (simulationism).[4] In these terms, the question of mnemonic confabulation becomes the question of whether confabulation is best explained by the absence of an appropriate causal connection or an unreliable process. Bernecker points to structural issues with the debate as framed in this way. He outlines a dual-faceted problem that the current dispute faces. The first issue, according to Bernecker, is what he calls the *bootstrapping problem*. The worry here is that there is an inherent circularity to the debate as it stands. The criteria used to determine whether a given case qualifies as mnemonic confabulation rely on the very theory of confabulation that the case is supposed to provide evidence for. The second worry is what Bernecker calls the *red herring problem*: because accounts of confabulation are derivative of accounts of (successful) memory, the debate about confabulation is really just a proxy battle between the two leading accounts of memory—causalism and simulationism. For Bernecker, once the controversy between causalism and simulationism about memory is resolved, the debate about confabulation will also be resolved.

Bernecker then proposes a new way of framing the debate, which, he claims, breaks the causalist–simulationist stalemate. He proposes an explanationist account of memory. On this view, a subject's truly representing that P via the memory system in the given circumstances qualifies as remembering if it is better explained by the fact that P itself, than by some statement referencing coincidental factors. For Bernecker, causalism and simulationism are distinct ways of fleshing out the explanation relation constitutive of remembering, and hence the explanationist model can uncover issues that lie at the core of the dispute and reconcile rival causalist and simulationist intuitions.

Building on his previous work on the simulation theory of memory (Michaelian 2016b), **Michaelian** outlines a very different way of thinking about the nature of mnemonic confabulation—one that directly challenges existing accounts and explanations of the phenomenon. Motivated to adopt a naturalistic approach and align his account with empirical evidence, Michaelian begins by introducing two key features of confabulations. First, even though he leaves room for veridical confabulation, Michaelian observes that confabulations are typically false. Second, Michaelian notes that confabulations are not restricted to remembering but can also occur when imagining the future. Michaelian then proceeds to review extant philosophical theories of confabulation—false belief, causalist, simulationist, epistemic, and explanationist accounts—and articulates problems for each view. Of particular relevance here is how he tackles Bernecker's explanationist model. According to Michaelian, the apparent circularity found in the bootstrapping problem is illusory because the empirical sciences offer us independent evidence of the types of phenomena that an adequate account of confabulation must cover: causalists and simulationists must then offer competing accounts of these phenomena. Addressing the red herring problem, Michaelian recognises that a theory of remembering does amount to an account of successful remembering, while denying that it determines an account of memory error. He then suggests that a given account of memory error may rule out particular versions of a theory of remembering. Far from being a proxy battle, Michaelian suggests, the confabulation debate affords progress in the ongoing dispute between causalism and simulationism.

With the existing accounts of confabulation each facing problems, Michaelian argues in favour of his own virtue-theoretic version of the simulationist classification of memory error. This approach introduces an *accuracy-because-reliability* condition, which requires that, in successful remembering, an apparent memory be accurate *because* it was produced by a reliable process. On this view, it is important to recognise the dual-layered role that luck can play in errors and confabulation. Falsidical confabulation occurs when the accuracy and reliability conditions are not satisfied and the inaccuracy-because-unreliability condition is satisfied. Veridical confabulation occurs when the accuracy condition is satisfied and the reliability condition is not satisfied. In the end, for Michaelian, confabulation is classed as a clinical error, distinct from cases of mere false memory and misremembering, and an error that can also be future-oriented.

I.3.4 Part IV: What is the function of episodic memory?

What is episodic memory for? This question lies at the heart of the inquiry into the function of episodic memory. Yet, the question partially obscures an important ambiguity in the notion of function (Schwartz 2020). The function of a mental state or process can be understood in at least two important ways: etiological function (Millikan 1984), or causal role function (Cummins 1975). Determining episodic memory's etiological function involves adopting a teleological perspective, which is concerned with the features and factors that led to its selection and retention in evolution (Suddendorf & Corballis 1997). In describing episodic memory's causal role function, we want to understand its role in the cognitive economy of the subject, as one component in a broader system (Schacter 2012). These two perspectives may be related in interesting ways, but they are separate questions. Articulating their views about the function of episodic memory, the two authors in this section each employ a different sense of function.

Why do we remember the past in the way we do? And why does remembering play such a prominent role in our lives and relationships? **Mahr** describes a theory of remembering that provides answers to these questions. Adopting an etiological perspective on the function of episodic memory, Mahr provides an account of why episodic memory has been selected to have the features it has in contemporary human adults. To arrive at a view of the evolutionary function of episodic memory, Mahr employs form-to-function reasoning. In evolutionary biology, we can make inferences from phenotypic form to evolutionary function (Cosmides & Tooby 1997). For example, we can look the shape and size of an animal's teeth and make an inference as to their evolutionary function or what they were selected for (e.g., eating meat). Mahr employs a similar methodology, accounting for the evolutionary function of episodic memory based on the form it has.

What is the form of episodic memory? To answer this question, Mahr first distinguishes between *memory*, understood as a diachronic capacity to store information, and *remembering*, understood as a synchronic capacity to construct representations of certain kinds of events. The latter is crucial to Mahr's project: in order to understand the function of episodic memory, we need to understand what it means to remember. The relevant features upon which to infer an etiological functional account of episodic memory are the features of the episodic memory representation. According to Mahr, episodic memory representations are about particular, past, actual, and personal events. In addition to this, episodic memories are metarepresentational: they represent that they were caused by one's past experience of the event. By explaining how these features of episodic memory representations might have been selected for, Mahr arrives at an account of the function of episodic memory. He rejects the idea that the function of episodic memory is purely preservative—that it is (merely) for accurately representing the past. He also distances himself from the idea that the function of episodic memory is to imagine the future. Instead, Mahr proposes that episodic memory serves a communicative function: episodic memory allows us to track and claim epistemic authority about the past. Indeed, this epistemic authority, Mahr shows, has social benefits, enabling individuals to influence what others take to be the case in the present social world (e.g., in eyewitness testimony). Mahr's account hence shows the rich ways in which remembering is stitched into the texture of our social world.

In her contribution, **Robins** explores the striking claim that the function of episodic memory is not to remember the past but to imagine the future. Focussing on the Constructive Episodic Simulation Hypothesis (CESH) (e.g., Schacter & Addis 2007), Robins argues that the evidence for this hypothesis does not establish a future-oriented function of episodic memory. Robins demonstrates that when CESH theorists talk about the prospective function of episodic memory, they have in mind the causal role sense of function: they are concerned with how episodic memory works, and what role it plays in a larger system. The CESH claim about episodic memory's future function has two steps: first, that the process of construction is the same for all forms of episodic simulation; and second, that future-oriented episodic thinking is the primary activity of the neurocognitive system responsible for constructive episodic simulation. Robins tackles the first step of the move. She delineates three pivotal claims of the CESH, in which episodic remembering and imagining are (1) subserved by the same brain system, (2) act on the same information, and (3) are governed by the same rules of operation. Robins discusses each criterion and evaluates their relevance for determining the causal-role function of episodic memory.

Assessing the first claim, Robins notes that sharing a brain system is not sufficient for sharing a function. There are many examples of different cognitive functions (e.g., language processing and musical appreciation) sharing an underlying mechanism or brain region, and it may even be the case that neural systems are multifunctional. Considering the second claim, Robins provides examples of different cognitive activities with different functional profiles that nonetheless share an information base. For Robins, it is the third criterion—shared operations—that best speaks to questions of function. What is this shared operation between remembering and imagining? It is the notion that both involve processes that are constructive. Robins grants that both remembering and imagining involve construction, but argues that this is not sufficient to warrant claims about functional parity. The claim about construction, Robins observes, is typically cashed out in terms of associationist networks. But, as Robins shows, this associative characterisation of construction proves problematic in different ways for remembering and imagining. Indeed, for Robins, remembering and imagining are constructive in importantly different ways, with differences manifesting between the two in awareness of construction, control over construction, and response to error discovery. The function of episodic memory is not, Robins concludes, for the future.

I.3.5 Part V: Do non-human animals have episodic memory?

The question of whether non-human animals have episodic memory is a central one for both the philosophy and the psychology of memory. It has important implications for how we approach other controversial questions in those areas, such as whether memory and imagination are of the same kind (Part I) and what the function of episodic memory is (Part IV). Despite its theoretical importance, there is little agreement as to how the question should be tackled. On the one hand, those who favour a negative answer have appealed to the conscious experience of remembering (e.g., Tulving 2005) and the continuity of episodic memory with future-oriented episodic thinking (e.g., Suddendorf & Corballis 1997, 2007) to make the case for their views. On the other hand, those who favour a positive answer have relied on an increasing body of empirical evidence suggesting that non-human animals are capable of retrieving event-specific information (e.g., Clayton & Dickinson 1998) and that they possess the relevant neurological structures responsible for episodic memory in humans (e.g., Corballis 2013). There is no consensus, however, about which of these features should play a central role in our theorising on the matter. Building on this limitation, the two chapters in this part make important contributions towards clarifying what is at stake in the dispute over whether non-human animals have episodic memories.

In her contribution, **Boyle** offers a novel perspective on the debate over whether non-human animals have episodic memory. She argues that the disagreement between 'optimists'—i.e., those who think that nonhuman animals have episodic memory—and 'kind sceptics'—i.e., those who think that there are differences of kind between human and non-human memory—is best understood as a disagreement about what episodic memory should mean in the relevant contexts. As Boyle points out, different definitions of 'episodic memory' will become attractive depending on the kind of questions we are trying to answer and on the methodologies we adopt. For instance, she argues that if our goal is to understand the evolutionary origins of episodic memory, then a sparser and more abstract definition of the term, which is not overly tied to how episodic memory is manifested in humans, is likely to be preferable to conceive of its occurrence in simpler and older forms of life. In contrast, Boyle notes that if we are interested in finding out the effects of a certain drug on humans by studying how it affects rats' memories, then a stricter definition of 'episodic memory', which highlights the resemblances between memory in rats and humans, is going to be more useful. Building on these considerations, Boyle advocates for a form of pluralism, in which the question of whether non-human animals have episodic memory does not allow for a simple 'yes' or 'no' answer, but is rather dependent on contextual considerations pertaining to scientific practice. This novel way of looking at the debate raises important questions of interest at the intersection of the philosophy of memory and the philosophy of science that future work on the subject will need to consider in more detail.

Diverging from the pluralism defended by Boyle, **Keven** argues that episodic memory consists in a uniquely human capacity. His strategy consists in distinguishing between *event memories*, which are sensory-like representations of discrete events, and *episodic memories*, which are representations of multiple discrete events organised in temporal, causal, and teleological relations. While Keven accepts that event memory is shared across species, he thinks that episodic memory is restricted to humans, for we are the only species capable of representing certain temporal, causal, and teleological relations. To establish this, Keven considers each type of representation in turn. Concerning temporal representations, he argues that while animals may be able to represent how long ago an event took place, which on Keven's view is sufficient to explain why they perform the way they do in the relevant experimental tasks, they are incapable of representing events as standing in a before–after relationship to one another. The latter, he argues, is what is central for episodic memory. Similarly, when it comes to causal representations, Keven argues that evidence showing that animals' rather limited capacity to represent causal relations among objects provides strong reason for being sceptical of their capacity to represent causal relations among events, for the latter appears to be a much more demanding cognitive capacity. Finally, Keven argues that two central features of teleological representations—namely, that they are recursive and that they require mind-reading abilities—gives us reason for being sceptical that non-human animals are capable of entertaining such representations. Thus, he concludes that the evidence available suggests that non-human animals do not possess episodic memory.

I.3.6 Part VI: Does episodic memory give us knowledge of the past?

Episodic memory is one of the main sources—if not *the* main source—of many of the claims we make about our personal pasts. It thus plays an important role in our communicative and social practices. But do the claims that we make on the basis of episodic memory constitute knowledge? Their importance notwithstanding, discussions about the epistemology of episodic memory have been overlooked in the literature until very recently. This is, in part, due to the widespread acceptance of archivalist views of memory (or what Langland-Hassan, in this volume, calls the 'replay theory'), where memories are viewed as being mere copies of past experiences. However, with the advent of constructive views (e.g., Sutton 1998; De Brigard 2014; Michaelian 2016b), on which memories are no longer viewed as copies of the past, but rather as reconstructions of it based on information currently available to our memory systems, the question of whether we can claim to have knowledge of the past on the basis of episodic memory has been brought back to the fore. Taking different stances on the issue, the two chapters in this part discuss new questions and problems concerning the epistemology of episodic memory.

Adopting a reliabilist approach, **Senor** sets out to develop an account of the epistemology of episodic memory. He begins by noting that episodic memories, which he calls 'memory seemings', are characterised by quasi-sensory and non-propositional contents that represent past experiences. This raises the question of whether they can be objects of epistemic evaluation. As Senor points out, given the non-propositional nature of memory seemings, that is unlikely to be the case at least on traditional ways of thinking about epistemic evaluation. So, the challenge for any attempt to account for the epistemology of episodic memory is to identify what (if anything) in episodic memory is an object of epistemic evaluation. To answer this question, Senor appeals to Michaelian's (2016b) account of episodic memory. Building on mental time travel research, Michaelian argues that episodic memory and other forms of imagining are all products of the same cognitive system, which he calls the 'episodic construction system'. What distinguishes episodic memory from other forms of imagining is, on Michaelian's view, the fact that the former is produced by a reliably functioning episodic construction system that aims to represent an event in the subject's personal past. These representations do not, however, automatically lead to beliefs. According to Michaelian, for this to be the case, the outputs of the episodic construction system need to be 'endorsed' as memories by a metacognitive system. The products of this endorsement process, or simply 'episodic memory beliefs', are, according to Senor, the objects of epistemic evaluation in episodic memory.

Despite helping us identify what is epistemically evaluable in episodic memory, Senor finds Michaelian's 'two-fold' account of the epistemology of memory to be incomplete. This is because it does not explain how memory seemings, whose contents almost invariably outstrip the contents of the beliefs we form on their basis, are responsible for the formation of certain beliefs that are compatible with them, as opposed to other beliefs that are equally compatible with those seemings. Senor's solution to this problem consists in amending Michaelian's original proposal. He argues that another system, perhaps one involving metacognitive monitoring too, is required to ensure the reliability of the process responsible for the formation of episodic memory beliefs out of memory seemings. The addition of this new system leaves us with a 'three-fold' reliabilist account of the epistemology of episodic memory. On this view, a subject's episodic memory belief will count as prima facie justified iff: (a) the original experience that grounds a memory seeming is a reliable depiction of the past event, (b) both the episodic construction system and the metacognitive endorsement system reliably produce a memory seeming, and (c) the process responsible for extracting a particular propositional content from a memory seeming is working in a reliable manner.

Taking a more critical stance on the epistemology of episodic memory, **Frise** argues for the surprising thesis that episodic memory does not usually give us knowledge of the past. Despite the idea seeming counterintuitive at first glance, Frise raises important challenges for any attempt to establish that episodic memory is indeed a source of knowledge. He develops two arguments that come in support of his thesis. The first argument says that the beliefs generated by episodic memory, even if they turn out to be justified and true, are often based on falsehoods. According to Frise, the falsehood in question refers to the belief held by subjects that episodic memory functions as an archive where content originating in experience is preserved without being altered. Given, however, that episodic memory is not an archive but is rather reconstructive, it follows that the beliefs we form on the basis of episodic memory cannot constitute knowledge. As Frise puts it, we are often 'Gettiered' when forming beliefs on the basis of episodic memory.

Frise's second argument has the form of a dilemma. It starts with the observation that, given the constructive character of episodic memory, it is not surprising that it often misrepresents the past. Frise then states that either subjects have evidence that memory often misrepresents the past or they do not. In either case, he argues that the beliefs formed on the basis of episodic memory will not constitute knowledge. More specifically, the first horn of the dilemma has it that if subjects have evidence that episodic memory often misrepresents the past, the beliefs they form on the basis of episodic memory will not be justified. This is because the belief that memory often misrepresents works as partial defeater. In contrast, the second horn has it that if subjects do not have evidence that episodic memory often misrepresents, then the beliefs they form on the basis of episodic memory will depended on a falsehood: i.e., that episodic memory rarely or never misrepresents. Given that both horns lead us to scenarios where at least one defining feature of knowledge is not satisfied, Frise concludes that episodic memory does not usually give us knowledge of the past.

Acknowledgements

We would like to thank Andrew Beck, Marc Stratton, and John Turri for their editorial guidance, the authors for their commitment throughout the entire process, and the anonymous reviewers who provided valuable comments on early versions of the chapters. We are also grateful to the audience of Current Controversies in Philosophy of Memory, a conference held virtually in October 2020 that discussed the chapters featured in the book. This work is supported by the French National Research Agency in the framework of the "Investissements d'avenir" program (ANR-15-IDEX-02).

Notes

1 For a more detailed discussion of the episodic/semantic distinction, see Michaelian and Sutton (2017). While this distinction is becoming standard in philosophy, alternative distinctions have been proposed, including a distinction between propositional memory (corresponding roughly to semantic memory) and perceptual, experiential, personal, or recollective memory (corresponding roughly to episodic memory).
2 Cf. Sutton and O'Brien's contribution to this volume.
3 There are exceptions: the functionalist theory of memory (Fernández 2019) makes no explicit reference to memory traces.
4 In his chapter, Bernecker refers to 'simulationism' as 'reliabilism'.

References

Addis, D. R. (2020). Mental time travel? A neurocognitive model of event simulation. *Review of Philosophy and Psychology*, *11*(2), 233–259.
Bartlett, F. C. (1932). *Remembering: A Study in Experimental and Social Psychology*. Cambridge University Press.
Bernecker, S. (2010). *Memory: A Philosophical Study*. Oxford University Press.
Bernecker, S. (2017). A causal theory of mnemonic confabulation. *Frontiers in Psychology*, *8*, 1207.
Bernecker, S., & Michaelian, K. (2017). Editors' introduction: The philosophy of memory today. In S. Bernecker & K. Michaelian (Eds.), *The Routledge Handbook of Philosophy of Memory* (pp. 1–3). Routledge.
Clayton, N. S., & Dickinson, A. (1998). Episodic-like memory during cache recovery by scrub jays. *Nature*, *395*, 272–274.
Corballis, M. C. (2013). Mental time travel: A case for evolutionary continuity. *Trends in Cognitive Sciences*, *17*(1), 5–6.
Cosmides, L., & Tooby, J. (1997). *Evolutionary Psychology: A Primer*. https://www.cep.ucsb.edu/primer.html
Cummins, R. (1975). Functional analysis. *The Journal of Philosophy*, *72*(2), 741–765.

De Brigard, F. (2014). Is memory for remembering? Recollection as a form of episodic hypothetical thinking. *Synthese, 191*(2), 155–185.

Debus, D. (2014). 'Mental time travel': Remembering the past, imagining the future, and the particularity of events. *Review of Philosophy and Psychology, 5*(3), 333–350.

Fernández, J. (2019). *Memory: A Self-Referential Account*. Oxford University Press.

Furlong, E. J. (1951). *A Study in Memory: A Philosophical Essay*. Thomas Nelson & Sons.

Hutto, D. D., & Myin, E. (2012). *Radicalizing Enactivism: Basic Minds Without Content*. MIT Press.

Hutto, D. D., & Myin, E. (2017). *Evolving Enactivism: Basic Minds Meet Content*. MIT Press.

Langland-Hassan, P. (2021). What sort of imagining might remembering be? *Journal of the American Philosophical Association, 7*(2), 231–251.

Martin, C. B., & Deutscher, M. (1966). Remembering. *The Philosophical Review, 75*(2), 161–196.

Michaelian, K. (2016a). Against discontinuism: Mental time travel and our knowledge of past and future events. In K. Michaelian, S. B. Klein, & K. K. Szpunar (Eds.), *Seeing The Future: Theoretical Perspectives on Future-Oriented Mental Time Travel* (pp. 63–92). Oxford University Press.

Michaelian, K. (2016b). *Mental Time Travel: Episodic Memory and Our Knowledge of the Personal Past*. MIT Press.

Michaelian, K. (2020). Confabulating as unreliable imagining: In defence of the simulationist account of unsuccessful remembering. *Topoi, 39*(1), 133–148.

Michaelian, K. (2021). Imagining the past reliably and unreliably: Towards a virtue theory of memory. *Synthese, 199*(3), 7477–7507.

Michaelian, K., Debus, D., & Perrin, D. (2018). The philosophy of memory today and tomorrow: Editors' introduction. In K. Michaelian, D. Debus, & D. Perrin. (Eds.), *New Directions in the Philosophy of Memory* (pp. 1–9). Routledge.

Michaelian, K., Perrin, D., & Sant'Anna, A. (2020). Continuities and discontinuities between imagination and memory: The view from philosophy. In A. Abraham (Ed.), *The Cambridge Handbook of the Imagination* (pp. 293–310). Cambridge University Press.

Michaelian, K., & Sant'Anna, A. (2021). Memory without content? Radical enactivism and (post)causal theories of memory. *Synthese, 198*(Suppl. 1), S307–S335.

Michaelian, K., & Sutton, J. (2017). Memory. In E. N. Zalta (Ed.), *The Stanford Encyclopedia of Philosophy* (Summer 2017). Metaphysics Research Lab, Stanford University.

Millikan, R. (1984). *Language, Thought, and Other Biological Categories: New Foundations for Realism*. MIT Press.

Perrin, D. (2016). Asymmetries in subjective time. In K. Michaelian, S. B. Klein, & K. K. Szpunar (Eds.), *Seeing the Future: Theoretical Perspectives on Future-Oriented Mental Time Travel* (pp. 39–61). Oxford University Press.

Perrin, D. (2018). A case for procedural causality in episodic recollection. In K. Michaelian, D. Debus, & D. Perrin (Eds.), *New Directions in the Philosophy of Memory* (pp. 33–51). Routledge.

Perrin, D., & Michaelian, K. (2017). Memory as mental time travel. In S. Bernecker & K. Michaelian (Eds.), *The Routledge Handbook of Philosophy of Memory* (pp. 228–239). Routledge.

Robins, S. (2020). Defending discontinuism, naturally. *Review of Philosophy and Psychology, 11*(2), 469–486.

Robins, S. K. (2016a). Representing the past: Memory traces and the causal theory of memory. *Philosophical Studies, 173*(11), 2993–3013.

Robins, S. K. (2016b). Misremembering. *Philosophical Psychology, 29*(3), 432–447.

Sant'Anna, A. (2021). Attitudes and the (dis)continuity between memory and imagination. *Estudios de Filosofía, 64*, 73–93.

Schacter, D. L. (2012). Adaptive constructive processes and the future of memory. *American Psychologist, 67*, 603–613.

Schacter, D. L. & Addis, D. R. (2007). On the constructive episodic simulation of past and future events. *Behavioral and Brain Sciences, 30*, 299–351.

Schacter, D. L., Addis, D. R., Hassabis, D., Martin, V. C., Spreng, R. N., & Szpunar, K. K. (2012). The future of memory: Remembering, imagining, and the brain. *Neuron, 76*(4), 677–694.

Schwartz, A. (2020). Simulationism and the function(s) of episodic memory. *Review of Philosophy and Psychology, 11*, 487–505.

Suddendorf, T., & Corballis, M. C. (1997). Mental time travel and the evolution of the human mind. *Genetic, Social, and General Psychology Monographs, 123*(2), 133–167.

Suddendorf, T., & Corballis, M. C. (2007). The evolution of foresight: What is mental time travel, and is it unique to humans? *Behavioral and Brain Sciences, 30*(03), 299–313.

Sutton, J. (1998). *Philosophy and Memory Traces: Descartes to Connectionism.* Cambridge University Press.

Tulving, E. (1972). Episodic and semantic memory. In E. Tulving & W. Donaldson (Eds.), *Organization of Memory* (pp. 381–402). Academic Press.

Tulving, E. (1985). Memory and consciousness. *Canadian Psychology/Psychologie Canadienne, 26*(1), 1–12.

Tulving, E. (2005). Episodic memory and autonoesis: Uniquely human? In H. S. Terrace & J. Metcalfe (Eds.), *The Missing Link in Cognition: Origins of Self-Reflective Consciousness* (pp. 3–56). Oxford University Press.

Werning, M. (2020). Predicting the past from minimal traces: Episodic memory and its distinction from imagination and preservation. *Review of Philosophy and Psychology, 11*(2), 301–333.

Part I

What is the relationship between memory and imagination?

1 Remembering, imagining, and memory traces

Toward a continuist causal theory

Peter Langland-Hassan

1.1 Introduction

Those who argue that remembering is a kind of imagining, and those moved to deny it, must share some idea of what it is to be an imagining. They must, and they do. But, often, the idea is not made very clear. This creates problems, as the resolution of their debate can be no clearer than the sense of 'imagination' at issue.

A few cases in point: Kourken Michaelian (2016c) defends a 'simulationist' theory of episodic remembering that 'simply equates remembering with imagining the past' (p. 110). Remembering is thus held by Michaelian to be continuous with other instances of imagining (such as envisioning the future) that are not cases of remembering. This assimilation of remembering to imagining has become known as *continuism* (Perrin, 2016; Perrin & Michaelian, 2017). However, Michaelian does not specify what it is about remembering, or envisioning the future, that qualifies either as imagining. Likewise, Donna Rose Addis defends 'a theoretical framework that views memory and imagination as the *same* process', proposing that 'memory and imagination are indeed one neurocognitive system'. This is in contrast to 'the dominant perspective' in cognitive neuroscience which, she explains, 'does not go so far as to conclude that memory is imagination' (Addis, 2020, pp. 237, 239, emphasis original). While Addis details many features shared by both rememberings and episodes of envisioning the future, she does not specify what qualifies them as instances of imagining. Nor are matters clearer among the 'discontinuists' who deny that remembering is a kind of imagining. Denis Perrin, for instance, argues that episodic remembering and envisioning the future are 'different in nature, one being memory and the other imagination', without specifying the sense in which only future-directed thought qualifies as imagination (2016, p. 41). Similarly, Carl Craver notes the 'momentous differences in attitudinal stance one takes with respect to a past in event in remembering as opposed to imagining' (2020, p. 277), again without explaining what he means by 'imagining'.

Of course, 'imagine' and 'imagination' are common words. They seem to need no introduction. However, within this dispute—which I will follow others in calling the *(dis)continuism debate* (Perrin & Michaelian, 2017)—'imagination' is not being used in its most familiar senses. Or so I will argue in the next section, echoing and expanding on my (2021). My suggestion will be that the sense

DOI: 10.4324/9781003002277-3

of 'imagining' at issue is *constructive imagining*, which, on reflection, is a relatively obscure sense of 'imagining', in need of elucidation. Having shown that the (dis)continuism debate is a debate about whether remembering (and envisioning the future) is constructive imagining, I then argue (in Sections 1.3 and 1.4) that settling that dispute will hinge on whether the memory traces (or 'engrams') that support remembering impose *a*rational, perception-like constraints that are too strong for remembering to constitute a kind of constructive imagining. In Section 1.5, I articulate two conceptions of memory traces—the replay theory and the prop theory—that return conflicting answers to that question. The prop theory's vision of traces is suggestive of continuism, while the replay theory's is a natural fit for discontinuism. Which view of traces is in fact correct remains undetermined by current empirical work. Nevertheless, it may already be possible to reach a compromise in the (dis)continuism debate. I conclude (in Section 1.6) by sketching a conciliatory *continuist causal theory*. This view—only outlined here—accepts the continuism-friendly prop theory of traces, while still requiring that genuine remembering fulfils an appropriate causation condition, as required by the kinds of causal theories of remembering typically favoured by discontinuists.

1.2 'Imagining' in what sense?

It is not hard to see that some of the most common senses of 'imagination' are not the ones at issue in the (dis)continuism debate. Witness the first definition of 'imagination' (definition 1a) in the *Oxford English Dictionary*: 'The power or capacity to form internal images or ideas of objects and situations not actually present to the senses, including remembered objects and situations' (OED, 2009). Here, imagination is said to represent objects and situations not actually present to the senses, '*including* remembered objects and situations' (emphasis added). Yet, as mentioned earlier, Addis tells us that the dominant perspective in cognitive science sees imagining and remembering as distinct. Has the *OED* broken ranks with the orthodox view that remembering is *not* an instance of imagining? That seems unlikely. This must not be the sense of 'imagination' at issue in the (dis)continuism debate.[1]

The *OED*'s second definition (1b) for 'imagination' reads: 'An inner image or idea of an object or objects not actually present to the senses; often with the implication that the idea does not correspond to the reality of things' (OED, 2009). Here again, we have the suggestion of image-like 'ideas' of things not present to the senses. If we stop there, remembering again remains a clear case of imagining. Yet, in this definition we get the added condition that (at least often) imagining occurs 'with the implication that the idea does not correspond to the reality of things'. Supposing we take the latter condition for a *necessary* condition on imagining, this understanding of imagination coheres fairly well with the broadest characterisation of 'imagine' given by Liao and Gendler (2020) in their *Stanford Encyclopedia of Philosophy* (*SEP*) entry on imagination: '*To imagine* is to represent without aiming at things as they actually, presently, and subjectively are'. Craver (2020) appears to invoke a similar understanding of imagination, when he contrasts it to remembering by noting a 'discontinuity of commitment' between the two.

However, this second sense of 'imagination'—seemingly shared by the *OED* (definition 1b) and *SEP*—has the converse problem of that seen with the first: it seems to preclude episodic remembering from being a kind of imagining, just as a matter of definition. When we episodically remember, we aim to represent things as they *really were* in our past; we don't aim to represent merely fictional or make-believe worlds. This much is accepted, and even emphasised, by continuists. Michaelian (2016b) explains that his theory 'discriminates between memory and episodic counterfactual thought by the requirement that [in the case of episodic remembering] the episodic construction system must aim at simulating an episode from the [actual] personal past' (p. 108). It seems clear that Michaelian and other continuists will freely grant that episodic remembering is not imagining in any sense that implies a lack of commitment to things having been as they are represented. This suggests that the *OED* definition 1b and the *SEP*'s commitment-free characterisation of 'imagination' simply aren't the senses of 'imagination' at issue.

What, then, do continuists mean by 'imagination'? It is not until the *OED*'s fifth (and final!) definition for 'imagination' that we get the beginnings of an answer. On this definition, imagination is, 'the mind's creativity and resourcefulness in using and inventing images, analogies, etc.' (OED, 2009). Creativity and 'resourcefulness' are not things traditionally associated with memory. Generally speaking, a good memory is one that sticks to the facts, one might think, with the scientific study of episodic memory being the study of how we manage to stick to those facts when representing our personal pasts. It is easy to see why discontinuists might deny that remembering is imagining in this actively creative sense. On the other hand, there is no flat contradiction in holding that remembering is importantly creative, requiring resourcefulness on the part of the cognitive system—an ability to draw together pieces of information from disparate areas to arrive at an appraisal of past events. Indeed, these are the very sorts of claims continuists make about memory in highlighting its 'reconstructive' nature (Addis, 2020; De Brigard, 2014a; Michaelian, 2021).

While there is fine-tuning yet to be done, we seem to have found a sense of 'imagining' that could be the one at work in the (dis)continuism debate. Happily, it corresponds to a kind of imagination also discussed in the philosophical literature—albeit less frequently than some others[2]—namely: *constructive imagining* (Van Leeuwen, 2013). Constructive imagining, Van Leeuwen (2013) explains, is 'a constructive process of assembling mental representations' (p. 221). When we say that *X* imagines *c*, in the constructive sense, we 'express that *X* is engaged in a process of coming up with mental representations that have *c* content' (p. 224). When we speak of constructive imagination as a capacity or faculty, we refer to 'the capacity to form novel representations' (p. 224).

This notion of constructive imagining shares with the *OED*'s fifth definition of 'imagination' the idea that imagining is a creative, actively constructive process involving the manipulation of mental representations of some kind. It also (unlike the *OED* definition 1b) omits any suggestion that imaginings can only represent mere possibilities, or things we take to be unreal. Further, unlike definition 1a, it avoids simply stipulating that episodic remembering is a kind of imagining. Let's proceed, then, with the understanding that the (dis)continuism debate concerns whether episodic remembering is a species of constructive imagining.

1.3 Whether remembering is constructive imagining depends on the kinds of constraints imposed by memory traces

What would it take to show that episodic remembering is a species of constructive imagining? The main barrier is to overcome the impression that remembering is subject to *constraints* that stand in the way of its being inherently 'creative', an active process of 'assembling representations', or simply a matter of resourcefully associating one thing with another. Consider, by analogy, ordinary perception. On the one hand, it is true that the human perceptual system makes 'top down' contributions to perceptual input. Perceiving the world is never simply a matter of passively receiving input at our sensory transducers. However, the way we perceive the world to be remains tightly constrained, moment to moment, by how the world is before us. Perception would be useless to us were it not so constrained. In calling a mental process 'constructive imagining', we seem to have in mind a process that is *much less* constrained by the way the world is before us, and *much more* creative.

Of course, remembering is also unconstrained by how the world *presently* is before us, and so is unlike perception in that regard. Nevertheless, remembering is constrained by the external world in the sense that we can only (successfully) remember events that in fact occurred; further, on most views of memory, the remembering of an event can only be successful to the extent that it coheres with how we experienced the event to be (some continuists demur on this last point; see, e.g., Michaelian, 2016c, 2021). However, those kinds of constraints are not the ones most obviously at odds with the idea that remembering is deeply creative, or constructive. There is still a deeper, more perception-like, form of constraint that applies to remembering from within the terms of the Causal Theory of Memory (CTM) (articulated most influentially by Martin & Deutscher, 1966). While there are importantly different versions of the CTM (Bernecker, 2010; Debus, 2017), a core commitment of most is that successful remembering involves, as a necessary condition, the *preservation* and *transmission* of representational content from an initial experience that is remembered. Typically, such content is said to be preserved and transmitted through the work of a persisting *memory trace* (Bernecker, 2010; Martin & Deutscher, 1966). While the precise analysis of what it is to be a memory trace is a matter of dispute— one we will explore later—the general idea is of a mental state that is caused by an act of perception, encodes information (i.e., representational content) about the perceived event, and continues to store that information until some later moment when, by suitably causing an episode of remembering, it allows the event that originally caused it, and about which it carries information, to be remembered (De Brigard, 2014b; Robins, 2016). According to the CTM, an event is successfully remembered when the episode of remembering preserves content from one's perception of the event, thanks to the remembering's being suitably caused by a memory trace.

If the world before us constrains perception—and thereby prevents perceiving from being constructive imagining—advocates of the CTM may hold that memory traces (which aim to record these perceptions) pass along these constraints to remembering, thereby preventing remembering from being constructive imagining as well. They may hold this even if they allow for successful memory to involve some addition and deletion of content to and from the original experience, and so provide for a degree of construction in successful memory—as countenanced by 'constructive' versions of the causal theory (De Brigard, 2014b; Michaelian, 2011). The constrains are 'passed along' to an act of remembering in just the way that the constraints met by a video camera—grounded its ongoing causal interaction with the recorded world—are passed on to any subsequent replay of the recording.

By contrast, one of the most provocative claims put forward by continuists is that 'one can remember without drawing on information originating in one's experience of the remembered episode', and that 'one can in principle remember even where one did not actually experience the episode to begin with' (Michaelian, 2016c, p. 118). Here we seem to have a view of memory that leaves it unconstrained by past perception and, hence, free of any perception-like constraints that might prevent remembering from being constructive imagining. Indeed, this is where the (dis)continuism debate typically occurs: between simulationists, like Michaelian, and 'causal theorists', such as Perrin (2016) and Debus (2014), who hold that at least some content preservation-via-causation-by-a-trace must occur in successful remembering. Thus, Perrin and Michaelian's (2017) conclusion, in an overview of the (dis)continuism debate, is that 'the continuist–discontinuist debate may bottom out in a clash of intuitions over the necessity of causation for remembering' (p. 236).

Before moving forward, it is worth noting that, even on the continuist view, remembering is constrained by the external world in the sense that there is a norm in place for any act of remembering to accurately represent the way the world was. This sort of accuracy constraint, I suggest, is compatible with being a constructive imagining—with actively assembling representations—as ordinary acts of reasoning, which are also subject to norms of truth-preservation, are similarly constrained. By contrast, the CTM sees memory traces as imposing *a*rational constraints—what I have called 'perception-like' constraints—akin to those imposed on perception by the external world, where one's internal state is under the control of an outside stimulus. In the case of remembering, this *a*rational constraint is passed along a chain from the external world, to an encoded memory trace, to an act of remembering that makes available the information stored in the trace. It is this sort of *a*rational, perception-like constraint that, I suggest, is incompatible with the kind of creativity required for constructive imagining.[3]

1.4 Even the committed continuist may have to concede that memory traces prevent remembering from being constructive imagining

With the (dis)continuism debate now clearly in view, I want to map a new route to defending continuism. Doing so will require first explaining why Michaelian's (2016a, 2016c) existing defences of the view remain incomplete. We have seen that Michaelian allows for cases of successful memory that are not caused by memory traces and that, in exceptional cases, occur in the absence of any corresponding experience had during the remembered event. The possibility of such lays bare a key disagreement between the CTM and Michaelian's brand of simulationism as, on the CTM, it is a requirement on a mental representation's being a successful case of remembering that it was in fact caused—via a mediating memory trace—by an experience of the event remembered.

Yet, when it comes to assessing whether remembering—considered as a *type* of mental process—is well-conceived as constructive imagining, matters are not settled by the fact that the simulationist will count some mental episodes as successful rememberings that the causal theorist will not. This is because Michaelian never denies that memory traces frequently play a role in remembering. To the contrary, he holds that, while we should abandon the CTM in favour of the simulation theory of remembering, 'the simulation theory likewise invokes [memory] traces' (Michaelian, 2016b, p. 77). He further explains that the 'simulation of a given past episode presumably *often* draws on information originating in the agent's experience of that particular episode', while emphasising that 'it will rarely draw *exclusively* on such information, and in principle it need not draw on such information *at all*' (Michaelian, 2016b, p. 103, emphases in original). In short, while Michaelian emphasises the *possibility* of one's (successfully) remembering an event without drawing on something like a memory trace, nothing in his account suggests that rememberings are not *usually* caused (in part) by relevant memory traces. On his (continuist) simulation theory, remembering happens whenever a 'properly functioning episodic construction system … aims to represent the personal past'. And this is quite compatible with a properly functioning episodic construction system usually drawing on memory traces as a central resource (Michaelian, 2016b, p. 97).

The upshot is this: if memory traces really do impose perception-like constraints on the rememberings they cause, and thereby prevent such rememberings from being constructive imaginings, it appears that even Michaelian may be committed to remembering not being a form of constructive imagining. For while his brand of simulationism allows for the possibility of *instances* of remembering that are also instances of constructive imagining, this does not entail the more ambitious claim that remembering just *is* imagining. So long as *most* episodes of remembering are caused, and thereby constrained, by memory traces, remembering (as a type of state) need not be seen as continuous with constructive imagining.

For the continuist, two avenues of response suggest themselves: either deny that memory traces are even *typical* causes of episodic rememberings; or, alternatively, hold that memory traces don't impose constraints on rememberings that prevent the latter from being constructive imaginings. One way to pursue the second strategy—explored in Section 1.6—is to argue that memory traces are *also* typical causes of mental states that we antecedently think of as (constructive) imaginings, including cases of imagining one's future and imagining how things could have gone differently in one's past. If, in pursuing this path, it turns out that memory traces are not quite what the standard causal theory of memory took them to be, the two avenues of response may merge: memory traces, as conceived by the causal theory, are not typical causes of rememberings (because memory traces of *that* sort do not exist); however, the memory traces that *do* exist, and that typically cause rememberings, also cause counterfactual and future-directed imaginings. Therefore, once memory traces are properly understood, there is no conflict in being caused by a memory trace and being a constructive imagining.

The balance of this chapter will assess the prospects for this kind of continuist response. We will see that, going in this direction, we face the question of whether remembering can still be distinguished from episodes of accurately representing the personal past that, intuitively, are not cases of remembering. By chapter's end I will sketch a *continuist causal theory* that aims to accept a continuist picture of memory traces while also building in causal requirements for remembering that distinguish it from the (mere) accurate representation of one's past (and from 'deviant' causal dependencies as well, such as are involved in 'relearning' (Martin & Deutscher, 1966).[4] To get there, I first need to contrast two ways we might think of memory traces and their relation to remembering.

1.5 Two views of memory traces and the constraints they impose

I will now present two metaphors for understanding the relation of episodic remembering to memory traces. The first picture—which I will call the *replay theory*—is modelled on the view of memory traces, and their relation to remembering, that is either explicit or implicit in the versions of the causal theory of memory defended by Martin & Deutscher (1966) and Bernecker (2010). The second theory—which I will call the *prop theory*—is modelled on what I take to be the view of continuists such as Michaelian (2016b) and Addis (2020). In both cases, the metaphors are idealised and admittedly picturesque renderings of the respective theories, aimed at highlighting their differences. I will try to substantiate the accuracy of the metaphors where needed, though I encourage the reader to consider ways in which they may be inaccurate. My articulation of the metaphors is an attempt to understand the theories, not to obscure them. As there is no single understanding of what it is to be a memory trace at work in memory research (De Brigard, 2014b; Robins, 2016, 2017), these metaphors aim to highlight some of the important consequences for understanding them in slightly different ways.

On both metaphors, we can think of remembering as an event that occurs on a stage, with on-stage events serving as an analogue for the conscious mind. Our imagined person doing the remembering, in each case, will be Peggy. On the first picture—the *replay* theory—the stage contains a large movie screen. Remembering occurs whenever a memory trace causes a representation of an event from Peggy's past to be shown on the screen. On this view, memory traces are stored offstage in a very large library of such traces. For each trace in the library, there is exactly one event it allows Peggy (sometimes with prompting) to remember.[5] On the other hand, it is compatible with the replay theory that, in some cases, there are multiple traces in the library that enable the remembering of the very same event. Each trace stores content about the event it allows Peggy to remember by being a sketchy recording of her past perceptual (or introspective) experience of that event—a recording made at the time of the event and dutifully stored in the offstage library until such a time as it might be retrieved and replayed in an onstage act of remembering. Importantly, *which* event is remembered is fully determined by the memory trace being shown on stage. Even if the theatre advertises that memories from 1989 will be shown, and even if Peggy concludes the showing by judging that she has recalled events from 1989, should it turn out that the camera operator (an employee of Peggy's subconscious) has unwittingly selected and projected traces recorded in 1992, then it is episodes from 1992 that Peggy remembered in the showing. Compare this to Martin and Deutscher's (1966, pp. 167–168) case of the painter who, they claim, unwittingly remembers a farmyard scene from his childhood, despite thinking that he is only imagining it. The triggering of the relevant memory trace is sufficient for the remembering. Indeed, the fact that they take its use to be sufficient for the remembering of an event is one of the best indicators that they take each trace to allow the remembering of *only* one event. For if a trace could be used to remember multiple events, we would be left without an explanation of why the painter counts as remembering one of those events, to the exclusion of another, in cases where he does not even take himself to be remembering.

On the second picture—the *prop* theory—memory traces are more like stage sets used in a theatre production, where each set is composed of various (reusable) props. On this view as well, memory traces spend most of their lives offstage, in storage. However, just as a theatre company will not create multiple sets for every scene that occurs in the kitchen—but, sensibly, will reuse the same kitchen set for each scene that occurs in the kitchen—so, too, on this metaphor for remembering, are individual memory traces reused in the representation of distinct events. On the prop theory, episodic remembering occurs when, at Peggy's request, the stage manager brings out one or more props (that together compose a particular set) in a representation of an event from Peggy's past. (Whether *all* accurate representations of Peggy's personal past will qualify as *remembering,* on the prop theory, is a delicate question to be addressed later in this section.) Like the camera operator on the replay view, the stage manager is a denizen of Peggy's subconscious. Skilful though he is, the stage manager is not always accurate in his use of props to represent Peggy's past. However, he is reliable enough to keep Peggy out of trouble. In the occasional cases where he misrepresents the past, it thus makes sense to think of these as unsuccessful rememberings, as opposed to pure confabulations (cf., Michaelian, 2016b).

Sometimes, however, Peggy asks the stage manager to bring out props in the representation not of her actual past but, rather, of likely future events, or of ways things could have gone differently in her past. When he does so, what result are cases not of remembering, but of imagining the future, or imagining counterfactual pasts—even if the very same props (and sets) might have been used in an act of successful remembering. Here we have a difference with the replay theory, which does not allow a memory trace to be projected both during a remembering and an imagining of the future, as the projection of a memory trace is always sufficient for remembering the event it records, on the replay view.

Unlike the replay view—where traces are not substantially altered after they are first created—work continues on the props day to day, with details added or features removed (cf. Robins's 2016 explication of memory traces as 'distributed patterns'). Each prop helps Peggy to represent one or more past events by representing features of those events, during onstage performances of the past. New props and sets are constructed only as needed to accurately depict Peggy's life events. When she visits Alaska for the first time, the stage crew gets to work in creating sets corresponding to her new experiences. Otherwise, when she stays home, the stage crew busies itself with maintaining and elaborating existing sets. Unlike the replay view, the same memory trace (qua stage set) may be used in the remembering of distinct events. Thus, *which* event Peggy is remembering—and even whether she is remembering as opposed to imagining the future—is not determined by the memory trace (or traces) currently on stage. The prop theory distinguishes remembering from imagining the future, fantasising, or considering counterfactual pasts, by appeal to Peggy's intentions in bringing props on stage. Some prop theorists also consider the beliefs that Peggy acquires on the basis of having witnessed the performance as relevant to determining the kind of performance that took place (Fernández, 2019).

The prop theory leaves us with some obvious puzzles. First, what is the difference between Peggy's accurately representing one of her past experiences (as she might do on the basis of testimony, or after 'relearning' Martin & Deutscher, 1966) and her truly remembering it? The same props are called on stage in each case in the service of depicting events from Peggy's personal past. Second, how does the stage manager know *which* sets to bring on stage in the representation of an event from Peggy's past? If the answer is that he himself remembers what happened when and is drawing on that knowledge in the selection of sets, we will naturally want to know what sort of analogy should be used to describe the stage manager's memory. If we apply the prop picture to him as well, we are left with the question of how his own stage manager knows which sets to bring on stage. The prop theorist will have to face up to such questions.

However, there are corresponding puzzles for the replay theory. First, we are left without an account of the relation between remembering, on the one hand, and imagining the future and counterfactual pasts, on the other. We can see that the latter processes will not simply involve projecting memory traces, as that is what remembering consists in, on the replay view. Recall that, on the replay view, projecting a memory trace is sufficient for remembering. Moreover, the projection of a pre-recorded memory trace lacks the creativity inherent in imagining the future and counterfactual pasts. The replay theory must either hold that some other store of representations is exploited in constructive imagining, or, more likely, that during constructive imagining, memory traces are copied, cut up, and newly pasted together in ways that render them no longer memory traces (and that now qualify the acts as constructive imaginings). In any case, the replay theorist owes an account of the relation between memory traces and constructive imagining, whereas the prop theory already has one at hand. This is due, in part, to the replay theorist's *discontinuism* about the relationship between remembering and imagining.

What about the other question we raised for the prop theory, of how the stage manager knows which props to bring on stage in the remembering of an event, given that the same props can be reused for many different purposes, and in the accurate representation of distinct events from one's past? It might seem that the replay theory avoids such questions simply in virtue of reserving exactly one memory trace for each event that can be remembered. The camera operator just needs to find the correct trace and project it. But this is an illusion. To see that it is, suppose that, on the replay view, there is a librarian in charge of storing each newly encoded memory trace (where the 'librarian' is another figment of Peggy's subconscious mind). And suppose that this librarian simply tosses each new trace she receives into a giant bin, without labelling it. In that case, there is still exactly one trace for each event Peggy can possibly remember. But the camera operator faces a hopeless task when asked to project a memory of any specific event. He will have to rummage hopelessly through many thousands of traces, lacking any means for recognising the right one *as* the right one when it is found. (Lest we attribute to him pre-existing knowledge of what happened, which again raises the question about the appropriate metaphor for understanding *his* knowledge.)

An obvious way to solve this problem is for the librarian to organise the traces as they are stored, by the time of their encoding. For instance, she might place each trace in a protective sleeve and write, on the outside, the location and date at which it was recorded. The camera operator would then have a way of searching for memories by date. However, the limitations of ordinary human memory tell strongly against this tweak to the metaphor. Humans are generally very bad at retrieving memories *simply* on the basis of the time and date at which they occurred. Asked to think of nothing but an arbitrary date in the past—October 6, 2004, say—and to retrieve associated memories, there is normally very little we will come up with. It seems that we don't do anything akin to pulling out the *October 6, 2004,* trace to see what is recorded there. The search instead proceeds by an indirect, associative route, starting with the general period of time and the typical kinds of activities and schedules in place then. A more accurate extension of the replay metaphor may be of a lacklustre librarian—or a more harried one—who simply tosses each new trace into a bin with others that seem related in one way or another. There may be 'early 1992' or 'fall of 2010' bins, or 'baseball game' and 'camping trip' bins. Or, keeping the traces out of bins, the librarian might simply write labels on the protective sleeves of each trace that are less specific than the time and place it was recorded: they might read 'college', 'elementary school', and 'my sister's wedding', for example. In trying to retrieve relevant traces, the camera operator could then focus on specific bins or labels (even if how he successfully sorts from within those results remains unresolved). A complicating factor on this system is that many traces could fit into multiple bins or accept multiple labels. A trace from a camping trip taken with one's brother during college could be copied and placed into each of a 'college', 'camping', or 'my brother' bin, or accept such a label, for instance. Such copying of traces is compatible with the replay theory, so long as each trace still allows only the remembering of one event. However, it suggests a much larger, and more difficult-to-search, storage facility, with most bins containing many traces that also appear in other bins—or where the information on one trace's label is much the same as that on another.

What matters for present purposes is that some sort of filing system is needed on the replay theory; and, given what we know about the limits of human memory, the system will not organise memory traces by the exact time and place of their occurrence, but by more general features. Importantly, there is no barrier to the prop theory's hiring a librarian to do the same kind of sorting as on the replay view. In cases where new props and sets are created, they can be sorted by the librarian into bins based on their subject matter ('parent's kitchen', 'sister's wedding') or the general time frame to which they are relevant ('college years', 'late 80's'). On both views, the labels on the bins can later be updated by the librarian to reflect their contents' new relevancies in light of subsequent experience. Though, keeping human limits in mind, these labels will remain at a high level of generality. The key point here is that the prop theory's doing without traces of the sort featured in the replay theory—that enable one-to-one mappings between traces and successful episodic memories—does not prevent it from employing much the same storage and retrieval system, and therefore does not place it at a special disadvantage in explaining how appropriate props are retrieved and displayed in acts of remembering.

Now, if the prop theory is a fairly accurate metaphor for remembering, imagining the future, and imagining counterfactual pasts, it is easy to see all these processes as cases of constructive imagining. In each instance, the stage manager draws from among the same collection of props to creatively assemble a representation of some episode. Unlike the camera operator on the replay view, he is not locked into simply replaying pre-recorded sequences. In fact, there are no such recordings to make use of. It is true that the stage manager works under real *constraints* as soon as he sets upon the project of representing an episode from Peggy's actual personal past. He cannot freely put out whichever props might strike his fancy—not without putting Peggy at epistemic risk. But similar constraints are operative when he is asked to represent likely future events, or events that would have occurred had some counterfactual event occurred. In each case, it is important to Peggy's well-being that he represent things accurately—either as they will be, or as they would have been. All three acts—remembering, imagining the future, and imagining the counterfactual past—remain sufficiently creative and stimulus-independent to be seen as constructive imagining.

The prop theory offers a sketch, then, of how continuism could be true (and remembering a kind of constructive imagining), even if memory traces are typical causes of remembering. This is not yet to show how continuism could be made consistent with the idea that remembering requires appropriate causation by an earlier experience of the event remembered (as required by the CTM). We do not yet have a *causal* continuist view on the table; sketching that possibility is the project of the next section. For now, we simply have a main ingredient: an otherwise plausible conception of memory traces that allows for their frequent involvement in acts of remembering that are well viewed as constructive imaginings.

1.6 Sketch of a way forward for continuism and the prop theory of traces

In my view, it remains an open empirical question which metaphor—the prop theory or replay theory—provides a more accurate picture of memory traces.[6] Nevertheless, there are ways theorists can support the prop theory (and the brand of continuism it allows) in the interim. We have seen that the prop theory, as outlined, does not offer an obvious means for distinguishing successful remembering from (merely) accurately representing one's personal past. Nor does it distinguish remembering from accurate representation via *deviant* causal chains—such as occur in Martin and Deutscher's (1966) cases of relearning and a person's reliance on 'suggestible states'. These gaps will, for many, stand as a barrier to accepting the prop theory's vision of memory traces, whatever virtues the prop theory otherwise possesses. It was, after all, the *raison d'être* of the replay view's appeal to memory traces to distinguish remembering from other instances of accurately representing one's past (Martin & Deutscher, 1966). Indeed, while I cannot argue for this now, I think that a theory of remembering that fails to draw these distinctions is incomplete. It would certainly help the prospects of the prop theory, and the kind of continuism it allows, if a general means for articulating such a distinction were available—one that does not, inadvertently, give up on the prop theory. I will end by pointing the way to such a view.

The key to making the prop theory (and continuism) more plausible is to show how a causal condition *of the right kind*—an 'appropriate' causation condition—can be fulfilled by successful rememberings, even if memory traces are as the prop theory imagines them. To see how we might get there, let us begin with a statement of a very general causal theory, where what constitutes appropriate causation is left open:

> *Causal Theory*: S's representation *r* is a remembering of event *e* iff: S observed *e*, *r* represents *e* within certain limits of accuracy, and *r* is appropriately caused by S's observation of *e*.

This is essentially what we find in Martin and Deutscher (1966) and Bernecker (2010) before they go on to explicate what it is for *r* to be *appropriately* caused by *S*'s observation of *e* in terms of a memory trace. Note, however, that in principle, this Causal Theory *could be* true even if traces are as the prop theory sees them. We would simply need an alternative account of what it is for representation *r* to be appropriately caused by *S*'s observation—one that does not cash it out in terms of causation by a replay-style memory trace. What other options are there? There is not room here for a full development of any, but I will end by pointing the way to some possibilities.

On the constructive view of episodic remembering—a natural fit for the prop theory of traces—remembering is less perception-like and more inference-like. In generating a single act of remembering, we draw upon a variety of cognitive cues and representations in order to construct (what we take for) an accurate representation of a past event. These include memory traces (as the prop theory sees them), but also background beliefs about one's past and feelings of fluency or ease at representing an event (Bastin et al., 2019; Whittlesea & Williams, 2000). It may be that one or more of these other states can at times bear the burden of providing an appropriate causal link between the event and its remembering, in lieu of a memory trace.

For example, in remembering the enormous pillars inside Barcelona's La Sagrada Familia basilica, my belief that I have ventured inside that building only once may be an essential component to the episodic remembering—a piece of information partly relied upon in fostering a representation of a specific *event* (my visit to La Sagrada Familia) and not simply an atemporal representation of the pillars themselves. If we suppose that this belief was caused by my visit that day, and that I would not seem to remember the visit were it not for this belief, then—at least in this instance—this persisting belief may be the state that guarantees that there is an appropriate causal relation between my observing the pillars and my remembering them. The idea here is that, while I could perhaps accurately represent the pillars themselves without this belief, I would not remember *the event* of being at La Sagrada Familia without the additional contribution of the event-caused belief that I once visited there. (This proposal is further developed in Langland-Hassan (2022).

Alternatively, it has been shown that people process a stimulus more quickly and easily—i.e., with greater *fluency*—if they have perceived it recently (Whittlesea, 1993; Whittlesea & Williams, 2001). Let mental state *F* be a state that is caused by one's perceiving of *S* and that causes one to be fluent for stimulus *S*. Suppose now that I recently turned off the stove and am trying to remember whether I have done so. I can easily generate props suitable for representing my turning off the stove, as I've perceived myself doing so many times. But I may only have the sense of *remembering* turning off the stove when those props are generated with fluency. Let us suppose that this fluency results from mental state *F*, which itself causally results from recently perceiving myself turn off the stove. In this sort of example, it may be mental state *F*—fluency for stimulus *S* (the stove)—that guarantees that there is an appropriate causal relation between my observing myself turn off the stove and my remembering doing so. This can be the case even if the remembering draws on states (such as suitable memory traces), in addition to F. What is important is the counterfactual that, had I not just perceived myself turning off the stove, I would not now seem to remember doing so—the truth of which is guaranteed by the causal relevance of F, a state of fluency.[7]

On this (revisionary) approach to the causal theory—call it a *causal constructive theory*—there is not just one way for a representation r to be appropriately causally dependent on an observation of event e. There may be several—a disjunction of appropriate causes—where the answer to which cause assures an appropriate causal link to the remembered event may vary from case to case, in keeping with the idea that multiple sources of information are drawn upon in ordinary cases of remembering. It will be an empirical project to determine what kinds of states and processes fall within this disjunction of appropriate causes. In order for this proposal not to be vacuous, consisting in a completely open-ended list of what may count as an appropriate cause, there will ultimately need to be some fixed set of such causes, the activity of which typifies a healthy episodic memory system. The guiding idea (well, *hunch*) behind this proposal is that there will indeed be some limited number of them (considered as types of causes) at work in cases where, intuitively, we judge there to be a non-deviant causal chain in place. We should not expect ourselves to be able to enumerate them all now, prior to a more complete empirical investigation.

I have given the barest sketch of two such causal chains, by finding a possible causal role for beliefs of a certain sort and for feelings of fluency. Importantly, in the cases described, these may seem to be non-deviant causes of (genuine) remembering, *even though* they do not involve memory traces as the relevant causes. Showing this to be an open possibility is the main point of this section. Once we view remembering as a complex inferential process, involving, in each instance, the collaboration of multiple mental states, we have correspondingly many candidates for the mental state or process that (partly) enable the remembering and that may provide an appropriate causal link to an observation of the event remembered. Memory traces need not always bear that burden. We may now see, in the offing, a kind of compromise between constructivist continuism and the causal theory.

1.6.1 Postscript: Reply to Schirmer dos Santos, McCarroll, and Sant'Anna

I find much to agree with, and a few things that perplex, in Schirmer dos Santos, McCarroll, and Sant'Anna's (Chapter 2, this volume) meditation on the (dis)continuism debate. They and I agree that it would sell the debate short to suggest that continuists and discontinuists are talking past each other—each using different senses of the term 'remembering' and, for that reason, arriving at conflicting conclusions about the relation of remembering to imagining. Yet Schirmer dos Santos, McCarroll, and Sant'Anna (hereafter, 'SMS') nevertheless want to emphasise that the debate is in some sense linguistic, resulting from each side's meaning something different by 'remembering'. For SMS, this difference in the meaning of 'remember' in the mouths of each group does not detract from the substance of the debate. They think we should see causal theorists and simulationists as involved in a 'metalinguistic negotiation' over what the meaning of 'remember' *ought* to be. Causalists prescribe that 'remember' should be defined such that remembering requires the fulfilment of an appropriate causation condition. Whereas simulationists propose to define 'remembering' so that its instances—including even its *successful* instances—need only result from the reliable functioning of an episodic construction system.

Supposing this is correct, what, exactly, is *metalinguistic* about this dispute? I am not sure. SMS are clear that they do not see the (dis)continuism debate as a (confused) metalinguistic debate of the sort had when two people argue over the meaning of the word 'bank', each unwittingly using a different word (homonyms) with an entirely different meaning. In the case of 'remembering', they explain, there is one side that will ultimately have to cede to the other concerning its proper use. Why isn't this, then, a straightforward dispute about the nature of remembering? What makes it metalinguistic?

Their answer seems to lie in the idea that—to pull from their quotation of Ludlow (2008, p. 117)—this is a case where 'crucial aspects of word meaning depend upon facts about the world that remain open'. Each side can be seen as *prescribing* a certain use of the term, as a part of a research strategy, perhaps, until there are good empirical reasons not to use it in that way. The problem I see with this is that simulationists—such as Michaelian (2016c), De Brigard (2014a), and Addis (2020)—seem to think the facts are already in. They do not advocate the simulationist conception of remembering as a kind of bold guess about how to describe certain borderline cases of remembering. They think that the last two decades of work on episodic remembering already strongly favour a simulationist view, where appropriate causal connections are not essential to successful remembering. To accuse them of a metalinguistic negotiation seems a coy way of saying that one doesn't buy the empirical case that has been made. Well, perhaps one shouldn't buy it, but then the debate seems to be about the quality of the evidence for and against simulationism and not about the meaning of 'remember'.

So, while I agree with SMS that there is a real debate afoot between continuists and discontinuists, I do not fully see the benefit in framing it as metalinguistic in nature. As they note, I think the debate hangs on whether remembering is a kind of *constructive* imagining and not over whether remembering is a kind of *attitudinal* imagining. In Section 2.4, SMS emphasise that they see an important debate still to be had concerning the attitudes involved in each of remembering and imagining and are dissatisfied with my apparent dismissal of such a debate. To clarify my own view on the matter: I do maintain that there is no substantive debate to be had over whether remembering is a kind of attitudinal imagining (because all sides will agree it is not). However, I also think there are interesting questions to ask concerning whether some *imagistic* imaginings—that is, some occurrent uses of mental imagery—may involve the same kind of (judgment-like) attitude as remembering. I outline a way of framing that question (in Langland-Hassan, 2015, 2020), where I develop a view on which some imagery-involving states are judgments. (Though I do not in either paper adequately address questions surrounding remembering.) I think SMS also see this question as substantive and worth pursuing. Yet this is not the question of whether remembering is a kind of imagining (which we can call the (dis)continuism-about-imagination debate), but whether some judgments that make use of mental imagery involve the same attitude as remembering. This we can call the (dis)continuism-about-judgment debate. It revolves around the question of whether remembering is a kind of occurrent belief.

Notes

1 The *OED*'s definition 2 for 'imagination' also appears to allow both fantasy *and* memory to be cases of imagining: 'The mind considered as engaged in imagining; a person's mind, or a part of it, represented as the place where images, ideas, and thoughts are produced and stored, or in which they are contained' (OED, 2009).

2 More commonly discussed in philosophy are the notions of *attitudinal imagination* and *imagistic imagining*. On my favoured understanding of imagistic imagining, all uses of mental imagery constitute imagistic imagining (Langland-Hassan, 2020; Van Leeuwen, 2013). Though some favour a more demanding conception of imagistic imagining, where it requires both imagery and (something like) an attitude of imagining toward the content represented by the imagery (Arcangeli, 2020; Kind, 2001). It is common to understand attitudinal imagining as occurring when someone takes an imaginative attitude toward a content (Kind, 2016; Van Leeuwen, 2013), though I favour (what I see as) a more theoretically neutral characterisation where attitudinal imagining is any instance of rich, elaborated, and epistemically safe thought about the possible, fantastical, or unreal (Langland-Hassan, 2020).

3 Thanks to a referee for pressing me to clarify this point. The contrast in kinds of constraint that I have in mind will be further clarified via the two competing conceptions of memory traces—the replay theory and prop theory—outlined in Section 1.5.

4 In a standard case of relearning, a person's current representation of a past event is causally dependent upon his having witnessed the past event, but (intuitively, to most) not causally dependent *in the right way*. Specifically, information about the remembered event has been forgotten and "relearned" through another's testimony—where the availability of this testimony itself causally depends upon the person who originally had the experience having related its details to someone else, prior to forgetting it.

5 It is sometimes held—e.g., by Bernecker (2010, p. 137)—that memory traces are 'distributed' across nodes in neural networks. It might be thought their being distributed in this manner conflicts with the idea that only one event can be remembered through the use of each trace. Indeed, Robins (2016) argues that there is such a conflict, and, further, that there being such a conflict clashes with the causal theory of memory that Bernecker aims to defend. For present purposes, what matters is that Bernecker—and other existing defenders of the Causal Theory of Memory—are committed to traces allowing for this sort of 'one trace to one experience rememberable' mapping, whether or not that is ultimately compatible with their view of how traces are stored in the brain.

6 While I cannot adequately review the relevant empirical literature here, a few observations can be made. Much of the behavioural and neuroimaging evidence put forward by continuists—involving co-occurring deficits in remembering and imagining the future (Hassabis, Kumaran, Vann, & Maguire, 2007; Hassabis & Maguire, 2009), and co-activation of a core neural network during each (Schacter & Addis, 2007;

Schacter, Addis, & Buckner, 2007; Szpunar, Watson, & McDermott, 2007)—is equally consistent with a replay conception of traces where traces are a resource common to both remembering and imagining the future, being modified and recombined in new ways only during the latter. Simulationists have also highlighted the fact that systematic errors are common in episodic memory; and it has been shown that one's sense of whether one is remembering can be manipulated in predictable ways (Garry, Manning, Loftus, & Sherman, 1996; Loftus & Pickrell, 1995). This makes sense if, as on the prop theory, remembering involves the active attempt of a stage manager to assemble relevant representations, as the stage manager may be sensitive to various cues that, at times, could lead him astray. However, as we saw earlier, the question of *how* relevant traces are organised, and the means by which they are retrieved, is far from straightforward even on the replay view, having much to do with the general labels attached to them. Errors in retrieval are to be expected there as well. Perhaps more telling in favour of the prop theory is recent empirical work indicating that memory traces are subject to processes of reconsolidation, during which stored traces are "reopened" so as to be updated and refined in the light of new experiences (Dudai, 2012; Nadel, 2007; Sara, 2000). If a single trace is causally shaped by multiple distinct experiences, it is plausible to think that the matter of *which* experience is being remembered through use of the trace is not determined by the trace itself. Such a trace could then be seen as a kind of prop that can be used to remember the various different experiences from which it derives. It is possible, however, for there to be traces that are subject to process of reconsolidation processes yet that are still only used to remember one event. This could be the case if, for instance, the information added to the trace during reconsolidation still only pertained to the original event during which the trace was produced. Whether, and how often, reconsolidation in fact results in trace promiscuity seems to me unsettled by current empirical work.

7 This does not entail that *all* cases where there is experienced fluency for a stimulus will result in genuine remembering, as fluency for a stimulus can be caused by things other than perceiving it (such as imagining it). (Thanks to a reviewer for noting this.) The point is simply that, in some cases, a state of fluency for a stimulus may be what provides an appropriate causal link to a past perception of the stimulus. See Langland-Hassan (2022) for further development of this proposal.

References

Addis, D. R. (2020). Mental time travel? A neurocognitive model of event simulation. *Review of Philosophy and Psychology*, *11*(2), 233–259. doi:10.1007/s13164-020-00470-0

Arcangeli, M. (2020). The two faces of mental imagery. *Philosophy and Phenomenological Research*, *101*(2), 304–322.

Bastin, C., Besson, G., Simon, J., Delhaye, E., Geurten, M., Willems, S., & Salmon, E. (2019). An integrative memory model of recollection and familiarity to understand memory deficits. *Behaviour Brain Science*, *42*, e281. doi:10.1017/s0140525x19000621

Bernecker, S. (2010). *Memory: A Philosophical Study*. New York: Oxford University Press.

Craver, C. F. (2020). Remembering: Epistemic and empirical. *Review of Philosophy and Psychology*, *11*(2), 261–281.

De Brigard, F. (2014a). Is memory for remembering? Recollection as a form of episodic hypothetical thinking. *Synthese*, *191*(2), 155–185. doi:10.1007/s11229-013-0247-7

De Brigard, F. (2014b). The nature of memory traces. *Philosophy Compass*, *9*(6), 402–414. doi:10.1111/phc3.12133

Debus, D. (2014). 'Mental time travel': Remembering the past, imagining the future, and the particularity of events. *Review of Philosophy and Psychology*, *5*(3), 333–350. https://doi.org/10.1007/s13164-014-0182-7

Debus, D. (2017). Memory causation. In S. Bernecker & K. Michaelian (Eds.), *The Routledge Handbook of Philosophy of Memory* (pp. 63–75). London: Routledge.

Dudai, Y. (2012). The restless engram: Consolidations never end. *Annual Review of Neuroscience, 35*(1), 227–247. doi:10.1146/annurev-neuro-062111-150500

Fernández, J. (2019). *Memory: A Self-Referential Account.* New York: Oxford University Press.

Garry, M., Manning, C. G., Loftus, E. F., & Sherman, S. J. (1996). Imagination inflation: Imagining a childhood event inflates confidence that it occurred. *Psychonomic Bulletin & Review, 3*(2), 208–214.

Hassabis, D., Kumaran, D., Vann, S. D., & Maguire, E. A. (2007). Patients with hippocampal amnesia cannot imagine new experiences. *Proceedings of the National Academy of Sciences of the United States of America, 104*, 1726–1731.

Hassabis, D., & Maguire, E. A. (2009). The construction system of the brain. *Philosophical Transactions of the Royal Society B: Biological Sciences, 364*(1521), 1263–1271.

Kind, A. (2001). Putting the image back in imagination. *Philosophy and Phenomenological Research, 62*(1), 85–109.

Kind, A. (2016). Introduction: Exploring imagination. In A. Kind (Ed.), *The Routledge Handbook of Philosophy of Imagination* (pp. 1–12). New York: Routledge.

Langland-Hassan, P. (2015). Imaginative attitudes. *Philosophy and Phenomenological Research, 90*(3), 664–686. doi:10.1111/phpr.12115

Langland-Hassan, P. (2020). *Explaining Imagination.* Oxford: Oxford University Press.

Langland-Hassan, P. (2022). Propping up the Causal Theory. *Synthese, 200*(95), https://doi.org/10.1007/s11229-022-03635-9

Liao, S.-Y., & Gendler, T. (2020). Imagination. In E. N. Zalta (Ed.), *The Stanford Encyclopedia of Philosophy* (Summer 2020 ed.). https://plato.stanford.edu/archives/sum2020/entries/imagination/

Loftus, E. F., & Pickrell, J. E. (1995). The formation of false memories. *Psychiatric Annals, 25*(12), 720–725. doi:10.3928/0048-5713-19951201-07

Ludlow, P. (2008). Cheap contextualism. *Philosophical Issues, 18*, 104–129. https://www.jstor.org/stable/27749902

Martin, C. B., & Deutscher, M. (1966). Remembering. *The Philosophical Review, 75*(2), 161–196. doi:10.2307/2183082

Michaelian, K. (2011). Generative memory. *Philosophical Psychology, 24*(3), 323–342. doi:10.1080/09515089.2011.559623

Michaelian, K. (2016a). Against discontinuism. In K. Michaelian, S. B. Klein, & K. K. Szpunar (Eds.), *Seeing the Future: Theoretical Perspectives on Future-Oriented Mental Time Travel.* Oxford: Oxford University Press.

Michaelian, K. (2016b). Confabulating, misremembering, relearning: The simulation theory of memory and unsuccessful remembering. *Frontiers in Psychology, 7*, 1857.

Michaelian, K. (2016c). *Mental Time Travel: Episodic Memory and Our Knowledge of the Personal Past.* Cambridge, MA: MIT Press.

Michaelian, K. (2021). Imagining the past reliably and unreliably: Towards a virtue theory of memory. *Synthese.* doi:10.1007/s11229-021-03125-4

Nadel, L. (2007). Consolidation: The demise of the fixed trace. In H. L. Roediger, Y. Dudai, & S. M. Fitzpatrick (Eds.), *Science of Memory Concepts* (pp. 177–182). Oxford: Oxford University Press.

OED. (Ed.) (2009) *Oxford English Dictionary* (3rd ed.). Oxford: Oxford University Press.

Perrin, D. (2016). Asymmetries in Subjective Time. In K. Michaelian, S. B. Klein, & K. K. Szpunar (Eds.), *Seeing the Future: Theoretical Perspectives on Future-Oriented Mental Time Travel* (pp. 39–61). Oxford: Oxford University Press.

Perrin, D., & Michaelian, K. (2017). Memory as mental time travel. In S. Bernecker & K. Michaelian (Eds.), *The Routledge Handbook of Philosophy of Memory* (pp. 228–239). New York: Routledge.

Robins, S. (2016). Representing the past: Memory traces and the causal theory of memory. *Philosophical Studies, 173*(11), 2993–3013. doi:10.1007/s11098-016-0647-x

Robins, S. (2017). Memory traces. In K. Michaelian & S. Bernecker (Eds.), *The Routledge Handbook of Philosophy of Memory* (pp. 76–87). London: Routledge.

Sara, S. J. (2000). Retrieval and reconsolidation: Toward a neurobiology of remembering. *Learning & Memory, 7*(2), 73–84.

Schacter, D. L., & Addis, D. R. (2007). The cognitive neuroscience of constructive memory: Remembering the past and imagining the future. *The Philosophical Transactions of the Royal Society B: Biological Sciences, 362*, 773–786.

Schacter, D. L., Addis, D. R., & Buckner, R. L. (2007). Remembering the past to imagine the future: The prospective brain. *Nature Review Neuroscience, 8*(9), 657–661.

Szpunar, K. K., Watson, J. M., & McDermott, K. B. (2007). Neural substrates of envisioning the future. *Proceedings of the National Academy of Sciences, 104*(2), 642–647.

Van Leeuwen, N. (2013). The meanings of 'imagine' part I: Constructive imagination. *Philosophy Compass, 8*(3), 220–230. https://doi.org/10.1111/j.1747-9991.2012.00508.x

Whittlesea, B. W. A. (1993). Illusions of familiarity. *Journal of Experimental Psychology: Learning, Memory, and Cognition, 19*(6), 1235–1253. doi:10.1037/0278-7393.19.6.1235

Whittlesea, B. W. A., & Williams, L. D. (2000). The source of feelings of familiarity: The discrepancy-attribution hypothesis. *Journal of Experimental Psychology: Learning, Memory, and Cognition, 26*(3), 547–565. doi:10.1037/0278-7393.26.3.547

Whittlesea, B. W. A., & Williams, L. D. (2001). The discrepancy-attribution hypothesis: I. The heuristic basis of feelings and familiarity. *Journal of Experimental Psychology: Learning, Memory, and Cognition, 27*(1), 3–13. doi:10.1037/0278-7393.27.1.3

2 The relation between memory and imagination

A debate about the right concepts

César Schirmer dos Santos, Christopher Jude McCarroll, and André Sant'Anna

2.1 Introduction

Episodic memory and imagination both represent absent events, and do so similarly, involving a rich, quasi-sensory phenomenology. Yet, is this similarity substantive? Is there a difference in kind between memory and imagination, or simply a difference in degree? Indeed, what precisely is the relation between memory and imagination? According to discontinuists, memory and imagination are different kinds of states or processes. According to continuists, any difference between memory and imagination is a difference in degree. This is the (dis)continuism debate about memory and imagination (Perrin 2016).

The (dis)continuism debate has been mostly articulated as a debate about causation and has resulted in two different factions—*causalism* and *simulationism*. According to causalists, memory is defined in terms of an appropriate causal connection to a past experience (Martin and Deutscher 1966). Because no such connection is present in imagining, causalists argue that memory and imagination are mental states of different kinds (Debus 2014). According to simulationists, memory and imagination are mental states produced by the same cognitive system, and as such, are states of the same kind (Michaelian 2016b). Because a causal connection of the relevant sort is unnecessary for imagining, the simulationist argues that it is not required for remembering either. This has led Perrin and Michaelian (2017) to suggest, in a recent overview of the debate, that the dispute concerning the relationship between memory and imagination boils down to the question of whether a causal connection is necessary for remembering.

Even though this debate focuses to some extent on *describing* the mechanisms of memory, given the focus on the necessity of an appropriate causal connection, one might wonder whether there is not a sense in which the debate is also *conceptual*. That is, maybe these different ways of conceiving the relationship between memory and imagination result from causalists and simulationists defining 'remembering' very differently. This, in turn, might imply that they are talking past each other. Compare the two natural language sentences, 'Mary moved to the bank' and 'Mary went to the bank'. In determining whether Mary ended up at the side of a river, or a financial institution, we need to know which sense of the word 'bank' these sentences are picking out. In the same way that the word

DOI: 10.4324/9781003002277-4

'bank' may express different meanings in different sentences, perhaps causalists and simulationists use the word 'remembering' in different ways? Indeed, there is a constant risk of reducing a substantive debate to a merely verbal dispute when it comes to philosophical discussions. It happens, for instance, when an observer tries to be charitable to the truth of the claims of all the participants in a debate, even though the participants may be using the same word in different ways, and concludes that everybody is right about different themes (Thomasson 2017). It also happens when one disputant interprets the opponent uncharitably, or, as we will argue in this chapter, when one fails to acknowledge the intentions of, or how the debate is conducted by, those involved in it.

These problems, it might be argued, threaten to trivialise the debate between causalists and simulationists in philosophy of memory, and, consequently, the debate about the relationship between memory and imagination. We suggest in this chapter that the debate is about *using the right concepts*, without being merely a verbal dispute. The use of 'remember' in the (dis)continuism debate is not the same as the different senses of 'bank' invoked earlier. We show that the debate between causalists and simulationists in particular, and the debate about the relation between memory and imagination more generally, are substantive ones. Importantly, we depart from recent approaches in that we think the substance of the debate lies not in an attempt to *describe* the mechanisms responsible for remembering and imagining, but rather in determining how the terms 'remember' and 'imagine' *should* be used. In a nutshell, we propose the reinterpretation of these debates as *normative* or *prescriptive*—instead of *descriptive*—disputes.

The chapter progresses as follows. Section 2.2 begins by introducing the causalism–simulationism and (dis)continuism debates. Section 2.3 then argues that, reinterpreted as prescriptive, the causalism–simulationism debate is about substantive questions relative to how the concept of 'remembering' *should* be used: it is important to look at the *intention* for using a concept in a particular way. According to our proposal, the causalist *prescribes* an appropriate causal connection between an accurate representation of an event *e* and the previous experience of the same event as the difference-maker between remembering and merely imagining (Martin and Deutscher 1966). In contrast, simulationists *prescribe* that memory is an inherently constructive capacity, thus arguing that this is reason for rejecting the causalist prescription (Michaelian 2016b, 13).

Finally, Section 2.4 considers an important implication of the prescriptive approach. We argue that it opens the logical space for a discussion of two problems, rather than only one problem, concerning the relationship between memory and imagination. In particular, we argue that focusing on the necessity of a causal connection is only *one* way of thinking about the continuism–discontinuism debate. We explore an alternative view, which involves conceiving of the continuism–discontinuism debate in terms of the *attitudes* that characterise remembering and imagining (Robins 2020; Sant'Anna 2021).

This proposal relies on a common way of characterising mental states in philosophy of mind, which consists in distinguishing between their *contents* and their *attitudes* (Searle 1983). The content is what the mental state represents, whereas the attitude is the stance taken toward what is represented. This distinction between attitude and content helps explain why we can have *different* mental states, which play different roles in our cognitive economies, that have the *same* content. Remembering and imagining are intentional states—they are states that represent or are about some object or state of affairs. While it is important to think of the relation between them in terms of content, and whether their content involves a causal connection to a past event, it is also essential to adequately characterise their respective attitudes.[1] Considering this alternative will lead to a more refined understanding of the precise issues involved in thinking about the relation between memory and imagination.

2.2 Causalism, simulationism, and the (dis)continuism debate

One way of thinking about the relation between memory and imagination is to think of it in terms of the necessity of a causal connection to the event represented by those mental states. Is a causal connection necessary for remembering and not imagining? The idea that present memories stand in a causal relation to past events has been articulated by a number of philosophers and can perhaps even be traced back to Aristotle, who tells us that memory images are produced in our soul *as a result of* former perception.[2] But the first systematically developed version of the causal theory, and the one that most informs contemporary research in philosophy of memory, is from Martin and Deutscher (1966).

The causal theory of memory, or simply *causalism*, says that remembering occurs only when a representation is appropriately causally connected to a past perceptual experience.[3] This is often expressed by the idea that remembering requires a *memory trace*,[4] understood as a brain state that encodes and stores information at the time of experience and that is later retrieved to cause memories of those events. Thus, causalists have proposed that a causal connection is appropriate when a memory trace, laid down at the time of the original event, connects a particular past event to a current representation of it.

The requirement for a causal connection in remembering has led causalists to argue that memory and imagination are mental states of different *kinds*. According to them, if there is an appropriate causal connection between a subject's current mental representation of an event and his previous experience of it, the representation will count as a case of remembering; in contrast, if such a causal connection is missing, the representation will count as a case of imagining.[5] Memory and imagination are, in other words, *discontinuous* (e.g., Debus 2014; Perrin 2016).

Causalism has, however, been challenged by a wealth of recent empirical evidence, which demonstrates that remembering is an active, constructive and reconstructive process, using information generated in the present (Addis 2018). Memories are constructed in—and alive to—the context of the present. To remember is not to retrieve a representation of a past event in the form of a memory trace, but rather to generate a representation that may incorporate content that was unavailable at the time of the original experience of the event and hence was not stored in a trace. Even though the classical causal theory can be updated and modified to reflect memory's creativity (e.g., Michaelian 2011), another line of research seems to further dissolve the boundaries between memory and imagination. According to this body of research, (episodic) memory and (episodic) imagination are just two specific occurrences of a more general cognitive capacity that we have for mental time travel in subjective time: while remembering is the specific ability we have to mentally travel into past subjective time, so as to "re-live" or "re-experience" an event, imagining corresponds to the specific ability we have to mentally travel into future subjective time, so as to simulate the experience of a possible event.[6] This research on memory as mental time travel (MTT) provides further motivation to abandon the necessity of a causal condition.

Inspired by the evidence on constructive memory and MTT, the simulation theory makes just such a move: it rejects the idea that a causal connection is necessary for remembering. The simulation theory, or simply *simulationism*, proposes that remembering is just a form of *imagining* the past (Michaelian 2016b, 103, 111). On this view, successful remembering occurs when a representation of a past event is produced by a reliably (properly) functioning *episodic construction system*, a neurocognitive system that also constructs representations of other scenarios, such as future and counterfactual episodes (see De Brigard 2014a).

Simulationism thus suggests that remembering and imagining are *continuous*; that is, they are mental states of the same kind at the most fundamental level.[7] The continuity between memory and imagination motivates the simulationist argument against the necessity of a causal connection for remembering. According to simulationists, mental time travel research implies that memory and imagination are mental states of the same kind. Given that imagination does not require a causal connection to what is imagined, it follows that a causal connection is not necessary for remembering.[8]

Thus, as is clear from this brief overview, the current dispute between causalists and simulationists has, in the context of the philosophy of memory, been closely associated with the dispute over whether memory and imagination are mental states of the same kind, or whether they are continuous with one another. On the one hand, causalists side with *discontinuists*, who believe that there is a fundamental difference between memory and imagination; on the other hand, simulationists side with *continuists*, who believe that there is no such fundamental difference. Some, such as Perrin and Michaelian (2017), have even gone as far as to say that the continuism–discontinuism dispute boils down to the causalism-simulationism dispute (see also Michaelian, Perrin, and Sant'Anna 2020). We believe, however, that reducing the former debate to the latter is problematic, for reasons articulated elsewhere (Sant'Anna 2021). Rather than rehearse those arguments here, in what follows, we will argue that there is a different way of formulating the dispute over the (dis)continuity between remembering and imagining. Motivating this alternative will require, as a first step, getting clear on what we mean by 'memory' and 'imagination', a task to which we turn our attention in the next sections.

2.3 Defining 'remembering'

Let us begin by looking into what we mean by 'remembering'. As we will see, one worry arising in the context of causalism–simulationism is that the participants in the debate seem to be defining 'remembering' in different ways. This might suggest that the debate is merely verbal, that is, that causalists and simulationists are just talking past one another. We will argue, however, that this is not the case. We show that even though they have different conceptions of remembering, the debate is a substantive one. Getting clear on the terms of the causalism-simulationism debate, we suggest, will afford us a way of getting clearer about the relation between memory and imagination.

If causalists and simulationists are not talking past one another, then what is the sense in which the debate is a substantive one? Answering this question requires identifying two ways in which a philosophical debate might unfold. On the one hand, the debate might be about *facts*, in the sense that it is about the nature or existence of an object, property, or relation. For example, in the debate about the relation between memory and imagination, the question of whether there is a property or relation, such as vivacity or causation, that pertains primarily or only to mnemonic states, is a debate about a fact concerning memory and imagination. On the other hand, the debate might be about *language*, in which case it is about the meaning of a word—for instance, when we want to know what 'remembering' means.

It might be argued that, if there is a sense in which the causalism–simulationism debate is substantive, it must be a debate about facts. A factualist interpretation along these lines is actually suggested by Michaelian (2016b, 97). On this way of seeing the dispute, the causalist proposes that an appropriate causal relation between a past experience and a present representation marks the difference between remembering and imagining. The simulationist, in contrast, argues that this difference has to do with the operations and aims of the episodic construction system—i.e., with whether the system is functioning reliably and whether it aims to represent an event in the personal past, the counterfactual personal past, or the personal future. Thus, the debate about what the criterion of mnemicity is—i.e., what makes a mental state a memory—boils down to the question of which view, causalism or simulationism, gets the relevant facts about 'remembering' right.

A problem with this factualist view of the debate is that there is no evidence of causalists or simulationists rejecting facts about memory and imagination. It is quite the opposite. For instance, both sides try hard to propose research compatible with the discoveries about mental time travel (Michaelian 2016a, 2016b; De Brigard 2014a; Robins 2020; Werning 2020). Indeed, another important issue that separates causalists and simulationists is whether remembering requires that a subject previously experienced the remembered event. While causalists argue that this is a requirement, simulationists deny it (Michaelian 2016b; see McCarroll 2020 for discussion). Thus, the dispute is *not* about the relevant facts for distinguishing memory from imagination. Instead, we propose, it is about the *meaning* of 'remembering'.

Of course, this proposal can be challenged. After all, causalists and simulationists seem to agree about the meaning of 'remembering'. For instance, both use the word to refer to the mental representation of an episode of one's personal past. But, as we saw in the last section, they disagree about the nature of remembering. More specifically, they disagree about the continuity between remembering and imagining. And, as we said in the last paragraph, they agree about the facts. How to interpret this situation? Carl Craver (2020) provides a source of inspiration. He notes that "[t]he construct 'remembering' is equivocal between an *epistemic sense*, denoting a distinctive ground for knowledge, and *empirical sense*, denoting the typical behavior of a neurocognitive mechanism" (2020, p. 261, our emphasis).

While we will not speak of 'epistemic' and 'empirical' remembering in what follows, we believe that Craver's overall diagnosis that there is an ambiguity in the notion of 'remembering' is on the right track. Building on this, we want to explore the hypothesis that causalists and simulationists disagree about the meaning of 'remembering'. For simplicity, we will refer to the causalist usage of the term as 'REMEMBERING$_C$'. In opposition, we will refer to the simulationist's use of 'remembering' as 'REMEMBERING$_S$'. A problem with this path, understood in this way, is that if the dispute is about language, and no fact is disputed, then there does not seem to be much substance to the debate after all, for it can be dissolved by the parties simply acknowledging that there are two concepts of 'remembering' at play.

A debate *can* be dissolved this way. But the causalism–simulationism debate is not. Why is it not? We propose that the explanation concerns the participants' *intentions*. Both causalists and simulationists know very well that they use 'remembering' differently. Thus, mere awareness of this situation does not suffice to end the debate. So, the question that becomes central is, why does the debate continue? Our suggestion is that the causalism–simulationism dispute is ultimately a debate about what the word 'remembering' *should* mean, given the facts we know about its nature. To further motivate this point, we need to look back at the distinction between debates about facts and debates about language introduced earlier. We tend to assume that only debates about facts can be substantive. However, there can be substantive disputes about what a word *should* mean.

Let us consider an example to illustrate. Suppose that one wants to assess the debate between two philosophers, M. and B., on the reality of time. Both accept that the time of physics is different from commonsensical time and that we can experience time. Thus, M. and B. accept the same facts. But while M. claims that 'time' means 'physical time', B. claims that 'time' refers to a feature of experience. M. and B. know very well each other's position. Still, in a debate, they manifest disagreement:

M.: Time does not exist.
B.: No. Time exists.

What is happening in this dispute? If we interpret the debate as a dispute about the literal meaning of 'time', then there is no substantive disagreement between M. and B. But if we understand the conversation as a dispute that is not centred on literal meaning, we can make explicit the point of disagreement (Plunkett and Sundell 2013, 7). One option is that, in their conversation, as a way of manifesting disagreement, M. and B. use 'time' *metalinguistically*, i.e., to show how the word should be used (Plunkett and Sundell 2013, 3). In this case, there is substantive disagreement, but it is not about facts. In this sense, M. and B. are not involved in a merely verbal dispute. There is something *substantive* at stake: how one *should* understand a concept (Thomasson 2017, 2–3).

Our claim is that, similar to the dispute between M. and B. about 'time', the dispute between causalists and simulationists about 'remembering' is not merely verbal. Rather, it is a substantive dispute about how we should use the word 'remembering' (and other cognate terms) based on facts. So, despite causalists and simulationists using the word 'remembering' differently, it does not follow from this that they are talking past each other. Instead, they are negotiating what 'remembering' *should* mean given the relevant facts for the appropriate use of this term. Following Plunkett and Sundell (2013, 3), we call *metalinguistic negotiation* 'a dispute … that employs competing metalinguistic usages of an expression, and that reflects a disagreement about the proper deployment of linguistic representations'.

Two points are worth highlighting here. The first is that metalinguistic negotiations can be tacit. Thus, the fact that the disputants involved in a debate sometimes fail to be explicit about how they are using certain words—e.g., they do not say things such as 'by "W" I mean …'—does not imply that they are not involved in a metalinguistic negotiation. For it is often charitable in those contexts to interpret the *use* that the disputants make of the word 'W' as a way of claiming what 'W' should mean. And when we interpret them in this way, we take the disputants to make a metalinguistic usage of the words, in the sense that we view them as making a claim similar to 'by "W" I mean …'. The second point is that, although the claim of a disputant can be interpreted as being about the meaning of a word, it does not follow from this that the dispute is merely verbal. As we pointed out before, the question of what a word *should* mean is a substantive one, in the sense that it is based on reason or evidence for the prescription of an extension or intension for the word in question.

As we said, Craver's (2020) proposal inspired us to explore the hypothesis that causalists and simulationists use 'remembering' differently. However, going beyond Craver's proposal, and adopting a view proposed by Plunkett and Sundell (2013), we propose that the dispute is about what *should* be in the extension of 'remembering.' Causalists and simulationists thus use 'remembering' differently because "crucial aspects of word meaning depend upon facts about the world that remain open" (Ludlow 2008, 117). Their dispute is therefore one about the difficult task of identifying *which* facts should figure in our understanding of the word 'remembering.' There are no facts of the matter about whether remembering necessarily requires a causal connection, nor are there facts of the matter about whether remembering requires that one necessarily previously experienced the past event. These claims are being negotiated in light of the correct way of articulating what we mean by 'remember'. In other words, the dispute between causalists and simulationists revolves around a metalinguistic negotiation about the proper way of using the concept of 'remembering'.

The idea of a metalinguistic dispute between causalists and simulationists can be further motivated with the help of a little science fiction. Suppose that a scientist wants to build a *Mnem-O-Matic* machine that differentiates remembering from imagining personal episodes from the actual past. The plan for this device must respect some conception of remembering. However, there is no relevant empirical data sufficient for planning the machine, and there is more than one philosophical conception of remembering. Therefore, more than one plan for a Mnem-O-Matic device is possible.[9]

Consider, first, a Mnem-O-Matic machine built according to the causalist concept of remembering. Call this the *C-Mnem-O-Matic* machine. In line with the causalist definition offered before, the main thing tracked by *C-Mnem-O-Matic* is the causal history of a memory representation. Consider, second, a Mnem-O-Matic machine built according to the simulationist concept of remembering. Call it the *S-Mnem-O-Matic* machine. In line with the simulationist definition offered before, the main thing tracked by *S-Mnem-O-Matic* is whether a representation produced by a reliably functioning episodic construction system tries to simulate an event in the personal past.[10] Importantly, both machines reflect different prescriptions about what should be tracked when assessing the nature of an alleged state of remembering. In this sense, deciding which *Mnem-O-Matic* machine should be built is equivalent to negotiating (in a metalinguistic sense) how the word 'remembering' should be used.

Now, to illustrate how the dispute between causalists and simulationists unfolds, consider a couple of different puzzles.

Puzzle 1

Alice goes in the *C-Mnem-O-Matic* machine. Alice represents an episode E in her mind. *C-Mnem-O-Matic* identifies that there is an appropriate causal connection between Alice's previous experience and her present representation of E and her episodic construction system is working unreliably. Does Alice REMEMBER E?[11]

There are two possible answers here. By relying on REMEMBER$_C$, the causalist will say: 'The participant REMEMBERS$_C$ because there is an appropriate causal connection between the present representation and experience'. In contrast, by adopting REMEMBER$_S$, the simulationist will provide a different answer: 'This is not REMEMBERING$_S$ because REMEMBERING$_S$ requires the reliable operation of the episodic construction system'.

Consider now the second puzzle:

Puzzle 2
John goes in the *S-Mnem-O-Matic* machine. John represents an episode E in his mind. *S-Mnem-O-Matic* identifies that there is not an appropriate causal relation between John's previous experience and his present representation of E and his episodic construction system is working reliably and aims to simulate the actual past. Does John REMEMBER E?

Like Puzzle 1, there are two possible answers here. Relying on $REMEMBER_C$, the causalist will say that: 'The participant does not $REMEMBER_C$ because $REMEMBERING_C$ requires a causal relation between the present representation and experience'. In contrast, by relying on $REMEMBER_S$, the simulationist provides a different answer: 'The participant $REMEMBERS_S$ because the episodic construction system is working reliably and aims to simulate the actual past'.

The upshot of Puzzles 1 and 2 is that there is a disagreement about what empirical facts matter for the use of 'remembering'. The machines track different facts—causal chains in the case of the C-Mnem-O-Matic machine, reliable operation in the S-Mnem-O-Matic machine case. Thus, the participants in the debate observe and accept the same facts. They also understand how the machines work. But they disagree about which facts are relevant for understanding or explaining what 'remembering' is. Their disagreement about the explanatory facts manifests itself as a disagreement about the meaning of 'remembering'. In Puzzle 1, the causalist uses C-Mnem-O-Matic to prescribe when $REMEMBERING_C$ should be used, namely, only when there is causal connection between experience and representation of an event. The simulationist, of course, disagrees with this prescription. Likewise, in Puzzle 2, the simulationist uses S-Mnem-O-Matic to prescribe when $REMEMBERING_S$ should be used, namely, only when the episodic construction system works reliably and aims to simulate the actual past. And the causalist, of course, disagrees with this prescription.

Thus, the Mnem-O-Matic machine thought experiment allows us to clearly see that the causalism–simulationism debate is not merely a debate about how to describe what 'remembering' is, but rather a debate about how we should use the term 'remembering.' In other words, it is not a *descriptive*, but rather a *prescriptive* debate about 'remembering'. Since the relevant *facts* about 'remembering' remain open (Ludlow 2008, 117), it is natural to expect the existence of different conceptions designed to capture those facts. Hence, far from being a merely verbal dispute, the causalism–simulationism debate is a substantive dispute about the normativity of language.

One could object that the problem of the criterion of mnemicity concerns the metaphysics of memory, and metaphysics, arguably, is about joint-carvingness (Sider 2011). Thus, the metaphysician must commit ontologically to the kinds of objects, events, and properties postulated by the best science available.

According to this objection, there is no space for prescriptive conceptual nego-tiation. Either the metaphysician commits ontologically to the suitable entities, or she does not.

In response, we do not think that these considerations threaten our argument: we provide two distinct replies to this objection. First, while we can accept that, if possible, a metaphysician must carve nature at its joints according to the best science available, we point out that the empirical evidence about the relation between memory and imagination is at best ambiguous. There is empirical evidence to support both continuism and discontinuism about memory and imagination (Perrin & Michaelian 2017; Michaelian, Perrin, & Sant'Anna 2020). Science does not tell us the answer, so part of the debate is precisely negotiating how to best interpret what science is telling us and what evidence should line up with the concept of remembering. Second, the objection rather neglects the importance of *conceptual ethics*, the field of investigation concerning the "concepts [we] should … use to think and talk about the world" (Burgess and Plunkett 2013, 1091). In other words, the objection assumes that, under-stood as a concept, remembering is unequivocally a joint-carving concept. However, it is not obvious that this is the only or even the main function of the concept, for it may also have an epistemic function (Craver 2020). So, even metaphysical research motivated by naturalistic concerns has to answer to ques-tions about "the right concepts" (Kitsik 2020, 1046). And this, we argue, is precisely what is going on in the causalism–simulationism debate.

2.4 Defining 'imagining'

Getting clear about the concept of 'remembering' is thus an important issue. Yet, to understand the nature of the relationship between memory and imagina-tion, we need to get clear not only on what 'remembering' means, but also what 'imagining' means. We have spent time considering different ways to define 'remembering'. Let us now consider 'imagining'.

Although 'imagining' and cognate terms have played a major role in recent discussions in philosophy of memory, the term is rarely defined in an explicit way. For 'imagination,' the thought goes, is a term that we seem to have a secure enough grasp of. Yet, there are different ways of understanding imagination too, and hence different ways that the debate about the relation between memory and imagination can be formulated. So, we cannot get clear about whether remembering is a form of imagining if we do not have a clear picture of what we mean by 'imagining'.

Addressing the debate about the relation between memory and imagination in precisely this way, and getting clear about the second term in the relation, Peter Langland-Hassan (2022; Chapter 1, this volume) surveys different ways of understanding imagination that might be at play in the (dis)continuism debate. Langland-Hassan identifies three different senses of the term imagination— imagistic imagining, attitudinal imagining, and constructive imagining[12]—and seeks to isolate the one that is of relevance for (dis)continuism.

He begins by considering *imagistic imagining* as a candidate. Imagistic imagining requires—as a necessary feature—the use of mental imagery. As such, Langland-Hassan suggests, this is not the type of imagining assumed in the (dis)continuism debate. Both sides of that debate—continuists and discontinuists—agree that imagination and episodic memory typically involve mental imagery. It would be trivially true that episodic memory is continuous with imagination if imagistic imagining is the sense of imagination we have in mind.

Similarly, Langland-Hassan rejects the idea that the sense of imagining in the (dis)continuism debate is *attitudinal imagining*. Attitudinal imagining involves taking an attitude, typically understood as a belief-like attitude, towards a content. To imagine, in this sense, "is to represent without aiming at things as they actually, presently, and subjectively are" (Liao and Gendler 2019). Thus, Langland-Hassan adds, attitudinal imagining is not the type of imagining assumed in the (dis)continuism debate either, for both continuists and discontinuists will happily accept the claim that remembering is not attitudinal imagining. The argument supporting this claim appeals to Michaelian's (2016b) claim that one of the conditions for remembering to happen is that it is produced by a reliably functioning episodic construction system that 'aims' at representing an event from one's personal past. This condition, Langland-Hassan argues, places unique epistemic constraints on remembering that do not hold for attitudinal imagining. As he puts it:

> to say that the episodic construction system "aims at" an episode from one's actual personal past is to say that its products are in epistemic need of revision when that aim isn't met—viz., when the episodic memory does not accurately represent an episode from one's actual personal past.
>
> (Langland-Hassan 2022; Chapter 1, this volume)

Langland-Hassan thus concludes that the type of imagining assumed in the (dis)continuism debate is best described as *constructive imagining*, which refers to "the capacity to form novel representations" (Van Leeuwen 2013, 204). In this sense, imagining is a creative, actively constructive process. Saying that memory just is imagination, then, is to say that memory is constructive imagination (Langland-Hassan 2021; Chapter 1, this volume).

This way of understanding the (dis)continuism debate, as a question of whether memory is a form of constructive imagination, crucially depends on how the representations of remembering and imagining are constructed. Discontinuists hold that the representations of memory will be constructed at least partially from content experienced at the time of the original event and stored in a memory trace. In other words, memory representations are constrained so that they cannot be (at least not entirely) creative acts of constructive imagining. Continuists reject this. Hence, framed in terms of constructive imagining, the (dis)continuism debate again boils down to the question of whether an appropriate causal connection is necessary for remembering.

We now want to explore whether this way of framing the debate, in terms of constructive imagination, is correct. We suggest that there is an important way in which the (dis)continuism debate is about the attitudes involved in remembering and imagining (Sant'Anna 2021). This is not, however, to say that the debate is about attitudinal imagining, or the capacity "to represent without aiming at things as they actually, presently, and subjectively are" (Liao and Gendler 2019). As we will discuss, there are forms of imagining that involve distinctive attitudes that are not captured by the notion of attitudinal imagining, such as cases of imagining the actual (Munro 2021). The question of whether memory and imagination are (dis)continuous is, therefore, the question of whether occurrences of remembering involve the same or similar attitudes to certain occurrences of imagining.

The suggestion that the (dis)continuism debate should be settled by considering the relationship between the attitudes of remembering and imagining has been articulated recently. For instance, Sarah Robins (2020) has argued that the attitude of "seeming to remember", which she takes to be characteristic of occurrences of successful and unsuccessful remembering alike, and which involves entertaining a content as being past and as having happened, is clearly distinct from the attitude of imagining. The latter, she argues, involves entertaining a content as being fictional or possible (Van Leeuwen 2013). Thus, by equating the attitude of imagining with attitudinal imagining, Robins argues that remembering and imagining are discontinuous. In a similar vein, Daniel Munro (2021) has argued that remembering is discontinuous with what he calls "hypothetical imagining" because they involve different attitudes towards contents. Unlike Robins (2020), however, Munro thinks that there is at least one type of imagining that is continuous with remembering—namely, what he calls 'actuality-oriented imagining', or situations in which one imagines actual scenarios, such as imagining the layout of a restaurant where one is going to dine. Crucially, Munro's strategy for defending this view involves arguing that remembering and actuality-oriented imagining involve attitudes of a very similar type. Thus, despite their differences, these two attempts share a more general motivation to resolve the (dis)continuism debate by offering characterisations of the attitudes of remembering and imagining.

How does the view that the (dis)continuism debate should be framed in terms of the attitudes involved in remembering and imagining mesh with what we have said in this chapter? We saw previously that there are different ways of thinking about the term 'remembering': remembering$_c$ and remembering$_s$. On our understanding, Langland-Hassan's focus on the notion of constructive imagining, as the key to understanding the relation between memory and imagination, is to adopt a related point of view on the debate. Langland-Hassan is interested in the mechanisms or processes by which the representations of remembering and imagining are constructed, and whether they are inherently creative or constrained. This type of focus brings with it the question of whether an appropriate causal connection, which is maintained by a memory trace, is necessary for remembering.

However, the debate could be reframed to consider the attitudes involved in remembering and imagining. If the notion of constructive imagining forces us to think about the debate from an empirical point of view, where the processes of constructing representations are important, viewing the debate from an epistemic point of view brings the attitudes involved in remembering and imagining into sharp relief. From an epistemic perspective, remembering is a way of making a claim about how the world was in the past: it involves an assertoric commitment (Mahr and Csibra 2018; Craver 2020). It is in this sense that the attitudes of remembering and imagining importantly differ:

> If we attend to the commitments one undertakes when one asserts to remember epistemically, or what is going on when one in fact remembers, the physiological, phenomenological, or mechanistic overlap among biological mechanisms is less important than the momentous differences in attitudinal stance one takes with respect to a past event in remembering as opposed to imagining.
>
> (Craver 2020, 277)

Langland-Hassan seems to anticipate this type of move in a response to Robins, and suggests that this way of thinking is to take a deflationary perspective on the debate between continuists and discontinuists:

> We could instead interpret the debate … as concerning which kind of psychological kind is most fundamental—attitudinal kinds or, say, neurocognitive kinds—with Robins arguing that a difference in attitudinal kinds is the one that should matter. But this is to take a deflationary perspective on the (dis)continuism debate. Continuists and discontinuists are then no longer disagreeing over whether EMs [episodic memories] are cases of imagining; they are, instead, talking past each other, using 'imagining' in different senses—and disagreeing, if implicitly, over which sense corresponds to a more fundamental kind.
>
> (Langland-Hassan 2021, pp. 237–238)

Yet, this is to ignore the type of metalinguistic negotiation that is taking place in the debate. As we argued earlier, settling how the relevant terms should be used and what the correct way of framing the discussion about the relationship between memory and imagination constitutes a *substantive* debate. It is not a mere verbal dispute that can be resolved by simply specifying which senses of 'remembering' and 'imagining' are being used by each party in the debate. In other words, the kind of dispute in which (dis)continuists are involved in when they disagree about whether 'memory' and 'imagination' are (dis)continuous is *not* the same type of dispute that, for instance, two parties might be involved in when they disagree over whether Mary went to the 'bank', where one party takes 'bank' to mean the financial institution and the other takes it to mean the side of a river. If our argument in the previous sections is correct, only the latter, but not the former, can be resolved by specifying the terms at play in the dispute. So, rather than 'deflating' the debate, the focus on attitudes provides us with a way to articulate a different prescriptive stance on the nature of remembering, imagining, and their relationship, that departs in important senses from the prescriptive stance, exemplified by Langland-Hassan's approach, which focuses on their underlying mechanisms.

2.5 Concluding remarks

By way of conclusion, let us revisit the more general question of the relationship between memory and imagination. If our argument in this chapter is on the right track, there are two distinct notions of 'remembering' that need to be considered when asking this question: namely, REMEMBERING$_C$ and REMEMBERING$_S$. If we approach it through the lens of REMEMBERING$_C$, then the issue is whether remembering and imagining involve the same attitudes. From this perspective, the question of whether a causal connection is necessary for remembering is not central.[13] In contrast, if we approach the initial question through the lens of REMEMBERING$_S$, then the issue is whether remembering is constructive imagining. And, from this perspective, the question of whether a causal connection is necessary for remembering is indeed central.

Does this mean that there are two separate questions about the relationship between memory and imagination? If we are right that the debate should be interpreted as a prescriptive one, then the answer is no. For, on the prescriptivist approach, both the causalism–simulationism debate and the continuism–discontinuism debate can be conceived as being about normative semantics. On the one hand, continuists prescribe that 'remembering' should be REMEMBERING$_S$ and that 'imagining' should be constructive imagining. On the other hand, discontinuists prescribe that 'remembering' should be REMEMBERING$_C$ and that 'imagining' should be attitudinal imagining. Thus, viewed in this light, the question about the nature of the relationship between memory and imagination is ultimately a question about which facts the notions of 'remembering' and 'imagining' *should* track.

Importantly, characterising the facts that remembering and imagining should track will involve getting clear about both the attitudes and content involved in remembering and imagining. There are different ways of specifying the attitudes of remembering and imagining, which may lead one to either a continuist (Munro 2021) or a discontinuist (Robins 2020) position. Indeed, contra what has been articulated in the current debate between causalists and simulationists, it may turn out that both remembering and imagining draw on memory traces, and that one can opt for a form of causal continuism (Langland-Hassan 2021; Chapter 1, this volume). We hope to have shown that both components of intentionality—attitudes and content—are important to the debate. Yet, the debate is not just about similarities and differences between remembering and imagining; rather, the debate involves a normative dimension that has to do with normative semantics. The debate will not be won by simply stipulating the definitions of the terms. The debate is about *the normativity of* these definitions themselves. In other words, it is a debate about the *right concepts*.

So, if, once the relevant metalinguistic negotiation is 'over,' we establish that REMEMBERING$_C$ and attitude imagining are the appropriate notions to conceive of the debate, then discontinuists will triumph over continuists, for, with the exception of perhaps a few types of imagining (Munro 2021), the attitude of remembering is clearly different from the attitude of imagining (Robins 2020). However, if we establish that REMEMBERING$_S$ and constructive imagining are the appropriate notions, then continuists will triumph over discontinuists, for neither remembering nor imagining require an appropriate causal connection.

Acknowledgements

This study was financed in part by the Coordenação de Aperfeiçoamento de Pessoal de Nível Superior–Brasil (CAPES)—Finance Code 001, processes 8881.310246/2018-1 and the French National Research Agency in the framework of the 'Investissements d'avenir' program (ANR-15-IDEX-02). The authors thank the participants of the Centre for Philosophy of Memory's internal seminar for helpful discussion on this chapter.

Notes

1 Some readers may worry that it is not obvious what it means to say that 'remembering' is an attitude. One helpful way to look at this is suggested by Langland-Hassan (2015): '[a] rough-and-ready way to conceive of attitude … is simply that aspect of a mental state's typical functional role that cannot be accounted for by its content' (667). Thus, for instance, if one thinks that part of what it means to remember is to entertain a content as past, but nonetheless thinks that the content of remembering does not include any temporal information (e.g., De Brigard & Gessell 2016; Mahr & Csibra 2018)—perhaps the content is simply a mental image of an event—one can account for the 'past orientation' of remembering by claiming that its attitude is such that, when one entertains the relevant contents under that attitude, one takes those contents to represent events in the past. There are, of course, concerns with this characterisation—e.g., there are cases where we entertain contents as being past that are not occurrences of remembering—but it is not our goal to defend it here. This is just meant to be an illustration of what it means to say that remembering is an attitude. So, while there is room to dispute how we should characterise the attitude of remembering, speaking of it as involving an attitude is not particularly mysterious or unmotivated.
2 See Sorabji (1972/2004) and Chappell (2017, 400) for details about causality in Aristotle's theory of memory. And see Bernecker (2008, 17) for a list of philosophers who speak of a causal connection in memory.
3 For an overview of the different versions of the causal theory, see Michaelian and Robins (2018).
4 Martin and Deutscher (1966) were the first to argue for this idea in the recent philosophy of memory literature. Despite the popularity of the causal theory, and despite being central for all subsequent versions of the theory (see Michaelian and Robins 2018 for a review), the idea of a memory trace has been the subject of many criticisms. See Sutton (1998, ch. 16) for discussion; see also De Brigard (2014b); Robins (2017).

5 Martin and Deutscher (1966) were also at pains to distinguish remembering from *relearning*, which occurs when there is a deviant causal connection to a past event. For example, relearning may occur when a subject experiences an event, recounts it to someone else, entirely forgets it, is told about the event by the person to whom he recounted it, entirely forgets being told about it, but then, under the influence of what he has been told, comes to entertain a representation that happens to be accurate with respect to the event in question. See, for example, Robins (2019), Michaelian (2016c).

6 See Tulving (1993, 2002, 2005); Addis (2018, 2020); Addis, Wong, and Schacter (2007); Schacter, Addis, and Buckner (2007); Schacter et al. (2012). See Perrin and Michaelian (2017) for a more detailed philosophical discussion.

7 See Michaelian (2016a, 2016b); Michaelian, Perrin, and Sant'Anna (2020); Sant'Anna (2020).

8 The attempt to show that memory and imagination are continuous is not the only motivation that leads Michaelian to deny that a causal connection is necessary for remembering. Another equally important reason is the possibility of there being memory representations that are fully accurate but that are not causally connected to the original events—e.g., memories whose contents are derived from testimony or memories whose contents are derived from causal connections to events other than the event remembered. See Michaelian (2016b, ch. 6) for discussion.

9 The available data warrant more than just one empirical account of what makes a mental state a memory. Here are two examples: the 'classic' and the 'refined' versions of the constructive episodic simulation hypothesis. In the classic version of this hypothesis, remembering is similar to imagining, and the adaptive function of the episodic memory system is to imagine the future (Schacter, Addis, & Buckner 2007, 659). But the refined version of the hypothesis is agnostic about the adaptive function of the episodic memory system (Addis 2018, 82).

10 See McCarroll (2020) for a worry about the simulationist understanding of the personal past.

11 This classification of remembering comes out on the classical version of the causal theory (Martin & Deutscher 1966). There might be differences in the classification depending on the version of the causal theory one endorses, however. For example, Michaelian (2011) revises the classical causal theory and introduces the notion of a reliably functioning episodic memory system, which rules out as cases of remembering instances where the system draws on a trace to construct the representation but does so unreliably and hence by chance. Nonetheless, the classical causal reading is a real possibility. Consider the case of H.M., one of the most famous individuals studied by memory researchers. Even though he was profoundly amnesic, and hence it could be said that he had a profoundly unreliable episodic construction system, he nonetheless was able to recall at least two events from his personal past in great detail and consistently over multiple retellings (Corkin 2013). In this case we can imagine that, just like in our puzzle, some trace of the past was left in H.M., and that the *C-Mnem-O-Matic* would classify him as remembering those events. Perhaps there are ways to rethink the notion of reliability, such that H.M.'s memory representations were generated by a reliable process in these cases, but the basic point is simply that on the classical causal theory remembering only requires a causal connection and not a reliably functioning system.

12 See, for example, Currie and Ravenscroft (2002); Langland-Hassan (2020); Van Leeuwen (2013, 2014).

13 It might be argued here that appeal to a causal connection is fundamental for characterising the attitude of remembering. We do not have space to address this objection here. For a more detailed discussion of this and other related points, see Sant'Anna (2021).

References

Addis, D. R. (2018). Are episodic memories special? On the sameness of remembered and imagined event simulation. *Journal of the Royal Society of New Zealand*, *48*(2–3), 64–88.

Addis, D. R. (2020). Mental time travel? A neurocognitive model of event simulation. *Review of Philosophy and Psychology*, *11*(2), 233–259.

Addis, D. R., Wong, A. T., & Schacter, D. L.. (2007). Remembering the past and imagining the future: Common and distinct neural substrates during event construction and elaboration. *Neuropsychologia*, *45*(7), 1363–1377.

Bernecker, S. 2008. *The Metaphysics of Memory*. Springer.

Burgess, A., & Plunkett, D. (2013). Conceptual ethics I. *Philosophy Compass*, *8*(12), 1091–1101.

Chappell, S.-G.. (2017). Aristotle. In S. Bernecker & K. Michaelian (Eds.), *The Routledge Handbook on Philosophy of Memory* (pp. 396–407). Routledge.

Corkin, S. (2013). *Permanent Present Tense: The Unforgettable Life of the Amnesic Patient, H.M.* Basic Books.

Craver, C. F. (2020). Remembering: Epistemic and empirical. *Review of Philosophy and Psychology*, *11*(2), 261–281.

Currie, G., & Ravenscroft, I. (2002). *Recreative Minds*. Oxford University Press.

De Brigard, F. (2014a). Is memory for remembering? Recollection as a form of episodic hypothetical thinking. *Synthese*, *191*(2), 155–185.

De Brigard, F. (2014b). The nature of memory traces. *Philosophy Compass*, *9*(6), 402–414.

De Brigard, F., & Gessell, B. (2016). Time is not of the essence: Understanding the neural correlates of mental time travel. In K. Michaelian, S. B. Klein, & K. K. Szpunar (Eds.), *Seeing the Future: Theoretical Perspectives on Future-Oriented Mental Time Travel* (pp. 153–179). Oxford University Press.

Debus, D. (2014). 'Mental time travel': Remembering the past, imagining the future, and the particularity of events. *Review of Philosophy and Psychology*, *5*(3), 333–350.

Kitsik, E. (2020). Explication as a strategy for revisionary philosophy. *Synthese*, *197*(3), 1035–1056.

Langland-Hassan, P. (2015). Imaginative attitudes. *Philosophy and Phenomenological Research*, *90*(3), 664–686.

Langland-Hassan, P. (2020). *Explaining Imagination*. Oxford University Press. https://philpapers.org/rec/LANEI-2.

Langland-Hassan, P. (2021). What sort of imagining might remembering be? *Journal of the American Philosophical Association*, *7*(2), 231–251.

Langland-Hassan, P. (2022). Remembering, imagining, and memory traces: Toward a continuist causal theory. In A. Sant'Anna, C. J. McCarroll, & K. Michaelian (Eds.), *Current Controversies in the Philosophy of Memory*. Routledge.

Liao, S., & Gendler, T. (2019). Imagination. In E. N. Zalta, U. Nodelman, & C. Allen (Eds.), *Stanford Encyclopedia of Philosophy*, 8 October. https://plato.stanford.edu/entries/imagination/.

Ludlow, P. (2008). Cheap contextualism. *Philosophical Issues*, *18*. https://www.jstor.org/stable/27749902.

Mahr, J. B., & Csibra, G. (2018). Why do we remember? The communicative function of episodic memory. *Behavioral and Brain Sciences*, *41*(January), e1.

Martin, C. B., & Deutscher, M. (1966). Remembering. *The Philosophical Review*, *75*(2), 161–196. http://www.jstor.org/stable/2183082.

McCarroll, C. J. (2020). Remembering the personal past: Beyond the boundaries of imagination. *Frontiers in Psychology*, *11*(September), 585352.

Michaelian, K. (2011). Generative memory. *Philosophical Psychology*, *24*(3), 323–342.

Michaelian, K. (2016a). Against discontinuism." In K. Michaelian, S. B. Klein, & K. K. Szpunar (Eds.), *Seeing the Future: Theoretical Perspectives on Future-Oriented Mental Time Travel* (pp. 62–92). Oxford University Press.

Michaelian, K. (2016b). *Mental Time Travel: Episodic Memory and Our Knowledge of the Personal Past*. MIT Press.

Michaelian, K. (2016c). Confabulating, misremembering, relearning: The simulation theory of memory and unsuccessful remembering. *Frontiers in Psychology*, 7 (November).

Michaelian, K., Perrin, D., & Sant'Anna, A. (2020). Continuities and discontinuities between imagination and memory: The view from philosophy. In A. Abraham (Ed.), *The Cambridge Handbook of the Imagination*. Cambridge University Press.

Michaelian, K., & Robins, S. K. (2018). Beyond the causal theory? Fifty years after Martin and Deutscher. In K. Michaelian, D. Debus, & D. Perrin (Eds.), *New Directions in the Philosophy of Memory* (pp. 13–32). Routledge. https://philpapers.org/rec/MICBTC.

Munro, D. (2021). Remembering the past and imagining the actual. *Review of Philosophy and Psychology*, *12*(2), 175–197.

Perrin, D. (2016). Asymmetries in subjective time. In K. Michaelian, S. B. Klein, & K. K. Szpunar (Eds.), *Seeing the Future: Theoretical Perspectives on Future-Oriented Mental Time Travel* (pp. 39–61). Oxford University Press.

Perrin, D., & Michaelian, K. (2017). Memory as mental time travel. In S. Bernecker & K. Michaelian (Eds.), *The Routledge Handbook of Philosophy of Memory* (pp. 228–239). Routledge. https://philpapers.org/rec/PERMAM-4.

Plunkett, D., & Sundell, T. (2013). Disagreement and the semantics of normative and evaluative terms. *Philosophers' Imprint*, *13*(23). www.philosophersimprint.org/013023/.

Robins, S. K. (2017). Memory traces. In S. Bernecker & K. Michaelian (Eds.), *The Routledge Handbook of Philosophy of Memory* (pp. 76–87). Routledge.

Robins, S. K. (2019). Confabulation and constructive memory. *Synthese*, *196*(6), 2135–2151.

Robins, S. K. (2020). Defending discontinuism, naturally. *Review of Philosophy and Psychology*, *11*(2), 469–486.

Sant'Anna, A. (2020). The hybrid contents of memory. *Synthese*, *197*(3), 1263–1290.

Sant'Anna, A. (2021). Attitudes and the (dis)continuity between memory and imagination. *Estudios de Filosofía*, *64*, 73–93.

Schacter, D. L., Addis, D. R., & Buckner, R. L. 2007. Remembering the past to imagine the future: The prospective brain. *Nature Reviews Neuroscience*, *8*(9), 657–661.

Schacter, D. L., Addis, D. R., Hassabis, D., Martin, V. C., Spreng, R. N., & Szpunar, K. K. (2012). The future of memory: Remembering, imagining, and the brain. *Neuron*, *76*(4), 677–694.

Searle, J. R. (1983). *Intentionality: An Essay in the Philosophy of Mind*. Cambridge University Press.

Sider, T. R. (2011). *Writing the Book of the World*. Clarendon Press.

Sorabji, R. (1972/2004). *Aristotle on Memory*. University of Chicago Press.

Sutton, J. (1998). *Philosophy and Memory Traces: Descartes to Connectionism.* Cambridge; Cambridge University Press.

Thomasson, A. L. (2017). Metaphysical disputes and metalinguistic negotiation. *Analytic Philosophy, 58*(1), 1–28.

Tulving, E. (1993). What is episodic memory? *Current Directions in Psychological Science, 2*(3), 67–70.

Tulving, E. (2002). Episodic memory: From mind to brain. *Annual Review of Psychology, 53*, 1–25.

Tulving, E. (2005). Episodic memory and autonoesis: Uniquely human? In H. S. Terrace & J. Metcalfe (Eds.), *The Missing Link: Origins of Self-Reflective Consciousness* (pp. 3–56). Oxford University Press.

Van Leeuwen, N. (2013). The meanings of 'Imagine' part I: Constructive imagination. *Philosophy Compass, 8*(3), 220–230.

Van Leeuwen, N. (2014). The meanings of 'Imagine' part II: Attitude and action. *Philosophy Compass, 9*(11), 791–802.

Werning, M. (2020). Predicting the past from minimal traces: Episodic memory and its distinction from imagination and preservation. *Review of Philosophy and Psychology, 11*(2), 301–333.

Further Readings for Part I

Debus, D. (2014). 'Mental time travel': Remembering the past, imagining the future, and the particularity of events. *Review of Philosophy and Psychology*, *5*(3), 333–350.

An early argument for discontinuism.

Langland-Hassan, P. (2021). What sort of imagining might remembering be? *Journal of the American Philosophical Association*, *7*(2), 231–251.

A recent exploration of the relationship between remembering and imagining from the perspective of the philosophy of imagination.

Michaelian, K. (2016). Against discontinuism: Mental time travel and our knowledge of past and future events. In K. Michaelian, S. B. Klein, & K. K. Szpunar (Eds.), *Seeing the Future: Theoretical Perspectives on Future-Oriented Mental Time Travel* (pp. 63–92). Oxford University Press.

Defends continuism against Perrin's argument for discontinuism (in his chapter in the same book).

Michaelian, K., Perrin, D., & Sant'Anna, A. (2020). Continuities and discontinuities between imagination and memory: The view from philosophy. In A. Abraham (Ed.), *The Cambridge Handbook of the Imagination* (pp. 293–310). Cambridge University Press.

A recent survey of arguments for continuism and discontinuism.

Perrin, D. (2016). Asymmetries in subjective time. In K. Michaelian, S. B. Klein, & K. K. Szpunar (Eds.), *Seeing the Future: Theoretical Perspectives on Future-Oriented Mental Time Travel* (pp. 39–61). Oxford University Press.

An empirically informed argument for discontinuism.

Perrin, D., & Michaelian, K. (2017). Memory as mental time travel. In S. Bernecker & K. Michaelian (Eds.), *The Routledge Handbook of Philosophy of Memory* (pp. 228–239). Routledge.

Argues that the continuist–discontinuist debate concerns the necessity of appropriate causation.

Robins, S. K. (2020). Defending discontinuism, naturally. *Review of Philosophy and Psychology*, *11*(2), 469–486.

An empirically informed argument for discontinuism.

Sant'Anna, A. (2021). Attitudes and the (dis)continuity between memory and imagination. *Estudios de Filosofía*, *64*, 73–93.

Argues that the continuism–discontinuism concerns the attitudes involved in remembering and imagining.

Study Questions for Part I

1) Is Langland-Hassan right to claim that a continuist causalism would be coherent? Would a discontinuist simulationism be coherent?

2) How are the prop theory and the replay theory described by Langland-Hassan related to the conceptions of traces discussed by Hutto and by Sutton and O'Brien in Part II?

3) If the causalist-simulationist debate is normative rather than descriptive in character, as Schirmer dos Santos, McCarroll, and Sant'Anna claim, and, if different norms are appropriate in different contexts, might there be a sense in which both causalists and simulationists are right? If there is a sense in which both causalists and simulationists are right, what follows concerning the continuism–discontinuism debate?

4) Continuists and discontinuists have generally not taken their debate to be about the attitudes involved in remembering and imagining. How might the debate change if it is reconceived along these lines, as Schirmer dos Santos, McCarroll, and Sant'Anna argue it ought to be?

5) If Schirmer dos Santos, McCarroll, and Sant'Anna's take on the continuist–discontinuist debate is right, what becomes of Langland-Hassan's argument for a continuist causalism?

Part II

Do memory traces have content?

3 Remembering without a trace?

Moving beyond trace minimalism

Daniel D. Hutto

3.1 Introduction

It can be compelling to think that remembering, or at least remembering of the episodic sort, depends on—and is only possible due to—the existence of memory traces of some kind. Many find the idea of memory traces intuitively appealing and explanatorily indispensable. The idea that memory depends on memory traces has enjoyed longstanding support from illustrious champions down the ages, and it figures prominently in the history of Western philosophy (De Brigard 2014a; Dupont 2014; Robins 2017). Indeed, without exaggeration, Robins (2017) observes that, 'memory traces feature in nearly every account of memory' (p. 76).

Traditional accounts of memory, however, typically do not draw distinctions between the various kinds of remembering that are recognised today: they do not distinguish between procedural, semantic, and episodic varieties of remembering. Instead, it is evident from the parade cases used down the ages that it is an episodic remembering of events from one's personal past that is, de facto, the primary explanatory target of such accounts.

Episodic remembering is also the central focus of this chapter. This is not because a case cannot be made for positing memory traces in order to explain procedural or semantic forms of remembering. Rather, it is because the apparent need to posit memory traces seems strongest and most compelling when considering episodic remembering, which Robins (2017) describes as the 'quintessential' form of remembering.[1] Moreover, the considerations that this chapter supplies for doubting the explanatory tenability of positing memory traces apply generally, and with equal force, to any attempt to posit memory traces in order to explain any kind of remembering.

The 'Remembering Requires a Trace' thesis, or RRT for short, gains its greatest support by reflecting on a familiar, intuitively attractive, and oft-invoked philosophical picture of episodic memory and how it works.

According to an age-old picture, successful acts of episodic remembering require that a remembered perceptual experience will have made a mark on the minds of one who remembers—leaving some sort of lasting, or at least recoverable, causally efficacious impression. Typically, the RRT is construed such that

DOI: 10.4324/9781003002277-6

it is by leaving such a mental mark—aka, a memory trace—that the content of a remembered perceptual experience, or a surrogate thereof, is somehow preserved and, ultimately, causally implicated in enabling the person to recall of the event in question (For discussion of different varieties and strengths of the RRT, see Aronowitz 2019; Bernecker 2018; Michaelian & Robins 2018).

Philosophical accounts down the ages have not only assumed that memory traces are necessary for remembering but that memory traces do their special preservative work in virtue of having representational properties. The reigning consensus in the philosophy of memory has long been that remembering requires, or is best explained in terms of, the storage and retrieval of mental contents of some sort—contents that are usually assumed to be located inside the brains or minds of individuals.

What has been, until recently, the received view—that memory traces are contentful—is no longer unchallenged orthodoxy today. Reflections on empirically oriented memory research revealing the reconstructive character of episodic memory have put pressure on the assumption that the function of biological memory systems can be that of producing accurate representations of specific past events at all (De Brigard 2014b; Robins 2016).

Considerations about the reconstructive and creative character of remembering and how it might work in detail has pushed theorists to rethink the nature of memory traces. Some now entertain the possibility of contentless, dispositional traces (Michaelian & Sant'Anna 2021).

These developments also raise doubts about the RRT. Researchers now advance post-causal and non-transmissionist theories of memory—theories which hold that successful remembering does not require causal connections linking current memories to past experiences (Perrin 2018; Michaelian & Sant'Anna 2021).

For example, simulation theories of remembering have emerged that characterise episodic remembering as a kind of imagining (see, e.g., De Brigard 2014b; Michaelian 2016). The most daring, non-transmissionist version of the simulationist theory of remembering does not presuppose that, in every case, successful remembering requires reproduction or recovery of component states of mind that are causally connected to a particular past experience.[2] The non-transmissionist version of simulation theory explicitly rejects RTT and obviates the need to posit memory traces in at least in some cases of remembering (Michaelian & Sant'Anna 2021).

This chapter takes things a step further. It provides analyses that compel us to abandon memory traces altogether and look beyond even their most minimal version in our attempts to understand and explain episodic and other forms of remembering. The action unfolds as follows.

Section 3.2 reviews what motivates the positing of memory traces and the explanatory work they were introduced to perform. This helps us to get a fix on their minimal defining characteristics.

Section 3.3 lays out reasons why some have been sceptical about the very idea of memory traces and their explanatory value as well as sketching a first-pass alternative vision of how remembering might be achieved without assuming the existence of memory traces.

Section 3.4 articulates the key assumptions of the causal theory of memory which provides the starting point for contemporary attempts to provide a workable theory of memory traces. A potentially crippling problem is highlighted that faces any account of memory traces committed to representationalism.

Section 3.5 focuses on an inventive attempt to avoid that crippling problem in the shape of Werning's (2020) minimal notion of a memory trace—a notion that does not presuppose the existence of any preserved representational content. This section identifies those assumptions Werning's trace minimalism retains from the causal theory of memory and which assumptions it, importantly, leaves behind. Specifically, trace minimalism holds out hope to proponents of memory traces precisely because it abandons the troublesome assumption that memory traces bear representational content.

Section 3.6 poses a dilemma for trace minimalism. Going with the first horn, it looks first at the prospect of weak trace minimalism, which assumes that only a limited amount of non-contentful information is preserved from an original remembered experience and plays a part in generating a memory of said episode. It is argued that understood under the auspices of weak trace minimalism, memory traces are rendered empirically respectable only at the cost of becoming theoretically vacuous and explanatorily hollow. Put otherwise, they buy their empirical respectability at the cost of washing away all vestiges of the properties that memory traces need to have in order to do their unique work—not only their contentful properties but also their causal powers. If so, weak trace minimalism is too weak—it paints a picture of memory traces that surrenders too much. Memory traces lose their minimal defining properties and can no longer satisfy the explanatory needs that they were originally introduced to answer.

In reply to this worry, it might be thought best to beef up minimal traces and to defend strong trace minimalism, which assumes that memory traces have some kind of content that falls short of representational content and that such content is capable of doing the special causal work asked of memory traces. Those who make this move must face the second horn of the dilemma. Strong trace minimalism may appear, *prima facie*, better placed to answer the requisite explanatory needs, but on closer inspection, this is not so. It must commit to a notion of content with special causal powers that is theoretically ad hoc and empirically unmotivated.

In the final analysis, there are compelling reasons to go beyond trace minimalism, abandoning hope of concocting a naturalistically respectable and explanatorily robust notion of a memory trace. It is concluded that the fate of trace minimalism is shared by any explanatory proposal about remembering that appeals only to contentless, dispositional traces but which also still assumes that, somehow, such minimal traces preserve causally efficacious information that somehow plays a part in reproducing remembered experiences. If the arguments this chapter supplies for leaving memory traces behind altogether prove sound, then, if we are to understand and explain remembering, we have every reason to look more seriously at enactivist and simulationist alternatives that make no commitment to memory traces.

3.2 What are memory traces?

Ought memory traces to figure in our best explanations of remembering? Is remembering without a memory trace even possible?[3] If we are to answer these questions, we must first get clear about what philosophers and cognitive scientists are minimally committing to when they posit memory traces. What are the core defining properties of memory traces? We can get a provisional grip on such commitments by clarifying the special explanatory work that memory traces are supposed to perform.

First and foremost, memory traces are meant to do a particular kind of causal work: they are meant to account for the special kind of causal connection that links a current act of remembering to a specific experience of a past event. This sort of causal connection takes centre stage in the very earliest thinking about memory traces. In Plato's *Theaetetus*, attention is given to the way memories leave marks on our minds: this is taken to be analogous to the way signet rings leave impressions in wax. Another analogy, made popular by St. Augustine and later by the British empiricists, also gets at the heart of the idea of memory traces doing this sort of preservationist work by comparing them to archived items in a mental storehouse.[4]

Though crude, these analogies capture something centrally important about what memory traces are imagined to be and the special kind of work that is earmarked for them. Yet, as we shall see in Section 3.5, rather than assuming that a memory trace entails an enduring structural change, it may be enough to conceive of a memory trace, in a more relaxed manner, as somehow figuring or featuring in a reliable process that has the capacity, under the right conditions, to create the required causal links that connect the current memory and the experience of the past event.

Robins (2017) provides a handy summary of the core properties that memory traces are assumed to have, and the key explanatory work they are meant to do. She writes:

> Memory traces provide a connection to the past by storing or somehow making available information about and from one's previous encounters. For this reason, traces are widely considered to be mental representations: mental states whose content reflects the facts, faces, and feelings previously encountered.
>
> (Robins 2017, p. 76)[5]

Minimally, memory traces must play a special part in establishing and maintaining the requisite causal links between current memories and past experiences. Yet, because those causal links are imagined to do special work, memory traces are required to do something more: they are meant to account for the content-ful similarities, or overlap, that are presumed to exist between a current memory and the experience of the remembered event.

3.3 Scepticism about memory traces

Philosophers are divided about whether there could be anything with the set of properties that memory traces are assumed to have that could do the special explanatory work demanded of them.[6] There are those who think the notion of a memory trace is either conceptually incoherent or deeply empirically suspect, or both.

Putting aside other differences, radical behaviourists, followers of Wittgenstein, and radical enactivists are united in their outright scepticism about both the RTT and the explanatory need for, and even the possibility of positing, memory traces.

Sustained attacks on the conceptual coherence of the very idea of memory traces and challenges to the need to posit such entities can be found in the work of Malcolm (1977), Heil (1978), and Bennett and Hacker (2003). The locus classicus of, and inspiration for, these critiques, of course, is Wittgenstein's famous comment in *Remarks on the Philosophy of Psychology*, Vol. I.

> I saw this man years ago: now I have seen him again, I recognize him, I remember his name. And why does there have to be a cause of this remem-bering in my nervous system? Why must something or other, whatever it may be, be stored-up there in any form? Why must a trace have been left behind? Why should there not be a psychological regularity to which no physiological regularity corresponds? If this upsets our concepts of causality then it is high time they were upset.
>
> (Wittgenstein 1980, 905)

On a standard reading, Wittgenstein is only denying that a psychological regu-larity logically requires a physiological (or neural) regularity. This has been taken by many as a reminder that we should not let our philosophy dictate, a priori, how things must stand with the world. Noting its modal force, this reading is compatible with Wittgenstein's denial that there *has* to be something stored up in a person's nervous system that causes a current remembering.

Moyal-Sharrock (2009) takes these ideas a step further and, with reference to the science of memory, argues in the light of empirical findings that there isn't, *in fact*, anything stored up in our nervous systems. She follows the enactivist lead in thinking of remembering as an ability grounded in dispositions that does not involve the recovery of any stored representations.

The radically enactivist view—that remembering is a non-representational ability that is, in part, neurally realized—is compatible with a non-transmissionist version of the simulationist hypothesis about episodic remembering in which memory traces pay no part at all (Hutto & Myin 2017).

Simulationist theories of episodic memory hold that the capacity to episodically remember involves and depends upon the re-instantiation of specific neural patterns. Simulationists about memory propose that such remembering is best understood as a form of recreative or simulative imagining that enables us to construct and entertain possible episodes (De Brigard 2014b; Michaelian 2016). Inspired by scientific developments, some simulationists about episodic remembering are prepared to accept that there is no intrinsic difference between remembering and imagining. Starkly put, some proponents of the simulation theory of episodic memory hold that 'to remember, it turns out, is just to imagine the past' (Michaelian 2016, p. 14; see also p. 120).

There is convincing empirical support for simulation theories of episodic memory in that there appears to be a common cognitive basis for acts of memory and imagination (Schacter & Addis 2009; Schacter, Addis, & Buckner 2007; Szpunar, Watson, & McDermott 2007). Novel scientific work on mental time travel has repeatedly confirmed the existence of some strong similarities in the patterns of neural activity associated with the sorts of cognitive procedures employed in thinking about our past and imagining our possible futures (Hutto & McGivern 2016).

Some defenders of the simulation theory of episodic memory commit to the existence of memory traces (Michaelian 2016). Yet, it is technically possible to defend such a simulation theory of memory while rejecting the existence of memory traces altogether. Radical enactivists embrace a non-transmissionist variant of the simulation theory of episodic remembering (for a full discussion of this option, see Michaelian & Sant'Anna 2021).

Embracing this option shows that it is possible to be sceptical about memory traces for philosophical reasons while also seeking to motivate a move away from memory traces by attending to empirical findings and assessing the needs of memory scientists. Using both of these strategies, radical enactivists seek to establish that there is not a theoretically tenable prospect of, nor any need to, posit memory-trace-middlemen.

Acts of recall in which specific events or episodes are re-experienced—for example, when we remember what it was like for us to enter a particular classroom for the first time—can be understood in terms of acts of re-creative imagination that involve neural reactivation. A non-transmissionist simulationist theory of episodic remembering is supported by the general observation that the brain often opportunistically reuses or co-opts its existing neural apparatus for novel tasks (Anderson 2010, 2014).

This means that, though a qualitatively rich, current remembering may have a proximate trigger—such as the smell of Proust's madeleines—there is no sense in which such a remembering might be said to be caused by a preserved copy, complete or partial, of the previous experience or its content. Assuming any recreated neural patterns are, de facto, similar enough to those that occurred during the original experience, their re-occurrence suffices for the features of a current remembering. The explanation appeals to a standing tendency or disposition, but just as Wittgenstein, the behaviourists, and the enactivists would have it, said disposition is nothing like a copy or a representation or anything containing the content of the prior experience, that is somehow stored up inside the person. Nothing like a memory trace plays any part in this dispositional explanation.

3.4 The classic causal theory of memory, and its problems

Contemporary defenders of memory traces tend to follow in the footsteps of Martin and Deutscher (1966), who proposed a highly influential, and indeed now canonical, causal theory of remembering. According to the causal theory of memory, to remember something a person must, within certain limits of accuracy, represent a past experience, and that past experience itself must have been 'operative in producing a state or successive states [that are, in turn] finally operative in producing [the person's current] representation' (Martin & Deutscher 1966, p. 166).

In its classic formulation, the casual theory of memory perfectly captures the idea that memory traces are representational middlemen. They are mental go-betweens, or intermediaries, that do special service by anchoring a current representation of a past experience to the past episode in question in causally appropriate and reliable ways. This is ensured to the extent that the putative content of the memory trace informs the content of the current remembering by some reliable process—where said process must ensure a current experience is accurate enough to count as remembering the particular past episode in question.

As depicted by the original, old-school version of the causal theory, memory traces do double duty: they not only provide a causal link to past experience, but they are also causally responsible for the current remembering's contentful similarity to the remembered experience. Mental traces achieve this, so the story goes, by bearing representational content that, through a reliable process, generates the content of a remembering. Putatively, the trace represents the content of the remembered experience sufficiently closely to qualify as an accurate or accurate enough remembering.[7]

How close is close enough? That is unclear. It is agreed by proponents of the causal theory of memory that memory traces must also preserve the content to be remembered – if not perfectly, then at least partially. The content of a memory might only partially match the content of the remembered experience, but the content of the memory trace must preserve enough of the content of the past experience to ensure that what is remembered is sufficiently similar to what was originally experienced so as to qualify as a remembering of that specific event.

Highlighting what is needed for a state or states to play this content-preserving role, Martin and Deutscher (1966) add an additional clause to the core of their theory—one that apparently emphasises the representational status of memory traces. They write, 'the state or set of states produced by the past experience must constitute a structural analogue of the thing remembered, to the extent [those states] can accurately represent the thing' (1966, p. 173).

Another core commitment of the classical causal theory's conception of memory traces is that, in addition to assuming that memory traces are mental states that do special causal work based on their contents, memory traces are also traditionally assumed to be internal states or processes: typically, memory traces are understood to be identical with neural states that reside inside the skin and skull of the remembering creature or person.[8]

The most recent cognitive revolution, which issued in contemporary representational-computational cognitive science, created the best possible conditions for developing sophisticated accounts of memory traces that satisfied the demands of the classic causal theory or memory. Nevertheless, that theory is 'not now widely endorsed' (Michaelian & Robins 2018, p. 16).

Why so? Some maintain that the classical causal theory—at least in its strong preservationist versions—is at odds with the epistemically ampliative character of episodic remembering.[9] The classical causal theory, at least in some versions, makes it hard to account for the fact that we can learn new things, such as where I left my keys this morning, by bringing to mind and attending the content of past experiences.

It has also been argued that the classical causal theory is empirically inadequate. Its strong preservationist versions seem incredible in light of what we have discovered about the fragile and corruptible nature of biological unaided episodic memory (De Brigard 2014b; Hutto 2017).

The most fundamental problem for the classical causal theory and its story about memory traces is its explanatory hollowness. This hollowness is connected to the fact that, despite many promises, we do not yet have an answer to the Hard Problem of Content.[10] Which is to say that we do not yet have a workable, scientifically respectable, naturalistic theory of content. We have no explanation of how content of the semantic variety can be identified with or otherwise derived from information of the covariational sort that poses no metaphysical mysteries for the hard sciences. Nor do we have an uncontested naturalistic theory of content that explains how it derives from other natural properties or processes, such as resemblance or biological function.

Without a naturalistic theory of content, we lack an account of how content, of any sort, can be literally possessed, stored within, processed or represented by brains. Indeed, going exactly the other way on this issue, we have positive reasons to think that brains simply do not do that sort of thing. Summarising his analysis of the current state of the art in memory science, Rosenberg (2018) cites the Nobel Prize-winning findings of Kandel and colleagues as showing that:

> neural circuits didn't store information by *representing it*, being *about it, having it as their content*. They showed that storing explicit memories was a matter of neurons being connected to one another to produce certain kinds of results, events inside the brain, in the neural networks, and eventually in behavior that other animals, like humans, could detect.[11]
>
> (p. 131)

These reflections alone ought to give us sufficient reason to steer clear of the classic causal theory of memory.

We can see the problem that arises from lacking a workable theory of content by considering the attempts by Sutton (1998, 2015) and Sutton and O'Brien (Chapter 4, this volume) to update the causal theory, and why and where they fundamentally fall short. Sutton (2015) proposed moving beyond the idea that memory traces are static, archived items of the sort posited by the language of thought, offering instead 'a mechanistic alternative to the idea of atomic, independently-stored, localist representations' (Sutton 2015, p. 413).

Drawing on connectionism, Sutton (1998) proposed that memory traces could be best understood as distributed, superpositionally stored entities with implicit content. As described in Michaelian and Sutton (2017), the explicit content of episodic memories is, according to this proposed account, 'generated from *information stored only holistically* in connection weights' (emphasis added). Sutton's (1998) proposal is as follows:

> we might prefer to see memories as tendencies to motion. It is in this latter sense that there can be many memories overlapping in the same place, *as implicit representations* which can all potentially be rendered explicit or actualised. Where explicit representations are transient, implicit representations endure. They are dispositions which allow for or ground the recreation of the explicit patterns ... without which ... reconstruction would be impossible.
>
> (p. 154, emphasis added)

Notably, both Bernecker (2010) and Michaelian (2016) are attracted to the idea that memory traces are distributed. And, on the face of it, this notion appears to be a good fit with empirical findings about the constructive character of episodic remembering. Yet, as Robins (2016) astutely observes, neither of these authors 'elaborates on the nature of these traces in much detail' (p. 3003).

When we look more closely at this proposal, a quite general worry about the notion of distributed memory traces emerges: such accounts generate what might be called the specificity problem. As Robins (2016) puts it, 'the account of superpositional storage makes clear how memories become blended ... But it does so at the expense of retaining the specifics of any particular past event' (Robins 2016, p. 3005). Since the whole point of having memory traces is to explain how we are able to reliably remember the specific details of particular past episodes, the specificity problem proves to be a deep problem for any attempt to update the classical causal theory with a connectionist account of superpositional storage of implicit contents. As Robins (2016) notes, 'Distributed memory traces are incompatible with the [causal theory of memory or CTM]. If memory traces are distributed patterns of event ... then the CTM cannot be right' (p. 2993).

An even more fundamental explanatory problem with the distributed memory trace proposal is that we are not given any account as to how or why the dispositions in question can or should be identified with traces understood as representations bearing implicit content.[12] Here the Hard Problem of Content kicks in to remind us that if we lack workable accounts of information or representational content, then we lack the fundamental explanatory resources needed to supply a causal theory of contentful memory traces. Worse still, even having those answers alone would not suffice: we would also need an explanation of how such putative kinds of content could do the causal work asked of them by memory trace theories.

Robins (2016) captures the challenge facing theorists on this score well in the following passage:

> All theorists who appeal to representations when explaining the mental capacities of humans and other cognitive creatures owe an answer to the Content Determination Question. In addition to an account of what is represented one must also provide an account of how this is achieved—in virtue of what do mind/brain states have the semantic properties that they do?
>
> (Robins 2016, p. 2995)

Sutton (1998, 2015) and Sutton and O'Brien (Chapter 4, this volume) assume the existence of content, but they neither provide nor point to a theory of content that can answer their needs. Nor do they provide a compelling reason why dispositions in connectionist networks can or should be thought to imply the existence of representations carrying implicit content. At best, they show how such content would be stored in a connectionist network, if it existed.

At this juncture, it is worth noting that it is perfectly possible to embrace the claim that biologically unaided remembering is implemented in a connectionist architecture while also abandoning any commitment to the view that such remembering is content-involving. It is worth quoting Perrin (2018) at length on this issue:

> Philosophers usually consider that connectionism substitutes a new conception of mnemonic traces—henceforth, distributed, superpositional, and constructed—for the old one. I propose to go further and see connectionism as discarding the very notion of a representational trace at the neural level. According to connectionism, each connection between two neural nodes has a weight. The only reality retention has at this level consists of this weight. Thus, the network at a certain stage of dynamics consists of a set of different weights of connection. Now the so configured network could yield, for certain input stimulus, an output representation. But this in no way implies that a representation would be deposited in the network, which (to repeat) only includes weights and potential reactions to stimuli…. the very notion of a trace, whether local or distributed, is to be rejected … on connectionism properly understood, what is retained is dispositions to react.
>
> (p. 40)

To be fair, O'Brien (2015a, 2015b) and O'Brien and Opie (2004, 2009, 2015) have worked to develop and defend a similarity-based theory of content and the notion of structural representations. However, even if that account were to prove viable, it would at best provide a support for the structural analogue account of the content of memory traces as opposed to an account of content of the kind that would support a distributed view of memory traces. As such, even if such a theory could be made to work, it would not suit the needs of contemporary memory science researchers who have independent reasons for rejecting structural analogue theories of content (see Robins 2016). Even so, in any case, there are reasons to think that structural analogues do not qualify as structural representations since, on their own, such states do not suffice for representational content (see Segundo-Ortin & Hutto 2021).

The Hard Problem of Content must be dealt with by any theory of memory traces that assumes memory traces bear representational content. This is so whatever particular proposals those theories make about formats or vehicles of the imagined implicit representations and whether these are assumed to be realised in local or distributed states, and whether those processes that are assumed to be only inside the head or to stretch beyond it.

For example, Sutton (2015) recognises that, when it comes to understanding episodic memory, 'for significant reasons, connectionism did not on its own provide sufficient tools' (p. 413). He proposes that we should follow the new trend of looking beyond the brain and to think of memory as grounded in distributed cognitive ecologies. Such a framework disavows internalism and individualism in favour of 'stronger, more integrative and practice-oriented views of the situated or distributed mind' (Sutton 2015, p. 414).

Yet any move outside the heads of individuals takes us no further in our understanding of how memory traces gain their content so long as the Hard Problem of Content remains unaddressed. Indeed, on the face of it, even if we bracket the issue concerning content, such a move only serves to raise further questions about Sutton and O'Brien's (this volume) general account of memory traces, since it raises questions about how external traces could be distributed in character or implemented in connectionist networks. Indeed, it would seem that very possibility of extended memory traces breaks faith with the idea that memory traces are always putatively superpositionally stored as implicit contents via in-the-head connectionism networks. The tension is immediately obvious if we consider the kind of discrete and unchanging information about the location of MoMA found in Otto's notebook—information that is assumed to function just like a memory trace in the most famous example of extended memory from Clark and Chalmers (1988).

In the end, it is no good to try to avoid the Hard Problem of Content by deflecting our attention away from it. Nor does taking stock of that problem and responding to it need to result in disagreements that are wholly negative or 'unnecessarily divisive' (Sutton 2015, p. 415). Doing so does not, *pace* Sutton, present 'barriers to integration and cooperative engagement between philosophy and the sciences of remembering' (Sutton 2015, p. 415). Nor does it 'set unnecessary limits to constructive theory-development' (Sutton 2015, p. 415). On the contrary, recognising the seriousness of the challenges that the Hard Problem of Content poses for us can push us to pursue and develop theoretical options that abandon RRT and memory traces. Alternatively, it can push us to attempt to develop other and more inventive ways of defending RTT and memory traces as credible posits.

3.5 Enter trace minimalism

Is it possible to fashion a deflated notion of memory traces that differs from the classic notion and yet which retains enough of its key properties to do the relevant explanatory work asked of memory traces?

Werning (2020) thinks so. He proposes borrowing the core machinery of predictive processing accounts of perception to understand episodic remembering in a way that commits to a minimal conception of memory traces that satisfies the aforementioned description. On Werning's account, episodic remembering is to be understood as a prediction about one's past experience based only on sparse hippocampal information combined with knowledge of learned statistical regularities.

Episodic remembering, on this theory, is a matter of generating a representation of the remembered experience in the here and now. Even though knowledge of the learned statistical correlations does much of the predictive work, a representation of the past experience will be verisimilar enough to serve the purposes of episodic remembering only if it also draws on sparse hippocampal information and that information is, in fact, reliably connected to the particular past episode being represented.

So conceived, a minimal memory trace is an 'internal process that causally links experience and remembering and is operated by the system in a truth-approximating reliable way' (Werning 2020, p. 321). On this account, memory traces can be minimal because, allegedly, they need only provide a very slender informational basis in order to support reliable enough inferences about how things stood in one's past on specific occasions. A current inference about a specific past experience will be reliable enough if the probability of its being true or accurate is greater than a certain threshold probability, where the notion of probability in play here is that of objective probability in the frequentist sense.

How does the process work? Werning's (2020) proposal assumes that our world is rife with statistical correlations—correlations that we take for granted in the background when we make predictions. We are surrounded by information-carrying structures that we systematically respond to all the time without our knowing or noticing. In Werning's terms, the unrecognised, unnoticed statistical correlations to which we are systematically attuned and responsive are 'cognitively sub-categorial'—they are not, and need not be, represented by cognisers when going about their workaday cognitive business.

Such correlations are only ever brought before our minds—in the sense of being uncovered and categorised—in our scientific practices, with the aid of advanced and special purpose tools and techniques. Werning (2020) gives the example of colour constancy as a cognitively sub-categorical phenomenon. Vision scientists discovered and categorised correlations that perceivers are sensitive and responsive to but which they do not cognitively represent. These include correlations between light reflectancies and edges, between perceived colours and shapes, and so on.

Since informational correlations of this kind are standard statistical regularities in our familiar environments, it would be cognitively wasteful for us to represent and categorise them. The path of least resistance is for cognitive systems to be sensitive to these information correlations without representing them as such. This frees up cognitive resources, allowing minds to focus on those aspects of events and happenings that are more unexpected and less predictable.

This is where the idea of a minimal information trace does its special work. Against this backdrop, it is supposed that only a fraction of additional information—information about the unique past event—would be needed in order for the brain to make accurate enough predictions about the details of a particular past experience.

Memory traces are thus minimal in two senses on this theory. Firstly, trace minimalism only subscribes to a very minimal, indeed sparse, content preservation. Only a small amount of information needs to be preserved in order for there to be an appropriately strong and reliable causal link from an episodic memory to a specific past experience.[13]

Secondly, trace minimalism denies that any representational content is preserved by minimal traces. Only information is preserved. Information is understood wholly in terms of probabilistic co-variation holding between states of affairs (Dretske 1981, 1988). Putatively, information is the kind of thing that tree rings carry about the age of trees, and that bi-metallic strips carry about the ambient temperature. Since minimal traces are not assumed to bear any intrinsic representational content, they do not, *a fortiori*, preserve such content from experience to remembering, not even partially.

3.6 A dilemma for trace minimalism

At first glance, trace minimalism may seem like an attractive way of keeping memory traces in the game; showing that they do just enough to be explanatorily useful while, at the same time, showing that they are not so robust as to be explanatorily problematic. Yet, if we look more closely, it becomes evident that trace minimalism faces a dilemma.

Read weakly, trace minimalism is too weak. The pivotal question is: How should we understand the nature of the hippocampal information that is, *ex hypothesi*, preserved in a minimal memory trace? On a weak reading, such sub-categorical information is purely correlational; nothing more than a statistically reliable covariance between states of affairs.

Here we might think that 'a memory trace is an entity that contains *a quantity of information* that matches or exceeds what the subject recalls about the relevant event' (Michaelian & Robins 2018, p. 16, emphasis added). Yet, merely knowing that a brain state carries information and that we can quantify the information it carries gives us exactly no reason to think that episodic remembering involves extracting and decoding such information, nor does this give us any clue about how such extraction or decoding could be achieved.

On the assumption that covariance is not any kind of content, it follows that no content, neither informational nor representational, is stably preserved over time. As such, there is nothing in the ultra-stripped-down version of the minimal trace theory that explains how the brain can make current predictions about past events based on contentless correlational, covariational information. For such an account to work, it would have to be supposed that the brain is already capable of treating information *as evidence* of certain things being the case and that it is able to do so based on the fact it is aware that certain correlations hold. Thus, the brain would need to be able to treat, say, the fact of a tree having three rings as *evidence* of the tree being three years old. But for the brain to treat information as evidence and to make such inferences entails that it already has representational and conceptual capacities, and that such capacities do all the heavy epistemic lifting, not the covariational information itself.

Proponents of the predictive processing account that weak trace minimalism relies on might simply bite the bullet at this point. They might posit unexplained, conceptually based representational and conceptual capacities on the part of the brain in addition to positing that neural states carry covariant information of a non-categorial sort.

Yet, biting that bullet brings such theorists face to face with the Hard Problem of Content once again. Until we at least have a workable account of the origins of brain-based representational contents and concepts, we have no account of how brains are in a position to carry out such epistemic operations (for arguments against this type of position, see Hoerl 2018; Hutto 2018; Rosenberg 2018).[14]

Werning (2020) speaks of place cells 'projecting into' the neocortex and combining with 'information flows' in ways that 'give rise' to the 'construction of a scenario'. But the most damning problem with the notion of minimal informational traces, as understood under the auspices of weak trace minimalism, is that they cannot themselves be causally operative in producing remembered experiences.

Minimal informational traces would be able to satisfy this condition only if stored minimal trace information could be the causal basis of the dispositions that enable the episodic remembering of specific events. Accordingly, minimal trace information might be thought of as dispositional information of a sort that is 'causally efficacious when the disposition is manifested' (Shea 2015, p. 79). But covariant information, in itself, is merely correlational and lacks causal powers. As such, it cannot be causally productive in the required way—even if the structures that reliably carry it can be.

Weak trace minimalism as defined above is too weak to explain how minimal memory traces do the explanatory work asked of them: hence, it provides no viable means of defending a deflated notion of memory traces.

Weak trace minimalism altogether relinquishes the idea of a memory trace in that it lets go of the idea of a state that preserves or transmits any kind of content as well as having to let go of the idea that the preserved covariant information is operative in producing, or otherwise causally involved in producing, any of the content of a current remembering. Weak trace minimalism thus drops all of the core defining features of memory traces, ergo it leaves no trace of the idea of a memory trace.

Is there another way to go? What about adopting strong trace minimalism? Strong trace minimalism holds that some kind of informational content, which falls short of representational content, is preserved through minimal traces and operative in producing episodic memories. Such informational content would need to be something more, and other than, information understood in purely covariance terms. We might think of it as information with a built-in intentionality such that a minimal trace would be 'preserving information *about* that event' (Michaelian & Robins 2018, p. 17, emphasis added). But what exactly is this more robust notion of informational content, and how is it better placed to explain the epistemic mechanics of the brain's alleged predictive capacities?

If it is possible to make good on an idea of informational content that has such properties and causal powers, then it might be possible to rescue a sufficiently strong notion of a memory trace—one that could perform the required explanatory roles and yet which is also minimal enough to avoid the problems faced by more robust versions of memory traces that posit the existence of unexplained representational contents. The trouble is that, as things stand, there is no such halfway-house, just-so notion of causally efficacious information content on today's naturalistic market—a notion of information that neither deflates into mere covariance nor inflates into full-blown representational content. There is no such in-between notion that is stable enough to pull off this delicate explanatory balancing act non-mysteriously.

3.7 Moving beyond trace minimalism

It seems, whichever way we choose to go, we have no option but to go one step beyond trace minimalism. As such, we are brought full circle. As De Brigard (2014b) observes, in the end:

> it may be best to think of a memory trace, not as a neural network constantly carrying a particular memorial content from encoding to retrieval, but rather as instantiating the dispositional property to reinstate, as closely as possible, the complex hippocampal-neo-cortical pattern of neural activation the brain was in during encoding, at the time of retrieval
>
> (p. 411).

A dispositional account of this kind could easily be accepted by those who are most sceptical about the existence of memory traces—behaviourists, Wittgensteinians, radical enactivists, post-causalists, and non-transmissionist simulationists alike. Only, when we follow through on the reasoning, we are left with dispositions, not contentless dispositional traces. On a pure dispositionalist account of episodic remembering, there is no content that is preserved over time—no informational contents, no representational contents, not even contentful instructions for reproducing such contents. Nor is there preserved, causally efficacious trace information at play in episodic remembering.

It is possible to assume, as per the non-transmissionist simulation theory, that episodic remembering only requires the replication of a current neural pattern that is, *de facto*, sufficiently similar to that which underwrote the original, remembered experience. It is possible to assume that such patterns carry measurable, non-representational information-as-covariance without assuming that these replications of neural patterns involve any kind of information storage or transfer.

To go this way raises taxonomical questions about how to distinguish memory from imagination, but this need not be done by looking to internal processes to secure that distinction. We might instead look at the different roles memory and imagining play in our everyday practices for guidance. But investigating the viability of such a proposal is a job for another time and place.

3.8 Conclusion

Many modern-day defenders of RTT and memory traces seek to provide an updated, contemporary version of classic causal theory, in some way or another. Yet both the classic causal theory of memory and the updated versions that posit distributed traces fail so long as we have no answer to the Hard Problem of Content.

These failures can make trace minimalism appear attractive as a way to defend a deflated and defensible conception of memory traces. However, trace minimalism itself faces an intractable dilemma. Its defenders can try to deliver the required explanatory goods by using only a respectable notion of information-as-covariance. But that notion is too weak to do the jobs asked of it. Defenders of trace minimalism can alternatively embrace the idea that minimal memory traces preserve some kind of causally efficacious informational content. But this introduces mysteries in the account which also render it incapable of delivering the explanatory goods.

Either way, we are compelled to move beyond even trace minimalism and to let go of all traces of memory traces in our theorising about memory.

Notes

1 It is contentious whether procedural or semantic remembering requires memory traces; prominent theorists in the field are divided on this issue (see Robins 2017). For a detailed discussion of the potential need and prospects of positing memory traces to explain such forms of remembering, see Michaelian and Sant'Anna (2021).
2 Michaelian and Sant'Anna (2021) present the reasoning that motivates rejecting the RTT vis-à-vis the transmissionist variant of the simulation theory as follows: 'given what we know about how the memory (or episodic construction) system works, we

have to assume that the same reconstructive process may be at work even when none of the content of the retrieved representation is transmitted from the content of the experience of the apparently remembered event. And this suggests that a retrieved representation may qualify as a genuine memory of the apparently remembered event even when *no content at all is transmitted from experience to retrieval*. If this is right, then satisfaction of the appropriate causation condition (understood in transmissionist terms) is not necessary for memory' (p. S328, emphasis added). It is to run the same line of argument in purely dispositionalist terms under the auspices of a non-transmissionist version of simulation theory, as these authors also do in the same paper.

3 Arguments in favour of RRT and the necessity of memory traces are advanced under different guises and in different ways. Some hold that the existence of memory traces is guaranteed because they are somehow entailed by, or somehow conceptually built into, the very idea of remembering. Others hold that memory traces have a secure place in the metaphysics of mind because there are compelling reasons to think they will show up in our best scientific explanation of episodic remembering. Opponents of RRT need to be sensitive to which line of argument is being advanced when making counterarguments. Keeping track of these differences is especially important when evaluating arguments because sometimes these two kinds of argument are blurred, despite their evident incompatibility.

4 As Dupont (2014) notes, 'based on the Greek idea of typos, Western culture early on used two complementary images to express the embodiment of memories: memory as wax tablets on which information is recorded, and memory as store or inventory … From Greek metaphors onwards, the idea that memory must be associated with a physical change runs through the entire history of Western thought, from the clinical observations of Renaissance physicians to the cerebral physiology of the Enlightenment' (p. 18; see also Hutto 2016).

5 Foreshadowing much current thinking in analytic philosophy of mind and cognitive science, Aristotle offered us the standard, old-school account of remembering by means of a memory trace. His account of remembering conceives of it as requiring recovery of a 'preserved representation that is both a copy of, and caused by, a previous perception of a past object or event' (De Brigard 2014a, p. 403). As De Brigard (2014a) also points out, 'At the beginning of *De Memoria et Reminiscentia*, Aristotle follows a content-based approach—the idea, roughly, that cognitive faculties are individuated in terms of the contents they operate with" (p. 402). In doing so, importantly, 'Aristotle goes beyond the impression metaphor and offers a more elaborate solution, using of the Platonic notion of eikon or "copy". "An eikon of X", Sorabji (2006) reminds us, "is both similar to, and derived from, X." Moreover, for Aristotle, this derivation is causal (450a27-b11); the preserved eikon brought to mind when one remembers is both similar to and causally derived from the perceived object' (p. 403).

6 On this score Dupont (2014) remarks, 'For philosophers like David Krell, such debates are like an illusory quest for the Holy Grail … For others, like John Sutton, there is a healthy continuity between old ideas and contemporary connectionism (Sutton 1998)' (p. 17).

7 Ultimately, the job of a memory trace is to provide a distinct causal link via a state or states that generates distinctive, preserved content. This is why it is widely assumed, as Dupont (2014) puts it, 'the notion of trace implies representation' (p. 31). It is why Sutton (2015) talks freely of 'memory traces or other kinds of mental representation' (p. 418). It is also why Robins (2016) tells us that, 'A memory trace is a representation of the past event, providing a link that is informational as well as causal' (p. 2994).

8 See, for example, Werning (2020), who assumes that memory traces are internal to biological organisms. Anticipating the extended memory debates, Martin and Deutscher (1966) contend that internalism about memory traces is not 'strictly necessary' (p. 181). They muse that non-human memory could be functionally realised

in ways that go beyond the skin and skull while doing essentially the same work. Hence, they imagine non-human creatures that might use external boxes to house and store the contents of their memories. For further discussion, see Sutton and Windhorst (2009). I thank Chris McCarroll for providing pointers with respect to the latter discussions.

9   Werning (2020) argues the classical causal theory of memory—or at least those versions committed to strong preservationism—cannot account for the epistemic generativity of episodic memory. Epistemic generativity is thought by some to be incompatible with versions of the causal theory of memory that conceive episodic remembering to be a matter of the recovery of an exactly preserved remembered content. For this reason, Werning regards the classic causal theory to be phenomenologically and epistemologically suspect. Yet this is a point of contention in the field. For example, Boyle (2019) advances an account of episodic memory that defends both the idea it based on stored information about the past and that is also epistemically generative.

10   See Hutto and Myin (2013) for the original statement of the Hard Problem of Content. For further detail and an up-to-date explication of the problem, see Hutto and Myin (2017, 2018). For discussions of its implications for memory research see Hutto and Myin (2017); Hutto and Peeters (2018); Perrin (2018); and Michaelian and Sant'Anna (2021).

11   For further detail along these lines, see Rosenberg (2018), Chapters 7 and 8.

12   Others deliver a similar verdict on the explanatory vacuity of Sutton's (1998) proposal about how implicit contents are allegedly stored in a distributed superpositional manner. In an early review, Skrenes (2000) concludes that Sutton's attempt to defend distributed models of memory 'must be judged a failure' (p. 401). More recently, concurring with conclusions reached by Perrin (2018), it has been observed that, 'Though Sutton himself has sometimes referred to distributed traces as having "implicit" content, this is misleading at best. Distributed content is no content at all' (Michaelian & Sant'Anna 2021, p. S325).

13   Werning (2020) provides an analysis which suggests that this proposal is in keeping with Reichenbach's (1956) Common Cause Principle and hence that it adequately addresses the reliability requirement, which he identifies as the principal reason to postulate memory traces as a basis for a causal link in the first place.

14   To avoid this objection, it might be possible to advance a version of the predictive processing story that makes no such assumptions about the representationally based inferential capacities of the brain. Werning suggested such a possibility when discussing the aforementioned challenge to weak trace minimalism in reply to a version of this paper presented at the Bochum-Grenoble Memory Colloquium on 20 July 2021. Although such a non-representationalist version of predictive processing would avoid the particular problem about the ab initio source of inferential capacities raised by the Hard Problem of Content, it would not avoid the problem that covariant information is, in itself, causally inert.

References

Anderson, M. L. (2010). Neural reuse: A fundamental organizational principle of the brain. *Behavioral and Brain Sciences*, *33*, 245–266.

Anderson, M. L. (2014). *After Phrenology: Neural Reuse and the Interactive Brain*. MIT Press.

Aronowitz, S. (2019). Memory is a modeling system. *Mind and Language*, *34*(4), 483–502.

Bennett, M. R., & Hacker, P. M. S. (2003). *Philosophical Foundations of Neuroscience*. Wiley-Blackwell.

Bernecker, S. (2010). *Memory: A Philosophical Study*. Oxford University Press.

Bernecker, S. (2018). A causal theory of mnemonic confabulation. *Frontiers in Psychology*. https://doi.org/10.3389/fpsyg.2017.01207.

Boyle, A. (2019). Learning from the past: Epistemic generativity and the function of episodic memory. *Journal of Consciousness Studies, 26*(5–6), 242–251.

Clark, A., & Chalmers, D. (1988). The extended mind. *Analysis, 58*(1), 7–19.

De Brigard, F. (2014a). The nature of memory traces. *Philosophy Compass, 9*(6), 402–414.

De Brigard, F. (2014b). Is memory for remembering? Recollection as a form of episodic hypothetical thinking. *Synthese, 191*(2), 155–185.

Dretske, F. (1981). *Knowledge and the Flow of Information*. MIT Press.

Dretske, F. (1988). *Explaining Behaviour: Reasons in a World of Causes*. MIT Press.

Dupont, J.-C. (2014). Memory traces between brain theory and philosophy. In C. T. Wolffe (Ed.), *Brain Theory: Essays in Critical Neurophilosophy* (pp. 17–34). Springer.

Heil, J. (1978). Traces of things past. *Philosophy of Science, 45*, 60–67.

Hoerl, C. (2018). Remembering past experiences: Episodic memory, semantic memory, and the epistemic asymmetry. In K. Michaelian, D. Debus, & D. Perrin (Eds.), *New Directions in the Philosophy of Memory* (pp. 313–328). Routledge.

Hutto, D. D. (2016). Remembering without stored contents: a philosophical reflection on memory. In S. Groes (Ed.), *Memory in the Twenty-First Century: New Critical Perspectives from the Arts, Humanities, and Sciences* (pp. 229–236). Basingstoke: Palgrave Macmillan.

Hutto, D. D. (2017). Memory and narrativity. In S. Bernecker & K. Michaelian (Eds.), *The Routledge Handbook of Philosophy of Memory* (pp. 192–204). Routledge.

Hutto, D. D. (2018). Getting into predictive processing's great guessing game: Bootstrap heaven or hell?. *Synthese, 195*, 2445–2458.

Hutto, D. D., & McGivern, P. (2016). Updating the story of mental time travel: Narrating and engaging with our possible pasts and futures. In R. Altshuler & M. J. Sigrist (Eds.), *Time and the Philosophy of Action* (pp. 167–185). Routledge.

Hutto, D. D., & Myin, E. (2013). *Radicalizing Enactivism: Basic Minds without Content*. MIT Press.

Hutto, D. D., & Myin, E. (2017). *Evolving Enactivism: Basic Minds Meet Content*. MIT Press.

Hutto, D. D., & Myin, E. (2018). Going radical. In A. Newen, L. De Bruin, & S. Gallagher (Eds.), *The Oxford Handbook of 4E Cognition*. (pp. 95–115). Oxford University Press.

Hutto, D. D., & Peeters, A. (2018). The roots of remembering: Radically enactive Recollecting. In K. Michaelian, D. Debus, & D. Perrin (eds.), *New Directions in the Philosophy of Memory* (pp. 97–118). Routledge.

Malcolm, N. (1977). *Memory and Mind*. Cornell University Press.

Martin, C. B., & Deutscher, M. (1966). Remembering. *The Philosophical Review, 75*(2), 161–196.

Michaelian, K. (2016). *Mental Time Travel: Episodic Memory and Our Knowledge of the Personal Past*. MIT Press.

Michaelian, K., & Robins, S. K. (2018). Beyond the causal theory? Fifty years after Martin and Deutscher. In K. Michaelian, D. Debus, & D. Perrin (Eds.), *New Directions in the Philosophy of Memory* (pp. 13–32). Routledge.

Michaelian, K., & Sant'Anna, A. (2021). Memory without content? Radical enactivism and (post)causal theories of memory. *Synthese, 198*, 307–335.

Michaelian, K., & Sutton, J. (2017). Memory. In E. N. Zalta (Ed.), *The Stanford Encyclopedia of Philosophy* (Summer 2017 Edition). https://plato.stanford.edu/archives/sum2017/entries/memory/.

Moyal-Sharrock, D. (2009). Wittgenstein and the memory debate. *New Ideas in Psychology, 27,* 213–227.

O'Brien, G. (2015a). How does mind matter? Solving the content causation problem. In T. K. Metzinger & J. M. Windt (Eds.), *Open MIND.* MIND Group.

O'Brien, G. (2015b). Rehabilitating resemblance redux. In T. K. Metzinger & J. M. Windt (Eds.), *Open MIND.* MIND Group.

O'Brien, G., & Opie, J. (2004). Notes toward a structuralist theory of mental representation. In H. Clapin (Ed.), *Representation in Mind* (pp. 1–20). Elsevier.

O'Brien, G., & Opie, J. (2009). The role of representation in computation. *Cognitive Processing, 10*(1), 53–62.

O'Brien, G., & Opie, J. (2015). Intentionality lite or analog content? *Philosophia, 43*(3), 723–729.

Perrin, D. (2018). A case for procedural causality in episodic recollection. In K. Michaelian, D. Debus, & D. Perrin (eds.), *New Directions in the Philosophy of Memory* (pp. 33–51). Routledge.

Reichenbach, H. (1956). *The Direction of Time.* University of California Press.

Robins, S. (2016). Representing the past: Memory traces and the causal theory of memory. *Philosophical Studies, 173*(11), 2993–3013.

Robins, S. (2017). Memory traces. In S. Bernecker & K. Michaelian (eds.), *The Routledge Handbook of Philosophy of Memory* (pp. 76–87). Routledge.

Rosenberg, A. (2018). *How History Gets Things Wrong: The Neuroscience of Our Addiction to Stories.* MIT Press.

Schacter, D. L., & Addis, D. R. (2009). On the nature of medial temporal lobe contributions to the constructive simulation of future events. *Philosophical Transactions of the Royal Society B: Biological Sciences, 364,* 1245–1253.

Schacter, D. L., Addis, D. R., & Buckner, R. L. (2007). Remembering the past to imagine the future: The prospective brain. *Nature Reviews: Neuroscience, 8,* 657–661.

Segundo-Ortin, M., & Hutto, D. D. (2021). Similarity-based cognition: Radical enactivism meets cognitive neuroscience. *Synthese, 198,* 5–23.

Shea, N. (2015). Distinguishing top-down from bottom-up effects. In S. Biggs, M. Matthen, and D. Stokes (eds), *Perception and its Modalities.* (pp. 73–91). Oxford University Press.

Skrenes, C. (2000). Review of John Sutton, *Philosophy and memory traces: Descartes to connectionism. Dialogue: Canadian Philosophy Review, 39,* 400–402.

Sorabji, R. (2006). *Aristotle on Memory.* University of Chicago Press.

Sutton, J. (1998). *Philosophy and Memory Traces: Descartes to Connectionism.* Cambridge University Press.

Sutton, J. (2015). Remembering as public practice: Wittgenstein, memory, and distributed cognitive ecologies. In D. Moyal-Sharrock, V. Munz, & A. Coliva (Eds.), *Mind, Language, and Action: Proceedings of the 36th Wittgenstein Symposium.* (pp. 409–443). De Gruyter.

Sutton, J., & O'Brien, G. (n.a., Chapter 4, this volume). Distributed traces and the causal theory of constructive memory.

Sutton, J., & Windhorst, C. (2009). Extended and constructive remembering: two notes on Martin and Deutscher. *Crossroads: An Interdisciplinary Journal for the Study of History, Philosophy, Religion and Classics, 4*(1), 79–91.

Szpunar, K. K., Watson, J. M., & McDermott, K. B. (2007). Neural substrates of envisioning the future. *Proceedings of the National Academy of Sciences of the United States of America*, *104*, 642–647.

Werning, M. (2020). Predicting the past from minimal traces: Episodic memory and its distinction from imagination and preservation. *Review of Philosophy and Psychology*, *11*, 301–333.

Wittgenstein, L. (1980). *Remarks on the Philosophy of Psychology*, Vol. I. (G.E.M. Anscombe, Trans., G. E. M. Anscombe & G. H. von Wright, Eds.). Blackwell.

4 Distributed traces and the causal theory of constructive memory

John Sutton and Gerard O'Brien

4.1 Memory as causal

A student remembers her surprise birthday party (Selwood, Harris, Barnier, & Sutton 2020, p. 415). In her apartment after work, she found balloons, then found her friends hiding in the living room; there was cake, and a crown with her name on it, and she put on 'something nicer'; someone spilled wine on the carpet, its 'first red stain'. Then 'all of a sudden our neighbour was in our living room. The music stopped and everyone froze. Especially me. I sank down on the sofa, and was so embarrassed'. She had trouble getting people out, but 'everything was fine': they all went to the pub, and later ate pie on the way home.

Though elicited in the peculiar context of an experiment (in this case, a study of how remembering events on your own differs from recalling them collaboratively), this is an otherwise unexceptional report of a personally significant past event. That event was complex and structured: it occurred within a delimited time frame but extended over a number of component episodes. The student experienced it actively, interpreting what was happening in her own way, attending to select, salient aspects of the event. For her now, later, to remember it is to weave a complex mental tapestry of perceptual, affective, and conceptual threads: among others, sets of dynamic visual images of locations and scenes, and of detailed visual experiences of people, objects, and actions; related sets of olfactory, auditory, gustatory, and embodied images, of the smell, the chatter and the music, the cake and the drinks, the bodily feelings of pleasure, or of sinking in embarrassment; and an array of affects and concepts, images, and attitudes relating to her feeling and thoughts at the time, and to her take on the social and emotional relations among her friends.

This person, it's natural to think, remembers her surprise party partly *because* she experienced it. While remembering it now is an activity prompted by an experimenter's request and influenced by many other factors, the recalled episode has a more or less integrated place in her past as a result of *causal* connections of certain kinds between it and the present remembrance. Significant personal events are woven in to more or less coherent autobiographical narratives that form and maintain our sense of the causal connectedness of events and actions in time (J. Campbell 1997; Ismael 2016).

DOI: 10.4324/9781003002277-7

It's also natural to think that the memory is in some sense *embodied*, or *carried* with the person over time. It may be highly context-sensitive, in that what and how she remembers may change in light of later events, or in reports to different audiences, and in that the factual and emotional details, the accuracy, and the qualitative experience of remembering may vary over repeated retellings (Temler, Barnier, Sutton, & McIlwain 2020). But the student's capacity to recall these episodes is transportable, typically *not* tied to one context alone. Though there is no guarantee in any particular case, she takes her access to *some* such events in her personal past with her, even if her path through life takes her far from their location and from any direct reminders (Sutton 2009).

While remembering is a situated activity in the present, it also has vital *diachronic* aspects. It typically involves *past* events, and is one ingredient among others that make us creatures *with* a past to which, in remembering, we fallibly lay claim (S. Campbell 2004). The forms of causation in play here, across multiple experiences, memories, and emotions, and over the weave of a life, are neither simple nor easy to track. This is not the collision of isolated billiard balls, but rather causation as sedimentation, where causal connections are multiple, indirect, and context-dependent (Deutscher 1989, p. 61; Sutton 1998, p. 308).

4.2 The causal theory of memory

Such considerations motivate the causal theory of memory (CTM; Martin & Deutscher 1966). CTM aims to illuminate them by invoking causal processes operative in remembering a past event, and memory traces which are in some sense *about* (aspects of) the event from which they derive.

The causal theory of memory is intended as an objective, third-person account, to catch the causal basis of memory's significance. Martin and Deutscher respected the diversity and richness of our language and practices around remembering, while refusing to treat the individual subject's perspective as the final authority (Deutscher 1989; Sutton & Windhorst 2009). CTM seeks objective marks or criteria by which to identify remembering. Such criteria, it is hoped, distinguish genuine memory of a past event from other phenomena: from, for example, merely appearing to remember it, from (merely) imagining it, or from knowing about it from a source other than personal experience (such as relearning it, after previously forgetting it).

In the case of the student's memory of the surprise party, for example, we can ask how traces of the spilling of the wine or of the student's embarrassment operate causally within the complex processes driving her active remembering, alongside the experimenter's request for such a narrative. We can also ask how closely the remembered episode matches the student's original experiences, if for some reason we need to assess its status as a genuine memory.

These are not questions about *subjective* differences between remembering and (say) imagining, about how in psychological practice we come (fallibly) to *take* ourselves sometimes to be remembering, sometimes to be imagining

(Michaelian 2016, pp. 71, 120). CTM allows for genuine error: I may well take myself to be remembering, when in fact I am not.

While psychologists and cognitive neuroscientists working on memory have typically acknowledged its diachronic nature (Tulving 2007, p. 66), few show specific interest in the CTM. Their projects are empirical, explanatory, or descriptive: they study the nature, mechanisms, processes, and operations of human memory across interacting social, behavioural, phenomenological, cognitive, and neural dimensions. Many philosophers, of course, share these interests and aims, participating alongside scientists in what Michaelian calls 'the naturalistic project of describing memory as a psychologically real process' (2016, p. 69). CTM is often rightly modified to fit better with memory science, and we are about to add to decades of debate on the implications of the resulting constraints.

Before we get to this core business, though, we note in advance that we do not claim that an understanding of human memory is exhausted by reference to the neurocomputational processes in question. It is entirely compatible with (though strictly independent of) all we say here to see them, rather, as the bio-internal wings or components of broader systems spanning brain, body, and world. In particular, we suggest in our final section that these descriptive facts about memory neither dictate nor exhaust the content of the causal theory. We focus there on 'external' forms of context-sensitivity, to add to the rich 'internal' context-sensitivity which is our primary concern. Future work that treats these forms of context-sensitivity together, we will suggest briefly, may engender more realistic assessment of relations between CTM and the cognitive neurosciences of memory.

4.3 The causal theory of constructive memory

Our work in the 1980s and 1990s was firmly in that naturalistic camp, assessing in different ways the philosophical implications of connectionism, where the superpositional 'storage' of multiple memories over the same resources gives rise to *distributed* traces, with many 'representations' in any one 'representing' (Haugeland 1991; McClelland & Rumelhart 1986; O'Brien 1993; Sutton 1998; van Gelder 1991). While CTM was not our primary concern, it was clear that connectionism would require some standard notions of mental content and mental causation to be either rejected or substantially liberalised. We adopted the latter, revisionary option: O'Brien argued against the elimination of content in connectionism (O'Brien 1991; Ramsey, Stich, & Garon 1991), and Sutton (1998) defended a connectionist account of contentful memory traces against a variety of critics (pp. 298–316). These were ongoing discussions: an explicit debate with Deutscher over the extent to which 'the causal analysis is in some tension with the extent to which remembering is a constructive activity' (Sutton & Windhorst 2009, p. 79, with a helpful response in Deutscher 2009, pp. 97–98) suggests that we were not 'slow to recognize that the distributed conception of traces may be in tension with the contentful conception of traces' (Michaelian & Sant'Anna 2021, p. S323). We do accept that 'there is a pressing need for further work' on the causal theory of constructive memory (Michaelian & Robins 2018, p. 21), and so we aim here to combat claims that 'distributed memory traces are incompatible with the CTM' (Robins 2016, p. 2994) and that 'the widely-adopted distributed conception of traces … [leads] inexorably to the contentless conception' (Michaelian & Sant'Anna 2021, p. S319).

In what follows, we briefly rehearse relevant features of connectionism and assess its application to the forms of memory in question. We identify two important, related aspects of these forms of memory which are sometimes neglected, but which lie at the heart of connectionist approaches. Our primary focus (in Section 4.6) is in applying a novel account of content for distributed representations to the debate on memory. We also sketch an approach to explaining the context-sensitive causal roles of such distributed traces. Finally, as promised, we pan back, considering the causal theory of constructive memory in relation to the development and pragmatics of practices of remembering.

We focus on challenges to the causal theory of constructive memory that arise from consideration of specific features of distributed traces, rather than those motivated only by general concerns about mental content or mental causation. We adopt Michaelian's starting point, an investigation of human remembering 'as it unfolds in the real world', as opposed to deploying an 'analytic methodology' that seeks 'an account of remembering immune to all possible counter-examples' (2016, pp. 3–4). We do not seek sharp necessary and sufficient conditions that apply across all contexts. Clear cases of remembering, and cases which are clearly not remembering, can legitimately be identified even if other cases are uncertain, the subject of reasonable disagreement. Rather than watertight 'analysis', then, the empirically informed view we defend embraces some vagueness at the edges, not as 'a tolerable defect' (Michaelian 2016, p. 91) but as a pointer to memory's deep context-sensitivity.

There are good, independent reasons to retain both the causal theory of memory and the idea that the traces it invokes are distributed. So the conjunction of these views is worth defending. The challenges posed by holding both – by defending the causal theory of constructive memory, or CTCM – are real puzzles about memory and its place in our lives, not mere artefacts of theory. These are difficult topics, which require precisely navigated integrations of challenging and changing fields in neuroscience, cognitive and developmental psychology, and many areas of philosophy. There are principled reasons why it's difficult to pin down what counts as an 'appropriate causal connection' between past experience and present recall, both in general and in particular cases. The point that claims to truth in memory are often desperately hard to assess, in theory and in practice, should not be surprising, and should not be a reason to give up on them. Both causal approaches to memory and distributed traces are valuable: identifying possible tensions between them should motivate us not to jettison commitment to one or to both, but to find clearer and more creative responses.

4.4 Connectionism and episodic memory

As a neurally inspired rival to the classical computational theory of mind (Fodor 1975), connectionism captures structural and temporal properties of the brain's neural networks in virtue of the way it deploys transient *activation patterns* and enduring sets of *connection weights* (O'Brien & Opie 1999; for an overview, see Buckner & Garson 2019).

Each unit in a connectionist network has an activation level (modelled on a neuron's spiking frequency) that is communicated to other units in the network via modifiable, weighted connections (modelled on synapses). From moment to moment, each unit sums the weighted activation it receives and generates a new activation level that is some threshold function of its current activity and that input. This is how a network responds to its inputs, generating a stable pattern of activity across its constituent units. Altering the network's connection weights alters the activation patterns it produces. Consequently, a network can learn to generate a range of target patterns in response to a range of inputs. These stable patterns of activation, generated rapidly in response to the flux of input imping-ing on individual networks, are taken by connectionists to constitute a transient form of information coding, often referred to as *activation pattern representation*. Activation patterns are vehicles of *explicit* representation: there is a *one-to-one* relationship between a specific activation pattern and an element of the net-work's representational domain.

While activation patterns are transient features of connectionist networks, a trained network, in virtue of the particular configuration of its connection weights, has a longer-term capacity to generate a set of target activation pat-terns, in response to cueing inputs. This second form of information coding, referred to as *connection weight representation*, is the basis of long-term memory in connectionist systems. Such long-term storage of information, by contrast with activation pattern representation, is *superpositional* in nature, since each connec-tion weight contributes to the 'storage' of every stable activation pattern the network can generate. This is the connectionist implementation of *distributed* representation. The information stored in a network is not encoded in a physi-cally discrete manner. Instead, a single appropriately configured network encodes a set of contents in a way that grounds its capacity to produce a set of activation patterns: there is a *one-to-many* relationship between this complex of connection weights and the elements that compose its representational domain (Clark 1993; Churchland 1995).

Much connectionist research with individual networks is conducted at the level of relatively low-level perceptual and categorical tasks such as colour cat-egorisation and face recognition. Such tasks are modelled by networks of a small number of units and layers (relative to the brain, that is). The episodic form of memory exemplified by the surprise birthday example, in contrast, is a high-level cognitive achievement, implicating multiple sensory and executive path-ways, each of which involves a myriad of neural circuits across the brain. Social and contextual features of the retrieval context may iteratively influence ongoing neural processes: as I narrate a past experience, someone else's responses can shape the content, form, and course of my remembering, in continuous reciprocal interactive causation. The relevant neurocognitive architectures are multi-level, integrating diverse cognitive domains across nested networks of interacting networks (De Brigard 2014a, 2014b). Despite other theoretical differences, cognitive neuroscientists agree that memory 'systems are much more interactive than we once thought' (Moscovitch et al. 2016, p. 124). The forms of representation and computation at the heart of connectionist neurophilosophy do ground the high-level neurocomputational architecture of episodic memory. But contemporary connectionism on its own does not offer an exhaustive theory of memory and cognition. It needs to be supplemented, first and at least, by incorporation into a fuller cognitive neuroscience.[1]

Yet leading connectionists from the outset did intend to generate 'a distributed model of human learning and memory' (McClelland & Rumelhart 1986), and questions about integration across levels continue to drive research in this field.[2] For our purposes, connectionism remains the best mechanistic demonstration of how the computational processing of representations gives rise to properties of generalisation, integration, and context-sensitive pattern-transformation which are also apparent in the dynamics of human memory (Kumaran & McClelland 2012; McClelland 1995; see Section 4.5).[3]

Let's return to our student's remembrance of the surprise birthday party. In the context of our experiment, this memory likely arose through 'generative' retrieval, a top-down, cue-driven deliberate process, rather than effortless 'direct' retrieval (Harris, O'Connor, & Sutton 2015). We did not image the student's brain in this study, but the characteristic time course and spatiotemporal dynamics of such retrieval processes are fairly well understood (Daselaar et al. 2008; Greenberg & Rubin 2003). On any contemporary neurocognitive view, this episodic memory implicates processing across an enormously complex web of interconnected neural networks, including sensory, emotional, and higher cognitive pathways, together with circuits in the hippocampus and the prefrontal cortex. At this global level, activation spreads as we remember events, rising and falling across interconnected networks of the networks that operate together as we identify, relive, feel, and perhaps narrate such structured, personally significant past experiences in real time.[4]

Fast changes in the stabilisation of all these networks cascade across the brain, generating myriad local activation patterns over specific component networks as the experience takes its course. From a connectionist perspective, such rapid sequences of localised activation pattern stabilisations within each of these networks are the (often minimal or fragmentary) components of representational content, which combine to generate the complex cascades of molecular representational states that constitute ongoing experience. These more global states, in virtue of the activation patterns from which they are composed, are explicit representing vehicles with discrete representational contents. As, for example, memory of the cake and the crown gives way to memories of the spilled wine and of embarrassment at the neighbour's arrival, stabilised patterns in gustatory and visual cortex are replaced by further stabilisations in emotional and kinaesthetic networks, such sequences generating the dynamic quality of the remembering experience across a few seconds.

As this is *constructive* memory, the activation patterns generated during this experience may differ markedly from those that arose during the party itself: from such a diachronic perspective, they will likely be both selective (discarding many details of the original experience), and generative (adding extra details). Such changes arise in constructive processes at any stage along the way, with extra content integrated from other sources, or generated from traces of other experiences. For the causal theorist of constructive memory, the visual details the student now retrieves need not match her visual experience at the time, and can even go beyond it to some extent: but with its diachronic focus, the causal theory expects *some* similarity here, such that the remembered details should 'not go too far beyond' those that were experienced (Michaelian 2016, p. 92).

The ongoing sequence of activation patterns takes the form it does, according to connectionism, ultimately in virtue of the configurations of connection weights at the level of the constituent networks. These configurations were so modified during the birthday party (and afterwards, in ongoing consolidation and reconsolidation) that now, in remembering, they enable the reconstruction of the activation patterns that contributed representational contents to the original experiences, even if these patterns are in certain respects now partial, impoverished, or altered. These configurations of connection weights constitute the distributed memory traces that mediate between experiences and their retrieval. They are also the source of connectionism's greatest strength as an approach to memory, and of the critics' concerns about its compatibility with causal theories. We consider each point in turn.

4.5 Dispositional memory and causal holism

Connectionist networks differ markedly from their classical computational counterparts in encoding information superpositionally over the long term. We argue that this is a great strength of connectionist computation: since *all* of the information encoded across a network is causally implicated *every time* the network processes an input, there is no need to process individual items of information separately. For connectionists, this 'causal holism' has the potential to overcome the vicious problems of computational intractability that stymied classical AI (O'Brien & Opie 1999, 2009). We focus here on its additional and distinctive philosophical pay-off. Connectionism, as the heart of the causal theory of constructive memory, catches two important, related aspects of human remembering: the difference between occurrent and dispositional memory, and memory's constructive or generative nature. These are features familiar in both ordinary and scientific views of memory, not exclusive to any one discourse or project. While they are by no means universally appreciated, neither are they new discoveries. A theory of memory that respects or – better – offers detailed accounts of these features is to be preferred to one that says little about them.

When the student told us about the surprise birthday party, her remembering was an activity at a particular time: an *occurrent* memory. But before and again after this exercise of her memory, she still – in another sense – remembers the party, even when she is not actively, presently thinking about it at all: this enduring capacity of hers is *dispositional* memory. This distinction is easily grasped, and long acknowledged – it was clearly articulated by Aristotle and by Locke (Sutton 1998, 2020a). Although the student's memories of these events may be partial or incorrect in various ways, and may of course ultimately become inaccessible, she doesn't simply *forget* them when she is remembering something else, or when she is swimming, or sleeping. Our best sciences of memory should acknowledge and explain both forms of memory, and their relations.

It is natural to characterise dispositional remembering in two slightly more substantive ways. Not only, we reasonably think, do memories endure when non-occurrent, but they continue to matter or make a difference: they remain part of our history and of who we are, and they have ongoing causal efficacy even when not explicitly in mind. This is not to posit one integrated global memory trace that fixes or binds *all* events of the surprise party in some single, unitary form. It is merely to claim that those component traces do endure, in some form, fragmentary or dispersed or superposed as that may be: they are neither impotent nor lost, not dissipated entirely between experience and recall. It makes a difference to the student's ongoing mental life that she lived through those events and remembers them, however imperfectly. This was a vital plank in the connectionist resistance to classical cognitivism: mental causation does *not* (as Fodor thought) require explicit representation.

Further, such enduring dispositional memories operate holistically. It's not that each event in my personal past is retained separately, sitting passively in cold storage until accessed at will, pulled out again just as it was first experienced, to make a single causal contribution to ongoing processing. Rather, we are well aware of the dynamics and context-sensitivity of memory's ongoing operation. This is not a point about memory's frailty and fragility, its errors and confusions. It's that we are all accustomed to changes in the significance, implications, and content of what we recall, sometimes outside awareness or control, sometimes in line with our changing epistemic, emotional, or evaluative perspectives on our past (Goldie 2012, pp. 26–55). Experiences we recall more or less reliably need not show up in ongoing mental life in static form: they contribute both to other activities of remembering, and to an array of other psychological operations, even when not explicit. Much of what we remember is updated as we have other related experiences, and much of what we remember integrates into or guides our ongoing cognition and action even when it's not occurrently active. As well as – sometimes – successfully recalling specific past events, human minds also tend easily to link new experiences with relevant memories, and to generalise across memories with similar content.

Such causal holism falls naturally out of the connectionist picture of distributed memory traces we outlined earlier (O'Brien 1998, p. 82). Because superpositional 'storage' – which is not distinct from ongoing processing, as it is in classical computation – creates such 'composite' memories, it has long been recognised as a detailed mechanistic implementation of a non-archival model of memory, and of the alternative view of memory processes as creative, selective, generative, and dynamic.[5] So far, so good – the context-sensitivity and content-addressability of connectionist processing drives flexible generalisation, the capacity to extract the central tendencies of a set of experiences, and other apparent characteristics of human mental life (McClelland & Rumelhart 1986, p. 193; Clark 1989, p. 99). On this measure, distributed representations as postulated in connectionism clearly outperform old and new localist accounts of engrams or memory traces. These are, we submit, strong considerations in favour of the connectionist account of distributed traces as an approach to memory, before any countervailing challenges are considered.

4.6 Distributed traces, content transmission, and causal history

We now respond to the two central concerns about the compatibility of distributed memory traces with CTCM. The first is that distributed memory traces cannot *transmit content* from experience to remembering in the way that, for the causal theorist, distinguishes cases of remembering from non-memorial forms of retention. The second is that distributed memory traces cannot appropriately mediate the requisite *causal history* between original experiences and their retrieval. Our task now is to explain how connectionist computation, contrary to critics' concerns, has the representational resources to implement memory traces that can transmit content and mediate appropriate causal histories between experience and retrieval.

4.6.1 The challenge to contentful traces

We defend – albeit in significantly revised form – the standard causal theorist's claim that there is some transmission of content between experience and retrieval.[6] If the causal connection is sustained by memory traces, such traces must be *representing vehicles* that convey (at least some) content of experienced episodes to subsequent remembering. The connectionist CTCM seems to have this covered. As we have seen, connectionists talk in terms of information *stored* long-term as connection weight representations. These configurations of connection weights appear to be representing vehicles capable of conveying contents over time in memory, where no such content transmission will be operative in either relearning or merely imagining the events.

But some philosophers of memory are not so sure. They worry that talk of connection weights 'storing' information is misleading. Because connectionists set their caps against the static storage of discrete items typical of classical models, it is easy to think they are rejecting content entirely. Superposition is a form of 'storage', but of a non-conventional form that can be tricky to grasp. As Elman (1993) wrote, in connectionism, once a given pattern has been processed and the network has been updated, the data disappear. Their effect is immediate and results in a modification of the knowledge state of the network. The data persist only by virtue of the effect they have on what the network knows.

(p. 89)

So when De Brigard notes that '"storing" is a rather misleading term', and characterises a memory trace as a 'dispositional property to reinstate ... the complex hippocampal-neocortical pattern of neural activation' (2014a, p. 411, 2014c, p. 169), some commentators read him as *rejecting* content (Hutto & Peeters 2018, p. 105; Michaelian & Sant'Anna 2021, p.S314; Hutto, Chapter 3, this volume, pp. 75-76). Such critics are happy to describe connectionist memory traces in terms of the *dispositional* properties of neural networks, but take this to mean that 'strictly speaking, no content is stored' (Michaelian & Sant'Anna 2021, p.S324).[7]

Debate about the representational credentials of configurations of network connection weights is not new. William Ramsey noted that whereas in

> classical models it is typically the case that causally distinct structures encode commands for specific stages of the computation ... in trained connectionist models, this type of specificity is not possible. While it might be true that some connection weights contribute to some episodes of processing more than others, there is no level of analysis at which we can say a particular weight encodes a particular command or governs a specific algorithmic step in the computation. Instead, all the system's know-how is superimposed on all the weights with no particular mappings between the two.
>
> (Ramsey 1997, pp. 48–49)

Ramsey is targeting the specifically *distributed* nature of connectionist memory traces: the fact the information is *superpositionally* encoded across a network's connection weights, with a *one-to-many* relationship between this configuration of weights and the elements that compose the network's representational domain. This leads Ramsey to conclude that 'there doesn't appear to be any other level of understanding or explanatory motivation that requires us to view the weights as representations' (1997, p. 51).

If connectionist memory traces are not representing vehicles in good standing, they cannot transmit content from experience to retrieval. In defending a connectionist CTCM, therefore, we need to show that such scepticism about the representational credentials of connection weights is misplaced. Our novel response which follows differs in detail from those offered by other connectionists (Churchland 2012; Haybron 2000; Shea 2007). While it is true that direct application of these debates to the philosophy of memory in particular is relatively recent, critics of content in connectionism need to acknowledge and answer these distinct and detailed views. They should not simply ignore them while asserting that distributed content is incoherent.

4.6.2 Why we need contentful traces

We contest a 'purely' dispositional, contentless interpretation of connectionism by focussing on the *explanatory gap* between the microphysical properties of connectionist networks and their capacity to successfully navigate their task domains. Architecturally identical networks trained up on to the same task domain but from distinct random initial assignments of connection weights come to occupy different points in 'weight space'.[8] As a consequence, each trained network responds to the *same* inputs by generating patterns of activation that occupy *different* points in 'activation space'.[9] At the microphysical or barely neural level of individual weighted connections and unit activation values, therefore, these different networks have nothing in common. From this microphysical perspective, nothing distinguishes those networks capable of successful performance in the task domain from those that are not.

This is what's wrong with the attempt to explain episodic memory entirely 'without a trace'. Consider, for example, the alternative offered by Hutto to accompany his attack on 'the explanatory vacuity' of our accounts of implicit, content-carrying distributed representations (Chapter 3, this volume, note 12). On his view, remembering does involve or require some internal similarity over time. But, he insists, this is not similarity of *content*. Rather, such similarity is to be sought at the level of 'specific neural patterns' alone: it is not a *representational* similarity, not even a psychological similarity. At the micro-neural level to which Hutto directs us, he expects to find 'the re-instantiation' of such 'specific neural patterns'. Such 'recreated neural patterns' will 'suffice' for memory if in 're-occurring' they are 'similar enough to those that occurred during the original experience' (Chapter 3, this volume, p. 66). Hutto repeatedly invokes this kind of neural commonality over time, and it is all he offers as a putative explanatory mechanism for memory. The 'replication' of a 'neural pattern' must be 'sufficiently similar to that which underwrote the original, remembered experience' (Chapter 3, this volume, p. 76).

Given that Hutto claims to acknowledge the extent of dynamic neural redeployment in relevant systems, it is surprising that he is so confident about finding such similarity, about the genuine re-instantiation or replication of 'specific neural patterns' across time and context. It is an empirical matter, but we believe there is little reason to expect any such 're-creation' or 're-instantiation' of specific patterns identified at the microphysical or neural level alone. We might also expect to hear more from Hutto about what these 'specific neural patterns' might be; about how they change over time; and about what this 'similarity' consists in, or how it is even in principle to be identified. Such a thin alternative does not successfully fulfil Hutto's 'radical' wish to eliminate traces and memory content.

Like other theorists of distributed connectionist content, we aim in what follows to offer, in contrast, full and detailed accounts of the kind of commonality we *are* likely to find, across distinct occasions (for example) on which the student remembers the same surprise party. What, then, *explains* the successful performance of networks that have nothing in common at the microphysical or barely neural level? To answer, and to defend the contentful conception of traces, we have to ascend to a higher, emergent level of description, and to show why reference to the *representational* capacities of connectionist networks is ineliminable.

4.6.3 How we get contentful traces

Successful networks differ from their unsuccessful counterparts in that they embody, within their configuration of connection weights, sufficiently accurate *structural models* of the task domain. These structural models, multiply realisable in the microphysical substrate of connectionist networks, are acquired during a network's training regime. Once in place, they govern a network's response to any input and enable it to relax into a stable activation pattern that corresponds with the region of the embodied representational landscape that constitutes the response to the input. We now demonstrate that connection weight representing vehicles earn their explanatory keep by explaining how connectionist networks compute (O'Brien & Opie 2006).

It is a well-known feature of connectionism that a network trained on a corpus of inputs constructs an activation pattern landscape partitioned into separable regions corresponding to salient categorical distinctions between the elements that compose its task domain (Clark 1993; Churchland 1995). What is not always appreciated about these activation patterns, however, is that collectively, they *structurally resemble* aspects of the task domain over which the network has been trained.[10] Indeed, this structural resemblance relation anchors the representational interpretation of activation patterns (O'Brien & Opie 2004).[11] With this representational interpretation of activation patterns in hand, we can see what different connectionist networks trained on the same task domain have in common, despite their microphysical differences: they each realise the same activation pattern representational landscape.

The deeper commonality between networks trained up on the same corpus of inputs – the fact that their connection weights embody a structural model of the task domain – requires some teasing out. Key players in network processing are what O'Brien and Opie call *fan-ins* (2006). A fan-in is the vector of weights modulating the effect of incoming activity on a particular hidden unit. Any feedforward network has one fan-in per hidden unit, each being to a row of the network's hidden layer weight matrix. Fan-ins effect the transformation of the network's input space into its hidden unit activation space. Specifically, each fan-in determines how one hidden unit responds to input, by way of a product of input activation and fan-in values. This product is then modified by the hidden unit's activation function to produce the value along a single coordinate in activation space. A network's fan-ins thus interface directly with the structure of the vectors coded at the input layer, and ultimately determine the structure of activation space. Most importantly for our purposes, investigations of familiar feedforward networks trained to perform such tasks as face recognition and colour categorisation (Laakso & Cottrell 2000) reveal that the configurations of connection weights that compose fan-ins structurally resemble aspects of the network's task domain (for details, see O'Brien & Opie 2006).

This second relation of systemic or structural resemblance secures an interpretation of connection weights as representing vehicles. Furthermore, this representational interpretation of network connection weights explains the successful performance of microphysically divergent networks operating in the same task domain. Despite their microphysical differences, each of these networks in the course of its training regime has sculpted a configuration of connection weights that structurally resembles, and hence represents, the task domain. Because the connection weights are ultimately responsible for the patterns of activity that networks generate in response to their inputs, this also explains why each of these networks achieves the same representational landscape in activation space: the structural resemblance embodied in its connection weights is causally responsible for the structural resemblance embodied in its activation space. These commonalities between the networks are invisible at the microphysical level of description. They are revealed only when we ascend to the abstract level at which these structural resemblance relations reside. Hence, only at this emergent level is there an illuminating explanation of their performance.

The foregoing, we think, is a strong and detailed response to those critics who charge that the distributed memory traces invoked by connectionist versions of CTCM are incapable of transmitting content between original and remembering experiences. Our discussion of the representational credentials and computational dynamics of connectionist systems derives from analysis of relatively simple networks performing straightforward categorical tasks (O'Brien & Opie 2006), but there is no reason to think the lessons don't generalise to more complex systems and cognitive capacities. Network connection weights are contentful representing vehicles anchored in structural resemblance relations with their task domains. As such, they are capable of transmitting contents between the activation patterns that originally established these relations of resemblance and the subsequent activation patterns they are instrumental in recreating. Again – explaining episodic memory in terms of 'specific neural patterns' alone, with no invocation of content, does not work. Far from discarding the notion of a representational trace, we *require* reference not only to weighted connections, but to the contentful representing vehicles which they constitute.

4.6.4 *Distributed traces and causal history*

Commentators raise a second concern about the compatibility of distributed memory traces with CTCM. What makes CTCM a *causal* theory of memory is its commitment to an appropriate causal connection between experience and remembering, mediated by memory traces. Not any old causal connection is enough: this causal connection should distinguish memories from one another, and remembering from relearning. Thus 'the causal chain leading back to the experience must be distinguishable from other causal chains' (Michaelian & Robins, 2018, p. 17). Perhaps the connectionist rendering of CTCM violates this requirement, precisely because it holds that memory traces encode information in a superpositional fashion:

> The traditional conception of traces involves fixed, explicit contents carried by distinct local vehicles … Proponents of distributed conceptions challenge this matrix of ideas, arguing that we should give up at least some of the features of the traditional conception…. If [the connectionist view] is right, we may be able to refer to memory traces in a loose sense, since a specific experience will result in a specific modification of connections in the network, but … there are no traces in the sense of *distinct vehicles* carrying *distinct contents*…. [It thus] remains unclear how … distributed causal theorists would have us understand the nature of the causal connection between retrieved memories and experiences.
>
> (Michaelian & Robins 2018, p. 21, original emphasis)

Like humans, connectionist models are good at generalising and integrating information. But perhaps there is an unacceptable cost. Does connectionism rule out a capacity to remember specific items or events? For Robins, its characteristic blending effects come 'at the expense of retaining the specifics of any particular past event': because 'the effect of any particular pattern will wash out over time, … distributed traces do not have individually distinguishable causal histories' (2016, pp. 3005, 3008). But if the CTM requires 'the possibility of tracing the unique causal influence of a particular past event up until the time that it is remembered', Robins claims, 'memory must be structured so as to retain discrete traces for each past experience a person is capable of recalling' (2016, p. 3011). This line of thought, if successful, would rule out connectionism, with its distributed traces, as a model of human memory: 'distributed network accounts of memory traces do not provide a way to track the causal history of memories for particular past events' (Robins 2016, p. 3009).

We postpone an equivalently full response to this concern to another occasion, partly for reasons of space: we will be content if our treatment of distributed content finds favour. We also acknowledge the difficulty of meeting this challenge, and of understanding better the complex causal nexus in which distributed traces are involved, and the senses in which connectionist causation is a matter of degree (Haybron 2000, p. 367). We offer here only a few promissory remarks on how these issues might be approached.

First, while we agree that a theory must allow for humans to remember specific past events, even if often partially and imperfectly, such specificity should not be over-emphasised. Episodic memory very often does not involve or require uniquely distinguishable causal pathways back to sharply delimited past events, because very often its content is not singular: repeated, recurrent, generic, or phasic events are very often remembered (Andonovski 2020; Mac Cumhaill 2020; Schechtman 1994; Sutton 1998). In such cases, the pressure on

CTCM to provide a way of singling out a specific causal connection running back to one event alone is released.

Secondly, we accept that the connectionist approach must significantly liberalise the way we understand how specific past events are singled out in memory, when they are. In refusing to posit discrete enduring traces for each past experience, we are in a sense treating representations of individual events 'like the town of Brigadoon' (Damasio 1995, pp. 103–104; Sutton 2004, p. 513), coming into being again only on the spot and rarely. The causal residues of many past events are smeared into all ongoing processing in a network, such that the ongoing presence of the before in the after is composite. This is not to rule out all determinacy in the relevant causal pathways: experiences alter connection weights at particular times, modifying the causal powers of a network in a determinate fashion, such that the network is now capable of responding to further input in new, different, or specific ways. But in any or most episodes of remembering, many such causal pathways, back to many past events, will be partly contributing to the occurrent processing. Perhaps there are resources in treatments of complex causation in metaphysics and philosophy of science to support the idea of distinctions between these various causal pathways running from experience to remembering, so as to provide a way of singling out a specific causal contribution running back to one event. But if not, we suggest, connectionists can simply bite the bullet here and show that CTCM can survive even this.

So, thirdly, we can challenge the assumption that a causal theory of memory requires a unique and distinguishable causal connection running through from a particular experience to retrieval. Instead, we might propose that memory requires *some* causal connection between them (though not necessarily a unique and distinguishable one), and some appropriate relation of content between the experiences then and now. In other words, CTCM would not rely on a unique causal connection to ensure that a memory is tied to a particular event. Instead, it would rely on a (liberalised) causal connection plus similarity of content.

In some cases this will result in a degree of indeterminacy as to whether a subject is remembering one particular event among a range of similar events. But is this a problem? This is what memory is like. The causal connection postulated by CTM does not have to be useable in practice, the causal history not necessarily itself recoverable. What matters in practice, rather, in distinguishing memory of one event from another, or remembering from imagining, or personal memory from testimony, will sometimes be given not by tracing these internal causal pathways, but by way of features of the external context. This returns us to the point we flagged briefly earlier, about the scope of CTM in relation to the broader pragmatic contexts of remembering.

4.7 Causal theories in context: Pragmatics and development

The amounts and forms of similarity between patterns activated at experience and at retrieval vary substantially. Causal connections between experiences, memory traces, and acts of remembering are complex and variable. It may turn out that distinguishably unique causal pathways cannot be identified in the midst of such complex internal computational processing across long periods. We conclude by suggesting that this outcome would signal not that the causal theory of memory has failed, but merely that it is incomplete.

At their most ambitious, causal theorists hope to pin down criteria to distinguish genuine remembering from many other cognitive phenomena. The idea is that true remembering is intuitively different from mere imagining, and from falsely 'remembering' or merely seeming to remember. Remembering on the basis of personal experience differs from knowing something because it has been relearned, or on the basis of testimony. It is also different from thinking – even in an episodic way – about future events or counterfactual events.

Part of the task in making progress towards this goal is to latch on to our best sciences of memory, to understand better the neurocognitive mechanisms and operations in play over the many phases of these complex processes. We have sought to contribute to that naturalistic project of adjusting the causal theory for better fit with the cognitive neurosciences. But the concerns of the causal theory, we can now see, are also broader than this. The causal theorist is supplementing the naturalistic project with something extra, doing something beyond drawing lessons from empirical science. We conclude with some initial thoughts on this.

There are many distinctive versions of CTM (for examples from early in the recent revival of philosophy of memory, see Bernecker 2010; Debus 2010; Naylor 2012). Differences and disagreements between them are not due to misunderstanding of, or lack of access to, extra facts about neurocognitive processes or the paths of internal causal transmission. In assessing candidate criteria for genuine memory against thought experiments or real-world cases, philosophers disagree on what counts as, for example, 'a causal link of the right kind' between past experience and present recall, evaluating intuitions about what feels 'not quite right' (Debus 2017, pp. 67–68). Likewise when we turn from disagreement over theory, criteria, or general intuitions to disagreement over particular cases. In practice, in applying the norms or standards by which certain phenomena and not others are accepted as genuine cases of remembering, people (individually and collectively) do not typically treat further neurocognitive facts about a particular case as vital or decisive for assessing a memory claim. Such facts may be relevant in one way or another, but they will be assessed alongside 'external' facts about the history and situation, considerations of plausibility, and the many other context-dependent features we factor into our attempts to resolve uncertainty or disagreement about whether someone is really remembering an event.

In socio-cognitive practice, both these standards themselves and the thresholds at which they are applied change, and they operate differently in different settings. The criteria we apply to claims to remember are partly pragmatic: different thresholds and standards apply when narrating a past event in casual conversation among friends, compared to bearing witness in a court of law. Although complex cases or situations can stretch and trouble our shared practices, much everyday memory talk is effortlessly sensitive to context, as people adjust the standards by which they assess claims about the past to fit distinctive settings and functions, from courtroom to dinner table, or in conversations with their partners, therapists, or bosses. Such normative, epistemic, or pragmatic considerations, highlighted again in recent philosophy of memory (Andonovski 2021; Craver 2020), were often previously discussed as forms of deep context-sensitivity (Campbell 2006; Deutscher 1989; Neisser 1982; Sutton 2003).

Even within specific cultural and social contexts, there can be reasonable disagreement on whether a particular memory is appropriately connected to relevant past events, or is sufficiently similar to earlier experience. This is because of this variability in the intuitions and judgements we have learned to apply, about what counts as a memory. In this domain, there is room for informed judgement or decision. In relation to distinctions between genuine memory and other different cognitive phenomena, people have learned to apply norms or standards. These norms or standards may vary somewhat and have grey areas at their edges, and they can be difficult to access and render explicit. Through enculturation in development, we come to apply standards, norms, or conditions, both in assessing others' memory claims, and importantly also in deploying our own cognitive and metacognitive capacities so as to discriminate, interpret, and communicate our cognitive processes as memories or as something else (Craver 2020, p. 267; Fivush 2019; Jablonka 2017; Sutton 2020b).

The internal neurocognitive processes on which causal theorists – including ourselves – have typically focussed thus do not, we suggest, exhaust the relevant fields of evidence. Getting more facts about either the general operation of such mechanisms, or specific computational processes in a single case, will not always settle the issues of which causal connections matter, and what similarity is required over time. But this does not mean that there is no real distinction between remembering and (for example) imagining: assessments or applications of causal criteria in social and psychological practice are not random or subjective, but are intersubjectively constrained, by both descriptive 'external' or situational facts and by (changing) contexts. The involvement of pragmatic or social factors in assessing memory claims does not render such assessments relative. The existence of uncertain cases, where it's not clear whether the causal connections between past and present are appropriate, or whether there is sufficient similarity between what was experienced and what is remembered, should not encourage us to give up: given the complexity and variability of both neurocognitive and socio-cognitive processes, we should expect to be challenged in our assessments of particular cases.

Future causal theorists can expand their scope to attend to such factors, even if they must thereby give up on any dream of finding watertight criteria to apply across all cases and contexts. But our core business here has concerned the internal, neurocognitive components of these larger systems in which memory processes are embedded. In applying one connectionist account of how distributed traces have content and causal efficacy, we defend the idea that memory has special diachronic aspects, that – as highlighted by the causal theory of memory – memory makes a claim on the past.

Acknowledgements

Many thanks to the editors for helpful comments on an earlier draft, and for their extraordinary efforts in promoting the philosophy of memory. We are also grateful to Max Deutscher, Jon Opie, and Carl Windhorst.

Notes

1 Some connectionists, seeking decisive moves away from classical cognitivism, came to reject individualism and develop '4E' alternatives. But they did not thereby abandon connectionism. Rather, for Clark (1997; 2013, pp. 17–19), Rowlands (1999, 2010, pp. 41–52), and Sutton (2009), 'connectionism's alternative accounts of cognitive neurodynamics, though already enough to confirm that remembering is a constructive, furiously active process, had to be *supplemented* both by more direct critique of the individualism of classical cognitivism, and by stronger, more integrative, and practice-oriented views of the situated or distributed mind' (Sutton 2015, p. 414, emphasis added). As confirmed by the fact that the current authors hold opposing views about individualism, connectionism is compatible with both individualism and anti-individualism: questions about mental representation are orthogonal to questions about the location of cognition (Sutton 2015). There is no tension in combining connectionism and the extended mind, as Hutto (Chapter 3, this volume, p. 71) claims, because on the natural and influential 'second-wave' view, external representations *complement* and 'need not mimic or replicate the formats, dynamics, or functions' of traces in the brain (Sutton 2010, p. 194).

2 Notably, a longstanding computational concern that superposition might lead to catastrophic interference – where new learning overwrites existing memories – led to theories of complementary learning systems in the mainstream cognitive neuroscience of episodic memory (McClelland, McNaughton, & O'Reilly 1995). Recent innovations in deep learning are driving new developments on this front, some focussed more at systems level, others on different ways of modifying connections within individual networks (Hasselmo 2017; Kirkpatrick et al. 2017; Kumaran, Hassabis, & McClelland 2016; McClelland, McNaughton, & Lampinen 2020; Shea 2022).

3 Localist alternatives to distributed representation do survive in the neuroscience of memory. While we don't have space to discuss current theories that posit discrete and stable engrams in (for example) rats' fear memory, we note that what arguably remain dominant views still acknowledge substantial instability or 'representational drift' across distributed representations (Rule, O'Leary, & Harvey 2019).

4 Specifically, over periods of 10–20 seconds, in response to a question or cue, distinctive activation trajectories mark out explicit search and retrieval processes (involving the hippocampus), identification and metamemory monitoring processes (involving prefrontal and parietal cortex), sensory processes as the remembered scene is maintained and developed (including, in this case, a range of sensory cortical areas with visual cortex and precuneus likely dominant), and emotional dynamics (involving complex interacting networks across amygdala, somatosensory cortex, and more) (Rubin 2006, 2019).

5 The notions of distributed traces and superpositional storage are not uniquely tied to modern connectionist models, but operate at an abstract level. So we can identify them in radically different scientific contexts, such as the neurophilosophy of fleeting 'animal spirits' which animated Descartes' rich account of corporeal memory (Sutton 2000), and which elicited widespread early modern criticism for depicting memory and mind as sites of 'a great deal of preposterous confusion' (Henry More, in Sutton 1998, p. 129). Critics of constructive memory were often horrified at those who,

like Descartes, seemed to be recommending an 'assimilation of imagination and memory' (Foti 1986, p. 636; Sutton 1998, pp. 50–113).

6 Some non-standard views retain causal connections by way of traces, but suggest that these are 'contentless' traces (Werning 2020; see Michaelian & Sant'Anna 2021 and Hutto, this volume, for discussion). Though our view of traces is highly liberalised relative to some, we reject this final step. Our response below to those who deny traces altogether applies equally to 'contentless' conceptions of traces. For relevant prior discussions, see Matthen (2010); Vosgerau (2010).

7 For Perrin, connectionism is 'discarding the very notion of a representational trace at the neural level': there are only weighted connections between neural nodes (Perrin 2018, p. 40). For Hutto, episodic memory 'involves and depends upon' not transmitted content, but only 'the re-instantiation of specific neural patterns' (Chapter 3, this volume, p. 66).

8 The weight space of a network is a Euclidean vector space in which each of the network's connection strengths (corresponding to the strengths of the synapses between the neurons in a real neural network) is represented as the position along a distinct coordinate axis. The dimensionality of this space corresponds to the number of connections in the network. We can picture training a network as a trajectory through weight space, and different final positions in the space as alternative ways of successfully dealing with the task demands.

9 The activation space of a network is a Euclidean vector space in which the level of activity of each of the network's processing units (corresponding to individual neurons in a real neural network) is represented as the position along a distinct coordinate axis. The dimensionality of this space corresponds to the number of processing units in the network. A network responds to an input by stabilising at a particular point in this activation space.

10 One system *structurally resembles* another when the *physical* relations among the objects that comprise the first preserve some aspects of the relational organisation of the objects that comprise the second (O'Brien & Opie 2004). Activation space is a *mathematical* space used by theorists to portray the set of activation patterns a network generates over its hidden layer. Activation patterns themselves are physical objects (patterns of neural firing, if realised in a brain), and thus distance relations in activation space codify *physical* relations among activation states. The set of activation patterns generated across any trained-up connectionist network constitutes a system of representing vehicles whose physical relations sustain a structural relation with respect to the task domain over which the network has been trained.

11 This structural resemblance story is not intended as a general theory of mental representation: such resemblance relations are insufficient to ground representation on their own. Instead, structural resemblance is a theory of *content determination*, which in turn plugs into a broader account of mental representation. Representation is a *triadic* relation implicating *representing vehicles*, *represented objects*, and *interpretations* within a cognitive system (O'Brien 2015; von Eckardt 1993). Content determination concerns the relationship between representing objects and representing vehicles, such that the latter are capable of disposing cognitive systems to behave appropriately towards the former (O'Brien & Opie 2004).

References

Andonovski, N. (2020). Singularism about episodic memory. *Review of Philosophy and Psychology*, *11*, 335–365.

Andonovski, N. (2021). Memory as triage: Facing up to the hard question of memory. *Review of Philosophy and Psychology*, *12*(2), 227–256.

Bernecker, S. (2010). *Memory: A Philosophical Study*. Oxford University Press.

Buckner, C., & Garson, J. (2019). Connectionism. In E. N. Zalta (Ed.), *Stanford Encyclopedia of Philosophy*, https://plato.stanford.edu/archives/fall2019/entries/connectionism/.

Campbell, J. (1997). The structure of time in autobiographical memory. *European Journal of Philosophy*, *5*(2), 105–118.

Campbell, S. (2004). Models of mind and memory activities. In P. DesAutels & M. U. Walker (Eds.), *Moral Psychology: Feminist Ethics and Social Theory* (pp. 119–137). Rowman & Littlefield.

Campbell, S. (2006). Our faithfulness to the past: Reconstructing memory value. *Philosophical Psychology*, *19*(3), 361–380.

Churchland, P. M. (1995) *The Engine of Reason, the Seat of the Soul*. MIT Press.

Churchland, P.M. (2012). *Plato's Camera*. MIT Press.

Clark, A. (1989). *Microcognition*. MIT Press.

Clark, A. (1993). *Associative Engines: Connectionism, Concepts, and Representational Change*. MIT Press.

Clark, A. (1997). *Being There: Putting Brain, Body, and World Together Again*. MIT Press.

Craver, C. F. (2020). Remembering: Epistemic and empirical. *Review of Philosophy and Psychology*, *11*(2), 261–281.

Damasio, A. (1995). *Descartes' Error: Emotion, Reason, and the Human Brain*. Picador.

Daselaar, S. M., Rice, H. J., Greenberg, D. L., Cabeza, R., LaBar, K. S., & Rubin, D. C. (2008). The spatiotemporal dynamics of autobiographical memory: Neural correlates of recall, emotional intensity, and reliving. *Cerebral Cortex*, *18*(1), 217–229.

De Brigard, F. (2014a). The nature of memory traces. *Philosophy Compass*, *9*(6), 402–414.

De Brigard, F. (2014b). The anatomy of amnesia. *Scientific American Mind*, *25*(3), 39–43.

De Brigard, F. (2014c). Is memory for remembering? Recollection as a form of episodic hypothetical thinking. *Synthese*, *191*(2), 155–185.

Debus, D. (2010). Accounting for epistemic relevance: A new problem for the causal theory of memory. *American Philosophical Quarterly*, *47*(1), 17–29.

Debus, D. (2017). Memory causation. In S. Bernecker & K. Michaelian (Eds.), *The Routledge Handbook of Philosophy of Memory* (pp. 63–75). Routledge.

Deutscher, M. (1989). Remembering 'remembering'. In J. Heil (Ed.), *Cause, Mind, and Reality* (pp. 53–72). Springer.

Deutscher, M. (2009). In response. *Crossroads: An Interdisciplinary Journal for the Study of History, Philosophy, Religion, and Classics* 4(1), 92–98.

Elman, J. (1993). Learning and development in neural networks: The importance of starting small. *Cognition 48*, 71–99.

Fivush, R. (2019). *Family Narratives and the Development of an Autobiographical Self: Social and Cultural Perspectives on Autobiographical Memory*. Routledge.

Fodor, J. A. (1975) *The Language of Thought*. MIT Press.

Foti, V. (1986). The Cartesian imagination. *Philosophy and Phenomenological Research*, *46*, 631–642.

Goldie, P. (2012). *The Mess Inside: Narrative, Emotion, and the Mind*. Oxford University Press.

Greenberg, D. L., & Rubin, D. C. (2003). The neuropsychology of autobiographical memory. *Cortex*, *39* (4–5), 687–728.

Harris, C. B., O'Connor, A. R., & Sutton, J. (2015). Cue generation and memory construction in direct and generative autobiographical memory retrieval. *Consciousness and Cognition, 33,* 204–216.

Hasselmo, M. E. (2017). Avoiding catastrophic forgetting. *Trends in Cognitive Sciences, 21*(6), 407–408.

Haugeland, J. (1991). Representational genera. In W. Ramsey, S. P. Stich, & D. E. Rumelhart (Eds.), *Philosophy and Connectionist Theory* (pp. 61–78). Erlbaum.

Haybron, D. M. (2000). The causal and explanatory role of information stored in connectionist networks. *Minds and Machines, 10*(3), 361–380.

Hutto, D. D., & Peeters, A. (2018). The roots of remembering: Radically enactive recollecting. In K. Michaelian, D. Debus, & D. Perrin (Eds.). *New Directions in the Philosophy of Memory* (pp. 97–118). Routledge.

Ismael, J. (2016). *How Physics Makes Us Free.* Oxford University Press.

Jablonka, E. (2017). Collective narratives, false memories, and the origins of autobiographical memory. *Biology & Philosophy, 32*(6), 839–853.

Kirkpatrick, J., Pascanu, R., Rabinowitz, N., Veness, J., Desjardins, G., Rusu, A. A., ... & Hassabis, D. (2017). Overcoming catastrophic forgetting in neural networks. *Proceedings of the National Academy of Sciences, 114*(13), 3521–3526.

Kumaran, D., Hassabis, D., & McClelland, J. L. (2016). What learning systems do intelligent agents need? Complementary learning systems theory updated. *Trends in Cognitive Sciences, 20*(7), 512–534.

Kumaran, D., & McClelland, J. L. (2012). Generalization through the recurrent interaction of episodic memories: A model of the hippocampal system. *Psychological Review, 119*(3), 573–616.

Laakso, A., & Cottrell, G. (2000) Content and cluster analysis: Assessing representational similarity in neural systems. *Philosophical Psychology, 13,* 47–76.

Mac Cumhaill, C. (2020). Still life, a mirror: phasic memory and re-encounters with artworks. *Review of Philosophy and Psychology, 11,* 423–446,

Martin, C. B., & Deutscher, M. (1966). Remembering. *Philosophical Review, 75*(2), 161–196.

Matthen, M. (2010). Is memory preservation? *Philosophical Studies, 148,* 3–14.

McClelland, J. L. (1995). Constructive memory and memory distortions: A parallel-distributed processing approach. In D. L. Schacter (Ed.), *Memory Distortions: How Minds, Brains, and Societies Reconstruct the Past* (pp. 69–90). Harvard University Press.

McClelland, J. L., McNaughton, B. L., & Lampinen, A. K. (2020). Integration of new information in memory: New insights from a complementary learning systems perspective. *Philosophical Transactions of the Royal Society B, 375*(1799), 20190637.

McClelland, J. L., McNaughton, B. L., & O'Reilly, R. C. (1995). Why there are complementary learning systems in the hippocampus and neocortex: Insights from the successes and failures of connectionist models of learning and memory. *Psychological Review, 102*(3), 419.

McClelland, J. L., & Rumelhart, D. E. (1986). A distributed model of human learning and memory. In J. L. McClelland & D. E. Rumelhart (Eds.), *Parallel Distributed Processing: Explorations in the Microstructure of Cognition* (Vol. 2, pp. 170–215). MIT Press.

Michaelian, K. (2016). *Mental Time Travel: Episodic Memory and Our Knowledge of the Personal Past.* MIT Press.

Michaelian, K., & Robins, S. (2018). Beyond the causal theory? Fifty years after Martin and Deutscher. In K. Michaelian, D. Debus, & D. Perrin (Eds.). *New Directions in the Philosophy of Memory* (pp. 13–32). Routledge.

Michaelian, K., & Sant'Anna, A. (2021). Memory without content? Radical enactivism and (post) causal theories of memory. *Synthese, 198*, S307–S335.

Moscovitch, M., Cabeza, R., Winocur, G., & Nadel, L. (2016). Episodic memory and beyond: The hippocampus and neocortex in transformation. *Annual Review of Psychology, 67*, 105–134.

Naylor, A. (2012). Belief from the past. *European Journal of Philosophy, 20*(4), 598–620.

Neisser, U. (1982). Memory: What are the important questions? In U. Neisser (Ed.), *Memory Observed: Remembering in Natural Contexts* (pp. 3–19). Worth Publishers.

O'Brien, G. (2015). How does mind matter? Solving the content causation problem. In T. Metzinger & J. M. Windt (Eds.), *Open MIND: 28(T)*. MIND Group.

O'Brien, G., & Opie, J. (1999). A connectionist theory of phenomenal experience. *Behavioral and Brain Sciences, 22*, 127–148.

O'Brien, G., & Opie, J. (2004). Notes toward a structuralist theory of mental representation. In H. Clapin (Ed.), *Representation in Mind* (pp. 1–20). Elsevier.

O'Brien, G., & Opie, J. (2006). How do connectionist networks compute? *Cognitive Processing, 7*(1), 30–41.

O'Brien, G., & Opie, J. (2009). The role of representation in computation. *Cognitive Processing, 10*(1), 53–62.

O'Brien, G. J. (1991). Is connectionism commonsense? *Philosophical Psychology, 4*(2), 165–178.

O'Brien, G. J. (1993). The connectionist vindication of folk psychology. In S. M. Christensen & D. R. Turner (Eds.), *Folk Psychology and the Philosophy of Mind* (pp. 368–387). Erlbaum.

O'Brien, G. J. (1998). Being there: Putting philosopher, researcher and student together again (review of Clark, *Being There*). *Metascience (new series), 7*, 78–83.

Perrin, D. (2018). A case for procedural causality in episodic recollection. In K. Michaelian, D. Debus, & D. Perrin (Eds.). *New Directions in the Philosophy of Memory* (pp. 33–51). Routledge.

Ramsey, W. (1997). Do connectionist representations earn their explanatory keep? *Mind & Language, 12*(1), 34–66.

Ramsey, W., Stich, S., & Garon, J. (1991). Connectionism, eliminativism, and the future of folk psychology. In J. Greenwood (Ed.), *The Future of Folk Psychology* (pp. 93–119). Cambridge University Press.

Robins, S. (2016). Representing the past: Memory traces and the causal theory of memory. *Philosophical Studies, 173*(11), 2993–3013.

Rowlands, M. (1999). *The Body in Mind: Understanding Cognitive Processes*. Cambridge University Press.

Rowlands, M. (2010). *The New Science of the Mind: From Extended Mind to Embodied Phenomenology*. MIT Press.

Rubin, D. C. (2006). The basic-systems model of episodic memory. *Perspectives on Psychological Science, 1*(4), 277–311.

Rubin, D. C. (2019). Placing autobiographical memory in a general memory organization. In Mace, J. (Ed.). *The Organization and Structure of Autobiographical Memory* (pp. 6–27). Oxford University Press.

Rule, M. E., O'Leary, T., & Harvey, C. D. (2019). Causes and consequences of representational drift. *Current Opinion in Neurobiology, 58*, 141–147.

Schechtman, M. (1994). The truth about memory. *Philosophical Psychology, 7*(1), 3–18.

Selwood, A., Harris, C. B., Barnier, A. J., & Sutton, J. (2020). Effects of collaboration on the qualities of autobiographical recall in strangers, friends, and siblings: both remembering partner and communication processes matter. *Memory, 28*(3), 399–416.

Shea, N. (2007). Content and its vehicles in connectionist systems. *Mind & Language*, *22*(3), 246–269.

Shea, N. (2022). Moving beyond content-specific computation in artificial neural networks. *Mind & Language*. https://doi.org/10.1111/mila.12387

Sutton, J. (1998). *Philosophy and Memory Traces: Descartes to Connectionism*. Cambridge University Press.

Sutton, J. (2000). The body and the brain. In Gaukroger, S., Schuster, J., & Sutton, J. (Eds.), *Descartes' Natural Philosophy* (pp. 697–722). Routledge.

Sutton, J. (2003). Truth in memory: The humanities and the cognitive sciences. In McCalman, I., & McGrath, A. (Eds.), *Proof and Truth: The Humanist As Expert* (pp. 145–163). Australian Academy of the Humanities.

Sutton, J. (2004). Representation, levels, and context in integrational linguistics and distributed cognition. *Language Sciences*, *26*(6), 503–524.

Sutton, J. (2009). Remembering. In Aydede, M., & Robbins, P. (Eds.), *The Cambridge Handbook of Situated Cognition* (pp. 217–235). Cambridge University Press.

Sutton, J. (2010). Exograms and interdisciplinarity: History, the extended mind, and the civilizing process. In Menary, R. (Ed.), *The Extended Mind* (pp. 189–225). MIT Press.

Sutton, J. (2015). Remembering as public practice: Wittgenstein, memory, and distributed cognitive ecologies. In Moyal-Sharrock, D., Coliva, A., & Munz, V. (Eds.), *Mind, Language, and Action: Proceedings of the 36th International Wittgenstein Symposium* (pp. 409–443). Walter de Gruyter.

Sutton, J. (2020a). Movements, memory, and mixture: Aristotle, confusion, and the historicity of memory. In Fink, J. L., & Mousavian, S. (Eds.), *The Internal Senses in the Aristotelian Tradition* (pp. 137–155). Springer.

Sutton, J. (2020b). Personal memory, the scaffolded mind, and cognitive change in the Neolithic. In Hodder, I (Ed.), *Consciousness, Creativity and Self at the Dawn of Settled Life* (pp. 209–229). Cambridge University Press.

Sutton, J., & Windhorst, C. (2009). Extended and constructive remembering: Two notes on Martin and Deutscher. *Crossroads: An Interdisciplinary Journal for the Study of History, Philosophy Religion, and Classics*, *4*(1), 79–91.

Temler, M., Barnier, A. J., Sutton, J., & McIlwain, D.J. (2020). Contamination or natural variation? A comparison of contradictions from suggested contagion and intrinsic variation in repeated autobiographical accounts. *Journal of Applied Research in Memory and Cognition*, *9*(1), 108–117.

Tulving, E. (2007). Coding and representation: Searching for a home in the brain. In Roediger, H. L., Dudai, Y. E., & Fitzpatrick, S. M. (Eds.). *Science of Memory: Concepts* (pp. 65–68). Oxford University Press.

van Gelder, T. (1991). What is the 'D' in 'PDP'? A survey of the concept of distribution. In Ramsey, W., Stich, S. P., & Rumelhart, D. E. (Eds.), *Philosophy and Connectionist Theory* (pp. 33–59). Erlbaum.

von Eckardt, B. (1993). *What Is Cognitive Science?* MIT Press.

Vosgerau, G. (2010). Memory and content. *Consciousness & Cognition*, *19*, 838–846.

Werning, M. (2020). Predicting the past from minimal traces: Episodic memory and its distinction from imagination and preservation. *Review of Philosophy and Psychology*, *11*(2), 301–333.

Further Readings for Part II

De Brigard, F. (2020). The explanatory indispensability of memory traces. *The Harvard Review of Philosophy*, *27*, 7–21.

   Argues that an adequate account of remembering will necessarily invoke traces.

Hutto, D. D., & Peeters, A. (2018). The roots of remembering: Radically enactive recollecting. In K. Michaelian, D. Debus, & D. Perrin (Eds.), *New Directions in the Philosophy of Memory* (pp. 97–118). Routledge.

   An initial statement of the enactivist account of remembering as not involving stored content.

Hutto, D. D., & Myin, E. (2017). *Evolving Enactivism: Basic Minds Meet Content*. MIT Press.

   The second volume of Hutto and Myin's two-volume statement of radical enactivism; chapter 9 is devoted to memory.

Michaelian, K., & Sant'Anna, A. (2021). Memory without content? Radical enactivism and (post)causal theories of memory. *Synthese*, *198*(Suppl 1), S307–S335.

   Argues that the simulation theory is compatible with an enactivist approach to remembering.

Robins, S. K. (2016). Representing the past: Memory traces and the causal theory of memory. *Philosophical Studies*, *173*(11), 2993–3013.

   Argues that the causal theory may be incompatible with the distributed conception of traces.

Robins, S. K. (2017). Memory traces. In S. Bernecker & K. Michaelian (Eds.), *The Routledge Handbook of Philosophy of Memory* (pp. 76–87). Routledge.

   An accessible overview of work on memory traces.

Sutton, J. (1998). *Philosophy and Memory Traces: Descartes to Connectionism*. Cambridge University Press.

   Looks at memory traces from the perspectives of the history of philosophy and recent connectionist approaches to cognition.

Werning, M. (2020). Predicting the past from minimal traces: Episodic memory and its distinction from imagination and preservation. *Review of Philosophy and Psychology*, *11*(2), 301–333.

   The main statement of trace minimalism.

Study Questions for Part II

1) Suppose that we could solve the Hard Problem of Content. Would it then be desirable to invoke contentful traces in our theory of remembering?

2) How might a trace minimalist respond to the charge that his account does not succeed in avoiding the Hard Problem of Content?

3) Can enactivism be coherently combined with simulationism, as Hutto suggests? Can enactivism be coherently combined with causalism?

4) Do Sutton and O'Brien succeed in showing that a conception of traces as distributed is compatible with a conception of traces as contentful? Do they succeed in showing that a conception of traces as distributed is compatible with the causal theory of constructive memory?

5) Does Sutton and O'Brien's account of traces as distributed but contentful face the hard problem of content?

6) What sort of account of appropriate causation might a constructive causal theorist provide?

Part III

What is the nature of mnemonic confabulation?

5 An explanationist model of (false) memory

Sven Bernecker

5.1 Introduction

Mnemonic confabulation or 'false memory', as it is also called, is usually defined as fabricated memory believed to be true.[1] Confabulations can be about autobiographical events or semantic knowledge; and they can refer to the more remote past, the more recent past, the present, or the future (Johnson et al. 2000, p. 368). Here I focus on confabulations about one's personal past.[2]

Confabulating is *not* remembering. It is a memory *error*. While forgetting is an error of omission, confabulation is an error of commission. The error consists in the absence of a suitable relation between the event or experience the person seems to remember and the person's past—'either because there is no such event in their past or because any similarity to such an event or experience is entirely coincidental' (Robins 2020, p. 125).

Given that confabulation is a kind of non-memory, the account of confabulation is parasitic on the account of memory. For instance, if the account of memory appeals to traces to explain the preservation of information, then confabulation can be characterised as a state of seeming to remember where these traces are absent. And if the account of memory demands that the cognitive process underlying memory yields a high ratio of true to false representations, then confabulations can be characterised as representations that are either false or merely accidentally true. The point is that the account of confabulation tracks the account of memory.

Philosophical theories of memory can be sorted along two axes -- the archival vs. constructive axis and the causalist vs. reliabilist axis. On the *archival view*, memory is a faculty for registering, storing and reproducing representations of past events and experiences. *Constructivism*, on the other hand, takes memory to be a capacity for constructing representations of past events and experiences. While constructivism emphasises the productive function of memory, archivalism characterises memory as a reproductive faculty.

In philosophy, the most prominent constructivist accounts of memory are De Brigard's (2014) *episodic-hypothetical thinking account* and Michaelian's (2016a) *simulation theory*. According to the former, memory is said to belong to a system for 'self-referential mental simulations about what happened, and could have

DOI: 10.4324/9781003002277-9

happened to oneself' (De Brigard 2014, pp. 174–175). To remember success-fully is to construct plausible representations of what was likely to have occurred in the past, rather than accurate representations of what did happen. Plausible representations need not be accurate. De Brigard takes it to be a mistake 'to jump from the epistemic claim that one's memory is false to the psychological claim that one's memory's system malfunctioned'.[3]

Like De Brigard, Michaelian maintains that memory and imagination are part of the same cognitive system whose function it is to imagine (or simulate) a possible scenario. Michaelian's view differs from De Brigard's in that he takes memory to require both accuracy and reliability. The key idea is that to remem-ber is 'to imagine the past in a reliable manner' (Michaelian 2016b, p. 7). He calls his account 'a pure reliabilist theory' (ibid.). I focus on Michaelian's version of simulationist reliabilism because I take it for granted that memory implies truth. An utterance of 'S remembers that p' (where 'S' stands for a subject and 'p' stands for a proposition) is true only if p is the case.

On the archival view, the primary function of memory is to preserve mental contents (content preservationism) or epistemic properties such as justification and knowledge (epistemic preservationism). According to *content preservationism*, you remember only if your current representational state stands in a memory relation to a representational state you had in the past and the contents of both representational states are type-identical.[4] *Epistemic preservationism* states that a subject justifiedly believes (or knows) that p on the basis of memory only if in the past they justifiedly believed (or knew) on the basis of a source other than memory.[5] The negation of content preservationism is *content anti-preservationism*, which holds that the content of the representation fed into the memory process need not be type-identical to the content of the representation produced by the memory process. The negation of epistemic preservationism is *epistemic genera-tivism*, the view that a subject can justifiedly believe (know) that p on the basis of memory even if, in the past, S did not justifiedly believe (know) that p on the basis of a source other than memory.[6]

Typically, archivalism goes hand in hand with *causalism*. Proponents of the causal view maintain that to remember something, the present representation must not only correspond to, but also be suitably causally connected to, the corresponding representation in the past. Remembering a particular event is said to require a persisting memory trace connecting the event and its subse-quent representation in memory. Memory traces account both for the propaga-tion of the representational content and (together with the retrieval cues) for the production of the state of recall.

The main competitor to causalism about memory is *reliabilism*.[7] Reliabilism states that remembering requires having an accurate representation generated by a reliable memory process; the causal connection is not necessary. Reliabilism is compatible both with archivalism and constructivism. When reliabilism is com-bined with archivalism, remembering is analysed as having a reliably formed true representation that was previously acquired and preserved.[8] Michaelian's simulationism is a constructivist version of reliabilism.

The account of confabulation is parasitic on the account of memory. Given content preservationism, memory demands that the retrieved content be the same as the encoded content. On this view, the retrieved content differing from the encoded content may be deemed sufficient for the state of recall to qualify as an instance of confabulation. Content anti-preservationism, by contrast, holds that it is the very function of the memory system to not only store but also process information. Just because the retrieved content does not match the encoded content does not mean that it is not a case of genuine remembering.

Causalism and reliabilism are the leading theories of memory and confabulation. Proponents of causalism characterise confabulation in metaphysical terms. The hallmark of confabulation is the absence of an appropriate causal relation between the present representation, on the one hand, and a memory trace and a past representation, on the other. According to reliabilism, what distinguishes confabulation from memory is the modal relation to the truth, not the causal relation to traces and past representations. When accuracy and reliability are the hallmarks of memory, confabulation is either false or accidentally true. Veridical confabulation is to memory what Gettierised belief is to knowledge.[9]

On the basis of this general overview, we can now focus on mnemonic confabulation. Section 5.2 outlines the causal theory of memory and confabulation. Section 5.3 sketches the reliabilist theory of memory and confabulation. Section 5.4 points out structural problems of the current debate on confabulation. I argue that the debate needs a perspective beyond the causalism/reliabilism divide. Section 5.5 proposes such an external vantage point in the form of an explanationist model of memory. Section 5.6 gives some pointers on how to reorientate the philosophical debate on confabulation.

5.2 Causalism about (false) memory

Intuitively, to remember something requires that it was represented in the past and that the present representation is in some way due to the past one. According to the causal theory, the link between the past representation and its subsequent recall is of a causal kind and involves memory traces. The stipulation of traces is motivated by the idea that between any two causally connected diachronic mental events, there has to be a series of intermediary events, each of which causes the next, and each of which is temporally contiguous to the next. Memory traces are supposed to account for the propagation of information through time and the generation of the state of recall.[10]

The classical formulation of causalism due to Martin and Deutscher (1966) has two distinctive features. First, it allows for complete prompting[11] but excludes relearning from the ranks of memory. A state of recall brought about by a complete prompt is said to count as remembering only if the following counterfactual condition is met: unless the subject had the relevant past representation, they would not accept the prompted information and hence would not form the state of recall.[12] Second, a memory trace is said to represent a past experience in virtue of its structural isomorphism with that experience.

The structural similarity between the past experience and the trace is conceived along the lines of the relation between sounds and the grooves in a vinyl record. For each variation in the pitch, tempo, or volume of the music, there is a variation in the grooves of the record.

On my version of the causal theory (Bernecker 2010, chs. 4, 5), the dependence relation between a state of remembering and a trace is different from the dependence relation between a state of remembering a past representation. The dependence of memories on *traces* is analysed in terms of necessary and sufficient conditions. In cued recall, the memory trace must be at least an INUS condition for the subject's present representation.[13] In free recall, the trace may not be pre-empted by another independently sufficient condition for the present representation. The causal dependence of the present representation on the *past representation* is analysed in modal terms: if the subject had not represented in the past that p, they would not represent in the present that p. This conditional rules out cases where a highly suggestible subject recalls something on the basis of a complete prompt that happens to be true.[14]

In contrast to Martin and Deutscher, I reject structural analogues in favour of memory traces as distributed patterns of event features (Bernecker 2010, p. 137). Following Sutton (1998, p. 2), I maintain that traces are spread across connectionist networks. Memories are, in Sutton's words, 'blended, not laid down independently once and for all, and are reconstructed rather than reproduced'.[15]

Traditionally, causalists endorse content preservationism, that is, the thesis that for a present representation to stand in a memory-relation to a past representation, the content of both representations must be type-identical. Content preservation about memory faces two kinds of challenges. First, it cannot account for the widespread phenomenon of incomplete remembering. Frequently, the content of a belief retrieved from memory is informationally impoverished vis-à-vis the stored content. Let us call the view whereupon the content of the representation fed into the memory process may outstrip the content of the representation produced by the memory process *content abstractionism*. ('Abstract' here means abridgment, précis, or summary.) Second, content preservationism fails to acknowledge the constructive nature of memory. The content of a belief retrieved from memory may outstrip the content originally stored. Let us call this view *content constructivism*. Content abstractionism and content constructivism are two varieties of content anti-preservationism.

The main disagreement among contemporary proponents of causalism concerns the abstractionism/constructivism debate. I side with content abstractionism by setting forth the *entailment thesis* (Bernecker 2010, pp. 222–229). The entailment thesis states that a present representation is memory related to a past representation only if the contents of the present representation is relevantly entailed by the content of the past representation. Michaelian (2011) and Robins (2016a) defend content constructivism. They maintain that the generation of new content between experience and retrieval is compatible with remembering. Examples of (partially) constructed memory contents are gist memory, observer memory, and boundary extended scene memory.[16]

According to the causal theory of memory, confabulation consists in the absence of an appropriate causal relation between the present representation, on the one hand, and the memory trace and/or past representation, on the other (Bernecker 2017). Sometimes a confabulatory state purports to represent a particular past representation, but there is no past representation. In other cases, there *is* a past representation, but the state of recall does not track the past representation in the sense that had the past content been different, so would have the recalled content. The hallmark of confabulation is that if there is a correspondence between the recalled content and the past content, it lacks the modal stability required for remembering.[17]

The absence of the causal relation constitutive of remembering manifests itself either in the recalled content being patently false or in the recalled content failing to be sufficiently similar to the corresponding past content. The degree of content similarity required for remembering crucially depends on whether one endorses content preservationism, abstractionism, or constructivism.

5.3 Reliabilism about (false) memory

According to simulationist reliabilism, it is one and the same cognitive process by which we remember the past and imagine the future. The process draws on stored contents to generate representations of the past and the future. The stored contents that form the building blocks of a given representation are not traceable to the experiences of a particular event remembered but combine contents originating from a multitude of different past experiences. The relation between experienced events and remembered events is neither one-to-one nor one-to-many. Instead, past experiences merely provide the material from which new representations are more or less freely assembled. In light of this view, it is claimed that remembering does not presuppose a causal connection (Michaelian and Robins 2018, p. 27).

The proper functioning of the simulation process responsible for remembering is defined in terms of three conditions—accuracy, internality, and reliability. The *accuracy* condition states that the representational contents of memories must be true to the facts. The *internality* condition states that the remembering subject must contribute either retained or generated content to the memory representation (Michaelian, 2016b, p. 10). Finally, the *reliability* condition states that for the simulation process to function properly, it must have the tendency to produce mostly accurate representations. The simulation process is said to be governed by heuristics that favour information over misinformation. Moreover, the simulation process is overseen by a source monitoring system whose job it is to reject simulations that have gone too far afield. The combination of the three conditions is meant to make the causal condition for remembering superfluous. Rather than defining the proper functioning of the memory system in terms of causation-based retention of information, Michaelian (2016b, p. 7) defines it in terms of reliability.

Given simulationist reliabilism, there are two sources of mnemonic confabulation: (1) the recalled content violates the accuracy condition because it is patently false or self-contradictory; and (2) the process giving rise to the recalled content (accurate or inaccurate) fails to be reliable. 'Confabulation is about lack of reliability' (Michaelian 2016b, p. 5). Michaelian explains:

> In a healthy subject, the system recombines information, whether or not it originates in the target episode, following procedures designed to enable it to produce a representation of the episode which is (within certain limits) accurate. In the confabulating subject, in contrast, the system malfunctions, following procedures which tend to produce inaccurate representations.
>
> (Michaelian 2016a, p. 109)

While inaccurate confabulation is the norm, simulationist reliabilism can also account for accurate confabulation generated by unreliable processes.

Michaelian's most recent position is called 'virtue-theoretic simulationism'. It differs from his older view in that the internality condition has been replaced by an 'accuracy-because-reliability' condition, 'a condition requiring that the apparent memory be accurate because it was produced by a reliable process' (Michaelian, Chapter 6, this volume, Section 6.7). The rationale for introducing this condition is to provide a more fine-grained distinction of phenomena in the vicinity of remembering. 'Veridical confabulation occurs when the accuracy condition is satisfied but the reliability condition is not satisfied' (Michaelian, Chapter 6, this volume, Section 6.7). It is also possible for the accuracy and reliability conditions to be satisfied, but not the accuracy-because-reliability condition. This is the case when a suggestible subject is completely prompted by someone who 'intends to provide inaccurate information but inadvertently provides accurate information' (ibid.).

5.4 Problems with the current debate on mnemonic confabulation

The current philosophical debate about confabulation is mainly concerned with the extensional adequacy of competing theories of confabulation. Causalists and reliabilists criticise each other for being unable to account for specific confabulatory phenomena. Among the phenomena used to challenge the extensional adequacy of extant theories of confabulation are veridical confabulation, relearning, misremembering, justified confabulation, and future-oriented confabulation.

The problem with the current debate is twofold. First, the criteria used to determine whether a given case qualifies as confabulation rely on the very theory of confabulation, for which the case is supposed to provide evidence. Call this the *bootstrapping problem*. Second, given that the account of confabulation is derivative of the account of memory, the debate about confabulation is a proxy battle between the two leading accounts of memory—causalism and reliabilism. As soon as the controversy between causalism and reliabilism about memory is (re)solved, the debate about which phenomena belong to the extension of confabulation is resolved as well. Call this the *red herring problem*. These problems are two sides of the same coin.

The traditional method of analytic philosophy is *conceptual analysis* informed by common sense, linguistic intuitions, and thought experiments (Daly 2010; Cappelen et al. 2016). It consists in working back and forth among our considered linguistic judgments about particular scenarios, the general rules that govern them, and the values we take to bear on those judgments and principles, revising each of these elements until we reach a reflective equilibrium (Daniels 2016). If the method of conceptual analysis works at all, it works only for terms that are entrenched in ordinary discourse. But this is not the case for 'confabulation'.

The Middle English word 'confabulacion' meant 'casual conversation' or 'chat'. The contemporary term 'confabulation' was introduced in the early 1900s to describe certain symptoms of patients with Korsakoff's syndrome (Berrios 1998). It is important to realise that 'confabulation', the way the term is used today, is a technical term. Unlike certain medical terms (such as 'pain', 'depression', and 'flu') and certain philosophical terms (such as 'knowledge' and 'reliability') that have not only a technical but also an ordinary usage, 'confabulation' (unlike 'memory') is solely a technical term, much like 'brain lesion', 'vitamin B1 deficiency', and 'hippocampus' (Bernecker 2017, pp. 11–12).

In the absence of an entrenched linguistic intuition about the term, what kind of considerations can guide philosophical theorising about confabulation? Looking at the literature, one gets the impression that philosophers (unwittingly) adapt their definitions of confabulation to their preferred definitions of memory. What is or is not an instance of confabulation crucially depends on the presupposed conditions for remembering. And since the theory of confabulation is parasitic on the theory of memory, the criteria used to determine whether or not a given phenomenon qualifies as confabulation rely on the very theory the phenomenon is meant to confirm. To drive this point home, consider three examples.

(1) In psychology and psychiatry, it is common to define confabulation in terms of falsity. Fotopoulou, for instance, characterises confabulations as 'false memories produced without conscious knowledge of their falsehood' (Fotopoulou 2008, p. 543). Causalists and reliabilists, however, maintain that it is conceivable that someone makes up a story that the story feels like something they have experienced in the past and that happens to be true (Bernecker 2017, pp. 4–5; Michaelian 2016b, pp. 4–5; Robins 2016a, p. 125). What explains the agreement regarding the possibility of *veridical confabulation*? Presumably the reason is that factivity, while being necessary for remembering, is not sufficient. Given that confabulation is a kind of non-memory, at least one of the necessary conditions for remembering must be violated; but it need not be the factivity condition that is violated. Hence, the stipulation of veridical confabulation is motivated by the theory of confabulation which, in turn, relies on the underlying theory of memory.

(**2**) Michaelian argues that causalism conflates *misremembering* and *falsidical confabulation*, since both are characterised by inaccuracy.[18] According to Michaelian's own view, 'misremembering occurs when the reliability condition is met but the accuracy condition is not.... And falsidical confabulation occurs when neither the reliability condition nor the accuracy condition is met' (Michaelian 2016b, p. 7). This way of drawing the distinction between misremembering and falsidical confabulation clearly presupposes content constructivism, which is a feature of Michaelian's simulationist reliabilism about memory. Thus, the falsidical confabulation/misremembering distinction is taken to be evidence in favour of the reliabilist account of confabulation, although we already have to assume reliabilism about confabulation to draw the distinction in this way.

(**3**) Michaelian criticises causalism about confabulation for not being able to countenance *future-oriented confabulations*, that is, 'representations of future events that fail to correspond to events that [the subject is] likely to experience' (Michaelian et al. 2020, p. 307; see also Michaelian 2022, p. 129). He takes it to be an advantage of his own reliabilist framework that it can account for the possibility of future-oriented confabulations. Yet we already have to assume the simulationist approach for the characterisation of an unrealistic future expectation as an instance of *mnemonic* confabulation to make sense.

The current debate about confabulation is a proxy battle between causalist and reliabilist views of memory.[19] Since the account of confabulation is derivative of the account of memory, disputes about the extensional adequacy of a given theory of confabulation can be traced back to the underlying theory of memory. For this reason, it is unlikely that the controversies about the scope of confabulation can be solved without first solving the dispute between causalist and reliabilist theories of memory. Yet there is no indication that the controversy between the two theories of memory will be solved anytime soon. What are we supposed to do?

The philosophical debate concerning confabulation would benefit from a perspective beyond the causalism/reliabilism divide. While an Archimedean platform outside of history is clearly inaccessible, it *is* possible to adopt a perspective on mnemonic confabulation that does not commit us right away to take a side in the causalism/reliabilism dispute: The external vantage point proposed here is the *explanationist model of memory*.

5.5 An explanationist model of memory

Given the stalemate between causalist and reliabilist views about confabulation, I suggest we shift perspective. Instead of focusing on the differences between the rival theories, let us look for similarities. Both causalist and reliabilist theories of memory attempt to explicate what the epistemic success of remembering consists in and how remembering differs from related phenomena such as relearning and imagining. Maybe the epistemic success of remembering can be described at a level of abstraction that transcends the causalism/reliabilism dispute and that ultimately helps us overcome the stalemate.

On the explanationist model of memory, a representation qualifies as memory only if it bears the appropriate explanatory connection to the truth of the matter. What is the appropriate explanatory connection? When trying to determine whether someone's accurately representing that *p* is an instance of remembering we need to ask ourselves whether the fact that *p*, by itself, fully explains the fact that the subject ends up with an accurate representation in the way they do. In particular, we need to ask ourselves whether referencing coincidental circumstances would improve the explanation for why the subject ends up with a true representation in the way they do. A person remembers that *p* only if their true representation that *p* formed via the memory system in the circumstances is better explained by the fact that *p*, by itself, than by some statement referencing coincidental factors. In other words, S's truly representing that *p* via the memory system in the given circumstances qualifies as remembering if it is better explained by '*p*' than by 'it just so happens that *p*' or 'coincidentally *p*'.[20]

The fact that S accurately represents that *p* via the memory system in the circumstances is necessary but not sufficient for the truth of *p* being an adequate (complete) explanation of S's accurately representing that *p*. The truth of the representation that *p* is insufficient for the truth of *p*, by itself, being a better explanation for the representation's truth than the truth of *p* *and* some coincidental factors. In slogan form, the explanationist model holds that remembering amounts to memorially representing something because it is true.

Confabulation does not qualify as memory either because the representation in question is false or because it is true but it is better explained by some coincidental factor than simply by the fact of the matter. The appeal to coincidence is needed to close the explanatory gap between the subject's truly representing, on the one hand, and the way the representation is formed in the particular circumstances, on the other.

To drive this point home, consider the following example. Jane is a highly suggestible subject who endorses all sorts of plausible promptings—true and false—concerning her past experiences. Suppose Jane forms a veridical memorial representation on the basis of a complete prompt, and suppose that the prompt happens to be correct.[21] According to explanationism, Jane's veridical memorial representation does *not* qualify as remembering. For given her suggestible state, an explanation of her truly representing that *p* by means of the fact that *p*, by itself, is incomplete. It is incomplete because it does not acknowledge the fact that she would have endorsed *any* prompting, true and false. To close the explanatory gap, we need to reference the coincidence in the explanans. Jane does not remember because her epistemic success is better explained by *it just so happens that p* than by *p* alone.

The explanans contains only a single item—the fact that *p*. The explanandum, on the other hand, contains the fact that the representation is true, the method by which the representation is formed (viz., recalling), as well as the circumstances. The circumstances are epistemically relevant features of the physical and social environment mentioned in the vignette. Among these features are the subject's suggestible state, their pharmacological state, the retrieval cues at play, the subject's identity (including Parfittian fission and fusion), the physical environment (including Burgean slow switching), etc. (cf. Bernecker 2010, ch. 7). These circumstances need not be cognitively accessible to the remembering subject.

Explanationism about memory conceives of explanation along the lines of *inference to the best contrastive explanation*. The basic idea of inference to the best explanation (IBE) is that there is a relation between explanation and inference such that an inference is justified owing to the explanatory relations that hold between the hypothesis inferred and the phenomena explained.[22] Harman, who appears to have coined the term, characterises IBE in the following way:

> In making this inference one infers, from the fact that a certain hypothesis would explain the evidence, to the truth of that hypothesis. In general, there will be several hypotheses which might explain the evidence, so one must be able to reject all such alternative hypotheses before one is warranted in making the inference. Thus one infers, from the premise that a given hypothesis would provide a 'better' explanation for the evidence than would any other hypothesis, to the conclusion that the given hypothesis is true.
>
> (Harman 1965, p. 89)

This informal statement of IBE can be formalised as a four-step inference pattern:[23]

1. F is some fact or collection of facts.
2.   Hypothesis H_1, if true, would explain F.
3.   No available competing explanations $H_2, H_3, \ldots H_n$ would explain F better than H_1.
4.   Therefore, one is justified in believing that H_1 is true over its competitors.

The hallmark of the *best* explanation is that it exhibits inferential virtues to a higher degree than its rivals. Examples of inferential virtues are precision, scope, simplicity, fertility, and fit with background belief (Beebe 2009, pp. 609–611). The inferential virtue most relevant for our purposes is explanatory completeness. A hypothesis is explanatorily complete if it explains all of the observed (known) facts.

An explanation is an answer to a why-question, and why-questions are (implicitly) sensitive to a contrast class or relevance relation.[24] For example, when we say 'Jane ate the apple because she was hungry', the contrast can be 'she ate an apple rather than a pear' or 'she ate rather than gave away the apple'. The quality of an explanation has to be assessed relative to the reference class. The idea of inference to the best contrastive explanation is that the hypothesis is justified in virtue of its ability to explain some fact in the contrast class better than its competitors. In the case of explanationism about memory, the competing explananda are *p* vis-à-vis *it just so happens that p*.

Explanationism about memory is a model, not a theory. A model is less specific than a theory; it is a means to explore a theory (cf. Morgan and Morrison 1999). The model of memory proposed here is compatible with both causalism and reliabilism because the notion of a memory system, used in the explanationist formula, is characterised in purely functional terms. The memory system is conceived of as a black box whose job it is to take experiences as inputs and yield memories as outputs. Causalism and reliabilism differ with respect to the inner workings of the black box. Causalists claim that the memory system involves traces, while simulationists and reliabilists take it to house episodic simulation processes.

Since the explanationist model remains neutral about the inner workings of the memory system, it can also accommodate different theories of explanation. In philosophy of science, the three prominent theories of explanation are the covering law model (Hempel 1965), the causal model (Salmon 1984; Woodward 2003), and the unificationist model (Friedman 1974; Kitcher 1981). According to the covering law model, an explanation of an event consists in subsuming (or 'covering') it under a law. When the covering law is deterministic, the explanation takes the form of a deductive argument. And when the covering law is probabilistic or statistical, it yields statistical explanations of individual events. According to the causal model, two events stand in an explanatory relation only if they are connected by a causal process. Unificationist models claim that the goal of explanation is to show how a range of phenomena are unified under various modes of arguments or patterns. Inference to the best explanation is compatible with all three theories of explanation (Cabrera 2020). A hypothesis need not satisfy the conditions of any particular theory of explanation to be explanatorily virtuous and hence justified. What does the justificatory work in any application of inference to the best explanation is just that the hypothesis does well with respect to the explanatory virtues relative to some evidence.

If explanation is understood along causal lines, the fact that p explains S's truly representing that p via the memory system in the circumstances only if there is a causal nexus between the fact that p and S's representation of p. Usually the causal nexus is said to involve memory traces. This view gives rise to causalism about memory. On the nomological interpretation, however, explaining is a form of deductive reasoning. To explain something, one must deduce a sentence describing the explained phenomenon from a sentence that describes the explaining reality and at least one law-like generalisation. On this picture, memory requires the kind of modal stability reliabilists demand for knowledge. Memory and knowledge have in common that they require non-accidentality: it may not be a coincidence that the subject represents truly rather than falsely.

To recap, the explanationist model has it that for someone to remember that p, their truly representing that p via the memory system in the circumstances must be better explained by p, by itself, than by 'it just so happens that p' or 'coincidentally p'. This model is compatible both with causalism and reliabilism about memory. According to reliabilism, the explanation in question ensures that the state of recall 'tracks the facts', that it covaries with the truth through a sphere of close possible worlds. The explanation relation is the inverse tracking relation. According to causalism, for one's correctly recalling something to be explained by the truth in question, the right kind of causal mechanism must be at play. It may not be the case that the truth of the state of recall is better explained by some other mechanism such as relearning, suggestibility *cum* complete prompting, or genetic inheritance.

5.6 A reorientation of the debate on confabulation

Given the explanationist model of model, a subject's recalling that p does *not* qualify as memory if the following condition is met: the subject's truly representing that p via the memory system in the circumstances is better explained by *it just so happens that p* than by p. One way to meet the condition is to recall a falsehood. Arguably, however, recalling a falsehood is neither necessary nor sufficient for confabulation. It is not necessary because one can confabulate veridically. It is not sufficient because intuitively minor inaccuracies (e.g., missing a single digit in a phone number) do not seem to qualify as confabulation. The content of confabulation is (typically) grossly implausible or false.[25]

The explanationist model helps us resolve the stalemate between causalist and reliabilist views about memory and confabulation by uncovering the issues that lie at the core of the dispute. Investigating these issues does not automatically settle the causalism/reliabilism dispute, but it gives us a deeper understanding of the issues at hand. Here are two examples.

(1) It is widely acknowledged that causal assertions can make two different sorts of claims (Godfrey-Smith 2010; Hall 2004). A cause produces (brings about) the effect and is relevant to the production of the effect. Following Glennan (2010), we can label these aspects of causation *productivity* and *relevance*. Usually, productivity and relevance go hand-in-hand but sometimes they come apart. Cases in point are *causal overdetermination* and *causation by omission*. A staple example of overdetermination is a prisoner being executed by a firing squad. A particular soldier's shot produces a deadly wound, but the shot does not make a difference to the prisoner's death because each of the other shots is sufficient to cause the prisoner's death. Besides cases of production without relevance, there are cases of relevance without production. Suppose I rear-end a car because I fail to break. Clearly, my failing to break is relevant for the occurrence of the accident. The accident would not have happened had I braked. But my failing to break is not an event that can be said to produce the collision.

My version of causalism about memory distinguishes between the causal relation between the state of recall and the past representation and the causal relation between the state of recall and the memory trace. It is productivity that connects traces with states of recall, and it is relevance that connects past representations with states of recall (Bernecker 2010, ch. 5). Since my account operates with both notions of causation, it can account for the memory version of simultaneous overdetermination (Bernecker 2010, pp. 141–143) and causation by omission (Bernecker n.d.).

The reliabilist approach to memory is compatible with causal relevance but not with causal productivity, because it rejects memory traces and causation at a distance. For this reason, reliabilism seems ill-equipped to handle cases of relevance *sans* production. More precisely, reliabilism does not seem to be able to discriminate between memory of omission (factive absence memory) and forgetting. Compare two cases. First, S non-inferentially remembers that S did not φ.[26] Second, S fails to remember (forgets) that S did not φ when, in fact, S φed. Given that reliabilists focus only on the start and end points of the memory process but do not acknowledge any causal intermediaries (such as traces), it is *prima facie* not clear how they can distinguish these cases. Whether this is, in fact, so and, if it is, whether it puts reliabilism at an explanatory disadvantage vis-à-vis causalism is an issue for another paper.

(2) Mechanistic explanations describe a phenomenon in terms of the entities involved, the activities displayed, and the way these entities and activities are organized. Mechanisms are 'entities and activities organized such that they are productive of regular changes from start or set-up to finish or termination conditions' (Machamer et al. 2000, p. 3).[27] The activities of mechanisms are understood in terms of the ability to manipulate the value of one variable in the description of the mechanism by manipulating another. For this reason, mechanisms are different from mere input-output patterns of a black box. Input-output patterns can describe non-causal temporal sequences (e.g., input crowing rooster, output dawn), correlations between the effects of a common cause (e.g., input falling barometer, output storm), and can even support counterfactuals (e.g., if the rooster were to be crowing, dawn would be coming). The important thing to note, though, is that none of these input-output patterns are explanatory (Craver 2006, pp. 371–372).

The stipulation of memory traces is the causalists' attempt to give a mechanistic explanation for remembering and confabulation. Simulationists also give a mechanistic explanation. They stipulate a representation production unit as well as an endorsement and decision unit (Michaelian 2016a, ch. 8). In the end, the causalism/reliabilism debate comes down to an assessment of the competing mechanistic explanations. Once agreement has been reached regarding the kinds of memory behaviours a mechanism is supposed to explain, one can ask whether the mechanistic components and their organisation are real or fictional.

In sum, the explanationist model memory has it that S's truly representing that p via the memory system in the given circumstances qualifies as remembering if it is better explained by the fact that p, by itself, than by some statement referencing coincidental factors. Causalism and reliabilism are distinct ways of spelling out the explanation relation constitutive of remembering. The explanationist model helps to resolve the stalemate between causalist and reliabilist views about memory and confabulation by uncovering issues that lie at the core of the dispute.

Acknowledgements

A predecessor of this chapter was presented at the *Current Controversies in Philosophy of Memory* workshop at the University of Grenoble, 26–31 October 2020. I am grateful to the audience for challenging questions. Thank you to César Schirmer dos Santos, the editors, and two anonymous reviewers for comments on an earlier draft. Work on this paper was supported by an Alexander-von-Humboldt Professorship Award.

Notes

1 See https://www.yourdictionary.com/confabulation and https://www.definitions.net/definition/confabulation
2 Even if the term 'episodic' is omitted, all references to remembering should be understood as remembering episodically.
3 De Brigard (2014, p. 179). De Brigard's version of simulationism is compatible with the existence of a causal connection between diachronic representations.
4 I use 'representation' to indicate that memory can take the form of a number of different kinds of cognitive attitudes towards the content. Believing is one such attitude. 'Content preservationism' is synonymous with the 'identity theory of memory' (Bernecker 2010, pp. 217–221). I use 'to recall' to mean to ostensibly remember.
5 Epistemic preservationism is characterised in terms of belief because, on my view, propositional knowledge implies belief. The account of epistemic preservationism in terms of propositional knowledge can be generalised to other forms of memory. First, consider memory ascriptions that include an interrogative complement starting with 'who', 'whom', 'what', 'which', 'where', 'when', and 'why'. Both reductionists and anti-reductionists about memory-wh hold that memory-wh is reducible to memory-that. The disagreement only concerns the type of proposition that memory-wh is identical with. Next, consider remembering-how. The two main positions regarding procedural memory are intellectualism and anti-intellectualism. Intellectualism holds that remembering-how is a species of remembering-that while anti-intellectualism holds that the object of remembering-how is an ability. The characterisation of epistemic preservationism in terms of propositional contents carries over to the intellectualist reading of procedural memory.
6 Bernecker and Grundmann (2019, pp. 527–528) distinguish between basic and robust epistemic generativism about memory and argue for the latter position. The position stated here corresponds to basic epistemic generativism.
7 Other competitors to the causal retention theory are the evidential and the simple retention theory. See Bernecker (2010, pp. 105–113).
8 The combination of reliabilism with archivalism is a version of the epistemic theory of memory (Bernecker 2010, pp. 65–71). The epistemic theory states that to remember something is to know it, where this knowledge has been acquired in the past.
9 Gettier cases are named after Gettier (1963). These are cases where a person has justified true belief that *p* but lacks knowledge that *p*. Gettierisation is due to the lack of coordination between the satisfaction of the justification condition and the satisfaction of the truth condition.
10 For an overview over the causal theory of memory, see Michaelian and Robins (2018). Different conceptions of memory traces are discussed in Robins (2016b, 2017).
11 A subject is completely prompted when they cannot correctly reproduce more about the relevant past event than was already supplied by the prompt. The prompted

information is identical with the stored information. Complete prompts are also called 'copy cues' or 'identity cues'.

12 'In those cases where prompting is operative for the representation, [a subject's] past experience of the thing represented is operative in producing the state (or the successive set of states) in him which is finally operative in producing the representation, in the circumstances in which he is prompted' (Martin & Deutscher 1966, p. 185; see Bernecker 2008, pp. 55–57).

13 An INUS condition is where a 'cause is, and is known to be, an insufficient but necessary part of a condition which is itself unnecessary but sufficient for the result' (Mackie 1965, p. 247).

14 For the distinction between lucky and non-lucky veridical suggestibility cases see Michaelian (2022, pp. 137-139).

15 Robins (2016b) argues that distributed traces do not provide a way to track the causal history of individual memories. Distributed traces are stored as patterns of event features, but these patterns are superpositional such that similar memories are blended together in overlapping patterns.

16 Gist memory does not provide a pristine and detailed record of each event but instead provides a rough-and-ready summary. See Bernecker (2008, pp. 164–165), Brainerd and Reyna (2002, p. 165), and Michaelian (2011). McCarroll (2018) argues that observer perspectives can accurately reflect past experience. Boundary extension is the phenomenon whereby one remembers more of a scene than one actually saw (cf. Hubbard et al. 2010).

17 Veridical confabulation occurs when a state of seeming to remember is coincidentally true rather than counterfactually depending on the facts (i.e., the past event and the past representation)

18 This criticism is off target. Robins (2016a), for instance, makes space for the difference between misremembering and falsidical confabulation, because appropriate causation occurs in the former but not in the latter. Michaelian has since retracted this criticism.

19 Arguably the dispute between the causalist and reliabilist views of *memory* is itself a proxy battle between the causalist and reliabilist views of *knowledge*.

20 The explanationist model assumes the failure of deflationism about truth, that is, the view that claims that $p = p$ is true. I take it that 'p' to the left of the equation sign names a fact while 'p' to the right of the equation sign refers to a proposition that is true in virtue of this fact.

21 This example is modelled after an example by Martin and Deutscher (1966, p. 186), which is discussed in Bernecker (2010, pp. 151–154). For an empirical study on suggestibility and episodic memory, see Mendelsohn et al. (2008).

22 Rival theories of inference are Bayesianism, hypothetico-deductivism, and falsificationism.

23 See Josephson and Josephson (1994, p. 5), Lycan (1988, p. 129; 2002, p. 413) and Psillos (2002, p. 614).

24 See Lewis (1986), Lipton (2004), and van Fraassen (1980). It is an open question whether explanations are necessarily contrastive. See Gijsbers (2018).

25 Robins (2016a) distinguishes between confabulation and misremembering. In misremembering the error relies on the retained past event whereas in confabulation the subject is just making it up. Often misremembering errors are 'smaller' than confabulation ones (although not in veridical cases).

26 There are three reasons for thinking that absence memory may be non-inferential. First, absence memory can feel instantaneous and lacking in conscious effort. Second, suppose you ostensibly remember not having fed and you are presented with misleading evidence to the effect that you did feed after all. In this case you may continue to ostensibly remember not having fed. The (defeasible) informational insulation from one's knowledge suggests that the memory-based experience of

absence is not an inference-based belief. Third, the ability to automatically detect absence confers strong adaptive advantage only if it is automatic, provided it is not affected by interference from beliefs and higher cognitive states.

27 See also Bechtel and Abrahamsen (2005).

References

Bechtel, W., & Abrahamsen, A. (2005). Explanation: A mechanist alternative. *Studies in History and Philosophy of Science Part C: Studies in History and Philosophy of Biological and Biomedical Science, 36*, 421–441.

Beebe, J. (2009). The abductivist reply to skepticism. *Philosophy and Phenomenological Research, 79*, 605–636.

Bernecker, S. (2008). *The Metaphysics of Memory*. Springer.

Bernecker, S. (2010). *Memory: A Philosophical Study*. Oxford University Press.

Bernecker, S. (2017). A causal theory of mnemonic confabulation. *Frontiers in Psychology, 8*, 1207.

Bernecker, S. (n.d.). *Remembering absence*. Unpublished manuscript.

Bernecker, S., & Grundmann, T. (2019). Knowledge from forgetting. *Philosophy and Phenomenological Research, 98*(2019), 525–540.

Berrios, G. E. (1998). Confabulations: A conceptual history. *Journal of the History of the Neurosciences, 7*, 225–241.

Brainerd, C. J., & Reyna, V. F. (2002). Fuzzy-trace theory and false memory. *Current Directions in Psychological Science, 11*, 164–169.

Cabrera, F. (2020). Does IBE require a 'model' of explanation? *British Journal for the Philosophy of Science, 71*, 727–750.

Cappelen, H., Gendler, T. S., & Hawthorne, J. (Eds.) (2016). *The Oxford Handbook of Philosophical Methodology*. Oxford University Press.

Craver, C. F. (2006). When mechanistic models explain. *Synthese, 153*, 355–376.

Daly, C. (2010). *Introduction to Philosophical Methods*. Broadview.

Daniels, N. (2016). Reflective equilibrium. *Stanford Encyclopedia of Philosophy*. https://plato.stanford.edu/entries/reflective-equilibrium/

De Brigard, F. (2014). Is memory for remembering? Recollection as form of episodic hypothetical thinking. *Synthese, 191*, 155–185.

Fotopoulou, A. (2008). False-selves in neuropsychological rehabilitation: The challenge of confabulation. *Neurophysiological Rehabilitation, 18*, 541–565.

Friedman, M. (1974). Explanation and scientific understanding. *Journal of Philosophy, 71*, 5–19.

Gettier, E. (1963). Is justified true belief knowledge? *Analysis, 23*, 121–123.

Gijsbers, V. (2018). Reconciling contrastive and non-contrastive explanation. *Erkenntnis, 83*, 1213–1227.

Glennan, S. (2010). Mechanisms, causes and the layered model of the world. *Philosophy and Phenomenological Research, 82*, 362–381.

Godfrey-Smith, P. (2010). Causal pluralism. In H. Beebee, C. Hitchcock, & P. Menzies (Eds.), *Oxford Handbook of Causation* (pp. 326–337). Oxford University Press.

Hall, N. (2004). Two concepts of causation. In J. Collins, N. Hall, & L. A. Paul (Eds.), *Causation and Counterfactuals* (pp. 225–276). MIT Press.

Harman, G. (1965). The inference to the best explanation. *Philosophical Review, 74*, 88–95.

Hempel, C. (1965). *Aspects of Scientific Explanation*. Free Press.

Hubbard, T. L., Hutchingson, J. L., & Courtney, J. R. (2010). Boundary extension: Findings and theories. *Quarterly Journal of Experimental Psychology*, *63*, 1467–1494.

Johnson, M. K., Hayes, S. M., D'Esposito, M. D., & Raye, C. L. (2000). Confabulation. In J. Grafman, F. Boller, & L. S. Cermak (Eds.), *Handbook of Neuropsychology. Vol. 2. Memory and Its Disorders* (2nd ed., pp. 383–407). Elsevier.

Josephson, J., & Josephson, S. (1994). *Abductive Inference*. Cambridge University Press.

Kitcher, P. (1981). Explanatory unification. *Philosophy of Science*, *48*, 507–531.

Lewis, D. (1986). Causal explanation. In D. Lewis, *Philosophical Papers* Vol. II, Oxford University Press.

Lipton, P. (2004). *Inference to the Best Explanation* (2nd ed.). Routledge.

Lycan, W. G. (1988). *Judgement and Justification*. Cambridge University Press.

Machamer, P., Darden, L., & Craver, C.F. (2000). Thinking about Mechanisms. *Philosophy of Science*, 67: 1–25.

Mackie, J. (1965). Causes and conditions. *American Philosophical Quarterly*, *2*(4), 245–255.

Martin, C. B., & Deutscher, M. (1966). Remembering. *Philosophical Review*, *75*, 161–196.

McCarroll, C. J. (2018). *Remembering from the Outside: Personal Memory and the Perspectival Mind*. Oxford University Press.

Mendelsohn, A., Chalamish, Y., Solomonovich, A., & Dudai, Y. (2008). Mesmerizing memories: Brain substrates of episodic memory suppression in posthypnotic amnesia. *Neuron*, *57*, 159–170.

Michaelian, K. (2011). Generative memory. *Philosophical Psychology*, *24*, 323–342.

Michaelian, K. (2016a). *Mental Time Travel: Episodic Memory and our Knowledge of the Personal Past*. MIT Press.

Michaelian, K. (2016b). Confabulating, misremembering, relearning: The simulation theory of memory and unsuccessful remembering. *Frontiers of Psychology*, *7*, 1857.

Michaelian, K. (2022). Towards a virtue-theoretic account of confabulation. In A. Sant'Anna, C.J. McCarroll, & K. Michaelian (Eds.), *Current Controversies in Philosophy of Memory* (pp. 127-144). Routledge.

Michaelian, K., Perrin, D., & Sant'Anna, A. (2020). Continuities and discontinuities between imagination and memory: The view from philosophy. In A. Abraham (Ed.), *The Cambridge Handbook of Imagination* (pp. 293–310). Cambridge University Press.

Michaelian, K., & Robins, S. K. (2018). Beyond the causal theory? Fifty years after Martin and Deutscher. In K. Michaelian, D. Debus, & D. Perrin (Eds.), *News Directions in the Philosophy of Memory* (pp. 13–32). Routledge.

Morgan, M. S., & Morrison, M. (Eds.) (1999), *Models as Mediators: Perspectives on Natural and Social Science*. Cambridge University Press.

Psillos, S. (2002). Simply the best: A case for abduction. In A. C. Kakas & F. Sadri (Eds.), *Computational Logic: Logic Programming and Beyond* (pp. 605–626). Springer.

Robins, S. K. (2016a). Misremembering. *Philosophical Psychology*, *29*, 432–447.

Robins, S. K. (2016b). Representing the past: Memory traces and the causal theory of memory. *Philosophical Studies*, *173*, 2993–3013.

Robins, S. K. (2017). Memory traces. In S. Bernecker & K. Michaelian (Eds.), *The Routledge Handbook of Philosophy of Memory* (pp. 76–87). Routledge.

Robins, S. K. (2020). Mnemonic confabulation. *Topoi*, *39*, 121–132.

Salmon, W. (1984). *Scientific Explanation and the Causal Structure of the World*. Princeton University Press.

Sutton, J. (1998). *Philosophy and Memory Traces: Descartes to Connectionism*. Cambridge University Press.

Van Fraassen, B. (1980). *The Scientific Image*. Clarendon Press.

Woodward, J. (2003). *Making Things Happen: A Theory of Causal Explanation*. Oxford University Press.

6 Towards a virtue-theoretic account of confabulation

Kourken Michaelian

6.1 Introduction

There is an ongoing debate among philosophers of memory over the nature of confabulation and related memory errors.[1] Confabulation can—very roughly—be defined as an error in which a subject who is unable to remember instead makes up an event, either by dislocating events in time or by fabricating events to fill in gaps in memory (Goodwin 1989, p. 65).[2] The representations that result from these processes are sometimes implausible, but they are sometimes perfectly plausible—at least when considered in isolation. Consider two cases discussed by Dalla Barba (2009). First, patient MB,

> while he was hospitalized, said on one occasion that he was looking forward to the end of the testing session because he had to go to the general store to buy some new clothes, since he hadn't been able to the day before, because he had gotten lost in the center of Paris, where he had fortunately met a nurse who kindly took him back to the hospital.
>
> (p. 227)

Though implausible when considered in relation to the subject's circumstances at the time, the events described by MB are not intrinsically implausible. Second, patient SD, when asked what he had done the day before, replied: 'Yesterday I won a running race and I have been awarded with a piece of meat which was put on my right knee' (Dalla Barba 2009, p. 227). Though highly implausible, the event described by SD was composed largely of elements drawn from his personal past, though not from the previous day, illustrating both the dislocation of events in time and the fabrication of events: SD, Dalla Barba tells us, 'was actually involved in running races', and '[i]t was actually during a running race in the mountains that he fell, sustaining a severe head trauma and an open wound to his right knee' (p. 227).

These cases illustrate two characteristic features of the phenomenon of confabulation. First, confabulations are typically *false*. The event described by SD did not occur and could not easily have occurred. The event described by MB could more easily have occurred, but as a matter of fact he had not gotten lost the day

DOI: 10.4324/9781003002277-10

before, and it was highly unlikely that he would go to the store after the session. Second, confabulation occurs not only in remembering the past but also in *imagining the future*. MB, like many of the patients described by Dalla Barba (2002, 2009), confabulates both with respect to his personal past and with respect to his personal future. The first of these features has played an important role in the ongoing confabulation debate; indeed, we will see that the importance of falsity has, if anything, been overestimated. The second feature, however, while unsurprising in light of the firmly established link between episodic memory and episodic future thought (see Michaelian 2016b), has so far played little role in the debate.

In this chapter, I review the confabulation debate, giving space to all available philosophical accounts of confabulation but making a case for the superiority of an updated, virtue-theoretic version of the simulationist account—based on the simulation theory of memory (Michaelian 2016b), which views episodic memory as a form of imagination distinguished from episodic future thought merely by its temporal orientation—over the rival false belief, causalist, and epistemic accounts, with an emphasis on the causalist account. Adopting a naturalistic outlook, the chapter takes for granted that confabulation is typified by clinical cases of the sort reported by Dalla Barba and that an adequate philosophical account of confabulation will be responsive primarily to the features of such cases; in other words, it takes for granted that an adequate philosophical account of confabulation will harmonise with the relevant empirical science.[3]

I discuss the false belief account, an early version of the causalist account, an early version of the simulationist account, an updated version of the causalist account, and the epistemic account in Sections 6.2–6.6. I then formulate an updated, virtue-theoretic version of the simulationist account in Section 6.7 and respond to the explanationist model of confabulation proposed in Bernecker's chapter in this volume in Section 6.8. I conclude by summing up the case in favour of the virtue-theoretic version of the simulationist account in Section 6.9.

6.2 The false belief account

As its name suggests, the false belief account of confabulation is inspired by the fact that confabulations are typically false or inaccurate. Not every false apparent memory is a confabulation, and false belief accounts (see Berrios 1998 for a review) differ with respect to which other features they take to be necessary for confabulation. But they have in common that they take confabulations to be false memories that are such that the subject is unaware of their falsity.[4] As Dalla Barba (2002) sees it, for example,

> [c]onfabulation is a symptom which is sometimes found in amnesic patients and consists in involuntary and unconscious production of 'false memories', that is the recollection of episodes, which never actually happened, or which occurred in a different temporal-spatial context to that being referred to by the patient.
>
> (p. 28)

The false belief account may work in practice, but it does not work in theory, simply because *veridical confabulation* is possible (Hirstein 2005; Robins 2016b). Take Dalla Barba's patient SD. Suppose that, as a matter of fact, SD really had won a race the day before and been awarded with a piece of meat on his right knee, but change nothing else about the case. Suppose, in particular, that there is no connection whatsoever between SD's experience of that event and his apparent memory of it. (The event that induced his amnesia might, for example, have occurred after the race.) SD's apparent memory is then true, but it nevertheless remains a confabulation.

Because the false belief account makes sense of the fact that confabulations are *typically* false by taking them to be *necessarily* false, it fails to accommodate the possibility of veridical confabulation and can thus be ruled out. Before moving on to the causalist account, however, it is worth pausing to ask whether the false belief account can acknowledge future-oriented confabulation. Though Dalla Barba himself calls attention to the existence of future-oriented confabulation, he does not quite come out and say that future-oriented confabulations are false episodic future thoughts. This is understandable, given the existence of disagreements regarding the truth-aptness of representations of future events. On many views in the metaphysics of time, the future is open. If the future is open, representations of future events would seem either not to have determinate truth values or to be systematically false. If they lack determinate truth values, the false belief account is straightforwardly inapplicable to future-oriented confabulation. If they are systematically false, the false belief account would seem to imply that all episodic future thoughts are confabulations.

Debates in the metaphysics of time notwithstanding, we ordinarily assume that at least many representations of the future have determinate truth values and are not systematically false. If we take that assumption for granted, the false belief account can in principle acknowledge future-oriented confabulation. It nevertheless fares no better with respect to confabulatory future thinking than it does with respect to confabulatory remembering, simply because, if veridical past-oriented confabulation is possible, then, assuming that representations of the future can be true, veridical future-oriented confabulation is possible.

6.3 The causalist account

The false belief account has been and remains influential in the empirical sciences of memory, but—perhaps because philosophers are used to considering such unlikely but theoretically important possibilities as veridical hallucination[5]—it has played little role in the current debate, which has unfolded essentially between partisans of causalist and simulationist accounts. Indeed, the debate was triggered by Robins's (2016a, 2019) proposal of a causalist account.

Inspired by the causal theory of memory (Martin & Deutscher 1966), Robins proposed a classification of confabulation and other forms of unsuccessful remembering based on two conditions (see Table 6.1). The first is an *accuracy* condition, which requires that the subject form an accurate representation of the

Table 6.1 Robins's (2016) causalist classification

Appropriate causation		~ Appropriate causation	
accuracy	~ accuracy	accuracy	~ accuracy
successful remembering	misremembering	relearning	confabulation

past event. The second is an *appropriate causation* or retention condition, which requires that the subject's representation be causally linked to his original experience of the event via the retrieval of stored information deriving from that experience. If both conditions are satisfied, the subject *successfully remembers* the represented event. If neither condition is satisfied, the subject *confabulates*. This initial causalist classification recognises two errors in addition to confabulation. If the accuracy condition is satisfied but the appropriate causation is not, the subject has *relearnt* the event. If the appropriate causation condition is satisfied but the accuracy condition is not, the subject is not remembering but *misremembering*.

The notion of relearning can be illustrated by a hypothetical case described by Martin and Deutscher. Suppose that a subject experiences an event, recounts it to a friend, loses all memory of it, is told about the event by the friend to whom he recounted it, loses all memory of being told, and then comes, under the influence of what he has been told, to entertain a representation that happens to be accurate with respect to the event in question. In this case, there is a causal connection between the subject's current representation of the event and his original experience of it, but the causal connection goes via another person and is therefore inappropriate. The notion of misremembering can be illustrated by the DRM effect, in which the subject is presented with a list of thematically related words (e.g., *hospital, sick, nurse,* etc.) and later recalls having seen a thematically consistent but nonpresented lure word (e.g., *doctor*) (Gallo 2010). It can also be illustrated by the misinformation effect, in which inaccurate post-event information is incorporated into the subject's memory for an event, resulting in retrieval of an inaccurate memory (e.g., the subject receives the suggestion and ends up remembering that there was a stop sign at the scene of an accident that he witnessed, when in fact he saw a yield sign) (Loftus 1996). In both the DRM effect and the misinformation effect, there is an appropriate causal connection between the subject's current representation of the event and his experience, but his representation is nevertheless inaccurate. Note that, unlike confabulation, misremembering is not a clinical but rather an everyday error: the DRM effect and the misinformation effect can be produced in the laboratory, but even in the laboratory, the subjects who display them are perfectly healthy and have intact memory systems, and the conditions that produce them in the laboratory are not dissimilar to conditions encountered in everyday life.

Because it calls attention to the existence of these additional errors,[6] Robins's causalist classification represents an important advance over the false belief account. Because it takes confabulations to be necessarily false, it nevertheless inherits that account's main problem: it fails to accommodate the possibility of veridical confabulation. By the same token, it fails to accommodate the possibility of *falsidical relearning*. The possibility of veridical confabulation was established earlier. The possibility of falsidical relearning is equally easy to establish. Take the subject in Martin and Deutscher's friend case. Suppose that the subject's experience of the event that he later recounts to a friend is entirely hallucinatory, but change nothing else about the case. Suppose, in particular, that there is a causal connection between the subject's current representation of the event and his original experience of it but that the causal connection goes via another person and is therefore inappropriate. The subject's apparent memory is then false, but if the original case is an instance of relearning, so is this variant of it.

We will see that the causalist account can be revised so as to enable it to accommodate falsidical relearning and veridical past-oriented confabulation. It cannot, however, be revised so as to acknowledge future-oriented confabulation (whether veridical or falsidical). The notion of future-oriented confabulation makes little sense if the defining feature of confabulation is the absence of an appropriate causal connection between the represented event and the subject's experience of it: since future experiences cannot cause present representations, it is trivial that episodic future thinking can never involve appropriate causation. The causalist would seem to have a choice between two strategies. First, he might classify all episodic future thinking as confabulatory. To opt for this strategy would be to stretch the category of confabulation beyond all recognition. Second, he might treat the application of the concept of confabulation to episodic future thought as a category mistake. To opt for this strategy would be to preserve the meaningfulness of the concept of confabulation as it applies to episodic memory at the cost of parting ways with the empirical science. Neither strategy is satisfactory.

6.4 The simulationist account

Before ruling the causalist account out entirely, we will consider an updated version of the account developed in part in response to the simulationist challenge. The present section discusses the simulationist account; the revised causalist account is discussed in the following section.

Drawing on the simulation theory of memory, I proposed a classification of errors based on two conditions (Michaelian 2016a; see Table 6.2). The first is an *accuracy* condition equivalent to Robins's. The second is a *reliability* condition, which requires that the subject's representation be produced by a properly functioning and hence reliable episodic construction system (where the episodic construction system is the system responsible for carrying out episodic remembering and episodic future thinking) that aims to produce a representation of an event from the subject's personal past. If both conditions are satisfied, the subject *successfully remembers* the represented event. If neither condition is satisfied, the subject *falsidically confabulates*. If the accuracy condition is satisfied but the reliability condition is not, the subject *veridically confabulates*. If the reliability condition is satisfied but the accuracy condition is not, the subject is not remembering but *misremembering*.

Table 6.2   Michaelian's (2016a) first simulationist classification

Reliability		~ Reliability	
accuracy	~ accuracy	accuracy	~ accuracy
successful remembering	misremembering	veridical confabulation	falsidical confabulation

This initial simulationist classification is designed to accommodate veridical confabulation and can be extended so as to acknowledge future-oriented confabulation. There are two approaches to defining a *future-oriented reliability* condition. The first approach is to say that, just as episodic remembering is reliable to the extent that it tends to produce accurate representations of events that occurred in the subject's personal past, episodic future thinking is reliable to the extent that it tends to produce accurate representations of events that *will* occur in the subject's personal future. There are two difficulties with this approach. On the one hand, it presupposes both that the future is determinate and that episodic future thinking is a matter of attempting to predict the future. The future may or may not be determinate, but it is clear that episodic future thinking often does not aim at predicting events that will in fact occur in the personal future but, more modestly, at producing representations of events that are *likely* to occur in the personal future. The second approach is to say that episodic future thinking is reliable to the extent that it tends to produce accurate representations of events that are likely to occur in the personal future. The relevant class of events—what Dalla Barba (2002) refers to as 'the probable possible'—will have to be specified more carefully before the future-oriented reliability condition can be fully spelled out, but if this can be done, then the simulationist will be able to treat *successful episodic future thinking* as occurring if both the accuracy condition and the reliability condition are satisfied, *'veridical' confabulatory future thinking* as occurring if the accuracy condition is satisfied but the reliability condition is not, *'falsidical' confabulatory future thinking* as occurring if neither the reliability nor the accuracy condition is satisfied, and *the future-oriented analogue of misremembering* as occurring if the reliability condition is satisfied but the accuracy condition is not. The latter error has not so far figured in the confabulation debate but would be worth investigating.

The obvious problem for this first simulationist classification is that it does not acknowledge relearning (whether veridical or falsidical). In order to acknowledge relearning, I proposed a second simulationist classification (Michaelian 2016a; see Table 6.3). The second classification incorporates an *internality* condition requiring that the subject himself contribute content to the retrieved apparent memory. If he does, then he is either (mis)remembering or (veridically or falsidically) confabulating, as before. If he does not, then he is either veridically or falsidically relearning.

There are two problems for this second simulationist classification. First, as Bernecker (2017) points out, relearning does not always amount to an error.

Table 6.3 Michaelian's (2016a) second simulationist classification

	Reliability		~ Reliability	
	accuracy	~ accuracy	accuracy	~ accuracy
internality	successful remember-ing	misremem-bering	veridical confabula-tion	falsidical confabulation
~ internality	veridical relearning	falsidical relearning	veridical relearning	falsidical relearning

Take Martin and Deutscher's friend case. If the subject takes his apparent memory to originate in his experience of the apparently remembered event, then he commits an error. But he need not take his apparent memory to originate in his experience of the apparently remembered event, and, if he does not do so, then the case need not involve error. Second, the causalist should arguably want to treat relearning as an error, simply because the appropriate causation condition is not satisfied in cases of relearning. The simulationist, in contrast, arguably should not: given that he rejects the appropriate causation condition, it is unclear what motivation the simulationist might have for not treating the satisfaction of the reliability and accuracy conditions as being sufficient for remembering. The first simulationist classification thus appears to be more adequate than the second.

6.5 A revised causalist account

In order to accommodate veridical confabulation, the causalist could in principle propose a classification analogous to the first simulationist classification (see Table 6.4).[7] The difference between this classification and the simulationist classification is simply that it replaces the reliability condition with the appropriate causation condition.

Given that he wants to count relearning as an error, however, the causalist will not be satisfied with this classification, which does not acknowledge relearning. Robins (2020) proposes a revised classification that takes into account not only appropriate causation but also the sort of inappropriate causation that figures in the friend case. As proposed by Robins, the classification does not accommodate the possibility of falsidical relearning, but it can easily be modified so as to do so (see Table 6.5). On this variant of Robins's classification, the subject

Table 6.4 A potential revised causalist classification

Appropriate causation		~ Appropriate causation	
accuracy	~ accuracy	accuracy	~ accuracy
successful remembering	misremembering	veridical confabulation	falsidical confabulation

Table 6.5   *A variant of Robins's (2020) revised causalist classification*

Causation				~ Causation	
appropriate causation		~ appropriate causation		~ appropriate causation	
accuracy	~ accuracy	accuracy	~ accuracy	accuracy	~ accuracy
successful remembering	misremembering	veridical relearning	falsidical relearning	veridical confabulation	falsidical confabulation

veridically or falsidically confabulates if the *causation* condition (and hence, trivially, the appropriate causation condition) is not satisfied. If the causation and appropriate causation conditions are satisfied, the subject successfully remembers or misremembers. If the causation condition is satisfied but the appropriate causation condition is not, the subject has veridically or falsidically relearnt.

This revised causalist account is a clear improvement over the original causalist account, but it faces a number of problems. We have already encountered some of these. First, it is unclear whether relearning should be treated as an error. Second, and more seriously, the account cannot be made to acknowledge future-oriented confabulation. The second of these problems, in particular, may already provide sufficient reason to rule the account out, but it faces three additional problems that have not so far been discussed.

The first problem concerns the status of confabulation as a clinical error. Robins takes confabulation to be exemplified by the sort of error at issue in suggestibility studies such as that reported by Loftus and Pickrell (1995). 'These studies', Robins writes, 'show that, as a result of mildly suggestive questioning, participants can come to "remember" events they never experienced, such as being lost in a shopping mall as a small child or having been hospitalized overnight' (2016a, p. 434). In a typical 'lost in the mall' (LITM) case, the subject is given inaccurate information to the effect that he was lost in the mall as a child and, under the influence of this information, comes to seem to remember being lost in the mall as a child. It is no surprise that Robins takes LITM apparent memories to be confabulations. Indeed, since there is, in these cases, no causal connection between the subject's apparent memory and his experience of the represented event, the causalist is bound to treat them as confabulations: he must treat a typical LITM case as an instance of falsidical confabulation and an LITM case in which the subject is given accurate rather than inaccurate information—such cases do not typically figure in the empirical literature but obviously might occur both in the laboratory and in everyday life—as an instance of veridical confabulation. The problem is that the error at issue in suggestibility studies differs fundamentally from what we have been referring to as confabulation. Confabulations, we have supposed, occur in clinical subjects suffering from amnesia and other malfunctions of the memory or episodic construction system. LITM apparent memories, in contrast, occur (primarily) in ordinary, healthy subjects. Confabulations, moreover, because they occur in subjects with malfunctioning memory systems, are most often false. LITM apparent memories, in contrast, may most often be true: assuming that, outside of the laboratory, others do not typically attempt to mislead us about our personal pasts,[8] and given that LITM apparent memories occur primarily in subjects with properly functioning memory systems, veridical LITM apparent memories may well be more frequent than falsidical LITM apparent memories.[9] It is thus highly misleading to apply the term 'confabulation' to both phenomena: the causalist is free to use the term however he wants, but there are two things here, not one, and our terminology ought to reflect that fact.

The second, related problem is that, because it treats LITM apparent memories as confabulations, causalism may have difficulty explaining why confabulations should tend to be false. The fact that there is no causal connection between a subject's apparent memory of an event and his original experience of it does not, of course, guarantee that the apparent memory is false. (Again, veridical confabulation is possible.) If, as suggested earlier, veridical LITM apparent memories are more frequent than falsidical LITM apparent memories, and if LITM apparent memories are sufficiently widespread, then, if LITM apparent memories are confabulations, veridical confabulation may be more frequent than falsidical confabulation. Causalism thus may have difficulty recognising the fact that confabulations are typically false.

The third problem, which can likewise be illustrated by means of LITM apparent memories, concerns the relationship between confabulation and relearning. On the revised causalist account, the difference between confabulation and relearning boils down to the presence or absence of a causal connection between the apparent memory and the subject's original experience of the apparently remembered event: in relearning, there is such a causal connection (though it is inappropriate); in confabulation, there is not. The problem is that this way of distinguishing between confabulation and relearning makes the distinction depend on irrelevant factors. Falsidical LITM apparent memories do not pose any difficulty. Such memories do not satisfy the accuracy condition. And because the events that they depict did not occur, it is trivial that the relevant subjects did not experience them and hence that they do not satisfy the causation condition. The causalist account will thus necessarily classify them as instances of falsidical confabulation. But consider veridical LITM apparent memories. Such memories do satisfy the accuracy condition. But though it is natural to assume (as we did in the previous paragraph) that they do not satisfy the causation condition, this is not necessarily the case. We must distinguish here between two possibilities.

First, take a standard non-laboratory veridical LITM case in which the subject's parents give him accurate information to the effect that he was lost in the mall as a child and, under the influence of this information, he comes to seem to remember being lost in the mall as a child. Suppose that the information provided by the parents derives entirely from their own experience of the event. There is then no causal connection between the subject's experience of being lost in the mall and the information provided by his parents, and hence there is no causal connection between the subject's experience of being lost in the mall and his apparent memory of being lost in the mall. The causalist account will thus classify the case as an instance of veridical confabulation.

Second, take the same non-laboratory veridical LITM case. But now suppose that the information provided by the parents is based in part on what the subject told them about the event before childhood amnesia took hold and he forgot it. There is now a causal connection between the subject's experience of being lost in the mall and the information provided by his parents, and hence there is a causal connection between the subject's experience of being lost in the mall and his apparent memory of being lost in the mall. *The causalist account will thus classify the case as an instance not of veridical confabulation but rather of veridical relearning.*

The account therefore implies that an apparent memory can be turned from an instance of confabulation into an instance of relearning by altering factors that have nothing to do with the operation of the subject's own memory system. In both of the scenarios just described, the subject forgets an event and later forms a representation of it on the basis of information provided by his parents. The only difference between them is that, in the second scenario, he happened to tells his parents about the event before forgetting it. The causalist account thus makes the status of an apparent memory, as an instance of confabulation or an instance of relearning, depend not on how the subject's memory system operates in the present or even on how it operated in the past, but rather on how someone else learned about the event. Note that the point generalises: any instance of confabulation can be turned into an instance of relearning by performing an appropriate alteration to the causal chain, and vice versa. (Martin and Deutscher's friend case, for example, can be turned into a case of confabulation merely by supposing that the basis for the information provided to the subject by his friend was not the subject's experience of the event but the friend's own experience of the event.) This way of classifying memory errors is clearly at odds with the understanding of confabulation at work in the relevant empirical fields.

If the causalist must classify LITM cases as instances of confabulation or relearning, it would seem that the simulationist is bound to say that, as long as the episodic construction system operates reliably in producing an LITM apparent memory, then the subject is either misremembering or successfully remembering. Indeed, I have argued (Michaelian 2016b) that what goes wrong in a standard LITM case is not that the subject fails to remember but rather that he misremembers, drawing on information received from others to construct a representation of an event that did not actually occur. By the same token, it would seem that the simulationist should argue that nothing goes wrong in a veridical LITM case: given that, in such a case, the subject draws on information received from others to construct a representation of an event that did in fact occur, simulationism would seem to imply that he simply remembers.

6.6 The epistemic account

We will see below that the implications of simulationism for LITM cases are not quite so straightforward. Before turning to this matter, a brief discussion of the relationship between the simulationist account of confabulation and the epistemic account proposed by Hirstein (2005) is in order, as the latter is similar in certain respects to the simulationist account. Two points about the relationship between the accounts should be noted.

First, the accounts are similar in that both emphasise the role of metacognitive failure in confabulation. Hirstein defines confabulation, roughly, as ill-grounded belief that the subject ought to but does not know is ill-grounded.[10] Similarly, the revised simulationist account reviewed in the next section (Michaelian 2020) treats confabulation as involving unreliability both at the object level (the retrieval process itself) and at the meta level (metacognitive monitoring for unreliability in the retrieval process). While full-blown confabulation arguably involves some form of metacognitive failure (cf. Schnider 2018), there is insufficient space here to take this aspect of confabulation into account, and it will be set aside in what follows.

Second, the accounts are similar in that both appear to be epistemic accounts. Hirstein defines confabulation in terms of ill-groundedness, a notion closely related to that of unjustifiedness, and he notes that his account of confabulation may be compatible with reliabilist analyses of justification (Goldman 1979). I define confabulation directly in terms of unreliability. Bernecker (2017) thus groups Hirstein's and my accounts together, treating both as epistemic accounts. This is, however, a mistake. The fact that reliabilists employ the concept of reliability in their analysis of justification does not imply that reliability is itself an epistemic concept, any more than the fact that utilitarians employ the concept of happiness in their analysis of moral rightness implies that happiness is a moral concept. One is free to make use of the concept of happiness while rejecting utilitarianism, and one is free to make use of the concept of reliability while rejecting reliabilism. The simulationist account of confabulation, in other words, may be compatible with reliabilism, but it does not entail it. Thus, while Hirstein's account is an epistemic account, mine is not. Whether this represents an advantage for my account will depend on the empirical respectability of accounts that employ (epistemic, ethical, or other) normative vocabulary. Standard forms of naturalism suggest that an adequate account must not employ such vocabulary, but we will not explore this question any further.

6.7 A revised simulationist account

Misremembering and veridical confabulation would appear to involve a form of *luck*: in misremembering, a reliable retrieval process happens by chance to produce an inaccurate representation, whereas in veridical confabulation, an unreliable retrieval process happens to produce an accurate representation (see Table 6.6). The failure involved in misremembering is thus not attributable to the subject, just as the success involved in veridical confabulation is not attributable to him.

Though I previously (Michaelian 2020) treated the form of luck involved in misremembering and veridical confabulation as exhausting the extent of luck involved in attempted remembering, I have more recently (Michaelian 2021)

Table 6.6   The simulationist classification (grey cells indicate luck)

Reliability		~ Reliability	
accuracy	*~ accuracy*	*accuracy*	*~ accuracy*
successful remembering	misremembering	veridical confabulation	falsidical confabulation

argued that a distinct form of luck is involved in certain LITM cases. Consider, on the one hand, falsidical LITM cases. In such cases, the subject forms an apparent memory on the basis of inaccurate information received from an external source. This need not (as noted earlier) result in unreliability, and assuming that the retrieval process is reliable, the simulationist account will treat these cases as instances of misremembering. Consider, on the other hand, veridical LITM cases. In such cases, the subject forms an apparent memory on the basis of accurate information received from an external source. Assuming that the retrieval process is reliable, the simulationist might treat these cases as instances of successful remembering (Michaelian 2016b). He ought, however, to distinguish between two kinds of veridical LITM case. In *non-lucky* veridical LITM cases, the external source (e.g., a family member) intends to provide accurate information and does so. There is no luck at work in such cases, and it therefore makes sense for the simulationist to treat them as instances of successful remembering. In *lucky* veridical LITM cases, the external source (e.g., an experimenter) intends to provide inaccurate information but inadvertently provides accurate information. There is a form of luck at work in such cases, and it therefore makes sense for the simulationist to treat them as instances of unsuccessful remembering. The form of luck at work in these cases, however, differs from that at work in misremembering and veridical confabulation.

Misremembering and veridical confabulation involve a single 'layer' of luck: a reliable process happens to produce an inaccurate representation (bad luck), or an unreliable process happens to produce an accurate representation (good luck). Lucky veridical LITM cases, in contrast, involve two layers of luck: first, the subject is, for example, the victim of experimenters seeking to implant in him a false memory of being lost in the mall as a child (bad luck); second, unbeknownst to them, he happens in fact to have been lost in the mall as a child (good luck). This two-layer structure recalls the structure of the Gettier cases that demonstrate the inadequacy of the "justified true belief" analysis of knowledge (Zagzebski 1994). Suppose, for example, that a subject truly believes that it is 9:00. Suppose that the subject formed this belief by looking at a clock that has always kept good time and believing what it indicated. His truly believing that it is 9:00 may nevertheless be due to luck: the clock may have stopped at 9:00 the day before (bad luck) and the subject happened to look at it at precisely 9:00 today (good luck).

The analogy between the form of luck at work in lucky veridical LITM cases and that at work in Gettier cases suggests looking to epistemology for clues as to how to handle the latter.[11] In developing a form of virtue reliabilism designed to cope with Gettier cases, Sosa (2007) observes that what goes wrong in such cases is that, while the subject's belief is true and is formed by a reliable process, it is not true *because* it is formed by a reliable process—it is, instead, true due to luck. Taking this observation as my starting point, I propose a virtue-theoretic version of the simulation theory and a virtue-theoretic version of the simulationist classification by introducing an *accuracy-because-reliability* condition, a condition requiring that the apparent memory be accurate because it was produced by a reliable process (Michaelian 2021). This makes room for the form of 'bad luck cancelled out by good luck' involved in lucky veridical LITM cases. I similarly introduce an *inaccuracy-because-unreliability* condition, a condition requiring that the apparent memory be inaccurate because it was produced by an unreliable process, making room for an analogous form of 'good luck cancelled out by bad luck' (see Table 6.7).[12]

On the resulting classification, successful remembering occurs when the accuracy, reliability, and accuracy-because-reliability conditions are satisfied. Misremembering occurs when the reliability condition is satisfied but the accuracy condition (and hence, trivially, the accuracy-because-reliability condition) is not. Lucky LITM cases occur when the accuracy and reliability conditions are satisfied but the accuracy-because-reliability condition is not. Falsidical confabulation occurs when the accuracy and reliability conditions are not satisfied and the inaccuracy-because-unreliability condition is satisfied. Veridical confabulation occurs when the accuracy condition is satisfied and the reliability condition (and hence, trivially, the inaccuracy-because-unreliability condition) is not satisfied. The nature of the sort of error that occurs when the accuracy and reliability conditions are not satisfied and the inaccuracy-because-unreliability condition is not satisfied is not immediately obvious but merits further investigation.[13]

6.8 The explanationist model

In his contribution to this volume, Bernecker argues that an explanationist model of memory may enable us to 'overcome the impasse' between causalist and simulationist approaches to memory error.

Table 6.7   Michaelian's (2021) revised simulationist classification (grey cells indicate luck)

Reliability			~ Reliability		
accuracy		~ accuracy	accuracy	~ accuracy	
accuracy b/c reliability	~ (accuracy b/c reliability)			~ (~ accuracy b/c ~ reliability)	~ accuracy b/c ~ reliability
successful remembering	lucky veridical lost in the mall	misremembering	veridical confabulation		falsidical confabulation

The explanationist model is motivated by two supposed problems. The first is what Bernecker refers to as the 'bootstrapping' problem: 'the criteria used to determine whether a given case qualifies as confabulation', he writes, 'rely on the very theory of confabulation, which the case is supposed to provide evidence for'. The suggestion here is that, because confabulation is a technical concept, we cannot rely on folk intuition in order to determine whether a given case ought to be categorised as an instance of confabulation. This leads to reliance on our favoured theories and thus to circularity: causalists have causalist intuitions and therefore categorise cases in accord with the causalist approach, and these classifications are then used as evidence in favour of causalism; and likewise for simulationism. For example, Bernecker suggests, 'we already have to assume the simulationist approach for the characterisation of an unrealistic future expectation as an instance of *mnemonic* confabulation to make sense' (Bernecker, Chapter 5, this volume). This is, however, not true. The simulationist approach has played no role in the empirical literature on confabulation, but the existence of future-oriented confabulation, which arises under the same conditions as past-oriented confabulation and appears to be due to the same mechanisms as the latter, is nevertheless widely recognised in that literature. We are thus not invariably bound, when asking whether a given case is an instance of confabulation or another kind of memory error, to rely on intuition. Instead, we often have independent purchase on the kind of error in question, enabling us to categorise specific cases without relying on intuition. These categorisations, in turn, can serve as independent evidence in favour of or against causalist and simulationist classifications, allowing us to avoid circularity.

The second problem is what Bernecker refers to as the 'red herring' problem: 'the debate about confabulation', he writes, 'is a proxy battle between the two leading accounts of memory—causalism and reliabilism [i.e., simulationism]. As soon as the controversy between causalism and reliabilism is (re)solved, the dispute about the individuation of confabulation comes to an end' (Bernecker, Chapter 5, this volume). The correspondence between theories of remembering, on the one hand, and classifications of memory errors, on the other, is, however, not as close as the 'proxy war' metaphor suggests. A theory of remembering does, of course, amount to an account of successful remembering, but it does not determine an account of memory error. As we have seen, multiple causalist and multiple simulationist accounts have been proposed. In general, multiple accounts will be compatible with a given theory. A given account of memory error may, however, rule out certain versions of the corresponding theory. For example, the virtue-theoretic account described in Section 6.7 implies that the original version of the simulation theory of memory (Michaelian 2016b) must be replaced with a virtue theory (Michaelian 2021). Far from being a mere proxy war, then, the confabulation debate may provide a means of making real progress in the ongoing dispute between causalism and simulationism.

The motivation for explanationism is thus lacking. That the motivation for the view is lacking does not, of course, imply that explanationism may not nevertheless shed light on the relationship between causalist and simulationist approaches to confabulation. Ultimately, however, it fails to do so. Bernecker takes as his starting point the observation that both causalists and simulationists classify many of the same cases as instances of successful remembering and confabulation. This suggests that they may have something in common—a shared core. Explanationism, the view that 'remembering amounts to memorially representing something because it is true' (Bernecker, Chapter 5, this volume), is meant to capture this shared core, which Bernecker takes to be a matter of ruling out luck (the coincidental correspondence of a present apparent memory to a past experience). But, while causalists and simulationists may agree on the need to rule out luck, they disagree about the nature of the luck that needs to be ruled out. They thus disagree about how to classify many cases. This should come as no surprise: because reliability is possible without appropriate causation, the theories are fundamentally opposed to each other—they lack a shared core.[14] Cases of future-oriented confabulation provide one example. Cases of LITM memory provide another: standard non-lucky veridical LITM memories are treated by simulationism, but not by causalism, as instances of successful memory. The examples are harder cases than those that Bernecker has in mind, but this does not make them any less important. It is no surprise that causalism and simulationism agree about the easy cases; the causalist–simulationist dispute will undoubtedly be decided—as philosophical disputes usually are—on the terrain constituted by the hard cases.

6.9 Conclusion

Overall, the simulationist account, particularly in its virtue-theoretic version, is in better shape than its rivals. The foregoing discussion has identified problems for the false belief, causalist, and epistemic accounts. *The false belief account* can be ruled out simply because it cannot accommodate the possibility of veridical confabulation. *The causalist account* faces a number of serious problems. It treats relearning as an error, though it appears that many cases of relearning are not errors. It is unable to acknowledge future-oriented confabulation. In addition, it does not treat confabulation as a clinical error, has difficulty explaining why confabulations tend to be false, and is committed to an implausible view of the distinction between confabulation and relearning. It remains to be seen whether the account can be modified so as to handle luck, including the form of luck involved in lucky veridical LITM cases, but it is by no means obvious what a suitably modified account would look like. *The epistemic account* shares some of the virtues of the simulationist account but has the disadvantage of being of doubtful empirical respectability. The simulationist account thus appears—at least at present—to be our best bet.

Even if the simulationist account is on the right track, however, it is not, in the version developed here, fully satisfactory. To see this, note that, while it classifies both falsidical LITM memories and DRM memories as instances of misremembering, there is an important difference between these, in that, while falsidical LITM memories are wholly false, DRM memories are false in detail.

The simulationist account is not alone in failing to acknowledge this difference. Indeed, despite the fact that the distinction between misremembering and confabulation is naturally taken to be intimately related to the distinction between memories that are wholly false and memories that are false in detail, the latter distinction plays a role in none of the accounts of confabulation and related errors that have so far been proposed in the literature. Determining the appropriate role for that distinction will be an important task for partisans of the simulationist, causalist, and epistemic accounts as the literature continues to develop.

In addition to this shared worry, the simulationist account faces a worry that may not be faced by its rivals. As noted at the outset, the motivation for the simulationist account is naturalistic in character. It is natural, from a naturalistic standpoint, to suppose that the factors that determine whether an apparent memory is an instance of error and, if so, of what kind of error it is an instance pertaining to the operation of the memory or episodic construction system; 'external' factors are irrelevant. The involvement of luck—which, according to the virtue-theoretic version of the simulationist classification, makes the difference between veridical LITM memories that qualify as successful memories and veridical LITM memories that do not—would, however, appear to be precisely such an external factor. The virtue-theoretic version of the simulationist classification thus appears to be at odds with the naturalistic motivation for the simulationist account. While I grant that the introduction of the notion of luck represents a departure from previous versions of the simulationist account, I suggest that it is not incompatible with a naturalistic approach to memory error. Luck plays a role in determining success and failure in many domains other than remembering, and there is, on the face of it, nothing to prevent a naturalist from acknowledging this. If so, then the naturalist can presumably likewise acknowledge a role for luck in determining whether remembering, in particular, is successful or unsuccessful. Further work will, however, need to be done both to articulate the worry and to determine whether the suggested line of response is viable.

Acknowledgements

Thanks to the participants in the Centre for Philosophy of Memory's internal seminar and in the Current Controversies in Philosophy of Memory online conference for feedback on earlier versions of this chapter. Thanks also to two reviewers for helpful reports. This work is supported by the French National Research Agency in the framework of the 'Investissements d'avenir' program (ANR-15-IDEX-02) and by CAPES-COFECUB (grant Sh 967/20).

Notes

1   Confabulation is sometimes defined broadly, so that it includes both mnemic and nonmnemic errors. For example, Hirstein's (2005) epistemic account of confabulation (discussed in this chapter) is meant to apply to nonmnemic as well as mnemic confabulation. This chapter is concerned exclusively with mnemic confabulation.

2 Definitions of confabulation in the psychological literature (see Berrios 1998 for a survey) often refer both to temporal displacement and to gap-filling. These two mechanisms would, however, appear to be distinct, and confabulations resulting exclusively from the former might differ in interesting ways from confabulations resulting exclusively from the latter. This possibility has not so far been considered in the philosophical literature but would be worth investigating.

3 Robins, whose work was responsible for launching the confabulation debate and is discussed in detail later in this chapter, explicitly rejects this clinical conception of confabulation (Robins 2020). There is insufficient space here for a response to Robins's argument against the clinical conception.

4 The fact that confabulators are typically unaware of their confabulations is emphasised by the epistemic and revised simulationist accounts of confabulation discussed in this chapter but will not be discussed here in any detail.

5 On the comparison of confabulation to hallucination, see Robins (2020).

6 In fact, it is not entirely clear that relearning should be treated as an error. We come back to this point later.

7 Bernecker (2017) may have roughly such a classification in mind.

8 This is, of course, an empirical claim; see Michaelian (2013) for a defence.

9 In fact, some veridical LITM apparent memories may not amount to errors at all; see Section 6.7.

10 Hirstein's definition, which is meant to apply to nonmnemic as well as mnemic forms of confabulation, reads in full:

S confabulates if and only if:

S claims that *p*;

S believes that *p*;

S's thought that *p* is ill-grounded;

S does not know that her thought is ill-grounded;

S should know that her thought is ill-grounded;

S is confident that *p*. (2015: 187)

This rich definition merits a more detailed discussion than can be provided here.

11 Note that, though the revised simulationist account draws inspiration from epistemology, it employs no epistemic concepts and is no more an epistemic account than was the original simulationist account.

12 Like the classification proposed in Michaelian (2020), that proposed in Michaelian (2021) acknowledges the possibility of meta-level error; again, this will be set aside here.

13 One might suppose that, if lucky veridical LITM cases occur when the accuracy-because-reliability condition is not satisfied, lucky falsidical LITM cases occur when the inaccuracy-because-unreliability condition is not satisfied, but this is not right. An unlucky falsidical LITM case would be an LITM case in which the external source intends to provide accurate information but inadvertently provides inaccurate information. Such a case involves only one layer of (bad) luck, amounting to misremembering.

14 For an argument for the view that reliability presupposes appropriate causation, see Werning (2020).

References

Bernecker, S. (2017). A causal theory of mnemonic confabulation. *Frontiers in Psychology*, 8, 1207.

Berrios, G. E. (1998). Confabulations: A conceptual history. *Journal of the History of the Neurosciences*, 7(3), 225–241.

Dalla Barba, G. (2002). *Memory, Consciousness, and Temporality*. Springer.

Dalla Barba, G. (2009). Temporal consciousness and confabulation: Escape from unconscious explanatory idols. In W. Hirstein (Ed.), *Confabulation: Views from Neuroscience, Psychiatry, Psychology and Philosophy* (pp. 223–260). Oxford University Press.

Gallo, D. A. (2010). False memories and fantastic beliefs: 15 years of the DRM illusion. *Memory & Cognition, 38*(7), 833–848.

Goldman, A. I. (1979). What is justified belief? In G. S. Pappas (Ed.), *Justification and Knowledge* (pp. 1–23). Springer.

Goodwin, D. M. (1989). *A Dictionary of Neuropsychology*, Springer.

Hirstein, W. (2005). *Brain Fiction: Self-Deception and the Riddle of Confabulation*. MIT Press.

Loftus, E. F. (1996). *Eyewitness Testimony* (2nd ed.). Harvard University Press.

Loftus, E. F., & Pickrell, J. E. (1995). The formation of false memories. *Psychiatric Annals, 25*(12), 720–725.

Martin, C. B., & Deutscher, M. (1966). Remembering. *The Philosophical Review, 75*(2), 161–196.

Michaelian, K. (2013). The information effect: Constructive memory, testimony, and epistemic luck. *Synthese, 190*(12), 2429–2456.

Michaelian, K. (2016a). Confabulating, misremembering, relearning: The simulation theory of memory and unsuccessful remembering. *Frontiers in Psychology, 7*, 1857.

Michaelian, K. (2016b). *Mental Time Travel: Episodic Memory and Our Knowledge of the Personal Past*. MIT Press.

Michaelian, K. (2020). Confabulating as unreliable imagining: In defence of the simulationist account of unsuccessful remembering. *Topoi, 39*(1), 133–148.

Michaelian, K. (2021). Imagining the past reliably and unreliably: Towards a virtue theory of memory. *Synthese, 199*, 7477–7507.

Robins, S. K. (2016a). Misremembering. *Philosophical Psychology, 29*(3), 432–447.

Robins, S. K. (2016b). Representing the past: Memory traces and the causal theory of memory. *Philosophical Studies, 173*(11), 2993–3013.

Robins, S. K. (2019). Confabulation and constructive memory. *Synthese, 196*(6), 2135–2151.

Robins, S. K. (2020). Mnemonic confabulation. *Topoi, 39*(1), 121–132.

Schnider, A. (2018) *The Confabulating Mind: How the Brain Creates Reality* (2nd ed.). Oxford University Press.

Sosa, E. (2007). *Apt Belief and Reflective Knowledge. Vol I: A Virtue Epistemology*. Oxford University Press.

Werning, M. (2020). Predicting the past from minimal traces: Episodic memory and its distinction from imagination and preservation. *Review of Philosophy and Psychology, 11*(2), 301–333.

Zagzebski, L. (1994). The inescapability of Gettier problems. *The Philosophical Quarterly, 44*(174), 65–73.

Further Readings for Part III

Bernecker, S. (2017). A causal theory of mnemonic confabulation. *Frontiers in Psychology*, 8, 1207.

Outlines an account of confabulation in causal terms, such that in confabulation there is no counterfactual dependence of the state of seeming to remember on the corresponding past representation.

Berrios, G. E. (1998). Confabulations: A conceptual history. *Journal of the History of the Neurosciences*, 7(3), 225–241.

Provides a history of the concept of confabulation, outlining different ways in which the term has been used in theorising.

Bortolotti, L., & Sullivan-Bisset, E. (2018). The epistemic innocence of clinical memory distortions. *Mind and Language*, *33*, 263–279.

Explores the ways in which confabulations and memory errors may have certain psychological and even epistemic benefits.

Dalla Barba, G. (2016). Temporal consciousness and confabulation. In K. Michaelian, S. B. Klein, & K. K. Szpunar (Eds.), *Seeing the Future: Theoretical Perspectives on Future-Oriented Mental Time Travel* (119–134). Oxford University Press.

Outlines the view that confabulations can be future oriented, and provides an account of confabulation in terms of the distortion of temporal consciousness.

Hirstein, W. (2005). *Brain Fiction: Self-Deception and the Riddle of Confabulation*. MIT Press.

Argues for an epistemic account of confabulation in terms of ill-groundedness.

Michaelian, K. (2020). Confabulating as unreliable imagining: In defence of the simulationist account of unsuccessful remembering. *Topoi*, 39(1), 133–148.

Offers a simulationist account of confabulation that highlights the role played by failures of metacognitive monitoring.

Robins, S. K. (2020). Mnemonic confabulation. *Topoi*, *39*(1), 121–132.

Makes a distinction between confabulation understood in a broad sense and mnemonic confabulation, and argues that mnemonic confabulation has more in common with perceptual hallucination than broad confabulation.

Sant'Anna, A. (forthcoming). Unsuccessful remembering: A challenge for the relational view of memory. *Erkenntnis*.

Suggests that forms of unsuccessful remembering including confabulation pose a problem for relational accounts of memory, in which memory involves experiential relations to past events or objects.

Schnider, A. (2018). *The Confabulating Mind: How the Brain Creates Reality* (2nd ed.). Oxford University Press.

Investigates different forms of confabulation, including differences between provoked confabulation (confabulations in response to questions) and spontaneous confabulations (confabulations that are sometimes acted upon).

Study Questions for Part III

1) Can there be benefits (e.g., epistemic, emotional) to mnemonic confabulations? Can veridical confabulations provide us with knowledge?

2) Both Bernecker and Michaelian focus on confabulations in individuals. Can there be cases of group confabulations?

3) Should the term confabulation be restricted to clinical cases (e.g., in subjects with Korsakoff syndrome), as Michaelian suggests? If so, why? If not, why not?

4) Is Bernecker correct that an explanationist model of confabulation is neutral with regard to causalism and simulationism? Can the explanationist model be used to explain other memory errors?

5) Should the notion of future-oriented confabulation be part of the debate and theorising about mnemonic confabulation?

Part IV

What is the function of episodic memory?

7 Episodic memory

And what is it for?

Johannes B. Mahr

7.1 Introduction

One might think that the question of what the function of episodic memory is ought to be ancient: Why can we remember the past at all and why can we do it in the specific way we do? Surprisingly, however, this question has not been asked as explicitly as it deserves until a few decades ago. Endel Tulving, who introduced the term 'episodic memory' into the psychological literature, famously once sent a stack of research papers about episodic memory to the evolutionary psychologists Leda Cosmides and John Tooby with the note "And what is it for?" (Klein et al. 2009). Partly as a result of the efforts of Cosmides, Tooby, and colleagues, whose answer still remains one of the best developed in the literature (Cosmides & Tooby 2000; Klein et al. 2002), the question of the adaptive function of episodic memory has received increased attention in the last two decades in the psychological sciences. More recently, philosophers have also begun to take psychological research about episodic memory more seriously and, with it, started paying attention to questions about its function (e.g., De Brigard 2014; Michaelian 2016). In this chapter, however, I will not give an overview of the entire debate and the positions occurring within it. Instead, I will use my own view as a foil for other views. That is, I will introduce what I believe to be the right way to approach the question and how to answer it (see Mahr & Csibra 2018, 2020). Along the way, I will then point to other proposals and why they might not work.

A common sentiment in debates about episodic memory function remains that the answer must be trivially obvious. Episodic memory must be, after all, for remembering things! One way to avoid this air of triviality is to make explicit the confusion between what might be called 'memory' and 'remembering' (Klein 2015). If one thinks of memory as the ability to encode, store, and retrieve information, a 'diachronous' and 'preservative' cognitive activity, remembering can be thought of as the generation of a representation in the present, a 'synchronous' and 'generative' activity. Crucially, the question of the function of the ability to encode and store information for future use is entirely different from the question of the function of the ability to generate certain kinds of representations that are constructed on the basis of such stored

DOI: 10.4324/9781003002277-12

information (Donald 2012; Roediger 2000). To understand the function of episodic memory, I will claim, we have to first understand what it means to 'remember'.

The move from episodic memory to remembering is a common one; episodic memory is regularly operationalised as judgements of 'remembering' (as opposed to 'knowing') in psychology (Gardiner 2001; Tulving 1985). Nonetheless, equating episodic memory with 'remembering' is not meant to appeal to a linguistic criterion for identifying its instances. There are many uses of 'remembering' that don't appeal to episodic memory (see, e.g., Werning & Cheng 2017). Instead, my use of 'remembering' as a shorthand for episodic memory is meant to emphasise that episodic memory constitutes a *psychological activity in the present* resulting in certain representational mental states. That is, episodic memory occurs whenever one generates a specific kind of mental representation. In order to answer the question of what the function of episodic memory might be, we therefore have to understand what kind of mental representation it produces.

In the next section (Section 7.2), I will thus give an account of the representations making up episodic memories. This characterisation will, in effect, amount to a specification of the truth conditions of remembering: What does one take to be the case when one remembers? In Section 7.3, I will then briefly introduce the cognitive machinery underlying these representations, that is, the arguably empirically best-supported account of how episodic memories are generated (Mahr 2020). This will set the stage for the question of why episodic memory should have the truth conditions it has. Section 7.4 will develop this question and consider a few possible answers before I develop my own account in Section 7.5. My favoured answer will turn on the claim that episodic memory allows one to track whether one has epistemic authority about the past (Mahr & Csibra 2018).

Before I begin, however, let me make a short detour to clarify what notion of 'function' I am employing. As Schwartz (2020) has recently observed, the debate about episodic memory function has suffered from a conflation of at least two separate (not mutually exclusive) meanings of the term—'etiological' and 'causal role' functions. While 'etiological' functions (à la Millikan 1984) denote the performance features of a device that have led to its selection and retention over evolutionary time, 'causal role' functions (see Cummins 1975) describe how the device works, or 'what it does'. I am here interested in the former, that is, the 'proper function' of episodic remembering. That is, I seek to give an account of why episodic memory has come to be selected to have the features that it has in contemporary human adults. Of course, in the absence of phylogenetic evidence, this exercise is necessarily speculative in nature. One strategy to nonetheless generate hypotheses about the evolved function of remembering is the one I am employing here, namely, form-to-function reasoning (for an account following a similar strategy and reaching similar conclusions, see Jablonka 2017). At the very least, this strategy can make clear what a satisfactory account of episodic memory function would have to explain, and generate testable hypotheses to adjudicate between different possible accounts.

7.2 What are the truth-conditions of remembering?

7.2.1 *What are the relevant 'performance features' of remembering?*

In order to employ form-to-function reasoning, we need an account of the *form* of the system we are investigating. However, what should the target of such an account be in the case of episodic memory? In the case of remembering, I claim, the relevant 'performance features' for an etiological functional account correspond to the features of the episodic memory representation. Such a functional account has to rely on a prior specification of what remembering actually consists in, that is, what representations it produces.

One might object that such an approach does not amount to identifying features of remembering as such but instead merely identifies a *folk theory* of remembering. That is, one might think that what I am characterising is merely what people *think about* remembering rather than what they are *doing* when they remember. Therefore, one might object that an account of the form of episodic memory should target not the *product*, but rather the *process* of remembering. In other words, in order to understand what adaptive behaviours remembering enables, we should not primarily seek to understand what representations the remembering subject entertains but rather how these representations come about. From my perspective, however, an account of the mechanisms of episodic memory is primarily valuable for providing a functional account of remembering in the 'causal' sense, i.e. in the sense of how remembering 'works'. If we are instead interested in why episodic memory has been selected to have the features it does, merely trying to explain its mechanisms will lead us down a garden path. After all, any given representational capacity might be enabled in a myriad of different ways. Instead, we have to explain why episodic memories 'do' the things they do in the mind.

This is not to say that understanding the mechanisms of episodic memory will not be potentially valuable for an etiological functional account. In fact, the current debate between preservative and simulationist views of episodic memory has arguably been kickstarted by the insight that episodic remembering seems to rely on many of the same mechanisms as episodic imagination (though see Robins, Chapter 8, this volume, for a detailed analysis of this claim). Nonetheless, the products of episodic remembering and episodic imagination clearly play identifiably different roles in the human mind. And when we are asking for a functional account of remembering, we are arguably interested in 'why' (in an etiological sense) these products play the cognitive roles they inhabit. Therefore, we need to understand the episodic memory representation in order to give an account of the etiological function of this system.

7.2.2 *Particular, past, actual, and personal events*

So what features does the episodic memory representation have? One way to get an answer to this question is by thinking about what kind of things one represents to be true when one remembers (for a similar approach see Robins's 'seeming to remember'; Robins 2020). Others have approached this question as a matter of phenomenology (e.g., Dokic 2014; Perrin, Michaelian, & Sant'Anna 2020) but I prefer framing this approach in representational terms because this allows us to ask what behaviours remembering might support (see also Boyle 2019b).

Approaching it in this way, *episodic* memory represents *events*. To determine what it means to represent an event, we can turn to psychology. Zacks and Tversky (2001, p. 3) have usefully proposed an 'archetypical' definition of an event. According to them, to represent an event is to represent 'a segment of time at a given location that is conceived by an observer to have a beginning and an end'. In the case of remembering, it seems reasonable to identify 'the observer' with the remembering subject. The inclusion of such an observer in the definition of event representations points to a second feature of episodic representations: they are perspectival (e.g., Clayton & Russell 2009; McCarroll 2019), suggesting an imagistic character (Hoerl 2001).

Representing an event perspectivally is, however, not all one entertains in episodic memory. There are, after all, many possible kinds of event representations (Mahr 2020). We can represent event *tokens* and event *types* (one specific trip to the supermarket vs. 'going to the supermarket'; Campbell 1996; Zwaan & Radvansky 1998), *future* and *past* events (Atance & O'Neill 2001), *possible* and *actual* events (De Brigard & Parikh 2019), as well as events that happened to *ourselves* or to *somebody else* (Pillemer et al. 2015). Without having to answer what conceptual requirements each of these elements makes, we can ask where episodic memories fall within this space of possible event representations.

First, it seems clear that episodic memory concerns *particular* events. While it is possible to remember 'going to high school' (say), this is not the phenomenon we are targeting when we want to understand episodic memory. Instead, we are interested in cases like remembering 'my sixth birthday', a particular event. Second, uncontroversially, episodic memories are about *past* events. While the last decade has seen an increasing interest in the similarity of the cognitive operations between episodic memory and episodic future thought (e.g., Schacter et al. 2012; see Section 7.3), these phenomena can clearly be distinguished due to their differing temporal orientation (Mahr & Schacter 2022).[1] Third, while some have argued that episodic memory should be thought of as a form of 'counterfactual thought' (De Brigard 2014), remembering is commonly taken to be 'factive' (e.g., Bernecker 2008; Werning & Cheng 2017). In other words, episodic memories are about events one takes to have *actually occurred*.[2] Finally, fourth, episodic memories are about events that occurred to oneself. Even though it is possible to represent past events that happened to someone else ('vicarious memories'; Pillemer et al. 2015), one would arguably not take oneself to 'remember' those events in the same sense as events in one's personal past. Thus, episodic memories are about Particular, Past, Actual, and Personal events; let's call such event representations *PPAP-events*.

7.2.3 Second-order content

While there has been disagreement about the details of this characterisation (e.g., Andonovski 2020), I take this way of thinking about what we represent when we remember to be largely common ground among the participants in the debate about episodic memory function (e.g., Boyle 2019b; Mahr 2020; Perrin et al. 2020). Crucially, however, representations of PPAP-events are not yet instances of remembering. One can, after all, imagine such events, too. I can, for example, imagine myself snoring last night; an event that I believe to have *actually* happened, to *me*, at a *particular* time, in the *past*. What, then, distinguishes instances of remembering from those of imagining a PPAP-event? At this point, a common answer in philosophy has been to point to something like 'previous awareness' (e.g., Shoemaker 1970). However, the philosophical discourse in this area has commonly not investigated the truth conditions of episodic memory representations but rather sought to establish necessary and sufficient conditions for something to count as an instance of remembering (e.g., Martin & Deutscher 1966). Speaking in terms of representations, it seems that, in order to be distinguishable from an imagined event, we have to not only generate a PPAP-event, we also have to represent that we have experienced that event. Note that, for our current purposes, it does not matter whether one *actually* experienced the event in question; one merely has to represent that one did.

This might still not be sufficient to distinguish representations of remembered and imagined events, however, since one can just as well imagine a PPAP-event that one takes to have experienced. For example, I remember nothing of my sixth birthday even though I surely experienced it. Yet, I can very easily imagine it without getting confused about whether I am in fact remembering. It thus seems that something additional is still required to satisfy the representational distinction between remembering and imagining: I have to represent that my current representation of the event in question was *caused by* my past experience of that event (e.g., Dokic 2001; Fernández 2019; Perner & Ruffman 1995). This explains why I do not get confused about whether I might be remembering my sixth birthday when I'm imagining it: I do not take my current representation of this event to be caused by my past experience of it. Note further that episodic memory presents itself not as being merely 'somehow' caused by one's past experience, but rather as a product of 'direct retrieval' without intervening inference (for the same point, see also Robins, Chapter 8, this volume).

We now have a complete characterisation of what an episodic memory represents, namely:

1. An event that is
   o   Particular
   o   Past
   o   Actual[3]
   o   Personal

2. That (1) has been directly caused by one's own experience.

It is important to note at this point that, while (1) describes entirely first-order content, (2) is clearly meta-representational. Note also, again, that this characterisation specifies the truth-conditions of remembering. After all, if any of the aspects of the episodic memory representation turn out to be false, the remembering subject is engaging in misrepresentation. In other words, we can answer the question of 'what is remembering?' simply by pointing to the psychological activity that results in this kind of representation. However, if we want to know if someone is remembering 'correctly', we can check if all truth conditions that remembering makes are indeed fulfilled (for a similar view, see Craver 2020). Crucially, because part of the episodic memory representation makes a meta-representational claim about its own origin, in order to evaluate to what extent a given memory representation is accurate, we have to know how it was generated. Therefore, in order to evaluate whether a given instance of remembering is misrepresentational, it is not enough to determine whether the event it represents indeed occurred, in the past, at one particular point in time, to the rememberer. We have to also evaluate the causal origin of the mental representation of the event.

7.2.4 How are episodic memory representations generated?

Psychologists have known for a long time that human remembering is highly constructive (Bartlett 1932): it is as much due to processes occurring at retrieval, in the present, as it is due to processes occurring at encoding, in the past. More recently, however, evidence from various fields within the cognitive sciences has emerged suggesting that the scope of the constructiveness of episodic memory is drastically wider than traditionally assumed (Addis 2018; Schacter & Addis 2007; Hassabis & Maguire 2007; Schacter, Addis, & Buckner 2007). The view that has emerged from this research is that episodic memory is merely one among a number of different outputs of a single underlying 'episodic simulation' mechanism (Addis 2020). This mechanism generates the kind of event representations discussed earlier (e.g., Madore, Jing, & Schacter 2019) in the service of not just episodic memory but also a number of other capacities, such as episodic future thinking (Benoit & Schacter 2015), and episodic counterfactual thought (De Brigard et al. 2013). Moreover, evidence from neuro-imaging suggests that the same pieces of encoded information are retrieved in the service of both remembering and imagining events (Thakral et al. 2020). Remembered and imagined event representations seem to be the outputs of the same underlying event construction mechanism (albeit this mechanism might operate differently in each case).

This is not to say that episodic memory is not commonly reliable (Diamond, Armson, & Levine 2020). Nothing in this view of the mechanisms generating episodic memories precludes their first-order content from being commonly veridical. What these empirical results suggest, however, is that thinking of remembering purely in terms of 'retrieval' of information underestimates the amount of inference involved in the generation of episodic memory representations. Episodic memory is reliable not because it is the result of the direct retrieval of stored experiences. It is reliable because of sophisticated inference mechanisms at retrieval allowing our cognitive system to interpret incomplete trace information as evidence about what likely occurred (De Brigard 2014; Kang et al. 2019). Even though information encoded during the experience of the remembered event will commonly play a role in enabling these inferences (Werning 2020), other sources of information such as semantic schemas (Irish & Piguet 2013) and second-hand information (Loftus 2005) play similarly important roles. The content of any given episodic (memory) representation will likely be constructed from an amalgamation of different sources. In fact, in some cases, one's actual experience of a given event might not contribute at all to one's episodic memory of it (Michaelian 2016). This might be the case without the event representation thereby necessarily being inaccurate or ceasing to be represented as an instance of remembering.[4]

Given what I have said about the truth-conditions of remembering in Section 7.2, this leaves us with a puzzle. Remember that we determined one of the truth-conditions of episodic memory to be that it is directly caused by personal experience of the represented event. As it turns out empirically, however, any given episodic memory representation is commonly not caused directly by our past experience of the event in question. Instead, it is the result of an inference process making use of many different sources of information. It thus seems that the second-order component of episodic memory is at best only heuristically accurate and at worst misrepresentational (Michaelian 2018).

7.3 From form to function: Explaining the structure of episodic memory

One way in which we can reason (or, more accurately, speculate) about adaptive function is from form to function. In fact, in the case of episodic memory, given a lack of phylogenetic evidence, form-to-function reasoning is arguably the only available strategy. Given what I have said in Sections 7.2 and 7.3, two critical questions emerge for an account of episodic memory function trying to account for its representational form:

1. Why do the truth-conditions of episodic memory include a second-order component regarding its own causal origin in personal experience?
2. Why are episodic memories represented as originating directly in personal experience when, in fact, they are generated through an inference process based on many different kinds of evidence?

Let us consider the two most common accounts of episodic memory function in light of these questions. I will first evaluate traditional preservative views before looking at more recent 'generative' or 'simulationist' views of episodic memory function.

7.3.1 Is episodic memory for remembering the past?

Common-sense views of episodic memory function as 'preservative' take it that episodic memory functions to reliably remember the past (Boyle 2019a; Schwartz 2020). How can preservative views deal with the second-order representational structure of episodic memory? For preservative views of episodic memory function, question 1 is particularly puzzling. After all, if episodic memory is about accurately representing the past, why are its truth-conditions determined by whether it originated in personal experience? Why is the accuracy of episodic memory not determined solely by whether it accurately represents the event in question?

Preservative views have two ways to respond to this challenge. On the one hand, it has been proposed that, because episodic memory shares many representational features with imagination (see Section 7.3), a cognitive 'memory index' is required to distinguish remembered from imagined events (Klein 2014; Michaelian 2016). Episodic memory's second-order component might fill this role. There is, however, a problem with this response: it does not provide an answer for why the distinction between memory and imagination should fall in line with a representation's causal grounding in personal experience rather than (say) whether the event occurred or not. In other words, this view does not, in fact, account for the form of episodic memory in functional terms. After all, if episodic memory were merely about reliably representing the past, we would expect the distinction with imagination to fall in line with something like the difference between factual and counterfactual events or between accurate and inaccurate representations of events. As I have argued, however, human beings seem to distinguish imagined and remembered event representations on the basis of whether they were caused by personal experience.

On the other hand, one might think that episodic memory's second-order 'source' component serves an epistemic function by supporting the accurate representation of events. This would provide an answer for why the distinction between remembering and imagining should be drawn along the lines of a source in personal experience. One could, for example, suggest that tracking the source of our event representations in episodic memory allows us to estimate the certainty with which we should hold beliefs formed on its basis (e.g., Tulving 1985). Again, however, a need for tracking certainty would not quite explain why episodic memory's second-order content functions the way it does. First, epistemic certainty could be estimated through confidence estimation alone, a capacity which is critically different from (and much simpler than) source representations. While confidence, arguably, seeks to signal directly the reliability of a given representation, source representations describe its causal origin. Moreover, while people seem to hold an intuitive theory to the effect that first-hand evidence is *ceteris paribus* more reliable than second-hand evidence (Mahr & Csibra 2021), this theory is certainly not always correct (Nagel 2015). Secondly, this account does not answer question 2: It does not make intelligible why episodic memory's source ascription should commonly at best be inaccurate and at worst be entirely misrepresentational. After all, if the second-order component had an entirely epistemic function, we would expect it to maximise accuracy. In other words, we would expect source ascriptions in episodic memory to reflect *the extent to which* a given representation originates in personal experience. Source representation in episodic memory, however, seems to be all or nothing: Either you remember, or you don't. Of course, we can have different degrees of confidence with which we might seem to remember. Such confidence is, however, 'second-order' – it signals certainty about whether one's event representation originated in first-hand experience and not the accuracy of that representation.[5]

7.3.2 Is episodic memory for imagining the future?

In contrast to preservative views of episodic memory function, more recently, 'simulationist' (Michaelian 2016) views have become increasingly popular. According to such accounts, episodic memory is functional not primarily because of its preservative capacities (i.e., its ability to accurately represent the past) but rather due to its constructive character (De Brigard 2014; Schacter & Addis 2007). That is, episodic memory is thought to function so as to enable other constructive episodic simulations, in particular, the ability to generate representations of future events (or 'mental time travel'). Since Sarah Robins (Chapter 8, this volume) deals with future-directed accounts of episodic memory function in much greater depth, I will keep my own observations here rather short.

Authors arguing for the future-directed function of episodic remembering usually put less emphasis on episodic memory as a specific kind of representation resulting from the process of episodic simulation. Instead, these views are somewhat ambiguous between a conception of episodic memory as 'memory' and as 'remembering' – that is, as a capacity for storing details of events one has experienced and as the ability to generate representations in the sense discussed here. What exactly the simulationist claim about episodic memory function should be taken to be, therefore, depends on whether one interprets these views as targeting the former or the latter capacity.

If episodic memory is merely taken to be a form of 'memory', i.e., the ability to store specific event details to be later used for the processes of episodic simulation, the simulationist claim should be uncontroversial. Clearly, the capacity to store information learned from specific events functions in the service of the later retrieval of this information. And such retrieval has to be flexible enough to make use of event information to generate a wide range of outputs (Addis 2018). Things are less clear, however, if one interprets the simulationist claim to target 'remembering', that is, the ability to generate episodic memory representations as I have introduced them in Section 7.1. On this interpretation, the claim amounts to the idea that the representation of future events would somehow be facilitated by the ability to generate representations of past experiences first. However, a whole range of features of those representations are not clearly explained by the supposed function of episodic memory to support the representation of future events.

On the one hand, it is not obvious how this version of simulationism would account for the first-order features of particularity and past-directedness of the episodic memory representation. What role would the fact that an event occurred at a *particular* point in the *past* play in supporting simulations about the future? It seems that this role could be filled more effectively by event representations that stay mute with respect to when or how often a given event occurred before. In fact, this is exactly the role we would expect semantic information abstracted from individual experiences to play in enabling future simulations (Irish et al. 2012). On the other hand, episodic memory's second-order component seems to become mysterious on this version of simulationism. Why would it be relevant to know whether one has had personal experience of a given event in order to generate representations of the future? One might, again, point to some kind of epistemic function like the tracking of reliability or certainty, but, as I mentioned earlier, this doesn't quite explain the content of the representation in question. Moreover, if the structure of the episodic memory representation was selected for supporting the representation of future events, wouldn't we want it to estimate the reliability of our representations of the *future* rather than of the past? How would tracking the source of our episodic memories contribute to tracking the reliability of representations of the future? Simulationism has to provide answers to these questions if it is to account for the representational form of episodic memory in terms of its role in supporting future simulation.

7.4 A communicative function for episodic memory

7.4.1 *Tracking and claiming epistemic authority about the past*

Given what I have said so far, it seems that neither preservationism nor simulationism can provide a satisfactory account of the complete structure of the episodic memory representation in functional terms. In particular, the second-order 'source' component representing episodic memory as a direct outcome of personal experience remains unexplained on either account. Why do human adults represent how they came to know when they represent past events? One obvious reason why this might be important is because human beings learn information from a variety of sources and not just through personal experience. A large part of our beliefs about the world come from second-hand sources. This stands in stark contrast to how other animals learn about the world. In the absence of language, social learning is highly constrained and the possibilities for being misled highly reduced. Therefore, one reason why humans might have to track where their knowledge comes from is because so much of it doesn't come from their own experience. In that sense, the structure of episodic memory might, in part, be an outcome of selection pressures on our cognitive system as a receiver of social information. Tracking which of our knowledge comes from personal experience might allow us to quarantine it from contamination through social sources, which might be misleading or incompetent (see also Cosmides & Tooby 2000). Further, keeping track of source information allows us to decide when to revise our beliefs in the light of new information. Mechanisms developed in response to the selection pressures posed by the potential unreliability of communicated information have been termed 'epistemic vigilance' mechanisms (Sperber et al. 2010). Episodic memory's source component thus plausibly serves a communicative, 'epistemic vigilance' function.

Human beings are, however, also senders of information in communicative exchanges. Thus, keeping track of what information was acquired through first-hand experience is not only important for the 'epistemic hygiene' of our own minds. It also allows us to transmit our beliefs more effectively to others (Mahr et al. 2021). As mentioned earlier, people seem to treat information acquired at first-hand as more believable than information acquired at second-hand (Mahr & Csibra 2021).[6] Eyewitness testimony intuitively seems to be convincing and highly reliable (Benton et al. 2006) in spite of its proven limitations (Zaragoza et al. 2007). Of the 367 people the Innocence Project exonerated since 1989 in the United States, 69% were originally convicted on the basis of eyewitness testimony. Having first-hand experience about a circumstance, thus, seems to confer epistemic authority about that circumstance. In fact, tracking epistemic authority is often the only way we can decide whom and what to believe about the past. Tracking when we ourselves have such authority should therefore be highly beneficial.

Note that this also explains the heuristic inaccuracy that second-order source attribution processes display in episodic memory. Remember that question 2 earlier asked why episodic memory would inaccurately represent its own origin in direct personal experience. If the function of this representation is not entirely epistemic but rather for social consumption, we can make sense of this. Similar to other cognitive capacities producing the reasons for why we hold a given belief (Mercier & Sperber 2017), source representations in episodic memory might be tuned to the social benefits of having epistemic authority about a given circumstance. In this sense, we could think of episodic memory's source component as functioning similarly to 'self-deception' in the service of social manipulation (von Hippel & Trivers 2011). The potential costs of representing the source of our beliefs about the past somewhat inaccurately might be offset by the social benefits conferred by gaining epistemic authority about the past.

7.4.2 The social benefits of epistemic authority about the past

What are these social benefits? In order to offset the costs of potential misrepresentation, epistemic authority about the past needs to have benefits that go beyond the purely epistemic domain. Elsewhere, Gergely Csibra and I (Mahr & Csibra 2020) have argued that the social benefits of epistemic authority about the past are rooted in a social norm that seems to be fundamental to many aspects of human social life: that social realities in the present are justifiable ultimately only by recourse to history. You might know that you own your car, but if challenged about this fact, how will you be able to prove that this is indeed the case? Ownership is, after all, not perceivable but rather a matter of social agreement. While you might have a certificate of ownership (acquired when you bought your car and certifying that such buying indeed occurred), such documents were arguably not available for the majority of human history. In the village of Babulo in East Timor, for example, a norm of first possession traditionally arbiters debates of land ownership (Fitzpatrick & Barnes 2010). Whoever can narratively trace their lineage to an ancestor who settled the respective land first is given ownership over it. Narrative authority about the past thus seems to become supremely important in deciding a certain social fact (land ownership) in the present.

As this example illustrates, and as will certainly be familiar to most readers, the past is supremely important in coordinating what we take to be true in the social world. It is no coincidence that eyewitness testimony is most familiar in the legal context – an arena where the stakes of what social facts we take to be true are high and other forms of evidence are often not available. While the court is an extreme case of such reliance on epistemic authority in virtue of personal experience, similar, less formalised, lower-stakes situations permeate our everyday lives and the social discourses we are part of. The potential benefit of tracking when one has personally experienced a given event, therefore, is this: personal experience can convey authority which comes with the power to influence what is treated as social fact in the present.

7.4.3 Evolutionary path-dependence

Given that I have accused other accounts of episodic memory function of failing to explain the 'complete' structure of the episodic memory representation, one might rightly wonder whether I have done better. After all, the present account primarily targets the second-order 'source' components of this structure. Indeed, this account is broadly compatible with a preservationist view of episodic memory function regarding first-order episodic memory contents (PPAP-events). In fact, while the present account predicts some biases in the way episodic memory contents are constructed (see Mahr & Csibra 2018 for details), it requires that episodic memories be sensitive to actual occurrences.

Maybe unsurprisingly, different aspects of episodic memory are therefore likely explained by different functional considerations and might have been shaped by different forms of selection. After all, the neurocognitive system underlying episodic memory in humans and other animals is ancient (Allen & Fortin 2013) and has likely come under selection from different environmental pressures at different times. Seemingly contradictory functional perspectives on episodic memory might therefore be compatible if we consider the episodic simulation system to be a product of evolutionary path-dependence with different selection pressures operating in sequence. From this perspective, it is indeed highly unlikely that all features of episodic memory will be explained by one all-encompassing functional account since some of these features will be owed to such path-dependence. Moreover, it is possible, and in the human case even likely, that different kinds of evolutionary processes (including, e.g., cultural-group selection as proposed by Heyes 2018) have operated on this system. Therefore, even though I have argued here against both preservationism and simulationism, each of these views likely gets some things right about the function of episodic memory. An exploration of what these things are exactly will, however, have to take place elsewhere.

7.5 Conclusion

Why do we remember the past in the way we do? And why does remembering play such a prominent role in our lives and relationships? These are the questions that, from the perspective I have argued for here, any account of episodic memory function will have to answer. I have proposed that episodic memory represents not just particular past events but also how we came to know about them, namely, through personal experience. Further, I have argued that this representational structure is not accounted for by either purely preservative or by purely generative views of episodic memory function. As an alternative, I have argued that episodic memory serves a social function: the tracking of epistemic authority about the past. This capacity is required not only because it carries epistemic value, but also because it allows one to adaptively influence what others take to be the case in the present social world.

There are, of course, still questions to be answered for this account. Most importantly, according to the view I have detailed in this chapter, the structure of remembering has come under selection pressure from social norms governing epistemic authority and the historicity of social entities like commitments and entitlements. For this account to carry weight, however, these social norms would have to have emerged long ago and be stable enough to exert such evolutionary pressure. One source of evidence that might offer support for this view could come from cross-cultural ethnography. To my knowledge, such evidence is, as of yet, sparse. As such, the account I have offered here allows us to ask new and exciting questions about the organisation of human social life that have previously not been connected to investigations into the nature of remembering. Remembering is, after all, part of the fabric of our social world.

Notes

1 As others have noted, the past-directedness of episodic memories alone might be reason enough to abandon any account viewing them as entirely preservative (Burge, 1993; Matthen, 2010). After all, we don't encode/store events *as past* but rather attribute temporal orientation to event representations generated at retrieval (D'Argembeau 2020; Mahr 2020; Mahr, Greene, & Schacter 2021).

2 There are important questions about the relationship between 'beliefs in occurrence' and episodic memories (see, e.g., Scoboria et al. 2014). One way to think about this relationship is as episodic memories producing reasons for believing that the remembered event indeed occurred (Mahr & Csibra 2018; Werning 2020). For the sake of simplicity, I will leave these considerations to the side in what follows.

3 Again, there is more to be said here about the place of the belief about the actual occurrence of the event in the representational ontology of episodic memory. For simplicity's sake I have grouped it with other first-order elements of the content even though this belief might actually be the outcome of an inferential process occurring after the episodic memory representation has been generated (see Mahr & Csibra 2018 for a more in-depth treatment of this issue).

4 This way of characterising episodic memory retrieval is not meant to beg the question against the causal theory of remembering on which remembering always requires an appropriate causal connection from the experienced event to its memorial representation. Instead, I'm merely pointing out that, in order to represent an event as remembered, such a causal connection is not necessary and, indeed, sometimes absent without thereby necessarily sabotaging the general accuracy of its contents.

5 Note that these considerations don't speak against attributing a preservative function to our capacity to generate PPAP-events in terms of accurately remembering the past. Nonetheless, such a preservative function cannot be the whole story because it fails to explain the complete structure of episodic memories.

6 There are two possible reasons for why this might be the case (see Mahr and Csibra 2021). On the one hand, people might think that information is degraded through inference and thus track the amount of inference a piece of information has been subject to. On the other hand, claims to first-hand experience might commit the speaker more strongly to the truth of her assertion thus signalling to her audience higher reliability.

References

Addis, D. R. (2018). Are episodic memories special? On the sameness of remembered and imagined event simulation. *Journal of the Royal Society of New Zealand, 48*(2–3), 64–88.

Addis, D. R. (2020). Mental time travel? A neurocognitive model of event simulation. *Review of Philosophy and Psychology, 11,* 233–259.

Allen, T. A., & Fortin, N. J. (2013). The evolution of episodic memory. *Proceedings of the National Academy of Sciences, 110*(suppl. 2), 10379–10386.

Andonovski, N. (2020). Singularism about episodic memory. *Review of Philosophy and Psychology, 11*(2), 335–365.

Atance, C. M., & O'Neill, D. K. (2001). Episodic future thinking. *Trends in Cognitive Sciences, 5*(12), 533–539.

Bartlett, F. C. (1932). *Remembering.* Cambridge University Press.

Benoit, R. G., & Schacter, D. L. (2015). Specifying the core network supporting episodic simulation and episodic memory by activation likelihood estimation. *Neuropsychologia, 75,* 450–457.

Benton, T. R., Ross, D. F., Bradshaw, E., Thomas, W. N., & Bradshaw, G. S. (2006). Eyewitness memory is still not common sense: Comparing jurors, judges and law enforcement to eyewitness experts. *Applied Cognitive Psychology: The Official Journal of the Society for Applied Research in Memory and Cognition, 20*(1), 115–129.

Bernecker, S. (2008). *The Metaphysics of Memory.* Springer.

Boyle, A. (2019a). Learning from the past: Epistemic generativity and the function of episodic memory. *Journal of Consciousness Studies, 26*(5-6), 242–251.

Boyle, A. (2019b). The impure phenomenology of episodic memory. *Mind & Language, 35*(5), 641–660.

Burge, T. (1993). Content preservation. *The Philosophical Review, 102*(4), 457–488.

Campbell, J. (1996). Human vs. animal time. In M. A. Pastor and J. Artieda (Eds.), *Time, Internal Clocks and Movement.* Elsevier.

Clayton, N. S., & Russell, J. (2009). Looking for episodic memory in animals and young children: Prospects for a new minimalism. *Neuropsychologia, 47*(11), 2330–2340.

Cosmides, L. & Tooby, J. (2000). Consider the source: The evolution of adaptations for decoupling and metarepresentation. In: D. Sperber (ed.), *Metarepresentations: A Multidisciplinary Persepctive.* (pp. 53–115). Oxford University Press.

Craver, C. (2020). Remembering: Epistemic and empirical. *Review of Philosophy and Psychology, 11*(2), 261–281.

Cummins, R. (1975). Functional analysis. *The Journal of Philosophy, 72*(2), 741–765.

D'Argembeau, A. (2020). Zooming in and out on one's life: Autobiographical representations at multiple time scales. *Journal of Cognitive Neuroscience, 32*(11), 2037–2055.

De Brigard, F. (2014). Is memory for remembering? Recollection as a form of episodic hypothetical thinking. *Synthese, 191*(2), 155–185.

De Brigard, F., Addis, D. R., Ford, J. H., Schacter, D. L., & Giovanello, K. S. (2013). Remembering what could have happened: Neural correlates of episodic counterfactual thinking. *Neuropsychologia, 51*(12), 2401–2414.

De Brigard, F., & Parikh, N. (2019). Episodic counterfactual thinking. *Current Directions in Psychological Science, 28*(1), 59–66.

Diamond, N., Armson, J., & Levine, B. (2020). The truth is out there: Accuracy and detail in recall of verifiable real-world events. *Psychological Science, 31*(12), 1544–1556.

Dokic, J. (2001). Is memory purely preservative? In C. Hoerl & T. McCormack (Eds.). *Time and Memory: Issues in Philosophy and Psychology.* (pp. 213–232). Oxford University Press.

Dokic, J. (2014). Feeling the past: A two-tiered account of episodic memory. *Review of Philosophy and Psychology, 5*(3), 413–426.

Donald, M. (2012). Evolutionary origins of autobiographical memory: A retrieval hypothesis. D. Berntsen & D. C. Rubin (Eds.), *Understanding Autobiographical Memory: Theories and Approaches* (pp. 269–289). Cambridge University Press.

Fernández, J. (2019). *Memory: A Self-Referential Account.* Oxford University Press.

Fitzpatrick, D., & Barnes, S. (2010). The relative resilience of property: First possession and order without law in East Timor. *Law & Society Review, 44,* 205–237

Gardiner, J. M. (2001) Episodic memory and autonoetic consciousness: A first-person approach. *Philosophical Transactions of the Royal Society B: Biological Sciences* 356, 1351–1361.

Hassabis, D., & Maguire, E. A. (2007). Deconstructing episodic memory with construction. *Trends in Cognitive Sciences, 11*(7), 299–306.

Heyes, C. (2018). *Cognitive Gadgets: The Cultural Evolution of Thinking.* Harvard University Press.

Hoerl, C. (2001). The phenomenology of episodic recall. In C. Hoerl & T. McCormack (Eds.), *Time and Memory: Issues in Philosophy and Psychology* (pp. 315–336). Oxford University Press.

Irish, M., Addis, D. R., Hodges, J. R., & Piguet, O. (2012). Considering the role of semantic memory in episodic future thinking: Evidence from semantic dementia. *Brain, 135*(7), 2178–2191.

Irish, M., & Piguet, O. (2013). The pivotal role of semantic memory in remembering the past and imagining the future. *Frontiers in Behavioral Neuroscience, 7,* 27.

Jablonka, E. (2017). Collective narratives, false memories, and the origins of autobiographical memory. *Biology & Philosophy, 32*(6), 839–853.

Kang, Y., Mahr. J. B., Nagy, M., Andrási, K., Csibra, G., & Lengyel, M. (2019). Eye-movements reflect causal inference during episodic memory retrieval. *Poster presented at the 2019 Conference on Cognitive Computational Neuroscience*, Berlin, Germany.

Klein, S. B. (2014). Autonoesis and belief in a personal past: An evolutionary theory of episodic memory indices. *Review of Philosophy and Psychology*, *5*(3), 427–447.

Klein, S. B. (2015). What memory is. *Wiley Interdisciplinary Reviews: Cognitive Science*, *6*(1), 1–38.

Klein, S. B., Cosmides, L., Gangi, C. E., Jackson, B., Tooby, J., & Costabile, K. A. (2009). Evolution and episodic memory: An analysis and demonstration of a social function of episodic recollection. *Social Cognition*, *27*(2), 283–319.

Klein, S. B., Cosmides, L., Tooby, J., & Chance, S. (2002). Decisions and the evolution of memory: Multiple systems, multiple functions. *Psychological Review*, *109*(2), 306.

Loftus, E. F. (2005). Planting misinformation in the human mind: A 30-year investigation of the malleability of memory. *Learning & Memory*, *12*(4), 361–366.

Madore, K. P., Jing, H. G., & Schacter, D. L. (2019). Episodic specificity induction and scene construction: Evidence for an event construction account. *Consciousness and cognition*, *68*, 1–11.

Mahr, J. B. (2020). The dimensions of episodic simulation. *Cognition*, *196*, 104085.

Mahr, J. B., & Csibra, G. (2018). Why do we remember? The communicative function of episodic memory. *Behavioral and Brain Sciences*, e41.

Mahr, J. B., & Csibra, G. (2020). Witnessing, remembering, and testifying: Why the past is special for human beings. *Perspectives on Psychological Science*, *15*(2), 428–443.

Mahr, J. B. & Csibra, G. (2021). The effect of source claims on statement believability and speaker accountability. *Memory & Cognition*, *49*(8), 1505–1525.

Mahr, J. B., Greene, J., & Schacter, D. L. (2021). *A long time ago, in a galaxy far, far away: How temporal are episodic contents? Consciousness and Cognition*, *96*, 103224.

Mahr, J. B., Mascaro, O., Mercier, H., & Csibra, G. (2021). The effect of disagreement on children's source memory performance. *PLoS One*, *16*(4), e0249958.

Mahr, J. B. & Schacter, D. L. (2022). *Mnemicity versus temporality: Distinguishing between components of episodic representations. Journal of Experimental Psychology: General*. Advance online publication. https://doi.org/10.1037/xge0001215

Martin, C. B. & Deutscher, M. (1966). Remembering. *The Philosophical Review*, *75*(2), 161–196.

Matthen, M. (2010). Is memory preservation? *Philosophical Studies*, *148*(1), 3–14.

McCarroll, C. J. (2019). Looking at the self: Perspectival memory and personal identity. *Philosophical Explorations*, *22*(3), 259–279.

Mercier, H., & Sperber, D. (2017). *The Enigma of Reason*. Harvard University Press.

Michaelian, K. (2016). *Mental Time Travel: Episodic Memory and Our Knowledge of the Personal Past*. MIT Press.

Michaelian, K. (2018). Autonoesis and reconstruction in episodic memory: Is remembering systematically misleading? *Behavioral and Brain Sciences*, e41.

Millikan, R. (1984). *Language, Thought, and Other Biological Categories: New Foundations for Realism*. MIT Press.

Nagel, J. (2015). The social value of reasoning in epistemic justification. *Episteme*, *12*(2), 297–308.

Perner, J., & Ruffman, T. (1995). Episodic memory and autonoetic consciousness: Developmental evidence and a theory of childhood amnesia. *Journal of Experimental Child Psychology*, *59*(3), 516–548.

Perrin, D., Michaelian, K., & Sant'Anna, A. (2020). The phenomenology of remembering is an epistemic feeling. *Frontiers in Psychology*, *11*, 1531.

Pillemer, D. B., Steiner, K. L., Kuwabara, K. J., Thomsen, D. K., & Svob, C. (2015). Vicarious memories. *Consciousness and Cognition*, *36*, 233–245.

Robins, S. K. (2020). Defending discontinuism, naturally. *Review of Philosophy and Psychology*, *11*(2), 469–486.

Roediger, H. L. (2000). Why retrieval is the key process in understanding in human memory. In E. Tulving (Ed.), *Memory, Consciousness, and the Brain: The Tallinn Conference.* (pp. 52–75). Psychology Press.

Schacter, D. L., & Addis, D. R. (2007). The cognitive neuroscience of constructive memory: Remembering the past and imagining the future. *Philosophical Transactions of the Royal Society B: Biological Sciences*, *362*(1481), 773–786.

Schacter, D. L., Addis, D. R., & Buckner, R. L. (2007). Remembering the past to imagine the future: The prospective brain. *Nature Reviews Neuroscience*, *8*(9), 657–661.

Schacter, D. L., Addis, D. R., Hassabis, D., Martin, V. C., Spreng, R. N., & Szpunar, K. K. (2012). The future of memory: Remembering, imagining, and the brain. *Neuron*, *76*(4), 677–694.

Schwartz, A. (2020). Simulationism and the function(s) of episodic memory. *Review of Philosophy and Psychology*, *11*(2), 487–505.

Scoboria, A., Jackson, D. L., Talarico, J., Hanczakowski, M., Wysman, L., & Mazzoni, G. (2014). The role of belief in occurrence within autobiographical memory. *Journal of Experimental Psychology: General*, *143*(3), 1242–1258.

Shoemaker, S. (1970). Persons and their pasts. *American Philosophical Quarterly*, *7*(4), 269–285.

Sperber, D., Clément, F., Heintz, C., Mascaro, O., Mercier, H., Origgi, G., & Wilson, D. (2010). Epistemic vigilance. *Mind & Language*, *25*(4), 359–393.

Thakral, P. P., Madore, K. P., Addis, D. R., & Schacter, D. L. (2020). Reinstatement of event details during episodic simulation in the hippocampus. *Cerebral Cortex*, *30*(4), 2321–2337.

Tulving, E. (1985) Memory and consciousness. *Canadian Psychology*, *26*,1–12.

Von Hippel, W., & Trivers, R. (2011). The evolution and psychology of self-deception. *Behavioral and Brain Sciences*, *34*(1), 1.

Werning, M. (2020). Predicting the past from minimal traces: Episodic memory and its distinction from imagination and preservation. *Review of Philosophy and Psychology*, *11*(2), 301–333.

Werning, M., & Cheng, S. (2017). Taxonomy and unity of memory. In S. Bernecker & K. Michaelian (Eds.), *The Routledge Handbook of Philosophy of Memory* (pp. 7–20). Routledge.

Zacks, J. M., & Tversky, B. (2001). Event structure in perception and conception. *Psychological Bulletin*, *127*(1), 3–21.

Zaragoza, M. S., Belli, R. F., & Payment, K. E. (2007). Misinformation effects and the suggestibility of eyewitness memory. In M. Garry & H. Hayne (Eds.), *Do Justice and Let the Sky Fall: Elizabeth Loftus and Her Contributions to Science, Law, and Academic Freedom* (pp. 35–63). Lawrence Erlbaum Associates Publishers.

Zwaan, R. A., & Radvansky, G. A. (1998). Situation models in language comprehension and memory. *Psychological Bulletin*, *123*(2), 162–185.

8 Episodic memory is not for the future

Sarah K. Robins

8.1 Introduction

Memory is for the future. This claim has become increasingly common amongst memory scientists and philosophers of memory in recent years. It is striking. Memory involves retention of information and experience from the past, so it has traditionally been assumed that the function of memory should match this orientation. The motivations researchers have for turning memory toward the future are varied. Collectively, they have served to reignite interest in what once seemed a well-settled question: What is the function of episodic memory?

Here I focus on the Constructive Episodic Simulation Hypothesis (CESH), one of the most prominent accounts of episodic memory's prospective function (Addis, Wong, & Schacter 2007; Schacter & Addis 2007). CESH theorists claim they have 'redefined the function of episodic memory as primarily future-focused' (Addis 2018, p. 65). Despite the popularity of the view, I argue that CESH has not established that episodic memory's function is for the future.

The argument proceeds in two steps. First, I illustrate how the CESH claim that episodic memory's function is future-focused depends on episodic remembering and episodic imagining being the same cognitive activity. Second, I argue that this claim does not hold: episodic remembering and episodic imagining are *not* the same cognitive activity. Even if they are both constructive, as CESH theorists maintain, they involve importantly distinct forms of construction.

Before beginning, I note some points of contact with Mahr's paired chapter on this controversy over the function of episodic memory. While our approaches differ, there are some key claims on which we agree. We both advocate for more careful consideration of functions in this literature, and we agree that progress on the question of episodic memory's function requires more attention to the nature of remembering and its distinction from imagination. What's more, our accounts of remembering appear to be, at least largely, complementary. We part ways on the question of which approach to functions is more pressing and fundamental, and we differ in how we relate the account of remembering to the search for episodic memory's function. Mahr begins with an account of remembering, and

DOI: 10.4324/9781003002277-13

then uses this account to advocate for a particular view of episodic memory's etiological function. I focus first on its causal-role function, and then use that focus to highlight what is distinct about episodic remembering.

8.2 The constructive episodic simulation hypothesis

In 2007, *Science* declared the discovery of similar brain areas supporting memory and imagination one of its 10 breakthroughs of the year ("Areas to watch" 2007; Schacter & Addis 2007). The discovery was—and remains—exciting because it challenges the standard conception of episodic memory as a distinct capacity for faithfully resurrecting past events. There is now extensive research on the neural overlap between memory, imagination, and other forms of self-projective thinking, which recruit the same 'core network', including the medial temporal lobes, hippocampus, retrosplenial cortex, medial prefrontal cortex, and the inferior parietal lobule (Addis, Wong, & Schacter 2007; Schacter et al. 2015; Szpunar, Watson, & McDermott 2007).

These findings serve as the motivation for the *Constructive Episodic Simulation Hypothesis* (CESH), which has quickly become one of the most influential accounts of episodic memory. The account is novel because it breaks with the traditional focus on episodic memory as a distinct neurocognitive capacity focused on representing the past.

The CESH has three central claims.

1. *What it is.* Humans possess a single neurocognitive system for the purposes of constructive episodic simulation (CES). The system includes information acquired from past events that is stored in the memory system, and various simulation processes that act on this stored information. Information storage in the CES system is organised so as to facilitate this constructive process—i.e., information from particular past events is stored in a distributed manner that allows, and even encourages, flexible recombination of event details across simulations.

2. *How it works.* In simulations, the CES constructs representations by flexibly retrieving and recombining the event information in its memory system. The types of simulations involve remembering, imagining, counterfactual reasoning, and future planning. The constructed representations are episodically framed events (i.e., from a first-person, autonoetic perspective). These representations can be directed toward the past or the future, as well as to counterfactual and hypothetical scenarios.

3. *What it's good for.* The flexible nature of information storage in the CES system is beneficial for imagining, and for combining event details in novel ways so as to think about the future or counterfactual and hypothetical scenarios. The flexible storage is detrimental for one of the constructive activities—remembering the past—and so can result in errors in these cases. Overall, however, the CES system is adaptive.

These features of how the CES is organised and operated are meant to provide the warrant for thinking of episodic memory as having a prospective function. To see how this is meant to work, we must first explore the sense of function at issue and then how this function becomes future-focused. The next two subsections take up these inquiries.

8.2.1 How do CESH theorists understand function?

When CESH proponents talk about the function of episodic memory and other forms of simulation, what sense of function do they have in mind? CESH theorists themselves do not provide an answer. More generally, philosophers of memory have not engaged much with the extensive literature on functions in the philosophy of biology and philosophy of science.[1] Discussion of biological functions has generated two broad classes of functions: etiological and causal-role functions (Garson 2016). Most philosophers of biology are *pluralists* about these functions—i.e., they think each has a role to play in the biological sciences. Since there are multiple, viable accounts of biological function available, it is important to determine which the CESH is committed to, as each has distinct requirements and implications. My aim here is not to pair CESH with a particular account of function—that would require more space than is available in the present chapter. Instead, my aim is to situate the CESH with respect to the general divide between two broad categories of biological function.

Accounts of function focus on a specific trait, property, or characteristic. Etiological functions seek to explain the existence of the trait: *Why* does it exist? Etiological accounts thus appeal to teleology, selected effects, or fitness in order to answer the question. Causal-role accounts, in contrast, seek to explain the trait's role in the overall system in which it is currently embedded: *How* does the trait work? These accounts identify the trait's functional role and, depending on the particular account, may also include particular mechanistic (neural or biological) details. Which account of function one uses will depend on the trait in question and the methods and resources available and of interest to the researcher. In principle, however, both functional accounts could be given for any trait. Take, for example, the topographic organisation of the visual cortex—the part of the brain responsible for processing visual information that is structured so that adjacent parts of the cortex represent adjacent parts of the visual field (e.g., Wandell, Dumoulin, & Brewer 2007). We could ask about its etiological function—why does this organisational structure exist? An answer here would be given in terms of selective advantages of this trait, or its emergence as a by-product of some other trait, etc. We can also ask about its causal-role function—that is, how this organisation of the visual cortex influences the nature of processing in the visual system and cognition more broadly.

Given the choice between etiological and causal-role approaches to function, at first glance it appears that CESH is best understood as an etiological account of episodic memory's function. One of the central claims of CESH, as outlined earlier, involves consideration of the overall adaptiveness of this system, suggesting attention to questions of *why* this trait exists. Closer inspection, however, reveals that the sense of 'adaptive' at use in CESH is distinct from use of the term in evolutionary contexts. For CESH theorists, 'adaptive' is meant to characterise 'beneficial characteristics of an organism' (Schacter 2012, p. 604). CESH theorists connect use and enhancement of CES to decision-making, emotional regulation, and spatial navigation (Schacter, Benoit, & Szpunar 2017). Increasing the amount of constructive episodic simulation a person engages in is thought to help with a range of cognitive processes. Discovering that some of these roles confer benefits on the individual is interesting, but it is not an account of etiological function, where benefits are more narrowly construed in terms of selective and reproductive advantage.

Instead of considering the selective advantages of episodic simulation, CESH theorists are investigating the scope of this system, how it works, and what role it plays in our cognitive processing more generally. They are, in short, offering an account of the causal-role function of the CES system. Explorations of how the system is adaptive are part of this broader investigation of how CES works. In pursuing these possible benefits, however, CESH theorists should proceed with caution. Whether a cognitive process confers benefits on the individual is a separate question from what the cognitive process *is*. Identifying benefits of episodic simulation can provide an indication of the other cognitive processes to which CES is connected, but there is no general adaptive constraint on causal-role functions as there is for etiological ones. Going forward, all references to the function of episodic memory and the CES should be read as causal-role functions.

8.2.2 *How does CESH make episodic memory future-focused?*

CESH theorists characterise episodic memory, and its function, in terms of the broader CES system in which it is embedded. The function of episodic memory just is the function of the CES system —or at the very least, the function of episodic memory is parasitic on the function of the CES system. There are two key steps in the argument via which CESH theorists establish the prospective function of episodic memory and the CES.

First, CESH theorists defend the claim that all forms of episodic simulation are the same—they are particular expressions of one general ability (to construct episodically framed event representations). As Addis (2018) puts the point, 'memories are not special or different than imaginings; both are complex, multimodal event representations constructed via the integration of schema and informational elements stored in content-specific areas of the cortex' (p. 66). Forms of episodic simulation may differ in the tense assigned to the constructive representation that is generated: It may be represented as from the past, about the future, or as hypothetical or counterfactual. Aside from this tense assignment, the underlying process is the same. Episodic remembering is essentially the same activity as episodic imagining. All forms of episodic simulation can be understood in terms of a single function.

Second, in order for this primary function of the CES to be *for the future*, the CESH theorist needs episodic imagination/future thinking, rather than episodic remembering, to be the primary or central activity of the episodic memory system. CESH theorists are not particularly explicit about how they defend this claim. The defence comes, presumably, from a survey of the various forms of episodic simulation and an assessment of which forms are most reliable—i.e., generate the fewest errors. Here, episodic remembering and its tendency toward false memory fares poorly. Episodic imagination is comparatively stronger, and the benefits of simulating future events for other cognitive activities (Schacter, Benoit, & Szpunar 2017) offer reason for thinking of this as the primary activity of CES.

For the purposes of this chapter, my focus is on the first move in this argument: collapsing episodic imagining and episodic remembering into two instantiations of the same general cognitive operation. This equivalence grounds the claim that CES has a particular function, which is then articulated as a *prospective* one. CESH theorists have long defended the similarity of episodic remembering and episodic imagining. In a recent set of papers, Addis (2018, 2020) strengthens the claim, arguing for their equivalence. In the next section, I ask whether Addis's account can support the claim that episodic remembering and episodic imagining are the same cognitive activity.

8.3 Addis's (2020) criteria for episodic remembering and imagining

In this section, I ask whether episodic remembering and episodic imagining should be considered the same cognitive process, as CESH proponents propose in an effort to establish the claim that episodic memory's function is prospective. In a series of recent papers, Addis (2018, 2020) advocates for a strong reading of the CESH, according to which episodic memory and episodic imagination are the same neurocognitive process. Specifically, she claims that episodic remembering and episodic imagining are:

1. Subserved by the same brain system,
2. Act on the same information, and
3. Are governed by the same rules of operation (2020: p. 1).

I discuss each criterion in a distinct subsection in what follows, evaluating their relevance for determining the causal-role function of episodic memory. I argue that our focus should be on the third—being governed by the same rules of operation.

8.3.1 Same brain system

The first criterion is the one that initiated interest in the CESH—the finding that episodic remembering and episodic imagining rely on the same brain system. Neuroimaging evidence accumulated over the past decade and a half makes clear that there is significant overlap in the brain regions that are recruited when participants are asked to remember past events and when they are asked to imagine future ones. It's worth noting that the vast majority of these studies show *overlap* in the brain regions involved in these two activities, but for the purposes of this chapter, I am happy to accept the stronger claim that episodic remembering and episodic imagining are subserved by the same brain system. What I want to question is whether this is enough to ground a claim of shared function. As I will argue here, there are a number of reasons to be sceptical of that claim.

To start, a general point: Sharing a brain system is not sufficient for sharing a function. There are myriad instances of biological and cognitive functions sharing an underlying mechanism, even a brain region, when such inference is not warranted. Our sensory capacities of smell and taste, for example, are both based in chemoreception, but that does not establish a shared function between the gustatory and olfactory systems. Language processing and musical appreciation also rely on the same brain regions but are recognisably distinct functions (Peretz et al. 2015; for an extended argument on this point, see Robins & Schulz, 2022). Moreover, many philosophers and neuroscientists now advocate for an understanding of neural systems as *multifunctional* (Anderson 2015; McCaffrey 2015). If a shared function is to be found across brain systems, many neuroscientists now think that figuring out what it is will require a massive overhaul of our cognitive ontology (e.g., Price & Friston 2005; Poldrack et al. 2009).

CESH theorists are not claiming that sharing a brain system is sufficient for uniting the various forms of episodic simulation as a single function. The view does have its origins, however, in the discovery of their neural overlap (as discussed in Schacter 2019). How far can this identified brain system take us in understanding the function of episodic simulation? The brain system by which episodic remembering and episodic imagining are both subserved is the *Default Mode Network*, or DMN. As a recognised brain system, the DMN is a relative newcomer. The first paper suggesting its existence was in 1997 (Schulman et al. 1997). The DMN has, however, quickly become one of the most extensively investigated brain systems. As of 2015, more than 3,000 papers had been published about the DMN (Raichle 2015). This is in part because the DMN is large and somewhat diffuse. It has distinct subsystems, each of which has a somewhat distinct functional characterisation. As Raichle (2015) expresses:

> data from humans suggest that the default mode network instantiates processes that support emotional processing (VMPC), self-referential mental activity (DMPC), and the recollection of prior experiences (posterior elements of the default mode network). These functional elements of the default mode network can be differentially affected during task performance by the nature of the task.
>
> (p. 440)

Each of these subsystems has a broad functional characterisation, subsuming several cognitive abilities and activities. Even the posterior subsystem associated with episodic remembering and episodic imagining is also associated with story comprehension and mind-wandering (Buckner et al. 2008). To arrive at a functional characterisation that encompasses all of these activities, even of a DMN subsystem, is quite difficult. The shared structure may indicate similarities in function, but they fall far short of establishing that this range of cognitive activities as sharing a single, well-defined function.

8.3.2 Same information base

Addis's second criterion for treating episodic remembering and episodic imagining as fundamentally the same is that they act on the same information. As she elaborates, both activities 'draw on elements of experience from fine-grained perceptual details to coarser-grained conceptual information and schemas about the world' (Addis 2020).

As with the previous criterion, I do not wish to dispute the claim that episodic remembering and episodic imagining may be the same in this regard. Instead, I want to question whether this sameness is enough to warrant considering these two activities as having a shared function, or being the same neurocognitive process. It seems relatively straightforward to assume that remembering the personal past and imagining a possible personal future make use of the same information. If I want to think about what I might be doing at this time of the year a few years in the future, my thoughts about that possible future will likely be derived from my detailed knowledge of how events in my life (particularly during this time of year) have gone before, updated so as to reflect how they might be combined and reconfigured in the future. In fact, it is unclear what the alternative hypothesis would be. Where would the components of our thoughts about future events come from, if not from past event information?

The use of the same informational base in both episodic remembering and episodic imagining is especially unsurprising in the experimental contexts where CESH is investigated. In these studies, researchers are comparing the brain areas active during remembering and imagining. To do so effectively, experiments are designed to hold as many other features of the two tasks constant as possible. Participants are generally instructed to generate mental representations with a particular structure, differing only in whether they are directed at the past or the future. Take, for example, one of the original studies exploring the CESH: Addis, Wong, and Schacter (2007). In this study, participants were given a set of cue words (e.g., *dress, yellow, star*), which they would use to generate event representations. They were instructed to make the representations temporally and contextually specific (i.e., occurring in a particular place at a particular time). In response to the presentation of a cue, participants were instructed to either 'recall a past event' or 'envisage a future event'. They were also given a time frame: either recent (within a year) or remote (5–20 years in the past or in the future). In response to *yellow*, for example, a participant engaged in recent remembering might generate a representation of visiting a sunflower field last fall. A participant who received the same cue, but was instructed to imagine a remote future, might imagine buying a yellow house a decade from now.

The point can be put more broadly: There are many cases where two cognitive activities make use of the same information and yet remain importantly distinct functions. Balancing one's chequebook and estimating the number of people attending a rally both involve numerical representations and addition. Writing a poem and transcribing a city council meeting involve linguistic representations and spelling. Sharing an information base does not interestingly contribute to making two cognitive activities the same.

8.3.3 Same cognitive operation

I have argued that the first two of Addis's proposed criteria are not particularly useful for establishing that episodic remembering and episodic imagining are the same cognitive process. One criterion remains: That these two activities are governed by the same rules of operation. According to Addis, 'both are complex, multi-modal event representations constructed via the integration of schema and informational elements stored in content-specific areas of the cortex' (2020).

Unlike the previous two criteria, this one seems particularly well suited to considerations of function, as it is focused on the operative processes of both episodic remembering and episodic imagining. These processes are, or at least directly inform, the causal-role function. Determining whether they are in fact the same process is critical for determining whether episodic remembering and episodic imagination have the same function.

What is the shared operation? CESH claims that both of these activities are constructive: They involve the retrieval of event details from episodic memory, which are then built into representations of episodically framed events.[2] These event representations may be directed toward the past or the future, but the addition of tense is a mere add-on to what is, essentially, the same constructive operation. If this can be established, then episodic remembering and episodic imagination will have been shown to have the same causal-role function.

8.4 Episodic remembering and episodic imagining as associative networks

In the previous section, a shared constructive operation was identified as the feature that must be shared by episodic remembering and episodic imagining if they are to be considered to share a function. Addis (2020) defends the sameness of episodic remembering and imagining on these grounds, proposing that their shared cognitive operation is spreading activation across associationist networks. Here I evaluate that proposal, illustrating how associationism fails to capture the operation of either episodic remembering or episodic imagination.

Associationist networks are representations of connected elements of semantic information (e.g., Bechtel & Abrahamsen 2002; Plaut 1995). In such networks, each node is semantically evaluable (i.e., meaningful) and the connections between nodes indicate connections between semantic elements.[3] The stronger the connection, the stronger the semantic relation. Information acquired as the result of a particular event is distributed throughout the network, as a particular pattern of associations between the nodes corresponding to its semantic elements. A person's network might thus have nodes for items like beach, sand, water, bathing suit, and sunglasses, as well as nodes for individual friends and family members, etc. In such networks, the nodes are connected in ways that reflect the associations between the information designated by each node. The nodes for beach and sand, for example, are likely to be well connected (or at least, better connected than the nodes for sand and library). Each node, then, has an activation level, or strength, reflecting how often and how recently the subject has encountered the corresponding idea.

When a node in the network is activated—for example, as a result of the presentation of a cue—the activity spreads from this node to other nodes with which it is connected. The amount and direction of spread will depend on the underlying activation level of that node, the number of other nodes to which it is connected, and the strength of those connections. As with the activation level of any individual node, the strength of the connections between nodes is a combined function of recency and frequency. Nodes that have activated together often and/or recently will be more strongly connected than those that have not. If a node has a strong activation level and a series of weak connections to many other nodes, its activation will likely be sufficient to activate all of them. In contrast, a node with a weaker activation level, and connections to a few other nodes, where one is more strongly connected than the others, will likely, upon activation, only spread activation to the well-connected node. The set of nodes that become activated in response to a cue provide the elements that can be combined in the constructive act of forming a mental representation.

Addis (2018, 2020) views these associative networks as active in episodic simulation at multiple levels. These networks govern the operations 'between elements, within and between schemas, and between schemas and the emergent simulation' (p. 11). That is, all simulations involve combining event elements and schemas to produce an episodically framed event representation. This occurs in both episodic remembering and episodic imagining. Consider how this would work in Addis et al.' (2007) experiment discussed earlier. Participants are given a cue like *star* or *dress*, as well as instructions on the type of simulation to produce (remembering or imagining, recent or remote). This cue activates the corresponding node in their semantic network, and then participants search between the other nodes that are activated by its spread to construct a representation that meets the requested specifications.

Addis's account picks up on an important element of cognitive processing: Associative strength is a critical feature of many activities, including remembering and imagining. However, associative strength fails to capture the full and distinctive operations of either cognitive activity under consideration here and thus fails to provide the basis for their united function. In the case of episodic remembering, associative strength is too weak to account for how representations are generated. In the case of episodic imagination, episodic simulation is too strong.

Associative strength has a clear influence on remembering. When trying to recall past events, details that are associatively linked are easier to recall than those that are not. Similarly, when errors occur in this process, as in cases of misremembering, the errors often reflect substitutions that favour associative connections (Gallo 2006). That is, when I remember a past event, and some detail of that event is wrong, in many cases the error involves incorporating a similar and more familiar feature instead. Given their role in remembering, CESH theorists have long been suggesting that the entirety of remembering be accounted for in terms of associative processes. I have argued at length against this approach in previous work (Robins 2016b), which I will summarise here. Associations explain remembering (and its errors) in cases where the representation generated includes details that cohere with the two basic principles of spreading activation: what was encountered most recently and what is encountered most frequently. Many memories fit with these principles, but not all. At least sometimes, we remember events from the remote past, even when features of those events have been more recently and more frequently associated with other events. Put another way, associationist accounts predict that anomalous event features would wash out of network connections over time, as the connections between more frequently co-occurring details are strengthened. This makes clear predictions about the kinds of events we should remember, and not. Unfortunately, the evidence about how and what we remember does not fit with this prediction. Associationist networks are too weak to account for the operation of episodic remembering.

In the case of episodic imagining, associationist networks face the opposite problem: They explain too much. What appeared an advantage earlier—namely, the ability of associationist networks to predict how spreading activation will occur within a cognitive system, and so which representations will be generated—constrains imagination in ways that fail to reflect our understanding of this cognitive faculty. Patterns of spreading activation predetermine and regularise which representations and schemas will be activated and when. Imagination, particularly when considering hypotheticals, counterfactuals, and the future, needs to release or suppress many of these associations. Again, this is not to say that there is no role for associations in imagination. Associations may play a key role in activating elements and schemas for consideration. But the activity of combining them into a plausible and interesting representation that suits one's purposes is what makes the activity imagination—and to do this requires going far beyond what is most recent or most frequent via spreading activation. In short, associative networks seek to explain too much about imagination. Using them to account for the cognitive operation underlying episodic imagination would run afoul not only of how we standardly think about imagination, but also the steady stream of results supported and often touted by CESH theorists that point to the connections between episodic imagining, creativity, and divergent thinking (e.g., Addis, Pan, Musicaro, & Schacter 2016).

There are ways of developing associationist models to allow for more sophisticated relations beyond brute frequency and recency.[4] It is thus possible that a revised version of associationism could address these issues in capturing the nature of episodic remembering and imagining. The burden for showing this can be done is on Addis and other proponents of the CESH. And, given that the explanatory demands for remembering and imagining pull in opposite directions, there is reason to be sceptical that a single unifying revision could be found.

8.5 Episodic remembering and episodic imagining are distinct forms of construction

Even if Addis's (2020) proposal for the cognitive operation underlying episodic remembering and imagining fails, as I argued in the previous section, CESH theorists may continue to claim that they are the same and go looking for an alternative way of characterising their shared cognitive activity. CESH theorists are committed to the claim that episodic remembering and episodic imagining must be the same cognitive activity because they are both constructive processes. In what follows, I allow that both remembering and imagining are constructive, while denying that they are constructive in the same way (and so deny that they are the same process). There are important, fundamental differences in the kind of constructive processes involved in episodic remembering and episodic imagining.

In a recent paper (Robins 2020), I proposed that remembering and imagining should be treated as distinct psychological attitudes.[5] My intention was to draw a parallel with the more familiar propositional attitudes. Belief and desire are both mental attitudes toward propositional contents, and also understood as distinct. So too for remembering and imagining, although the contents of remembering and imagining are unlikely to be propositional. As orientations toward mental content, there are differences in the feel and function of each attitude. The activities of remembering and imagining feel different to people when they're engaged in them. Here I do not intend a strong claim about the phenomenology of either, only that people can easily recognise which attitude they are taking (remembering or imagining) and tell the difference between them. This can happen even if the content is the same—a person can remember eating lunch last Tuesday or imagine eating lunch last Tuesday.

In that paper (Robins 2020), I argued further that CESH theorists agree with me on this difference between episodic remembering and episodic imagining, at least implicitly. The experiments used to test CESH, like the Addis, Wong, and Schacter (2007) paper, instruct participants to engage in remembering in some conditions and imagining in others. These are treated as distinct experimental conditions and are analysed as independent variables in the subsequent statistical analyses. CESH theorists find, as they did in the Addis et al. (2007) paper, that the neural regions activated by these activities are the same (or highly overlapping, at least), but the activities themselves are treated as distinct.

My aim here is to build on this basic distinction between episodic remembering and episodic imagining, offering further grounds for differentiating between them in terms of the kinds of construction that they involve. Characterisations of construction, amongst CESH theorists but also memory theorists more broadly, are underspecified. Most theorists have devoted their energy to the contrast between construction and other, more preservative accounts of remembering. Memory is not simply retrieving well-preserved items from the mind's storage, most theorists insist; remembering is *constructive*. What constructive means, beyond the assembly of event details at the time of retrieval, is left unsaid.

In what follows, I am happy to accept this basic characterisation of construction, and further, to accept that both episodic remembering and episodic imagining are constructive in this sense. Even if so, there is room to differentiate between them and identify them as distinct forms of construction. As a significant step in this direction, I identify three features of the constructive process that differ across episodic remembering and episodic imagining: (1) awareness, (2) control, and (3) response to error.

When comparing these forms of construction, it is helpful to have clear examples in mind. To this end, it is incredibly helpful that one of the CESH papers, from Addis and colleagues' article (2007), provides participant examples in the appendix:[6]

Past event (5 years ago; cue = star)

> It was my birthday and I was about to leave for a trip with my family … And so my friend, he has just gotten his license, and he said, okay, you know, I'll take you out for your birthday before you leave … so we went to this place in Berkeley … famous for its deep dish pizzas. He had just gotten his license, I'm kind of oblivious [of this] … so when I got in the car I immediately started talking to him, and he's, um, okay I can't talk right now … We had the pizza and he took me to this place called Indian Rock in Berkeley and it was a very interesting place, and I had always heard of it but you need a car to get there, so perfect timing, so we walked up with the pizzas and it's this big rock on the top of this kind of hill at Berkeley. And when you're up at the top you can see the whole bay and you can see San Francisco … the view was gorgeous, and the sun was setting.

Future event (in 5 years; cue = dress)

> My sister will be finishing … her undergraduate education, I imagine some neat place, Ivy league private school … it would be a very nice spring day and my mom and my dad will be there, my dad with the camcorder as usual, and my mom with the camera as usual. My sister will be in the crowd and they'd be calling everyone's name … I can see her having a different hair style by then, maybe instead of straight, very curly with lots of volume. She would be wearing contacts by then and heels of course. And I can see

myself sitting in some kind of sundress, like yellow, and under some trees … the reception either before or after and it would be really nice summer food, like salads and fruits, and maybe some sweets, and cold drinks that are chilled but have no ice. And my sister would be sitting off with her friends, you know, talking with them about graduating, and they'd probably get emotional.

8.5.1 Awareness of construction

Episodic remembering and episodic imagining may both be constructive, but episodic imagining is transparently so while episodic remembering is not. The everyday person is aware of the constructive aspects of imagining; they are not similarly aware of the constructive aspects of remembering. That is, while engaged in the activity of episodically imagining, I may often experience the activity as mental assembly, building a representation from disparate event details. It seems like this may be what's going on in the future event case reported from the Addis et al. (2007) study, where the participant visualises what their sister will look like at her graduation ceremony. The participant updates various aspects of their image of the sister bit by bit—first her hair, then her glasses, and then her shoes and clothes. The combination of these representational features is transparent to the participant; they seem to be cognisant of the way in which each is added to the imagined scene.

The reported memory event is importantly different in this regard. The representation in this case may be equally as constructive, cobbled together at the time of retrieval. This construction does not appear to be apparent to the participant; at the very least, there is nothing constructive in the event description as given. This fits with the experience of remembering more broadly. It would likely take a person by surprise to learn that the act of remembering, which feels like retrieval, actually comes about in a very different way. The disconnect between how remembering feels versus what the process is actually like is part of why the findings from the psychology of memory have been so startling to many and so extensively discussed.[7] For those of us who do research in this area, it is easy to take these features of remembering as obvious and apparent, forgetting that in the act of remembering, they are not.

8.5.2 Control over construction

A second feature over which episodic remembering and episodic imagining differ concerns whether and how the person has control over each constructive process. Episodic imagination is under a form of direct cognitive control. A person who is episodically imagining a future event may not have full control over which event details or possibilities come to mind, but they do have control over which are selected and then incorporated into the event representation.[8] The participant in the Addis et al. (2007) study may have considered multiple ways that their sister's appearance would change in five years. They may have considered the sister's hair being both longer and shorter before deciding upon a representation of it as curly.

Episodic remembering, in contrast, is not similarly controlled. The person who is remembering a past event does not consider multiple ways the past event might have gone and then select amongst them to establish what happened. At least, this is not what happens at the level of awareness. It is possible that, subpersonally, this kind of activity is taking place. Without awareness of it, however, there is no opportunity for intervening in and controlling such a process. In this way, this feature of episodic construction is importantly connected to the previous.

Remembering does allow some opportunities for indirect control. If I am having difficulty calling an event to mind, I can engage in additional cue elaboration, or use peripheral details and semantic knowledge to help bring the desired information to mind. What's important for my purposes here is that the activity of doing this feels like promoting one's search for a particular event representation. It does not feel like the process of generating a range of options, between which one can select to form a memory. To put the point another way, in the case of episodic imagining it would make sense to ask the participant, '*Why did you include detail X?*' In the case of episodic remembering, such a question makes far less sense.

8.5.3 Response to error discovery

The third difference I want to highlight between episodic construction in the case of remembering and imagining concerns how the constructive process is viewed by the person who generated it after learning that the representation contained an error—i.e., involved a component that did not correspond to how the event actually occurred. Both episodic remembering and episodic imagining could contain such errors, although in the case of imagining it's more difficult to characterise them as erroneous, since they were generated prior to the event. Still, both forms of construction could be involved in cases where a person is required to confront a discrepancy between their representation and the represented event.

In episodic imagining, this could happen in a few distinct ways. First, the event could happen, and happen differently from how it was envisioned. Suppose the little sister, in the earlier example, decided upon an art institute rather than an Ivy League university. The person may note and reflect on the difference between what they expected would happen and what actually occurred, and they may even go so far as to identify flaws in the assumptions that they used to construct the representation of the event (e.g., attending too much to how their parents characterised the sister's ambitions, not attending enough to her love of drawing and painting). Second, a person could recognise an error in their construction of the future event even before it happens. The person could, for example, spend more time with their sister and come to recognise that the sister is far more attached to her glasses than they'd previously realised, or far too squeamish about touching her eyes to ever transition to contacts. In either case, it seems possible for the person to maintain the initial event representation as an imagined account of the event. The status and assessment of that representation are not threatened by their disconnect with the event itself.[9] In short, discovery of an error in the process of episodic imagining does not diminish or alter the status of the event representation that was generated.

Conditions are quite different in the case of episodic remembering. Episodic remembering also contains errors. Researchers debate how often and how significant such errors are, but even without empirical studies of the phenomenon, we are all aware of at least occasional discrepancies between our memories of particular past events and what actually transpired. Suppose there was an error in the memory representation reported in the Addis et al. (2007) study. Maybe the participant who reported getting pizza with a friend on their birthday was mistaken about some of the event's details—maybe they had sushi, not pizza, or sat on the opposite side of the bay, or maybe it was the friend's birthday, not theirs. Any such discovery (provided by conflicting testimony, photo or video evidence, etc.) would diminish the status of the representation *as an episodic memory*. The person would no longer endorse their report as a representation of the event. The person could hang on to the representation, and the feeling of remembering it generates, while denying the representation has the status that was previously presumed. In so doing, they might say something like, 'Wow, I really felt like I remembered us eating pizza. But I guess it was sushi.' Alternatively, the person might edit the representation to fit the details they now know were actually a part of the event. Doing so would be an instance of actively controlled, consciously aware construction. But, importantly, doing so would also mean that the person no longer treats the representation as a memory.

This is only a sketch; far more attention to the nature and details of these constructive processes is needed before we can determine whether the differences between these forms of episodic construction are as strong as I have suggested. My aim has been to describe and elaborate on three features on which the constructive processes of episodic remembering and episodic imagining differ from one another, even if both processes involve assembling event details to form episodically framed representations. In doing so, I am inspired in part by a similar distinction that has been drawn between forms of non-episodic imagination—i.e., the constructive formation of mental images, but without the episodic perspective. This form of constructive imagining can happen voluntarily. I can, for example, imagine a polar bear that has webbed feet and pointed ears. This form of imagining also occurs in non-voluntary contexts; most notably, while one is dreaming. Both of these activities are properly described as constructive imagining.[10] Both involve building a mental image from various object details. Researchers have recently noted, however, that these are importantly distinct forms of constructive imagining. This is best documented by the observation that damage to particular brain areas impedes the ability to engage in voluntary constructive imagining, but leaves constructive imagining during dreaming intact (Vyshedsky 2019). The two are both constructive processes, but importantly distinct ones.

8.6 Conclusion: What is the function of episodic memory?

CESH theorists are engaged in a research program that claims to have 'redefined the function of episodic memory as primarily future-focused' (Addis 2018, p. 65). This revision to our understanding of episodic memory, casting its function as prospective rather than retrospective, relies on treating all forms of episodic construction as essentially the same. That is, CESH theorists are committed to the existence of a single cognitive process—episodic simulation—by which event details are selected and assembled into episodically framed event representations.

In this chapter, I challenged the claim that all forms of episodic construction are effectively equivalent. Episodic remembering and episodic imagining differ not only in the tense assigned to the constructed representation, a difference CESH theorists acknowledge, but in three further, substantial ways. This is true, I suggest, even if we allow that they are both supported by the same brain system and draw upon the same mental reserve of information. Going further, I argued that episodic remembering and episodic imagining are importantly different *even if* they are both constructive processes.

The failure to unite these forms of episodic simulation as a single cognitive activity undercuts the claim that episodic memory's function has been redefined. The lack of an argument in favour of episodic memory's prospective function is not yet a defence of the traditional, retrospective account (see Boyle 2019 on this point). It is, instead, an incentive to continue exploring the full range of possible ways episodic memory's causal-role function could be understood.

CESH theorists may wish to revisit the distinction between accounts of function in Section 8.2, and renew their interest in the etiological function of episodic memory. Many of the concerns raised by CESH theorists suggest an interest in this, as researchers often ask, '*Why does episodic memory have the organisational structure that it does?*' This is an interesting and important question, and one on which CESH theorists and others can make more substantial progress once the standards for each form of function are better understood. Questions about evolutionary function are difficult, because they cannot always be answered as posed. That is, there might not be a reason that episodic memory has the structure that it does. Episodic memory could be a by-product of some other adaptive process—or an exaptation, or a spandrel. Pursuit of the full range of options will require transcending concerns about and features of our current human psychology and neural organisation, turning instead to consideration of what previous form these features may have taken and how prior environments may have differed from our present circumstances. Such work could yield a prospective account of episodic memory function, but episodic memory's role in the here and now remains an open question.

Notes

1 Schwartz (2020) is a notable exception.
2 Thinking of episodic remembering and episodic imagining as two forms of constructive imagination finds support beyond CESH (see Michaelian, Perrin, & Sant'Anna (2020) for a summary). Recently, Peter Langland-Hassan (2020) has argued that the sense of imagination that could best serve to unite episodic remembering and episodic imagining is constructive imagination. Ultimately, Langland-Hassan is sceptical that such an account will be successful, but the claim does find resonance with a broader class of theorists who wish to defend *continuism* between remembering and imagining.
3 For a discussion of semantically evaluable distributed networks in memory, see Robins (2016a).
4 I'm grateful to an anonymous reviewer for raising this point.
5 Technically, Robins (2020) focused on the state of *seeming to remember*—a state meant to be broad enough to catch both successful and unsuccessful cases. CESH theorists are not operating with a factive view of remembering. Their account of episodic remembering involves both successful and unsuccessful attempts. My use of 'seeming to remember' in that paper and the use of 'episodic remembering' by CESH theorists are similar enough for present purposes, so I'm framing my account in terms of CESH views here.
6 Later papers in the CESH framework follow a similar experimental design, but do not often include an appendix of participant reports.
7 Episodic remembering can be piecemeal. A person may assemble event details slowly as they're recalled. This may count, in a loose sense, as awareness of construction. But the sense of construction here is still quite different than that of episodic imagining. The distinction is akin to two ways one might build a house out of LEGO: by following the instructions in a kit and by using a non-curated pile of pieces to build one from scratch. Remembering is like the first, imagining like the second. Thanks to an anonymous reviewer for suggesting this kind of case.
8 Exactly how much control an individual has over their imagination is an open and interesting empirical question. However much it turns out to be, it seems safe to maintain that it's more control than exists in remembering.
9 As an anonymous reviewer has rightly noted, the plausibility of this claim depends on what the nature of imagining turns out to be, and whether there is a distinct form of imagination that is actuality-oriented along the lines suggested by Munro (2021).
10 Amongst philosophers, there is an active debate over whether dreaming involves imagination or perception (see Ichikawa (2009) for a defence of dreaming as imagination). In empirical work on the visual system, however, the term *constructive imagining* is often used to refer to the activity of both (e.g., Vyshedsky, 2019).

References

Addis, D. R. (2018). Are episodic memories special? On the sameness of remembered and imagined event simulation. *Journal of the Royal Society of New Zealand*, *48*, 64–88.

Addis, D. R. (2020). Mental time travel? A neurocognitive model of event simulation. *Review of Philosophy and Psychology*, *11*, 233–259.

Addis, D. R., Pan, L., Musicaro, R., & Schacter, D. L. (2016). Divergent thinking and constructing episodic simulations. *Memory*, *24*, 89–97.

Addis, D. R., Wong, A. T., & Schacter, D. L. (2007). Remembering the past and imagining the future: common and distinct neural substrates during event construction and elaboration. *Neuropsychologia*, *45*, 1363–1377.

Anderson, M. L. (2015). *After Phrenology: Neural Reuse and the Interactive Brain.* MIT Press.

Areas to watch: Breakthrough of the year. (2007, 21 December). *Science, 318,* 1848–1849.

Bechtel, W., & Abrahamsen, A. (2002). *Connectionism and the Mind: An Introduction to Parallel Processing in Networks* (2nd ed.). Basil Blackwell.

Boyle, A. (2019). Learning from the past: epistemic generativity and the function of episodic memory. *Journal of Consciousness Studies, 26*(5-6), 242–251.

Buckner, R. L., Andrews-Hanna, J. R., & Schacter, D. L. (2008). The brain's default network: anatomy, function, and relevance to disease. *Annals of the New York Academy of Sciences, 1124*(1), 1–38.

Gallo, D. A. (2006). *Associative Illusions of Memory: False Memory Research in DRM and Related Tasks.* Taylor & Francis Group.

Garson, J. (2016). *A Critical Overview of Biological Functions.* Springer.

Ichikawa, J. (2009). Dreaming and imagination. *Mind and Language,* 24, 103–121.

Langland-Hassan, P. (2020). What sort of imagining might remembering be? *Journal of the American Philosophical Association, 7*(2), 231–251.

McCaffrey, J. (2015) The brain's heterogeneous functional landscape, *Philosophy of Science, 82*(5), 1010–1022.

Michaelian, K., Perrin, P., & Sant'Anna, A. (2020). Continuities and discontinuities between imagination and memory: the view from philosophy. In A. Abraham (Ed.), *The Cambridge Handbook of the Imagination.* Cambridge University Press.

Munro, D. (2021). Remembering the past and imagining the actual. *Review of Philosophy and Psychology, 12,* 175–197.

Peretz, I., Vuvan, D., Lagrois, M.-É., & Armony, J. L. (2015). Neural overlap in processing music and speech. *Philosophical Transactions of the Royal Society London B, Biological Sciences, 370*(1664), 20140090.

Plaut, D. C. (1995). Semantic and associative priming in a distributed attractor network. *Proceedings of the 17th Annual Conference of the Cognitive Science Society* (pp. 37–42). Lawrence Erlbaum Associates.

Poldrack, R. A., Halchenko, Y., & Hanson, S. J. (2009). Decoding the large-scale structure of brain function by classifying mental states across individuals. *Psychological Science, 20,* 1364–1372.

Price, C. J., & Friston, K. J. (2005). Functional ontologies for cognition: The systematic definition of structure and function. *Cognitive Neuropsychology, 22,* 262–275.

Raichle, M. E. (2015). The brain's default mode network. *Annual Review of Neuroscience, 8,* 433–447.

Robins, S. K. (2016a). Representing the past: Memory traces and the causal theory of memory. *Philosophical Studies, 173,* 2993–3013.

Robins, S. K. (2016b). Misremembering. *Philosophical Psychology, 29,* 432–447.

Robins, S. K. (2020). Defending discontinuism, naturally. *Review of Philosophy and Psychology, 11*(2), 469–486.

Robins, S. K., & Schulz, A. (2022). *Episodic memory, simulated future planning, and their evolution. Review of Philosophy and Psychology.* https://doi.org/10.1007/s13164-021-00601-1

Schacter, D. L. (2012). Adaptive constructive processes and the future of memory. *American Psychologist, 67,* 603–613.

Schacter, D. L. (2019). Implicit memory, constructive memory, and imagining the future: A career perspective. *Perspectives on Psychological Science, 14,* 256–272.

Schacter, D. L., & Addis, D. R. (2007). On the constructive episodic simulation of past and future events. *Behavioral & Brain Sciences, 30,* 299–351.

Schacter, D. L., Benoit, R.G., De Brigard, F., & Szpunar, K.K. (2015). Episodic future thinking and episodic counterfactual thinking: Intersections between memory and decisions. *Neurobiology of Learning and Memory, 117,* 14–21.

Schacter, D. L., Benoit, R. G., & Szpunar, K. K. (2017). Episodic future thinking: Mechanisms and functions. *Current Opinion in Behavioral Sciences, 17,* 41–50.

Schwartz, A. (2020) Simulationism and the function(s) of episodic memory. *Review of Philosophy and Psychology, 11,* 487–505.

Shulman, G. L., Fiez, J. A., Corbetta, M., Buckner, R. L., Miezin, F. M., Raichle, M. E., & Petersen, S. E. (1997). Common blood flow changes across visual tasks: 2. Decreases in cerebral cortex. *Journal of Cognitive Neuroscience, 9,* 648–663.

Szpunar, K. K., Watson, J. M., & McDermott, K. B. (2007). Neural substrates of envisioning the future. *Proceedings of the National Academy of Sciences, 104,* 642–647.

Vyshedsky, A. (2019). Neuroscience of imagination and implications for human evolution. *Current Neurobiology, 10,* 89–109.

Wandell, B. A., Dumoulin, S. O., & Brewer, A. A. (2007). Visual field maps in human cortex. *Neuron, 56,* 366–383.

Further Readings for Part IV

Addis, D. R. (2020). Mental time travel? A neurocognitive model of event simulation. *Review of Philosophy and Psychology*, *11*, 233–259.

> *Argues that memory, imagination, and perception are supported by a domain-general simulation system, which functions to enable a mental rendering of experience.*

Boyle, A. (2021). The mnemonic functions of episodic memory. *Philosophical Psychology*, *35*(3), 327–349.

> *Argues that episodic memory encodes, stores, and retrieves the type of information typically associated with semantic memory, which plays a role analogous to that played by mind palaces in the method of loci, and may serve an evolutionarily adaptive function.*

De Brigard, F. (2014). Is memory for remembering? Recollection as a form of episodic hypothetical thinking. *Synthese*, *191*(2), 155–185.

> *Outlines a view in which remembering is a particular operation of a cognitive system that allows for the simulation of possible or hypothetical past and future events.*

Jablonka, E. (2017). Collective narratives, false memories, and the origins of autobiographical memory. *Biology & Philosophy*, *32*(6), 839–853.

> *Argues that autobiographical memory evolved in the context of human linguistic communication through selection for reliability in communication.*

Michaelian, K. (2016). *Mental time travel: Episodic memory and our knowledge of the personal past*. MIT Press.

> *Provides a systematic account of remembering as a form of imaginative simulation, providing an answer to the question of why episodic memory evolved.*

Schwartz, A. (2020). Simulationism and the function(s) of episodic memory. *Review of Philosophy and Psychology*, *11*, 487–505.

> *Outlines a functional pluralism—different ways in which the notion of function can be understood—that casts doubt on the simulationist revision of the proposed function of episodic memory as relating to storing and retrieving experiences.*

Suddendorf, T., & Corballis, M. C. (1997). Mental time travel and the evolution of the human mind. *Genetic, Social, and General Psychology Monographs*, *123*(2), 133–167.

> *Provides an account of the evolutionary function of episodic memory as part of a larger cognitive capacity for mental time travel, in which imagining future scenarios is particularly adaptive.*

Study Questions for Part IV

1) How do you think the two notions of the function of episodic memory—etiological and casual role—may be related?

2) Can you think of any problems with applying form-to-function reasoning to episodic memory? Is Mahr correct about what the form of episodic memory is?

3) What other types of evidence might support Mahr's evolutionary account?

4) Robins favours a preservative (past-directed) account of the function of episodic memory. How would this align with the idea that memory involves systematic errors?

5) What evidence would count in favour of a preservative view of the function of episodic memory?

Part V

Do non-human animals have episodic memory?

9 Episodic memory in animals

Optimism, kind scepticism and pluralism

Alexandria Boyle

9.1 Introduction

Episodic memory is memory for personally experienced past events—that is, events which were experienced or witnessed first-hand. It's often contrasted with semantic memory, which is a store of decontextualised information. If I remember taking a picnic on a frosty day on Dartmoor, I'm episodically remembering. If I remember that Devon is the only English county with two coastlines, but don't retrieve any event associated with that information, I'm semantically remembering.

Whether animals have episodic memory is a subject of some controversy.[1] On the one hand, two decades of research into this question have turned up dozens of results apparently confirming that animals remember past events (to be discussed in more detail in Section 9.2). As a result, many comparative psychologists think that episodic memory exists in at least some non-human species (Allen & Fortin 2013; Emery & Clayton 2004; Jozet-Alves et al. 2013). I'll call this position 'optimism'. On the other hand, there remain those I'll call 'sceptics', who propose that episodic memory is a uniquely human capacity. Some sceptics argue that the available evidence fails to show that animals have anything like episodic memory: It provides no reason to think that animals remember past events (Hoerl & McCormack 2019; Suddendorf & Corballis 2007). Nazım Keven (Chapter 10 in this volume) calls this position 'capacity scepticism'. But in this chapter, I want to focus on a different form of scepticism, which I'll name 'kind scepticism'. A kind sceptic acknowledges that the evidence suggests animals have something *similar* to episodic memory—they have some form of memory for events. Nevertheless, the kind sceptic argues, this memory capacity does not qualify as episodic memory, because it *differs in kind*.

I begin in Sections 9.2 and 9.3 by introducing optimism and kind scepticism in more detail. In Section 9.4, I'll offer a diagnosis of the dispute between kind sceptics and optimists. I suggest that this disagreement is not primarily about whether there are differences between human and non-human memory. Rather, it is about what episodic memory is, and what it would take for animals to have it. In Section 9.5, I consider how we might make progress. I argue that questions about the delineation of episodic memory can be settled by reference to

DOI: 10.4324/9781003002277-15

the theoretical goals we aim to satisfy by asking whether animals have it. Since we ask whether animals have episodic memory in the service of a number of projects, the resulting picture is a pluralist one: Different projects demand different delineations of episodic memory and can be expected to yield different verdicts about whether animals have it.

9.2 Optimism

Optimism, as I've said, is the view that animals have episodic memory. In this section, I'll give a brief overview of the evidence optimists take to support their view.

The pioneering studies on episodic memory in animals were conducted by Nicola Clayton and Anthony Dickinson (Clayton & Dickinson 1998, 1999), who investigated whether Californian scrub-jays were able to remember past events using the 'what-where-when' criterion—which looks at whether animals recall *what* happened, *where* it happened, and *when* it happened (Tulving 1972). In one experiment (Clayton & Dickinson 1999, experiment 1), birds were allowed to cache worms and nuts at approximately the same time. They were then allowed to return to the caching site after either a 4- or 124-hour interval, during which the food had been removed to eliminate olfactory cues. All else equal, scrub-jays prefer worms to nuts—so one might expect the scrub-jays to prefer to return to the worms' location. But worms decay faster than nuts; after 4 hours they would still be fresh, but after 124 hours they would be unpalatable. The birds had been familiarised with these differential patterns of decay. So, if they were able to remember not just what was buried where, but *when* the food had been buried, they should display a preference for the worms' location after 4 hours, but for the nuts' location after 124 hours. This pattern was, indeed, observed.

The 'what-where-when' criterion is still widely used as an indicator of episodic memory in animals, but a number of additional criteria have also been used to investigate animals' memory for events. These include:

- Integration (Clayton, Bussey, & Dickinson 2003): This criterion requires 'what', 'where' and 'when' components to be integrated into a single representation of the event, such that retrieval of one of these pieces of information about an event predicts retrieval of the others, and similar events can be discriminated from one another in memory.
- Flexibility (Clayton, Yu, & Dickinson 2003): According to this criterion, the subject should be able to use the memory flexibly, rather than always producing the same behaviour, it should support a range of appropriate behaviour in different informational and motivational contexts.
- What-where-which (Eacott et al. 2005): This criterion replaces the 'when' component with a 'which' component. The idea is that one need not be able to locate an event in time to episodically remember it, but one should be able to discriminate it from other, similar events.

- Source memory (Crystal et al. 2013): This criterion investigates whether subjects recall other contextual information besides 'what-where-when' or 'what-where-which'. For example, Crystal et al. (2013) looked at whether rats could remember whether they found their own way to a location or were placed there by an experimenter.
- Replay (Panoz-Brown et al. 2018): This criterion looks at whether subjects remember the order in which events occurred. For instance, Panoz-Brown et al. investigate whether rats can recall the order in which a series of odours were presented.
- Incidental encoding (Singer & Zentall 2007): On this criterion, the subject should be able to recall information which, at the time of the event, she was not expecting to need, and which she has not previously been rewarded for remembering. This criterion aims to discriminate episodic memory from semantic or rule-based memory.
- Hippocampal dependence (Crystal et al. 2013): This criterion looks at whether, in species with a hippocampus, hippocampal lesions impair performance on episodic memory tasks—as they would in humans.

Researchers have looked for episodic memory in a range of animals besides scrub-jays, using some or all of these criteria. Confirmatory results have been reported relative to at least one of these criteria in great apes (Martin-Ordas et al. 2010), black-capped chickadees (Feeney et al. 2009), magpies (Zinkivskay et al. 2009), rats (Babb & Crystal 2006), dogs (Fugazza et al. 2016), meadow-voles (Ferkin et al. 2008), honeybees (Pahl et al. 2007), cuttlefish (Jozet-Alves et al. 2013), and Yucatan minipigs (Kouwenberg et al. 2009), among other species. Some of these species have been tested using only one or two of these criteria, whilst others have 'passed' tests using multiple criteria. Perhaps the most impressive evidence comes from rats, which have 'passed' tests employing what-where-when (Babb & Crystal 2006), source memory (Crystal & Alford 2014; Crystal et al. 2013), replay (Panoz-Brown et al. 2018), integration (Crystal & Smith 2014) and hippocampal dependence (Crystal et al. 2013; Panoz-Brown et al. 2018) criteria.

This growing body of research has convinced many researchers that at least some non-human animals have episodic memory. Within optimism, a range of views about episodic memory's distribution and origins are represented. For instance, Timothy Allen and Norbert Fortin (2013) write that 'the core properties of episodic memory are present across mammals, as well as in a number of bird species' (p. 10384), proposing that this is likely to be due to a 'shared underlying neural ancestry' (p. 10379). Others propose that episodic memory has emerged convergently in a number of lineages (Emery & Clayton 2004; Jozet-Alves et al. 2013).

One caveat is worth noting. Most optimists stop short of claiming that non-human animals have episodic memory, preferring the term 'episodic-like memory'. This is because episodic memory is often characterised in terms of a distinctive experience of 'mentally reliving' a past event. Many take it to be impossible to determine whether animals have these experiences (e.g., Clayton & Dickinson 2010; Michaelian & Sutton 2017). The term 'episodic-like memory' is used as a way of side-stepping this issue: it is intended to indicate neutrality about whether non-human memories have the relevant experiential features. This is an important issue, which I have discussed at length elsewhere (Boyle 2020). For the purposes of this chapter, I set it aside. The dispute I'm concerned with in this chapter does not centrally turn on whether animals have *experiences* of mental reliving. As I outline in what follows, the kind sceptics discussed here resist optimism on the grounds that human and non-human memory capacities may differ in *other* important respects, in virtue of which they may differ in kind.

9.3 Kind scepticism

As I noted in Section 9.1, some—'capacity sceptics'—dispute whether the evidence briefly described in Section 9.2 establishes that animals have any form of event memory. In this chapter, however, my focus is not capacity scepticism, but *kind* scepticism. Kind sceptics argue that whilst the evidence may establish that animals have an event memory capacity *similar* to episodic memory, it does not establish that animals actually *have* episodic memory. This is because the relevant non-human memory capacities differ in kind from episodic memory, or because it is at least consistent with our evidence that they do.

What might it mean to say that animals' memory capacities may differ in kind from episodic memory? A popular view of science treats it as being in the business of investigating *natural kinds*—that is, groups of entities about which we can uncover laws or regularities, where those groups are 'natural' in the sense of being out there in the world to be discovered. Examples of natural kinds include gold, *Homo sapiens*, SARS-CoV-2, and haemoglobin: Each seems to be a natural group about which we might discover regularities or laws.

Exactly what natural kinds are is subject to debate. One influential view treats natural kinds as homeostatic property cluster kinds (Boyd 1989, 1991). A class C of entities is a homeostatic property cluster (HPC) kind if it satisfies the following conditions:

1. The members of C tend to share a cluster of properties;
2. That cluster of properties is methodologically significant, in the sense that it features in successful explanations, interventions, and predictions;
3. There exist one or more 'homeostatic mechanisms' that explain why the cluster of properties tend to be found together in the members of C; and
4. C is 'maximal' with respect to its methodological significance—there is no group of entities C' which is more inclusive than C and has the same methodological significance as C (supporting all the same predictions, explanations, and so on).

The HPC view is a popular approach to cognitive kinds—that is, the kinds investigated by the cognitive sciences, which might include things like emotions

(Griffiths 2008), concepts (Machery 2009) and—importantly for our purposes—episodic memory (Andonovski 2018; Cheng & Werning 2016). There
may be different ways to apply the HPC view to cognitive kinds, but one natural approach is to treat the cluster of properties characterising a cognitive kind in
functional terms (in terms of the role that the cognitive kind occupies in individuals' mental lives), and the homeostatic mechanisms in *neurobiological* terms
(in terms of the brain mechanisms that explain why those functional features
arise and cluster together). In what follows, I'll assume this picture of cognitive
kinds.

This provides two ways in which animals' memory capacities might differ in
kind from episodic memory. First, it might be that although they're similar in
some ways, they differ in some important *functional* respect. That is, they do not
behave in the same ways, or play the same roles in animals' cognitive lives.
Second, it might be that although they are functionally similar, they are underpinned by distinct neurobiological mechanisms. Kind sceptical views about
non-human memory come in both of these flavours.

On the functional side, Keven (Keven 2016, 2018) proposes that whilst animals form perceptual memories of events, these memories lack the structure
characteristic of humans' episodic memories. Episodic memories, in his view,
are characterised by temporal, causal, and teleological structure: They carry
information about the order in which events occurred, the causal relationships
between events, and their relationships to the subject's aims or goals. Keven
proposes that in humans, a 'narrative binding process' organises perceptual,
image-like event memories into these temporally, causally, and teleologically
structured episodic memories. Animals, lacking language, plausibly lack this
capacity for narrative binding—and whilst it's possible that another process
might provide non-human memories with the relevant kinds of structure, Keven
argues (in this volume) that there are independent reasons to doubt that non-
humans do have temporally, causally, and teleologically structured memories.
On his view, the non-human memories being uncovered in comparative psychology belong to a distinct cognitive kind, which he calls 'event memory'.[2]

On the mechanistic side, Sarah Malanowski (2016) has argued that establishing that animals have episodic memory requires showing that their memory
capacities are underpinned by the same kind of neurobiological mechanisms as
episodic memory. Malanowski sees this as key to the episodic memory research
programme realising what she takes to be its central aim—increasing our understanding of and ability to treat human episodic memory pathologies. As
Malanowski points out, experiments investigating non-human *behaviour* are not
obviously capable of establishing similarity at the level of mechanism. Moreover,
although lesion studies have shown that rats' performance in episodic memory
tasks is impaired by hippocampal damage, and although we have evidence for
mechanistic similarities between the hippocampi of rats and humans (Corballis
2013), this does not show that the underlying mechanisms are the same—since
the mechanisms may still differ when considered at a finer level of grain
(Malanowski 2016). So, even if rats or other animals have hippocampally

dependent event memories, their memories may nevertheless differ mechanistically from our episodic memories, and therefore differ in kind.[3]

9.4 What is episodic memory?

How should we make sense of the dispute between kind sceptics and optimists? Both of the kind sceptical views I've described involve an inference of the following shape:

P1: There are certain differences between non-human memory systems and human episodic memory (or at least, this is consistent with our evidence).
C: Non-humans lack episodic memory (or this is at least consistent with our evidence).

Understood in this way, we can locate the disagreement between kind sceptics and optimists in either of two places. It may be that optimists dispute that animals' memories differ from episodic memories in the ways kind sceptics claim. Or it may be that they dispute the legitimacy of the inference from P1 to C. In this section, I want to suggest that the disagreement is (at least primarily) concerned with the legitimacy of this inference—that is, it is about whether the differences identified by kind sceptics *make* the difference between a memory capacity 'counting' or 'not counting' as episodic memory.

It's important to distinguish this question from another, related question. The other question is: if human and non-human memory differ in the ways kind sceptics suggest, would that establish that the two differ in kind? Importantly, the answer to this question might be 'yes', without that showing that animals lack episodic memory—because there might be different kinds of episodic memory. Consider anatomical structures which are shared across species, such as the heart. It seems plausible to say, for instance, that the hearts of humans and zebrafish differ in kind—that *human heart* is one natural kind and *zebrafish heart* is another. Each of these plausibly satisfies conditions 1–4 described earlier, and each is maximal with respect to a particular sphere of methodological significance. There are important generalisations or laws that are true of human hearts and not zebrafish hearts, and vice versa. For instance, the human heart has four chambers, whereas the heart of a zebrafish has only two. But that there is a difference in kind between human hearts and zebrafish hearts does not show that zebrafish do not have hearts—since both human and zebrafish hearts may belong to the more inclusive kind, *heart*, which also satisfies conditions 1–4 and has its own methodological significance. More generally, establishing that two things differ in kind does not show that they aren't both members of a specific kind with which we're concerned.

Our question, then, is about which kind we're interested in. When we ask whether animals have episodic memory, what cognitive kind is 'episodic memory' supposed to pick out? And how is this kind to be delineated? What functional properties and mechanistic underpinnings does a memory capacity need to have in order to 'count' as a member of that kind?

These questions are not straightforward, because the comparative context in which they are asked vitiates certain natural ways of settling them. Suppose, for instance, that we discover a new species of duck, and we're interested in characterising the natural kind to which it belongs. Simplifying somewhat, we might begin by looking at the ducks we take to be typical or paradigmatic members of this new species, based on our observations to date. Of these ducks, we might ask: what do they have in common? What features do they tend to have in common, and by what mechanisms are these clustering properties underpinned? In this way, we might arrive at a characterisation of the kind, in terms of its properties and underlying mechanisms. Now suppose we want to settle the question of whether a new duck we've observed belongs to this species. We might naturally use the characterisation of the kind we've arrived at to address that question, by investigating whether the new duck has the relevant properties, underpinned by the relevant mechanisms.[4]

In the case with which we're concerned, however, this approach is problematic. We are interested in the proper characterisation of the kind episodic memory, a cognitive capacity whose only clear, uncontroversial instances are found in humans. So, our initial characterisation of the capacity will inevitably be based on what's known about the functional features and mechanistic underpinnings of episodic memory *in humans*. Yet, it's reasonable to think that, if episodic memory is a capacity shared across species, there may be species-specific aspects to its manifestation—just as there are interspecific variations in the anatomy of the heart. An investigation into the functional properties and mechanistic underpinnings of episodic memory based only on its human instances might yield an adequate characterisation of *human* episodic memory. But we cannot unproblematically assess whether a candidate *non-human* memory capacity 'counts' as an instance of episodic memory by considering whether it satisfies this characterisation of human episodic memory—it almost certainly will not.

Episodic memory plays functional roles in the cognitive lives of humans that it would almost certainly not play in the lives of animals, if they had it. For instance, Johannes Mahr and Gergely Csibra (2018) argue that episodic memory supports socio-communicative practices like making and enforcing commitments and evaluating testimony. Since animals don't speak, they can't possibly have a form of memory that plays these roles for them. Similarly, if episodic memory exists in non-human species, it is likely to differ from human episodic memory at the level of neurobiological mechanism, for two reasons. First, any differences in the functional profiles of human and non-human episodic memory would likely be mirrored at the level of neurobiological mechanism. Second, the brains of different species differ from one another; the more so, the more distantly related they are. For instance, the hippocampus is known to be a crucial structure for episodic memory in humans. But some of the species in which comparative psychologists investigate episodic memory, including cuttlefish and bees, lack a hippocampus altogether. So, if these non-hippocampal species did have episodic memory, the mechanisms underpinning their episodic memory could not be just the same as those underpinning the capacity in humans.

Despite these differences, we take it to be a sensible question, whose answer is not obvious in advance, whether animals have episodic memory. So, in asking this question, we cannot be asking whether animals have a form of memory *just like* human episodic memory. Rather, when we ask whether animals have episodic memory, we must be envisaging our capacity for episodic memory as a member of a more inclusive cognitive kind, within which there is room for interspecific variation.

But how should we characterise this more inclusive kind, and how should we evaluate whether animals' memory capacities belong to it? Here, there's room for disagreement—since we can envisage our capacity for episodic memory as falling into a range of more or less inclusive kinds, depending both on which features of its human manifestation we prioritise and on how concretely or abstractly we specify them. The disagreement between optimists and kind sceptics can be seen as a difference of opinion with respect to this question. In considering whether animals have episodic memory, optimists tend to adopt sparser characterisations of episodic memory, prioritising fewer of (human) episodic memory's features, and characterising them more abstractly. To see this, we can consider the functional features and the mechanistic underpinnings of episodic memory in turn.

With respect to episodic memory's functional features, Keven (Chapter 10 in this volume) argues that animals lack episodic memory because episodic memories bind event elements together into a single representation with temporal, causal, and teleological structure, and there are reasons for thinking that these structural properties are absent from non-human memories. At the same time, optimists conclude that animals have episodic memory on the basis of evidence adduced using the criteria for episodic memory listed in Section 9.2. The picture of episodic memory suggested by these criteria is one on which episodic memories bind event elements together into a single, structured representation of the event. But whilst this involves having a representation with spatial, and perhaps temporal, structure, there is notably no requirement that episodic memories have causal or teleological structure. In short, the criteria appealed to by optimists suggest a sparser conception of its functional features, on which episodic memories must be structured, but need not have all of the structural features by which Keven takes them to be characterised in humans. This, I take it, rather than a dispute over whether animals' memories have these structural features, explains their greater willingness to ascribe episodic memory to non-human animals.[5]

Similarly, Malanowski argues that it would be premature to declare that animals have episodic memory, because the mechanisms underpinning non-human memory could differ from those underpinning human episodic memory. The point that further research into the mechanisms of non-human memory is needed is well-taken. But a further question is what sort of evidence would be required to establish that the mechanisms underpinning human and non-human memory were the same—or, to put it another way, what 'sameness of mechanism' consists in. This question is complicated because, as Carl Craver (2009) argues, there is never just one way to specify the mechanisms underpinning our cognitive capacities. The same mechanism might be characterised at a coarser or finer level of grain, or in more abstract or concrete terms. How the mechanism is characterised will affect our judgements about whether a given mechanism counts as 'the same'. If we were to describe the mechanisms underpinning my own episodic memory capacity in sufficiently minute, concrete detail, then even the mechanisms underpinning *your* episodic memory would not count as examples of the same mechanism. On the other hand, if we described those same mechanisms very coarsely and abstractly, it is conceivable that mechanisms of the same kind might be found even in creatures with radically different brains.

Just as optimists assume a sparser characterisation of episodic memory's functional profile of episodic memory than sceptics do, I suggest that they also think of the mechanisms underpinning episodic memory in relatively sparse, abstract terms. For instance, Allen and Fortin (2013) write,

> The circuit [underpinning episodic memory in mammals] requires higher association areas to process the sensory information (neocortex), interface areas to communicate with the hippocampus (parahippocampal region), the hippocampus to integrate and retrieve information about the episode, and executive areas to produce the appropriate behaviour (prefrontal cortex) … [Birds] have a similar circuit that could perform the same fundamental operations. The corresponding system in birds involves a combination of homologous … and analogous … structures. Therefore, we hypothesise that a fundamental circuit may be shared between species that demonstrate episodic memory abilities.
>
> (p. 10383)

Allen and Fortin hypothesise that the mechanisms underpinning episodic memory are shared between birds and mammals because birds have a circuit that could perform the operations they take to be fundamental to the mechanisms of episodic memory in mammals—things like processing, integrating, and retrieving information, and putting it to use in directing behaviour. They offer this hypothesis despite being entirely aware that, when characterised exhaustively, in fine-grained and concrete detail, there will be many differences between the mechanisms operating in birds and mammals. This suggests that they operate with a relatively sparse and abstract picture of the mechanisms of episodic memory and take these differences between birds and mammals to be consistent with the hypothesis that the mechanisms are the same.

On the other hand, Malanowski is inclined to individuate the mechanisms of memory in less inclusive terms. She writes that, 'the description of the mechanism needs to be fine-grained enough to allow us to determine if a particular species would make a good model for studying human memory disorders'—suggesting a view on which sameness requires similarity at this more fine-grained level. On the subject of Allen and Fortin's claim, she suggests that the mechanisms of memory in mammals and birds 'are likely to be only similar on some broad scale of comparison … [and] work, neurobiologically, in different ways'. As such, she denies that these mechanisms are likely to be the same.

Summarising, I've suggested in this section that that the difference of opinion between optimists and kind sceptics does not primarily concern whether animals' and humans' memory capacities differ in the ways kind sceptics suggest. Rather, the dispute is about how this bears on whether animals have episodic memory—which in turn bottoms out in a dispute about how inclusively episodic memory should be characterised and delineated. Optimists, who characterise episodic memory in fairly sparse and abstract terms, are inclined to delineate it relatively inclusively, and so to hold that the differences to which kind sceptics advert are consistent with the claim that animals have episodic memory. Kind sceptics, who characterise episodic memory in richer and more concrete terms, disagree.

9.5 Moving forward

How might we make progress with this disagreement? A natural response, in light of what I've said so far, would be that we can't, because this is a trivial terminological dispute. When kind sceptics claim that animals lack episodic memory, they mean one thing. When optimists argue that animals have episodic memory, they mean something else. There's little to be gained by policing terminology, and no sense in asking what the term 'episodic memory' *really* denotes.

In a sense, this is right: this is a dispute about terminology. But not all terminological disputes are trivial. A dispute about the 'ultimate' or 'objective' meaning and extension of 'episodic memory' would be a waste of energy. But this dispute is about what 'episodic memory' picks out, or should pick out, *in a certain scientific context*—it's about how to delineate the object of the episodic memory research programme in comparative psychology. And this is not a trivial matter.

Suppose I develop a remedy that eliminates symptoms of a certain virus, and I take this to a virologist attempting to develop a cure. I tell her that she can halt her work, because I've cured the virus. She may rightly reply that I've done no such thing: I've merely developed a treatment. It will be no good for me to reply that, since I'm using 'cures' to mean 'eliminates the symptoms', our dispute is terminological, and that since there's no fact of the matter about what 'cure' *really* means, my use of the term can't be criticised. Quite clearly, it can. I intended to intervene in her project, but by using the term 'cure' in the way I do, I have only succeeded in changing the subject. Intervening in a scientific project is not a terminological free-for-all. It requires sensitivity to what scientists engaged in that project take themselves to be talking about, and to what they are trying to achieve.

This is not to say that we must defer entirely to scientists' uses of terminology, or to their characterisations of their objects of study—since it may be that another way of conceptualising phenomena would be more productive, from the point of view of their theoretical goals. For instance, it might be that in certain circumstances, the distinction between curing a virus and treating its symptoms is less important than in others: Perhaps there are viruses for which eliminating the symptoms is as good as a cure. But for other viruses, including those that spread asymptomatically, it is not. If my virologist's project concerned the first kind of virus, there might be something to be said for my intervention after all: Perhaps her goals would be well served by the adoption of a more inclusive characterisation of 'cure'.

All this is to say that whilst there might not be a single, ultimately correct way of characterising episodic memory, not all ways of characterising and delineating it will be equally suitable in all contexts. Different theoretical interests may call for different delineations of a phenomenon (Taylor 2021). So, having said that kind sceptics and optimists characterise episodic memory in different ways, we should not declare their dispute terminological and wash our hands of it. Instead, we should consider what those engaged in the episodic memory research programme in comparative psychology are up to and ask how episodic memory ought to be delineated relative to their theoretical interests.

At this point, Malanowski might point out that in making her kind sceptical argument, she did exactly this. She is explicit about the role theoretical interests play in determining how phenomena should be characterised and delineated. She suggests that the central goal of the episodic memory research programme in comparative psychology is to achieve a better understanding of how *human* episodic memory works, with a view to developing treatments for pathologies of memory (Malanowski 2016). It's with this in mind that she argues for a characterisation of episodic memory in fine-grained and concrete terms.

There's no denying that some comparative psychologists approach the question of non-human episodic memory with this theoretical interest in view. Babb and Crystal (2006), for instance, state that establishing a rodent model of episodic memory holds 'enormous potential' for understanding and treating memory pathologies. And it seems right that if our interest is in, say, using rats as a model for determining which drugs will be useful in treating Alzheimer's, then we had better delineate both the functional profile and mechanisms of memory sufficiently concretely to allow us to make reliable inferences about that. In fact, even if it is true that more work remains to be done, I take it that Crystal and his colleagues have studied rats so extensively, assessing them against a much wider range of criteria than have been applied to most species, for just this reason: Because their theoretical interests demand similarity between human and rat memory at a fine-grained and concrete level.

But this is not the only, or even the most central, goal driving episodic memory research in comparative psychology. Scientists ask whether animals have episodic memory with a view to satisfying a wider range of curiosities. For instance, some psychologists studying episodic memory in animals hope to draw conclusions about animal welfare. Amy-Lee Kouwenberg and colleagues (Kouwenberg et al. 2009, p. 171) suggest that their findings about memory in

Yucatan minipigs indicate 'the need for increased consideration of memory and learning in modern swine husbandry and housing guidelines', proposing that if pigs have episodic memory, they may benefit from environmental enrichments including more complex feeding systems.

When we ask whether animals have episodic memory with considerations of welfare in mind, it is not obviously productive to characterise episodic memory in just the same way that we would in the context of biomedical science. Here, our interest is in whether animals have a memory capacity that is of a kind with ours in a different sense—viz. one which carries at least some of the same ethical weight. Exactly how episodic memory should be characterised and delineated for this purpose is unclear and will turn on what we take the ethical weight of episodic memory to be, and on what gives it that ethical weight. Relative to this project, we may both prioritise different features of episodic memory and characterise them at a different level of abstraction than we would in a biomedical context. It's plausible that the fine-grained mechanistic underpinnings of episodic memory may be less important with respect to this project than with respect to the biomedical one—and we might be more inclined to prioritise interactions between episodic memory and other cognitive capacities, such as traumatic memory, boredom, and regret.

Perhaps most centrally, comparative psychologists ask whether animals have episodic memory with a view to furthering our understanding of its origins. Determining which animals have episodic memory is relevant to understanding when, why, in what circumstances, and how many times episodic memory emerged, as well as its relationship to other cognitive capacities. A comparative study of episodic memory may also reveal ways in which, if it is not uniquely human, it varies from species to species. Many comparative psychologists take these kinds of evolutionary questions to be at the heart of the comparative psychological project (Eaton et al. 2018). The central question of Allen and Fortin's paper, referenced earlier, is whether episodic memory evolved convergently in mammals and birds, as Emery and Clayton (2004) suggest, or before the mammalian/reptilian divergence. Similarly, Christelle Jozet-Alves and colleagues (2013) conclude their report about episodic memory in cuttlefish by suggesting that it represents 'a genuine case of evolutionary convergence', which may shed new light on the evolution of cognition.

If our interest is in tracking the development of episodic memory over evolutionary time, we had better not cleave too closely to its human manifestation in characterising it. Rather, we should characterise it sparsely and abstractly enough to enable us to detect evolutionarily older and simpler forms, and any species-specific forms that may have emerged. Similarly, whilst it is true that *bona fide* cases of evolutionary convergence require sameness of kind—similar functional properties underpinned by similar mechanisms—this need only be at a certain level of abstraction. The camera eyes of vertebrates and invertebrates, the paradigm case of evolutionary convergence, exhibit important differences at a fine-grained and concrete level in virtue of which one could certainly view them as different in kind. But claims of evolutionary convergence are made at a slightly more abstract level of description, and so tolerate this sort of variation. So again, claims about the evolutionary convergence of episodic memory must be made and evaluated with a relatively abstract and inclusive conception of episodic memory in view.

If this is right, and if non-human episodic memory researchers are often motivated by these evolutionary questions, the kind sceptic's objection will often amount to changing the subject. It may be true that humans' and animals' memories differ in the ways kind sceptics propose. But this doesn't obviously bear on the claim that animals have episodic memory, when it's made in the context of this evolutionary project. And nor should it: A sparse and inclusive characterisation of episodic memory, such as the one favoured by optimists, is appropriate relative to this project. At the same time, it's important to bear in mind that this inclusive characterisation of episodic memory won't be appropriate with respect to *every* project—and so evidence that supports the claim that animals have episodic memory in this inclusive sense may not establish anything about, say, animals' ethical status or their potential as models of human memory. Since our goals in asking whether animals have episodic memory play an important role in determining how 'episodic memory' ought to be delineated, our judgements about whether animals have episodic memory may vary from project to project. In short, the argument I've been making points toward a form of pluralism.

One might have concerns about this pluralist position. Isn't it confusing to suggest that episodic memory can be characterised and delineated in different ways for different purposes? Perhaps this will lead to communication problems: hearing from evolutionarily motivated researchers that cuttlefish have episodic memory, biomedical researchers might be led to conduct dead-end research on cuttlefish as models of human memory.[6] It's worth emphasising that this isn't a challenge to the substantive claim I have been making in this chapter: That comparative psychologists investigating episodic memory do so with different goals in view, and so (appropriately) characterise and delineate their object of study in different ways. Rather, it is a question about what we should do, having made that observation. Should we be pluralists, and treat them as characterising the same phenomenon in different ways, or should we be 'splitters', introducing new terminology to differentiate their objects of study?

Choices between pluralism and splitting are finely balanced, with risks to consider on both sides. As noted earlier, pluralism can generate confusion, and this can provide a legitimate reason to reject it (Taylor & Vickers 2017). On the other hand, splitting might lead us to disregard important connections between different research areas. For instance, it might turn out that the similarities between human and cuttlefish memory are such that it would be productive to explore cuttlefish as models of human memory—but we might miss this if we introduce terminological distinctions to separate the evolutionary and the biomedical project. How to balance these risks is a tricky question, and at least partly an empirical one. But one thing I have already mentioned tells in favour of pluralism—namely, that although researchers aiming to develop rodent models of memory pathologies draw on related research with evolutionary motivations, they operate with different evidential standards, seeking positive results against a more diverse range of criteria. So, matching the delineation of episodic memory to the demands of the task at hand is something comparative psychologists, to some extent, already do.

9.6 Conclusion

Answering whether animals have episodic memory requires a determination on how episodic memory should be characterised and delineated. The dispute between kind sceptics and optimists is rooted in a disagreement about this question. I proposed that we can make progress by considering what scientists are trying to achieve by asking whether animals have episodic memory. Different characterisations of episodic memory may be more appropriate than others, relative to particular theoretical goals. I argued that comparative psychologists ask whether animals have episodic memory in the service of a number of projects. But with respect to at least some of these projects—including attempts to understand the evolution of cognition—the narrow delineations of episodic memory insisted upon by kind sceptics are inappropriate, and kind scepticism misfires. So with respect to those projects at least, there are grounds for optimism.

More importantly, I've suggested that the various projects that motivate scientists to ask whether animals have episodic memory are incommensurate, in the sense that they require different characterisations of episodic memory. So, although I've suggested that optimism may be justified in certain contexts, I have not defended a straightforward 'yes or no' answer to whether animals have episodic memory. Rather, I've suggested that there isn't one: We can sensibly ask this question only with a particular project in view. In virtue of being incommensurate, different projects may yield different answers. This may not be entirely satisfying, but dissatisfaction is an occupational hazard. As Mary Midgley (2018, p. 50) writes,

> philosophy, in fact, is all about *how* to think in difficult cases … It is a set of practical arts far more like the skills involved in exploring an unknown forest than they are like the search for a single buried treasure called the Truth. And because of this, it is far more concerned with the kind of questions that we should ask than with how, at any particular time, we should answer them.

Acknowledgements

Versions of this chapter were presented at Cambridge, CEU and Ruhr University Bochum, as well as at the Current Controversies in Philosophy of Memory conference associated with this volume. I'm grateful to all those audiences for their helpful questions and comments, which greatly improved the chapter.

Thanks to the editors for the invitation to write this chapter, and to a reviewer for invaluable feedback. I'm indebted to Nazım Keven, my opposite number in this volume, for stimulating exchanges on this topic which have helped to clarify my thinking. Thanks also to Henry Taylor for feedback on the ideas in this chapter, and for many enriching conversations about natural kinds.

Notes

1 I use 'animals' as shorthand for 'non-human animals'.
2 Mahr and Csibra (2018) also draw a distinction between episodic and event memory, proposing that animals have only the latter. Their distinction differs from Keven's, but space prohibits a full discussion.
3 Malanowski also doubts that the evidence establishes that animals have a form of memory functionally similar to human episodic memory. For the purposes of this short chapter, I focus only on her arguments about mechanism.
4 One way in which this is a simplification is that the relevant properties and mechanisms might be present to a greater or lesser degree in a candidate entity—and so, in some cases, this approach will deliver no clear verdict on whether this entity 'counts' as an instance of the kind (Taylor, 2020). Another is that in sexually dimorphic species, including many ducks, male and female members of the species may differ significantly, resulting in distinct clusters of species-typical features (for discussion, see Magnus, 2012, pp. 149–165).
5 Those optimists who take temporal structure to be characteristic of episodic memory will also dispute Keven's claim that animals' memories lack this structure, perhaps appealing to evidence that rats' memories of events carry sequence information (Panoz-Brown et al., 2018). Too little evidence bears directly on this question to settle it with any certainty. In any case, I suggest, the remainder of the disagreement in this case concerns the characterisation of episodic memory. Moreover, some optimists take temporal information to be less central in characterising episodic memory (Eacott & Easton, 2010). Here, I suggest their dispute with kind sceptics is explained without remainder in terms of their differing characterisations of episodic memory.
6 Thanks to Nazım Keven for pressing this worry.

References

Allen, T. A., & Fortin, N. J. (2013). The evolution of episodic memory. *Proceedings of the National Academy of Sciences Jun 2013*, *110*(Supplement 2), 10379–10386.

Andonovski, N. (2018). Is episodic memory a natural kind? *Essays in Philosophy*, *19*(2), 178–195.

Babb, S. J., & Crystal, J. D. (2006). Episodic-like memory in the rat. *Current Biology*, *16*(13), 1317–1321.

Boyd, R. (1989). What realism implies and what it does not. *Dialectica*, *43*(1–2), 5–29.

Boyd, R. (1991). Realism, anti-Foundationalism and the enthusiasm for natural kinds. *Philosophical Studies*, *61*(1–2), 127–148.

Boyle, A. (2020). The impure phenomenology of episodic memory. *Mind & Language*, *35*(5), 641–660.

Cheng, S., & Werning, M. (2016). What is episodic memory if it is a natural kind? *Synthese*, *193*(5), 1345–1385.

Clayton, N. S., Bussey, T. J., & Dickinson, A. (2003). Can animals recall the past and plan for the future? *Nature Reviews Neuroscience*, *4*(8), 685–691.

Clayton, N. S., & Dickinson, A. (1998). Episodic-like memory during cache recovery by scrub jays. *Nature, 395*(6699), 272–274.

Clayton, N. S., & Dickinson, A. (1999). Scrub jays (Aphelocoma coerulescens) remember the relative time of caching as well as the location and content of their caches. *Journal of Comparative Psychology, 113*(4), 403–416.

Clayton, N. S., & Dickinson, A. (2010). Mental time travel: Can animals recall the past and plan for the future? In M. D. Breed & J. Moore (Eds.), *The New Encyclopedia of Animal Behaviour* (Vol. 2, pp. 438–442). Academic Press.

Clayton, N. S., Yu, K. S., & Dickinson, A. (2003). Interacting cache memories: Evidence for flexible memory use by western scrub-jays (Aphelocoma californica). *Journal of Experimental Psychology, 29*(1), 14–22.

Corballis, M. C. (2013). Mental time travel: A case for evolutionary continuity. *Trends in Cognitive Sciences, 17*(1), 5–6.

Craver, C. F. (2009). Mechanisms and natural kinds. *Philosophical Psychology, 22*(5), 575–594.

Crystal, J. D., & Alford, W. T. (2014). Validation of a rodent model of source memory. *Biology Letters, 10*(3), 20140064.

Crystal, J. D., Alford, W. T., Zhou, W., & Hohmann, A. G. (2013). Source memory in the rat. *Current Biology, 23*(5), 387–391.

Crystal, J. D., & Smith, A. E. (2014). Binding of episodic memories in the rat. *Current Biology, 24*(24), 2957–2961.

Eacott, M. J., & Easton, A. (2010). Episodic memory in animals: Remembering which occasion. *Neuropsychologia, 48*(8), 2273–2280.

Eacott, M. J., Easton, A., & Zinkivskay, A. (2005). Recollection in an episodic-like memory task in the rat. *Learning and Memory, 12*(3), 221–223.

Eaton, T., Hutton, R., Leete, J., Lieb, J., Robeson, A., & Vonk, J. (2018). Bottoms-up! Rejecting top-down human-centered approaches in comparative pschology. *International Journal of Comparative Psychology, 31*, 1–19.

Emery, N. J., & Clayton, N. S. (2004). The mentality of crows: Convergent evolution of intelligence in corvids and apes. *Science, 306*(5703), 1903–1907.

Feeney, M. C., Roberts, W. A., & Sherry, D. F. (2009). Memory for what, where, and when in the black-capped chickadee (Poecile atricapillus). *Animal Cognition, 12*(6), 767–777.

Ferkin, M. H., Combs, A., Delbarco-Trillo, J., Pierce, A. A., & Franklin, S. (2008). Meadow voles, Microtus pennsylvanicus, have the capacity to recall the "what", "where", and "when" of a single past event. *Animal Cognition, 11*(1), 147–159.

Fugazza, C., Pogány, Á., & Miklósi, Á. (2016). Recall of others' actions after incidental encoding reveals episodic-like memory in dogs. *Current Biology, 26*(23), 3209–3213.

Griffiths, P. E. (2008). *What Emotions Really Are*. University of Chicago Press.

Hoerl, C., & McCormack, T. (2019). Thinking in and about time: A dual systems perspective on temporal cognition. *Behavioral and Brain Sciences, 42*(e244), 1–69.

Jozet-Alves, C., Bertin, M., & Clayton, N. S. (2013). Evidence of episodic-like memory in cuttlefish. *Current Biology, 23*(23), R1033–R1035.

Keven, N. (2016). Events, narratives and memory. *Synthese, 193*(8), 2497–2517.

Keven, N. (2018). Carving event and episodic memory at their joints. *Behavioral and Brain Sciences, 41*(e1), 30–31.

Kouwenberg, A. L., Walsh, C. J., Morgan, B. E., & Martin, G. M. (2009). Episodic-like memory in crossbred Yucatan minipigs (Sus scrofa). *Applied Animal Behaviour Science, 117*(3–4), 165–172.

Machery, E. (2009). *Doing without Concepts*. Oxford University Press.

Magnus, P. D. (2012). *Scientific Enquiry and Natural Kinds*. Palgrave Macmillan.

Mahr, J. B., & Csibra, G. (2018). Why do we remember? The communicative function of episodic memory. *Behavioral and Brain Sciences, 41*(E1), 1–16.

Malanowski, S. (2016). Is episodic memory uniquely human? Evaluating the episodic-like memory research program. *Synthese, 193*(5), 1433–1455.

Martin-Ordas, G., Haun, D., Colmenares, F., & Call, J. (2010). Keeping track of time: Evidence for episodic-like memory in great apes. *Animal Cognition, 13*(2), 331–340.

Michaelian, K., & Sutton, J. (2017). Memory. In E. N. Zalta (Ed.), *The Stanford Encyclopedia of Philosophy* (Summer 2017 ed.). https://plato.stanford.edu/archives/sum2017/entries/memory/

Midgley, M. (2018). *What is Philosophy For?* Bloomsbury Academic.

Pahl, M., Zhu, H., Pix, W., Tautz, J., & Zhang, S. (2007). Circadian timed episodic-like memory - A bee knows what to do when, and also where. *Journal of Experimental Biology, 210*(20), 3559–3567.

Panoz-Brown, D., Iyer, V., Carey, L. M., Sluka, C. M., Rajic, G., Kestenman, J., Gentry, M., Brotheridge, S., Somekh, I., Corbin, H. E., Tucker, K. G., Almeida, B., Hex, S. B., Garcia, K. D., Hohmann, A. G., & Crystal, J. D. (2018). Replay of episodic memories in the rat. *Current Biology, 28*(10), 1628–1634.e7.

Singer, R. A., & Zentall, T. R. (2007). Pigeons learn to answer the question 'where did you just peck?' and can report peck location when unexpectedly asked. *Learning & Behavior, 35*(3), 184–189.

Suddendorf, T., & Corballis, M. C. (2007). The evolution of foresight: What is mental time travel, and is it unique to humans? *Behavioral and Brain Sciences, 30*(3), 299–351.

Taylor, H. (2020). Emotions, concepts and the indeterminacy of natural kinds. *Synthese, 197*(5), 2073–2093.

Taylor, H. (2021). Whales, fish and Alaskan bears: Interest-relative taxonomy and kind pluralism in biology. *Synthese, 198*(4), 3369–3387.

Taylor, H., & Vickers, P. (2017). Conceptual fragmentation and the rise of eliminativism. *European Journal for Philosophy of Science, 7*(1), 17–40.

Tulving, E. (1972). Episodic and semantic memory. In E. Tulving & W. Donaldson (Eds.), *Organization of Memory* (pp. 381–402). Academic Press.

Zinkivskay, A., Nazir, F., & Smulders, T. V. (2009). What-where-when memory in magpies (Pica pica). *Animal Cognition, 12*(1), 119–125.

10 What does it take to remember episodically?

Nazım Keven

10.1 Introduction

When we remember an experience, we can mentally travel back in time to relive that experience. The system that makes mental time travel possible is known as episodic memory. Episodic memory has several intriguing features distinguishing it from other types of remembering, such as semantic memory or recognition memory. On the one hand, with semantic memory, one could learn general facts about the world without first-hand experience. For example, I know that it rains a lot in London, but I have never been there. On the other hand, with recognition memory, one could identify many different types of cues such as faces, words, sounds, and objects without conscious recollection of encountering them earlier. For instance, I can recognise someone's face without remembering where we met before. In both of these cases, one can *know* that something is the case without *remembering* it. However, to remember episodically, one needs to have both first-hand experience and autonoetic awareness of personally having this experience in one's past (cf. Michaelian 2016).

It is debated whether episodic memory is a uniquely human capacity. On the one hand, defenders of human uniqueness generally build their arguments around the mental time travel metaphor and emphasise various distinctive features of episodic recall, particularly autonoetic awareness (Suddendorf & Corballis 2007; Tulving 1985) and meta-representation (Redshaw 2014). On the other hand, defenders of continuity across species reject defining episodic memory in ways that are not testable behaviourally and keep adding to their arsenal of evidence for memory-like capacities in various species (Crystal 2010; Salwiczek, Watanabe, & Clayton 2010).

I defend what Boyle (Chapter 9 in this volume) classifies as a kind sceptical view within this debate. I think non-human animals (hereafter: 'animals') have memories about their past experiences, but these memories are of a distinct kind than human episodic memory. Human episodic memories are organised differently from animal memories. In this chapter, I propose a distinction between perceptual and inferential contents of episodic memory to bring this crucial organisational difference to the forefront. As a first approximation, the perceptual content of memory consists of sensory information about observable

DOI: 10.4324/9781003002277-16

elements and their relations taken from an experience. Inferential content, however, consists of unobservable relations that are inferred, such as temporal, causal, and teleological relations among past events. In my view, to reconstruct an episodic memory of a personal experience is to establish these types of *inferential relations* between past events. I argue that although animals have memories with perceptual content, only humans have episodic memories with perceptual contents organised by inferential contents.

In Section 10.2, I begin with a brief overview of the uniqueness debate. Then, in Section 10.3, I propose a distinction between perceptual and inferential contents of memory. Finally, in the following three subsections, I go over three different types of inferential contents in detail with an eye towards whether animals can make temporal, causal, and teleological inferences. I show in each case that, so far, there is no evidence either in memory or in other cognitive domains that animals can make these types of inferences.

10.2 Is episodic memory uniquely human?

Endel Tulving (1972) originally defined episodic memory as a capacity to recollect personal experiences that involve remembering what, where, and when something happened. This content-based definition is known as the WWW criteria. Tulving (1985) himself abandoned the WWW criteria before any empirical study of episodic memory in non-human animals, as it is neither necessary nor sufficient for episodic memory (Suddendorf & Busby 2003). On the one hand, WWW content is not necessary because one can remember an experience even if one cannot remember where or when it happened. For instance, even though I can remember a present that I received on one of my birthdays, I may not be able to remember which birthday it was. On the other hand, WWW content is not sufficient either. One can know what happened and where and when without remembering the experience. For instance, everyone knows where and when they were born, but no one remembers their birth. It seems as though the WWW criteria fail to capture distinctive aspects of episodic memory.

Yet, this did not stop comparative psychologists from adopting the WWW criteria to reveal that animals can also satisfy it. Perhaps the most famous example is Clayton and Dickinson's (1998) ingenious study on scrub-jays' caching and retrieval behaviour that demonstrated that these animals can form memories of what, where, and when food was cached. Clayton and Dickinson utilised scrub-jays caching and recovering behaviour for food items that do perish and that do not perish over a retention interval. Birds learned that worms but not nuts decay over a 124-hour retention interval in several training trials. In the test trials, then, birds were given a choice between locations where they had hoarded worms (their preferred food) and locations where they had hoarded nuts. Birds preferred worms over nuts at 4 hours as their preferred food item. However, birds reversed their preference at 124 hours, when worms were degraded. Clayton and Dickinson interpret their results to show that birds remember what they cached (worms or nuts), where, and when they were cached. They argue that jays have a memory system akin to episodic memory, which they call episodic-like memory.

Although there may be some exceptions, it would be fair to say that philosophers are generally sceptical of rich interpretations of results such as these. At the far end of the spectrum, *capacity sceptics* argue that animals do not have any memory capacity. Hoerl and McCormack (2019), for instance, argue that animals are cognitively stuck in time, and they have no way to revisit the past. They think it is possible to explain away results such as Clayton and Dickinson's without postulating any memory capacity.

Others hold more moderate positions, which Boyle (Chapter 9 in this volume) refers to as *kind sceptics*. Unlike capacity sceptics, kind sceptics accept that animals have various memory capacities. However, they argue that the memory capacities of animals are different in kind from that of human episodic memory. In earlier work (Keven 2016), for instance, I propose a functional distinction between event and episodic memory. In my view, event memory is a snapshot-like memory for a change in the state of affairs, whereas episodic memory is a story-like memory for a course of events. I argue that the mnemonic abilities of animals (and young children) can be more appropriately captured by the notion of event memory. Mahr and Csibra (2018) concur to a large extent, although they have slightly different views about how to carve up this distinction. I will return to the event and episodic memory distinction in more detail later in the chapter.

Malanowski (2016) takes a different approach and raises a compelling line of ecological criticisms against Clayton and Dickinson's (1998) results. Based on evidence from the natural ecology of scrub-jays, she argues that scrub-jays do not need to remember what is cached and when they cached it in their natural habitat. She suggests that it is unnecessary to remember what is cached because observations in the wild reveal that scrub-jays exclusively cache either acorns or pine nuts depending on their respective regions (DeGange et al. 1989). It seems futile to keep track of what is being cached on each site if the food items are all the same. It is also unnecessary to keep track of when a nut is cached either, as nuts are not perishable. Even though scrub-jays eat worms, generally, they do not cache such perishable food items in the wild. They even check the quality of nuts before caching them to avoid spoilage from cracked or otherwise defective nuts. So, scrub-jays are quite meticulous.

Another reason why Malanowski thinks it is unlikely that scrub-jays would remember when they cached an item is their reburying behaviour. Scrub-jays frequently visit their cache sites to recover and rebury their caches without eating them. In fact, reburying is highly prevalent, with over 90% of recovered acorns reburied. It seems that, instead of a cognitively demanding strategy such as mentally travelling in time to visit each and every caching event individually, evolution favoured a far simpler behavioural strategy, namely physically travelling in space to revisit each cache site. Reburying helps scrub-jays to assess the quality of their nuts while reacquainting and rehearsing the birds with their locations. Taken together, it seems that merely a capacity for cognitive maps would be sufficient for scrub-jays. There is no biological need for episodic recollection in the natural ecology of scrub-jays.

According to Malanowski, researchers need to be wary when interpreting results such as Clayton and Dickinson's (1998). In her view, what an animal can do in an experimental setting needs to be double-checked against what they actually do in their natural ecology. If the relevant cognitive capacity is unnecessary in the wild, this raises the spectre that laboratory animals might find other ways to succeed in the experimental setting. Here, experimental training and participation in prior experiments could be the likely culprits. For instance, she points out, the scrub-jays used in Clayton and Dickinson's study had been involved in two other studies, each with its own training and pre-training periods. Needless to say, scrub-jays are quite intelligent creatures. So, it is likely that these experiment-savvy birds have learned that they can receive rewards if they perform in the way that the experimenter wants them to perform. And the sheer amount of training that these experiment-savvy animals receive before each task makes it difficult to figure out how they actually succeed in any given task. This becomes especially worrisome when their less experimentally savvy counterparts in the wild have no need or use for the purported cognitive capacity.

Kind scepticism offers a plausible resolution to the debate. It suggests a viable way to reconcile a large body of evidence in comparative psychology with the arguments of mental time travel theorists. However, Boyle (Chapter 9 in this volume) argues against kind scepticism and defends *kind pluralism* instead. In her view, there can be more than one way to delineate cognitive kinds depending on different theoretical interests. According to Boyle, comparative psychologists should spread their nets widely to find how much episodic memory is shared across species. Therefore, she argues that comparative psychology could benefit from a sparser characterisation of episodic memory to be more inclusive. I agree that comparative psychology could benefit from such a characterisation, but that sparse characterisation deserves its own name to avoid unnecessary terminological confusion. In fact, kind sceptics already offer a sparse characterisation, namely event memory, and carefully distinguish it from episodic memory.

Boyle, however, insists on calling that sparse characterisation episodic memory and argues that kind sceptics set the bar too high when they define episodic memory. She seems to overlook the opposite problem, though. If comparative psychologists operate with a sparse characterisation of episodic memory, there could be instances where some animals thought to have episodic memory may not actually have it. If researchers set the bar too low, then there could be many false positives. Among other potential problems, this could have detrimental effects for biomedical fields in which animals are used as model organisms. Although Boyle downplays this aspect of comparative psychology, one of the most important theoretical contributions of comparative psychology is to help identify model organisms. It is not possible to figure out where to set the bar unless we can distil the essential features of episodic recollection. In what follows, that is what I shall do.

10.3 Perceptual and inferential contents of episodic memory

To remember a personal experience is to reconstruct a mental state with content. It might be helpful to distinguish perceptual and inferential components of this mental content. When I remember an experience, a significant part of what I remember consists of sensory information such as colours, shapes, movements, and various other features. For instance, I remember working hard for my logic final. When I inspect this memory, I remember my dorm room, table, chair, bed, and so on. I also vividly remember the thick black logic textbook, jotting down notes and proofs on its pages all night. All of these places and objects that I remember constitute the perceptual content of my memory.

Crucially, perceptual content is limited to *observable* elements and their observable relations. When I remember my dorm room, the things that I remember were available for inspection in the original experience. I use the term 'observable' quite liberally to include any feature that can be assessed or measured by some sensory modality. For example, I could visually inspect the spatial relationships between different pieces of furniture and see that my bed was *next to* my cupboard, and my desk and my chair were *in front of* the bed. I can also estimate the distance between various items if need be. All of these items and their spatial relationships were perceptually available to me at the time. Perceptual content of memory does not include any information over and above what was perceivable in the original experience.

In earlier work (Keven 2016), I refer to memories based on perceptual content as event memories.[1] Event memory is supported by a growing body of evidence on dynamic cognition that reveals that humans track changing features in their environment, individuate their perceptual experience in terms of discrete events accordingly, and better remember these events in turn (for a review, see Radvansky & Zacks 2014). It is not possible to repeat my arguments and evidence here, but a brief recap might be helpful.

Event memory provides a perceptual record of a change in the *state of affairs*. For example, suppose a creature encounters a predator. This is a notable change in the current state of affairs: The situation has changed from safe to dangerous. The predator's appearance is thus an event for the creature. Events can be discriminated at a fine grain by tracking every minor change, or they can be discriminated at a coarse grain by tracking only major changes. Various organisms can discriminate different events at different grains of segmentation, depending on their capacities, tasks, needs, upbringing, and so on. For instance, many migrating animals track changes in the earth's magnetic field as a guide to navigate, but, for us humans, such a feat is not even conceivable. We, humans, parse bodily movements of our conspecifics into recognisable and discrete intentional acts to navigate our complex social world. To each their own.

Event memory utilises snapshot-like depictive representations. These snapshots are likely to be instantiated by using some form of mental imagery (e.g., Kosslyn 1994). Snapshot-like representations can be quite valuable for memory as they preserve much implicit information that can be recovered retrospectively.

From a snapshot, it is possible to retrieve a piece of information that was not explicitly considered during encoding. For example, how was the furniture layout in my dorm room? That was not part of my recollection initially, but I can visualise the room to answer. The layout information is implicit in my mental snapshot of the room, even though it was not considered at the time of encoding.

Whereas event memory provides snapshot-like records of a change in the *state of affairs*, episodic memory is primarily concerned with *course of events*. Thus, an entirely different kind of content is required to bind various events into a unified episode. In my view, to construct an episodic memory of a personal experience is to establish certain *inferential relations* between past events. In particular, these inferences can be temporal (e.g., event X happened before/after event Y), causal (e.g., event X occurred because of event Y), and/or teleological (e.g., event X occurred to bring about event Z). Episodic recollection, therefore, goes beyond perceptual content and snapshot-like depictive representations.

To give a simple example, reconsider the logic class example. To reconstruct such a straightforward memory, a bewildering array of inferences needs to be made. Besides retrieving perceptual contents of events, the memory systems need to infer across temporally distant events that I worked before the final, not afterward, that I worked hard because of the final and that I worked hard to pass the course. These types of temporal, causal, and teleological inferences bind a sequence of events into an episode. In my previous work (Keven 2016), I refer to this inferential process as *narrative binding*, as it is closely tied to our uniquely human storytelling capacities. These types of narratively bound episodes are the primary bearers of the inferential content of episodic memory.

Crucially, these inferential relations between events are not directly observable and cannot be provided by perceptual experience alone. In the logic class example, all I perceived was a series of perceptually distinct events scattered over different times and places. I took the final one day after I worked, I worked in my dorm room but took the final in a classroom, I passed the course many days after the final, and many other events happened before and after taking the final. So, constructing episodic memories requires selecting a specific set of events from memory. These are then placed into a sequence by establishing the proper temporal, causal, and teleological relations between those events. In other words, at its base, to reconstruct an episodic memory of a personal experience is to bind perceptually scattered events into a sequence of events. Event memory can support making these inferences by providing a temporary buffer for the construction of episodic memories. Unlike event memory, however, the mental states of episodic memories include both perceptual and inferential contents.

10.3.1 Temporal information and memory

It might be helpful to go over these inferential relations in more detail. Let me start with temporal information, which is the most basic inferential content type. Remembering when an event happened is usually treated as if it is a unitary construct. However, there could be many different ways to encode temporal information. Friedman (1993) distinguishes three different types of temporal information that can be utilised in memory. Firstly, one can track how long ago an event occurred. This type of temporal information provides a record of the distance of an event from the present time. It is generally referred to as *elapsed time*. Secondly, one can remember when an event occurred within a time scale. This is akin to a temporal tag such as a date that locates an event in a time frame, such as a calendar. Following Friedman (1993), I refer to it as *chronological time*. Finally, one can remember the order in which two or more events occurred in time. This is remembering whether an event happened before or after another event. I will use the term *sequential time* to refer to this third kind of temporal information.

For recent events, we can remember all three types of temporal information at the same time. We can easily remember how long ago an event happened, which date it happened, and whether it happened earlier or later than some other events. However, as time passes, these different types of temporal information deteriorate at different rates. Although sequential time seems to be the most stable of the trio, it is still possible to confuse the temporal order of various events, especially when the events are distant in time. Similarly, as time passes, elapsed time tends to lose its precision quickly, whereas chronological time is likely to be forgotten entirely. In fact, many studies reveal that chronological time is a very poor retrieval cue for the memory of an event (Barsalou 1988; Brewer 1988), which suggests that memories are not time-stamped during encoding. So, I will focus only on elapsed time and sequential time information, as chronological time does not seem relevant for memory.

Aside from different rates of deterioration, elapsed time and sequential time differ from each other regarding their content type. Whereas sequential time is inferential, elapsed time information appears to be perceptual. Elapsed time information can be observed or measured by two main sensory mechanisms (Staddon 2005). The first one is based on circadian rhythms, which is the daily cycle that governs feeding, sleeping, and other activities based on light onset and offset. The other one is interval timing, which can track how much time has passed since a particular event at intervals on the order of seconds and minutes. The exact nature and neural mechanisms of interval timing are debated, but according to a popular theory, interval timing is based on the accumulation of pulses emitted from a pacemaker (Gibbon 1977, 1991). Regardless of whether elapsed time information is based on observations of day and night cycles or whether an interval timing mechanism measures it, its content appears perceptual. Unlike elapsed time, however, sequential time cannot be observed or measured. The essential difference between elapsed and sequential time is that the temporal order of events is an *ascribed* relationship that needs to be inferred from memory after the fact.

Sequential time can be inferred based on many different types of information. One obvious candidate is the elapsed time itself. If elapsed time information is available for two events, based on the difference in elapsed time, it would be possible to infer which event happened earlier. These types of inferences can be beneficial when ordering recent events. Another strategy might be to use a salient event as a temporal marker and infer whether a particular event happened before or after that salient event. Such a strategy might be helpful for distant events. In some cases, it can be possible to exploit typical or logical relations between events. For instance, for the logic class example, it is possible to use typical relations such as people generally study before an exam, not afterward; taking the final is usually required to pass a course; and so on. Semantic memory can assist these types of inferences. Naturally, these different methods of inferring sequential time are not exclusive; they can be used in tandem to strengthen the inference. This is not meant to be an exhaustive list either; there could be other ways to infer sequential time as well.

Episodic memory reconstructions would cease to be about past experiences if they did not have sequential time content. Memory reconstructions would turn into a hodgepodge of events with no resemblance to the actual experience if the events do not unfold in their proper sequence in time. Without sequential time content, memory reconstructions would represent past experiences as much as a scrambled jigsaw puzzle represents its printed picture. Even if you have all the pieces, those pieces cannot represent the whole picture if they are not placed in the right place. Similarly, even if you remember all the events, those events cannot represent your past experience unless placed in the proper temporal sequence. To turn this hodgepodge of events into episodic memory, past experiences need to be organised in a memory reconstruction representing when specific events occurred in relation to each other. It is, therefore, this inferred sequential time that gives memories their episodic quality (cf. Cheng & Werning 2015).

Can animals infer sequential time in their memory reconstructions? Ample evidence indicates that animals are sensitive to time. For example, they can learn to go to specific places for food at a particular time of the day or learn to measure short periods precisely. However, closer scrutiny of these and similar cases reveals that their temporal sensitivity is based solely on elapsed time information. It is beyond the scope of this chapter to review all the relevant evidence (for such reviews, see Hoerl and McCormack 2019; Martin-Ordas 2020; Roberts 2002). Here I will consider just one example to illustrate how explanations usually go.

Let us return to Clayton and Dickinson's (1998) work with scrub-jays. Clayton and Dickinson's results have been interpreted to suggest scrub-jays can remember when an event happened. However, as we have seen, there are different types of temporal information that can be utilised in memory reconstructions. The critical question to ask here is whether scrub-jays use elapsed time or sequential time information. In Clayton and Dickinson's task, there is no need to encode caching events in relation to each other to reconstruct a temporally organised memory. If scrub-jays can keep track of how much time has passed since they cached worms, they can retrieve worms within a specific interval and retrieve nuts otherwise. Therefore, elapsed time information would be more than enough to succeed in this task. Scrub-jays only need to learn that a particular interval time is a good predictor of edible worms. And, as Malanowski (2016) points out, these highly intelligent and experiment-savvy animals go through many training trials to pick up these types of subtle cues, and they are highly motivated to do so. Therefore, scrub-jays in Clayton and Dickinson's study could only be using elapsed time information (for similar explanations, see Hoerl & McCormack 2019; Keven 2019).

Episodic memories are essentially temporally ordered. Sequential time provides the most basic form of inferential content, which binds events in episodic memory. Without such content, it is hard to see how a creature could construct episodic memories. I argued further that so far, there is no evidence to suggest that animals can use sequential time information in their memory reconstructions.

10.3.2 Causal inferences and memory

Inferences based on sequential time arrange events as one event following another. This is quite different from inferring that an earlier event causes a later event. Since causes precede their effects, in a sense, sequential time content is a prerequisite for causal inferences. But reconstructing episodic memories requires more than mere temporal ordering.

Consider the logic class example once again. The content of my memory includes more than me studying and then taking the final and passing the course. I do not just remember these events happening one after another, as mere temporal succession would have it. Crucially, my memory also incorporates the proud fact that I passed the course *because* I studied hard. Without this causal content, my memory would lack a crucial ingredient. Many memories include these types of cause-effect relations. I remember being late for a class because my alarm did not ring, I remember being stuck at home because of the coronavirus pandemic, and so on. In all of these and like cases, events are routinely causally related to each other in memory reconstructions, and the causal content of memory plays a vital role in binding events.

Various theories have been proposed to explain the psychological basis of causal inferences. On the one hand, according to one strand of theorising in psychology, humans infer the causes of events by identifying the pattern of elements that covary with the target effect (Cheng & Novick 1992). The idea behind the covariation approach is that a cause is an element that is present when the effect is present and absent when the effect is absent as well. Thus, the covariation approach is especially suited for learning new causes by identifying the pattern of elements that covary with the target effect. However, it seems ill-suited for memory reconstructions because episodic memories are generally about unique one-time occurrences. This makes observing a covariation difficult. On the other hand, according to the mechanistic approach to causal reasoning in psychology (Ahn & Kalish 2000), two events are causally related to each other when a plausible mechanism capable of transmitting causal power in that particular situation is recognised, recalled, or imagined. This process generally involves postulating a *causal mechanism* that explains the transmission of causal power.

The covariation and mechanism approaches are the two main views on causal inferences in psychology. In philosophy, David Lewis's (1973) influential counterfactual theory of causation offers a third, and perhaps the most plausible, alternative. According to the counterfactual theories of causation, if a later event is causally dependent on an earlier event, then the later event could not have happened without the earlier event. In other words, if the earlier event had not occurred, the later event would not have happened. That was certainly the case for my logic final. I know that had I not studied hard that night, I could have failed the course. Note that earlier events may not be sufficient to bring about later events, as there may be other causes. I did not pass logic solely because I studied for the final. I also attended all the classes, took the midterm, and so forth. But earlier events are counterfactually necessary for the occurrence of later events.

Covariation, mechanism, and counterfactual views all offer different but somewhat related ways to infer causes. And there are other theories of causation as well. It is hard to discern which approach is utilised in memory reconstructions, as there may not be an exclusive strategy. Instead, it is more likely that different methods (or various combinations of them) are employed in different recollections. However, it is worth mentioning that the counterfactual approach is the most plausible candidate in the case of episodic memory. The ability to construct possible events that could have happened in our past but did not happen is called *episodic counterfactual thinking*, which is psychologically and neurologically affiliated with episodic recollection (De Brigard et al. 2013). Episodic counterfactual thinking can help discern counterfactual dependencies between past events. When people reminisce about their past experiences, it is quite natural to wonder whether a later event could have occurred if an earlier event had not occurred. In our recollections, whereas some events seem to occur in due course, others seem to depend on the occurrence of certain events. Perhaps causal inferences in memory reconstructions are based on these types of episodic counterfactual thinking.

Can animals make causal inferences? A large body of evidence has accumulated on causal reasoning in comparative psychology since Wolfgang Kohler's famous studies at the turn of the last century on the ability of chimpanzees to stack boxes to reach an overhanging banana. Many animals are sensitive to causally relevant features, especially in the domains close to their natural tool-using behaviour. However, despite their sensitivity to causally relevant features, they usually fail to make causal inferences to unobservable features for outcomes they have observed. For instance, Povinelli and colleagues systematically studied chimpanzees' understanding of physical causal mechanisms (Povinelli 2000). They concluded that when various tool-use tasks are carefully reconstructed to tease apart observable and unobservable relations, chimpanzees predominantly focus on the observable relations and ignore unobservable causal mechanisms. Schloegl and Fischer (2017) provide an overview of more recent studies on causal reasoning in animals. Like Povinelli and colleagues, they also concluded that many animals, including most apes, have a relatively limited understanding of cause-effect relationships between two objects even though they are sensitive to causally relevant features.

To give one striking example, Call (2007) studied apes' understanding of how hidden objects influence the orientation of other objects. In one study, a food item was hidden under a small board. Given a choice between an inclined board and the other lying flat on the ground, the apes showed a clear preference for the inclined board. So, they seem to be aware that objects can influence the inclination of other objects. In the next phase of the study, the apes were allowed to choose between a small piece of banana and a large piece of carrot. They clearly preferred the banana. The same food items were then hidden underneath the boards. This time the apes were given a choice between two boards, with the one hiding the large carrot clearly having a steeper inclination than the one hiding the small banana. However, the apes failed to infer where the small banana was. Instead, they went for the board with the steeper inclination. Here a hidden food item needs to be inferred from the board's inclination, but apes fail to make this inference despite their awareness that objects can influence the inclination of other objects. Thus, the inclination of the board covaries with the size of the food item hidden behind; the larger the hidden item, the steeper its inclination will be. Apes, however, seem to be oblivious to this particular covariation relation.

Animals' causal reasoning over object-object relationships seems to be rather limited. Based on these types of evidence, what can we say about their causal reasoning abilities over event-event relationships from memory? It is quite likely that animals' causal reasoning over event-event relations would be even worse because causal reasoning over object-object relations is not as cognitively demanding as causal reasoning over event-event relations. First of all, causal reasoning over object-object relationships involves objects that are present, whereas event-event relations involve working on events that are absent. Although the food items were hidden, the boards and their respective inclinations were perceptually available to the apes to visually inspect in Call's study. In contrast, causal inferences in memory involve reasoning about event-event relationships among mental representations that are not perceptually available anymore. Unlike object-object relationships, event-event relationships are ephemeral. Episodic memories consist of unique one-time experiences that are non-recurring. So, in contrast to causal reasoning over object-object relations, an extra memory demand is added in the case of causal reasoning over event-event relations.

When I remember the logic final, none of the perceptual content of my memory is directly available to me anymore. Yet when I remember, I can causally infer that my behaviour in my dorm room caused my performance in the classroom and consequently resulted in my grade. Here, inferences form a causal chain across different times and places, in which one cause triggers an effect that triggers another one. These inferences are carried out on mental representations of events that lasted a short amount of time, never recurred, and are long gone. Yet, those ephemeral and nonrecurring events without any perceptual overlap are causally connected through the inferential content of my memory.

The second reason why causal reasoning over object-object relations is not as cognitively demanding as causal reasoning over event-event relations is that there is no temporal distance between cause and effect in the former case. In Call's study, for instance, the food items immediately cause differences in inclination when placed behind the boards. This may seem like a trivial observation, but it becomes quite significant when considering causal inferences from memory. As the temporal distance between cause and effect increases, it becomes harder to infer a causal relationship between them. One can almost perceive causality in events such as a billiard ball striking another. In contrast, it is challenging to establish a causal relationship between, say, smoking and lung cancer, where the effect appears years later. Although causes can be immediately followed by their effects in some cases, events have their effects delayed in many others. Therefore, it is much more challenging to decipher the cause of an event among many different circumstances and many different events that precede it.

10.3.3 Teleological inferences and memory

So far, I have considered temporal and causal inferences in memory. In this section, I will consider the last inferential content type, namely teleological inferences. Memory reconstructions are infused with teleological inferences simply because remembered events include various actors doing things with specific goals in mind. People remember themselves and others doing things for reasons, which are revealed through their beliefs and desires. In fact, human memory seems to be tuned to remember living creatures (Nairne, VanArsdall, & Cogdill 2017). Animacy is a critical cue for human episodic memory because the animacy status of an item seems to be one of the best predictors of its later recall. Across many different studies, people remember living targets better than matched non-living targets.

Whenever I remember something that I did or witness something that someone else did, a resort to teleological explanation is inevitable. A teleological explanation of why an event occurred is to say that it occurred *so that* a second event should occur or in order to produce a specific result. For instance, the man ran in order to catch the train. Here, the second event, catching the train, is the goal of running. Like causal inferences, teleological inferences also seek to answer the why-did-this-happen question. However, teleological inferences accomplish this by answering a prior what-is-its-goal question. They generally involve invoking psychological causes, namely mental states, to achieve this. For example, I worked hard for my logic final simply because I *wanted to* pass the course. To explain something teleologically is to cite the goal towards which it is naturally tending. Teleological explanations have a forward-looking character in this sense.

Two features of teleological inferences are worth emphasising. Firstly, teleological inferences characteristically involve attributing mental states such as beliefs, desires, suppositions, aims, drives, needs, and so forth. Mental states help explain what an actor is trying to do, what state of the environment she is trying to bring about, and what her goal is. If you see a man running towards the train station as a train is approaching the station, you infer that the man *wants to* catch the train. Here an unobservable mental state establishes a connection between two observed events. Similarly, what connects the events of studying in my dorm room and passing the course weeks later is an unobservable mental state. These events are spatiotemporally distinct, but they are connected in memory via my mental state of wanting to pass the course, which binds my memory into a whole. I wanted to pass the course, studied hard, and finally did it. Teleological inferences attribute mental states to establish relationships between observed events.

Secondly, teleological inferences are *recursive*. Recursion allows humans to embed different levels of mental representations when reconstructing the past (Redshaw & Suddendorf 2020). To be clear, some recollections can consist only of a simple goal that is achieved based on one attempt, and no recursion is needed in such a memory reconstruction. But more often than not, memories consist of more challenging goals and require a plan accompanied by a series of attempts until the desired outcome is reached. These plans usually involve devising subgoals, and in some cases even sub-subgoals, to overcome the obstacles encountered along the way. Several studies have shown that humans can represent up to five orders of embedded reasoning about mental states (Oesch & Dunbar 2017). If an attempt to achieve a goal fails, a new plan must be made to achieve the goal. These types of struggles with a back-and-forth between attempts and failures make great memories afterward. Passing the logic course was such a struggle for me, making my last-ditch effort at the end of the semester all the more memorable for me.

Can animals make teleological inferences? We can try to answer this question step by step by looking at whether animals can attribute mental states first, and then we can ask whether they can reason recursively. In a seminal paper, Premack and Woodruff (1978) asked whether chimpanzees can attribute mental states to others, and one of the most famous debates in comparative psychology ensued. Unfortunately, the debate could not produce a satisfactory answer to this question after over 40 years. I agree with Heyes's (2015) assessment that after countless studies on whether animals can understand various mental states carried out by different research groups, research methods, unfortunately, lost their vigour and rigor over time, and the debate stalled.

The animal mind-reading debate produced a plethora of findings that are difficult to interpret in their entirety. Although proponents favour rich interpretations (Call & Tomasello 2008) and sceptics continue to defend lean interpretations (Penn, Holyoak, & Povinelli 2008), both sides agree that mind-reading capacities of chimpanzees and other animals are nowhere near the belief-desire psychology of humans. It seems unlikely that animals can attribute unobservable mental states such as beliefs and desires to other animals. Nonetheless, some animals are quite socially savvy. Especially in food competition contexts, some animals can act in accordance with what a competitor animal can see or know (e.g., Clayton et al. 2007; Hare et al. 2006). Although these types of evidence do not support an explicit mind-reading capacity, they point towards the presence of some implicit social competence. Therefore, recent years have seen an increased interest in dual-process accounts that distinguish various implicit forms of behaviour-reading from explicit mind-reading abilities to reconcile these discrepant findings (for examples, see Butterfill & Apperly 2013: Gómez 2007; Whiten 1996). These kinds of dual-process accounts offer a promising avenue for future research.

Can animals embed events within events in a goal plan hierarchy? Recursion in animal cognition became a contentious issue after Hauser, Chomsky, and Fitch (2002) declared it the property that makes language uniquely human. Since then, it is debated whether animals' abilities in non-linguistic domains, such as hierarchical reasoning abilities in the navigation or tool-use tasks or their knowledge of dominance hierarchies in matrilineal kin groups, can count as evidence of some form of recursion in the animal kingdom (Parker 2006). Resolving the debate has proven to be difficult because, empirically, it is hard to distinguish recursion from similar processes such as embedding, iteration, and cognitive grouping (Martins 2012). However, it seems clear that no animal communication system exhibits true recursion in the sense of hierarchical embedding of linguistic structures (Corballis 2007; Jackendoff & Pinker 2005).

Taken together, these results suggest that animals would be highly unlikely to attribute mental states to establish event-event relations and embed events within events in a goal plan hierarchy. To reconstruct a goal sequence requires parsing an actor's behaviours in a way as to infer what the actor tries to achieve with that particular behaviour. Without an explicit mind-reading ability, animals cannot parse a continuous stream of behaviours into discrete actions by assigning them mental states to render them intentional. Moreover, without a capacity for recursion, it is not possible to turn these discrete actions into a hierarchically embedded goal sequence in which various subgoals and sub-subgoals are devised to achieve a principal outcome. Therefore, it seems highly unlikely that animals can make teleological inferences in their memory reconstructions.

10.4 Conclusion

In this chapter, I distinguished the perceptual and inferential contents of memory and analysed three different types of inferences that are essential in episodic memory reconstructions. I argued that to show that animals have episodic memory requires showing that their memories also have inferential content, that they can remember whether a specific event happened before or after another one, that they can distinguish which one caused the other and why these events happened. In other words, to show that animals can remember episodically at a minimum requires to show that animals can make temporal, causal, and teleological inferences. The evidence for memory-like abilities in animals only shows that animals can retain and retrieve perceptual content for some time. So far, however, there is no evidence of inferential content in animal memory.

Acknowledgements

This work was supported by the BAGEP Award of the Science Academy in Turkey.

Note

1 Rubin and Umanath (2015) also use the term 'event memory' to distinguish memories based solely on scene construction from episodic memories that are event memories accompanied by a sense of reliving involving the self. Actually, 'scene memory' would be a more apt term for their theory, as they are more concerned with scenes rather than events. Regardless, it seems that we both share the same intuition that there is a more basic memory type than episodic memory. However, we disagree as to the nature of that basic memory type. Rubin and Umanath take scene construction as fundamental. In contrast, I think we can go even lower, all the way down to perceptual event segmentation processes and reserve constructive processes for episodic memory. Moreover, they think the main difference between episodic and event memory is the presence or absence of autonoetic consciousness. In contrast, I think episodic memories require an entirely different kind of organisation than event memories based on a different kind of binding process

References

Ahn, W., & Kalish, C. W. (2000). The role of mechanism beliefs in causal reasoning. In F. C. Kiel & R. A. Wilson (Eds.), *Explanation and Cognition*. MIT Press.

Barsalou, L. W. (1988). The content and organization of autobiographical memories. In U. Neisser & E. Winograd (Eds.), *Remembering Reconsidered: Ecological and Traditional Approaches to the Study of Memory* (pp. 193–243). Cambridge University Press.

Brewer, W. F. (1988). Memory for randomly sampled autobiographical events. In U. Neisser & E. Winograd (Eds.), *Remembering Reconsidered: Ecological and Traditional Approaches to the Study of Memory* (pp. 21–90). Cambridge University Press.

Butterfill, S. A., & Apperly, I. A. (2013). How to construct a minimal theory of mind. *Mind & Language*, *28*(5), 606–637.

Call, J. (2007). Apes know that hidden objects can affect the orientation of other objects. *Cognition*, *105*(1), 1–25.

Call, J., & Tomasello, M. (2008). Does the chimpanzee have a theory of mind? Thirty years later. *Trends in Cognitive Sciences*, *12*(5), 187–192.

Cheng, P. W., & Novick, L. R. (1992). Covariation in natural causal induction. *Psychological Review*, *99*(2), 365–382.

Cheng, S., & Werning, M. (2015). What is episodic memory if it is a natural kind? *Synthese*, *193*(5), 1–41.

Clayton, N. S., Dally, J. M., & Emery, N. J. (2007). Social cognition by food-caching corvids. The western scrub-jay as a natural psychologist. *Philosophical Transactions of the Royal Society B: Biological Sciences*, *362*(1480), 507–522.

Clayton, N. S., & Dickinson, A. (1998). Episodic-like memory during cache recovery by scrub jays. *Nature*, *395*(6699), 272–274.

Corballis, M. C. (2007). Recursion, language, and starlings. *Cognitive Science*, *31*(4), 697–704.

Crystal, J. D. (2010). Episodic-like memory in animals. *Behavioural Brain Research*, *215*(2), 235–243.

De Brigard, F., Addis, D. R., Ford, J. H., Schacter, D. L., & Giovanello, K. S. (2013). Remembering what could have happened: Neural correlates of episodic counterfactual thinking. *Neuropsychologia*, *51*(12), 2401–2414.

DeGange, A. R., Fitzpatrick, J. W., Layne, J. N., & Woolfenden, G. E. (1989). Acorn harvesting by Florida scrub jays. *Ecology*, *70*(2), 348–356.

Friedman, W. J. (1993). Memory for the time of past events. *Psychological Bulletin, 113*(1), 44–66.

Gibbon, J. (1977). Scalar expectancy theory and Weber's law in animal timing. *Psychological Review, 84*(3), 279–325.

Gibbon, J. (1991). Origins of scalar timing. *Learning and Motivation, 22*(1–2), 3–38.

Gómez, J.-C. (2007). Pointing behaviors in apes and human infants: A balanced interpretation. *Child Development, 78*(3), 729–734.

Hare, B., Call, J., & Tomasello, M. (2006). Chimpanzees deceive a human competitor by hiding. *Cognition, 101*(3), 495–514.

Hauser, M. D., Chomsky, N., & Fitch, W. T. (2002). The faculty of language: What is it, who has it, and how did it evolve? *Science, 298*(5598), 1569–1579.

Heyes, C. (2015). Animal mindreading: What's the problem? *Psychonomic Bulletin & Review, 22*(2), 313–327.

Hoerl, C., & McCormack, T. (2019). Thinking in and about time: A dual systems perspective on temporal cognition. *Behavioral and Brain Sciences, 42*, 1–72.

Jackendoff, R., & Pinker, S. (2005). The nature of the language faculty and its implications for evolution of language (reply to Fitch, Hauser, and Chomsky). *Cognition, 97*(2), 211–225.

Keven, N. (2016). Events, narratives and memory. *Synthese, 193*(8), 2497–2517.

Keven, N. (2019). Let's call a memory a memory, but what kind? *Behavioral and Brain Sciences, 42*, e260.

Kosslyn, S. M. (1994). *Image and Brain: The Resolution of the Imagery Debate.* MIT Press.

Lewis, D. (1973). Causation. *Journal of Philosophy, 70*, 556–567.

Mahr, J. B., & Csibra, G. (2018). Why do we remember? The communicative function of episodic memory. *Behavioral and Brain Sciences, 41*, 1–16.

Malanowski, S. (2016). Is episodic memory uniquely human? Evaluating the episodic-like memory research program. *Synthese, 193*(5), 1433–1455.

Martin-Ordas, G. (2020). It is about time: Conceptual and experimental evaluation of the temporal cognitive mechanisms in mental time travel. *WIREs Cognitive Science*, e1530.

Martins, M. D. (2012). Distinctive signatures of recursion. *Philosophical Transactions of the Royal Society B: Biological Sciences, 367*(1598), 2055–2064.

Michaelian, K. (2016). *Mental Time Travel: Episodic Memory and Our Knowledge of the Personal Past.* MIT Press.

Nairne, J. S., VanArsdall, J. E., & Cogdill, M. (2017). Remembering the living: Episodic memory is tuned to animacy. *Current Directions in Psychological Science, 26*(1), 22–27.

Oesch, N., & Dunbar, R. I. M. (2017). The emergence of recursion in human language: Mentalising predicts recursive syntax task performance. *Journal of Neurolinguistics, 43*, 95–106.

Parker, A. R. (2006). Evolving the narrow language faculty: Was recursion the pivotal step? *The Evolution of Language*, 239–246. https://doi.org/10.1142/9789812774262_0031

Penn, D. C., Holyoak, K. J., & Povinelli, D. J. (2008). Darwin's mistake: Explaining the discontinuity between human and nonhuman minds. *Behavioral and Brain Sciences, 31*(02), 109–130.

Povinelli, D. (2000). *Folk Physics for Apes: The Chimpanzee's Theory of How the World Works* (in collaboration with J. E. Reaux, L. A. Theall, & S. Giambrone). Oxford University Press.

Premack, D., & Woodruff, G. (1978). Does the chimpanzee have a theory of mind? *Behavioral and Brain Sciences, 1*(4), 515–526.

Radvansky, G. A., & Zacks, J. M. (2014). *Event Cognition.* Oxford University Press.

Redshaw, J. (2014). Does metarepresentation make human mental time travel unique? *Wiley Interdisciplinary Reviews: Cognitive Science, 5*(5), 519–531.

Redshaw, J., & Suddendorf, T. (2020). Temporal junctures in the mind. *Trends in Cognitive Sciences, 24*(1), 52–64.

Roberts, W. A. (2002). Are animals stuck in time? *Psychological Bulletin, 128*(3), 473–489.

Rubin, D. C., & Umanath, S. (2015). Event memory: A theory of memory for laboratory, autobiographical, and fictional events. *Psychological Review, 122*(1), 1.

Salwiczek, L. H., Watanabe, A., & Clayton, N. S. (2010). Ten years of research into avian models of episodic-like memory and its implications for developmental and comparative cognition. *Behavioural Brain Research, 215*(2), 221–234.

Schloegl, C., & Fischer, J. (2017). *Causal Reasoning in Non-Human Animals* (M. R. Waldmann, Ed., Vol. 1). Oxford University Press.

Staddon, J. (2005). Interval timing: Memory, not a clock. *Trends in Cognitive Sciences, 9*(7), 312–314.

Suddendorf, T., & Busby, J. (2003). Mental time travel in animals? *Trends in Cognitive Sciences, 7*(9), 391–396.

Suddendorf, T., & Corballis, M. C. (2007). The evolution of foresight: What is mental time travel, and is it unique to humans? *Behavioral and Brain Sciences, 30*(03), 299–313.

Tulving, E. (1972). Episodic and semantic memory. In Tulving, E. & Donaldson, W., (Eds.), *Organization of Memory.* Yale University, 381–402.

Tulving, E. (1985). *Elements of episodic memory.* Oxford University Press.

Whiten, A. (1996). When does smart behaviour-reading become mind-reading? In P. Carruthers & P. K. Smith (Eds.), *Theories of theories of mind.* Cambridge University Press.

Further Readings for Part V

Boyle, A. (2020). The impure phenomenology of episodic memory. *Mind & Language*, *35*(5), 641–660.

>   *Argues that the focus on phenomenology does not rule out the possibility that non-human animals have episodic memory.*

Clayton, N. S., & Dickinson, A. (1998). Episodic-like memory during cache recovery by scrub jays. *Nature*, 395, 272–274.

>   *Argues that scrub-jays are capable of retrieving event-specific information.*

Keven, N. (2016). Events, narratives and memory. *Synthese*, *193*(8), 2497–2517.

>   *Argues for the event memory and episodic memory distinction in more detail. Also defends the idea that episodic memory requires narrative capacities.*

Malanowski, S. (2016). Is episodic memory uniquely human? Evaluating the episodic-like memory research program. *Synthese*, *193*(5), 1433–1455.

>   *Argues for a mechanistic approach to the question of whether non-human animals have episodic memory.*

Suddendorf, T., & Corballis, M. C. (1997). Mental time travel and the evolution of the human mind. *Genetic, Social, and General Psychology Monographs*, *123*(2), 133–167.

>   *Argues that the function of mental time travel is to imagine the future and hence that episodic memory is uniquely human.*

Tulving, E. (2005). Episodic memory and autonoesis: Uniquely human? In H. S. Terrace & J. Metcalfe (Eds.), *The Missing Link in Cognition: Origins of Self-Reflective Consciousness* (pp. 3–56). Oxford University Press.

>   *Argues that episodic memory involves a distinctive form of consciousness that is uniquely human.*

Study Questions for Part V

1) What is the difference, according to Keven, between event memory and episodic memory? Why is it important for him to draw such a distinction?
2) Why are teleological representations important for episodic memory? Why do they give us reason to think that episodic memory is uniquely human?
3) What are the main arguments in favour of 'optimism' and 'kind scepticism'? What is the problem that Boyle identifies with the current debate between proponents of these two approaches?
4) According to the form of pluralism advocated by Boyle, what would be required to establish that non-human animals have episodic memory?
5) How could a pluralist respond to the arguments put forward by Keven?

Part VI

Does episodic memory give us knowledge of the past?

11 The epistemology of episodic memory

Thomas D. Senor

11.1 Introduction

Epistemologists are primarily interested in the evaluation of belief. The epistemology of memory has been no exception to this rule. Using the terminology
of recent work in psychology, epistemologists have chiefly concerned themselves mostly with *semantic* memory. Very little attention has been paid to the
epistemology of what psychologists call *episodic* memory. This chapter cuts
against the epistemological tide. After introducing the relevant concepts, I'll
give a general characterisation of episodic memory before turning our attention
to epistemic matters. We'll go into some detail exploring Kourken Michaelian's
important contribution to the epistemology of episodic memory. In the end,
the position I defend owes a lot to Michaelian, although I will add what I take
to be an important new feature that allows for the epistemic evaluation of episodic memory belief.

11.2 Semantic and episodic memory

The term 'semantic' in *semantic memory* is unfortunate because it suggests a kind
of memory that only has to do with the meaning of terms or the content of
concepts. While semantic memory does include, e.g., your memory that the
word 'cat' refers to domesticated felines or that the concepts *floor* and *ground* are
similar yet conceptually distinct, it includes much else besides. Any kind of
factual memory that is propositional (rather than, e.g., imagistic) will count as a
semantic memory. An example of semantic memory is my belief that Abraham
Lincoln was assassinated in Ford's Theater. When I recall this, I'm conscious of
a bit of information; inasmuch as I'm aware of anything, it's typically of little else
than the propositional content of the belief.

In contrast to remembered belief is *episodic memory*. As a first approximation,
episodic memories are recollections of events that purport to be past first-person
experiences. In the summer of 2019, I travelled to France for the 'Issues in
Philosophy of Memory 2' conference. Presently, I have a memory of arriving by
train in Grenoble. While there are many pieces of semantic memory that
accompany my episodic memory (that I arrived by train, that I was carrying a

DOI: 10.4324/9781003002277-18

small backpack and pulling a large, blue suitcase, and that I was travelling with my wife), my episodic memory is phenomenologically quite different. When I recall these events, I bring to mind a series of images, sounds, and feelings that appear to me to be a sort of reliving of the past. When 18th-century Scottish philosopher David Hume famously described memories as ideas that are 'less vivid and forceful' than perception but more vivid and forceful than imagination, he undoubtedly was thinking of the experience of episodic memory (Hume 1739, 1978, section 85).

For our purposes, we'll think of episodic memory as being typified by a *memory seeming*.[1] When I recall exiting the train at the Grenoble station, it *episodically seems to me* that the weather was warm, that I was lugging a backpack, rolling a suitcase, and feeling very tired. Importantly, this seeming is quasi-sensory, or at least not merely the seeming that accompanies occurrent beliefs. The phenomenology of belief, e.g., of *doxastic seeming*, tends to be mild to non-existent. When I consciously reflect on something I believe to be true, that proposition *seems* true to me; I have some degree of felt confidence.[2] But what I'm calling a *memory seeming* is not (or at least not primarily) a seeming that a proposition is true. Rather, it is a seeming that includes some combination of images, sounds, feelings, smells, and tastes that are quasi-sensory. Recalling the sweet smell of the Sonora desert as you ran through it in a storm, the taste of the Panang curry you had for dinner last Christmas Eve, the rough texture of sandpaper from last summer's deck staining, the sound of your newborn child's cooing on the drive home from the hospital, or the sight of the sun's sinking into the ocean on your first trip to the Pacific—these episodes are not just a matter of contemplating propositions. Rather, these are experiences that purport to recreate (if imperfectly) sensory experiences you've had previously. While it is certainly not right to say that these experiences are sensory full stop, they come to us as quasi-sensory.[3] But not every aspect of episodic memories is quasi-sensory, where what qualifies as sensory is limited to the five senses: For example, I might remember how nervous I was before my first professional talk, how excited I was on my wedding day, or the fear I felt as the doctor was about to reveal the results of my spouse's lab work.

Episodic memories are not only (mostly) quasi-sensory, they present themselves as experiences from one's personal past.[4] What distinguishes my quasi-sensory memory of the smell of the rain on a particular run, for example, from just 'remembering what the desert smells like after a rain' is that the former, but not the latter, includes the seeming that a particular experience of that smell during a run was part of my personal history. That is, it is presented as a memory of a particular episode in my past.

One final aspect of episodic memory should be noted before we turn our attention to epistemic matters. As I've previously claimed, episodic memories are not only experiential but also quasi-sensory. One important aspect of perceptual experience is that it provides us with more data than we can process. For example, as I look out my window, I see my front yard, the street, and my neighbour's yard and house. My percept includes vastly more information than

I am able to pay attention to and explicitly process. But if I attend to certain features of my experience, I'll notice things that I hadn't been aware of before. For example, attending to the vegetation on either side of my neighbor's front porch, I can now see that the bush to the left is a darker green than the one on the right. My percept always represented the scene that way, but it wasn't until I paid attention to that aspect of my experience that I processed that information. In the same way, a memory seeming often has more content that is consciously appreciated by the subject. Here's an example: I recently had a Zoom meeting in which I gave a talk to five other people who had their cameras on. When it was over, I reflected on the meeting and had a quasi-visual experience of the picture on my screen. Scanning the scene in my mind's-eye, I noticed that one of the participants was in the lower left quadrant of his square (I could see a lot of wall and ceiling behind him, particularly to his left). Although the content of my memory seeming included this all along, it wasn't until I paid attention to it that I noticed that this was so. The lesson here is that, as with perception, there are aspects of memory seemings that are part of the content of the seeming but that are not picked up on by one's conscious reflection (see Boyle 2019).

So, how do we epistemically evaluate episodic memory? The first point to note is that, typically, memory seemings are not merely representational states with quasi-sensory content. As with their perceptual counterparts, these seemings have something that approximates assertive content; that is, they standardly come to us as representations of experiences that were part of our personal history. And this is crucial if they are to be epistemically evaluated at all. For example, a painting of a woodsy scene may represent a pine forest with a river bisecting it, and a bluff to the left. The painting can have all of this as content without the artist's intending it to represent an actual forest. On the other hand, when we perceive such a scene, our percept not only has content, but it comes to us as a representation of the way things are in a certain place. Of course, that is not to say that percepts *are* beliefs, entail beliefs, or even generally lead to them causally. Memory seeming is typically the same: it comes to us with not just representational content but suggesting (as it were) that this content represents past experience.

Is the fact that memory seemings are quasi-assertive enough to make them suitable objects of epistemic evaluation? Given that perceptual seemings are not justified or unjustified, rational or irrational, the answer is no—unless either we are wrong about perceptual seemings or there is some reason for thinking that memory seemings are different in this regard. What, then, can be said in way of epistemic evaluation for episodic memories?

In the next section we'll have a look at one of the more detailed discussions of this question, viz., the position found in Kourken Michaelian's (2016) important book *Mental Time Travel: Episodic Memory and Our Knowledge of the Personal Past*. While there is much to like about Michaelian's treatment, I'll argue it isn't adequate as it stands as an epistemology of episodic memory and suggest a significant alteration that corrects what I take to be the view's chief problem.

11.3 Michaelian's two-level system/metacognitive account

In order to clearly understand Michaelian's epistemology of episodic memory, it will be helpful to begin with his general account of what it is to remember an event. Michaelian is interested in giving neither an explication of the content of our concept of remembering nor an account of the semantics of the English word. Rather, his focus is on providing a psychologically adequate description of remembering the personal past.

According to Michaelian, subject S remembers event E just in case: (i) S now has a representation R of e, and (ii) R is produced by a properly functioning episodic construction system which aims to produce a representation of an episode belonging to S's personal past. There is no requirement that there is a causal connection between R and either a past representation or a past event in S's personal history. Furthermore, S's remembering E doesn't entail that E did in fact occur. These last two points (that there need not be a causal connection to a past representation or event and that the remembered event might not have occurred) are significant because they distinguish Michaelian's position from traditional causal theories that take memory to be factive. That is, standard accounts of memory require that a memory be causally related to an earlier event, and that if someone genuinely remembers an event, then that event actually occurred.

Michaelian's justification for rejecting these two standard features is that, as previously mentioned, he takes episodic memories to be outputs of a psychological process. Often, that process will operate on states that are causally related to past representations and experiences, but it need not do so. As has become standard in contemporary accounts of episodic memory, Michaelian's view is that memory is largely a reconstructive and constructive process. Our recollections of past events are not stored in our brains like a video file stored on a computer. Rather, they are reconstructed (if not outright constructed) at the time of recall. Episodic memories, then, are outputs of a properly functioning psychological process that aims to recreate events of one's personal past; there is no reason to think that this process requires a causal connection to earlier representations, and still less reason to think that all of its outputs are representations of events that actually took place.

Taking his cue from the work of Endel Tulving,[5] Michaelian thinks of memory as 'mental time travel' and that the process that produces it is the same psychological process that allows us to imagine future events and events that didn't happen (i.e., 'counterfactual imaginings'). His theory, then, is that the only thing that distinguishes *remembering* an event from *imagining* an event is that in the former case, the episodic construction system (note that the system is simply 'episodic' and not 'episodic memory construction system') is aiming to create a representation of an event the person experienced in the past. Because mental time travel is a matter of simulating both the past and the future, the position defended by Michaelian is called the 'simulation theory'.

Let's turn now to the epistemological part of Michaelian's theory. If the traditional archival view of memory were correct, then as long as we have reliable sensory systems, we would have good reason to trust our recollections. For when I, for example, see a bear on my camping trip, what happens is that I have a visual experience of the bear, this experience gets recorded and stored as is, and when I later recall it, that recorded experience is retrieved. Naturally, this picture of memory doesn't entail its reliability (various kinds of interference, not to mention forgetting, are still possible and would be expected from time to time) but there is *prima facie* reason to trust it. But when the account of episodic memory is constructive/reconstructive rather than archival, the chances of error become pronounced.

Michaelian offers reasons to be optimistic about the role that construction plays in episodic memory. The fact that information from, for example, testimony can be incorporated into first-person memories might sometimes provide information that will make those memories more reliable than they would have been had they not been aided by the incorporated information. Furthermore, since episodic memory is a key distinguishing feature of human psychology, and its unreliability would certainly make it less likely that we would live long enough to reproduce, there is a general argument from evolutionary fittedness for the reliability of our mnemonic processes.

Although getting into the finer details of Michaelian's account is unnecessary for our purposes, it will be helpful to see how he understands what we've been calling 'memory seemings' to be related to belief fixation and the processes' reliability. On Michaelian's view, we should think of episodic memory as a two-level process. The first level is the 'information producer', which presents a representation (constructed by the episodic simulation process). Michaelian calls level two the 'endorsement mechanism'. The idea is that the representation that the episodic simulation system generates is not automatically converted into a belief; rather, it is first subjected to a monitoring ('metacognitive') process that determines whether or not the representation is acceptable. I'll let Michaelian explain how episodic memories are produced by this two-level process.

> It is useful to conceive of the endorsement mechanism as implementing a policy (which need not be explicitly represented) consisting of a set of criteria against which produced information is evaluated together with a rule determining whether a given item of information is to be evaluated as accurate given the extent to which it satisfies these criteria …
>
> An endorsement mechanism need not produce explicit beliefs that a given representation is accurate or inaccurate. If it does, the overall process which produces the beliefs output by the system will be belief dependent, taking both received information and beliefs about its accuracy as input.
>
> (Michaelian 2016, pp. 150–151)

One last piece of the puzzle will be necessary before we discuss the implications of Michaelian's view of the epistemology of episodic memory.

> In general, metacognition may draw on either type 1 (heuristic, unconscious, fast) processing or type 2 (reflective, conscious, slow) processing; that is,

control operations can be based on either automatic or systematic monitoring. Metacognitive systems incapable of systematic monitoring are possible, but the systems on which the discussion will focus here … are capable of both types of processing. Even in these systems, (cheaper) type 1 processing executed by the relevant system itself occurs by default. But (more costly) type 2 processing executed at the level of the agent can also occur under certain circumstances: the agent can deliberately initiate systemic processing, or system processing might be triggered by the system itself under certain conditions.

(Michaelian 2016, pp. 153–154)

On Michaelian's view, then, one has an episodic memory when a simulation process is properly functioning and aiming to produce an episode from the subject's past, and it produces a representation.[6] This information-producing process is monitored by the information-endorsement mechanism; if the information is endorsed, a belief is formed with the relevant content. If the representation does not pass metacognitive monitoring, no belief is formed.

What we have so far is psychological rather than epistemological. Although he is pluralist regarding knowledge in general, Michaelian accepts what is known as 'process reliabilism' as the correct theory of memory knowledge. According to this theory, a memory belief counts as knowledge only if the cognitive processes upon which it depends tend to produce true belief. So, if the processes that produce the memorial representation are reliable, the belief will be justified (and if other conditions are met, an instance of knowledge).

11.4 Evaluating and expanding Michaelian's position

One important position that Michaelian argues for in his book is that the fact that episodic memory is reconstructive and constructive should not be taken to imply that it is not reliable. Indeed, the role it plays in our getting around successfully in the world is *prima facie* evidence of its reliability. That part of Michaelian's argument will not be our concern.

As we've seen, a crucial part of Michaelian's theory (and really, any theory of episodic memory) concerns the nature of the representation (or memory seeming) that is produced, either voluntarily or involuntarily as the case may be. Recall that it is the job of the information-producing process to generate the representation, and the job of the monitoring mechanism to either accept or reject the representation—that is, to form a belief or not. Now, one interesting question concerns the object of epistemic valuation. Recall that semantic memory is essentially memory belief; part of what is supposed to distinguish episodic memory is that it isn't captured by the standard propositional attitude that-clause. But if the target of epistemic evaluation for episodic memory is the belief at the end of the two-level process, then it looks like we've made epistemology relevant only after converting episodic memory to its semantic cousin. So, have we failed to do what we set out to do, i.e., offer an epistemology of *episodic* memory?

This is a tricky problem, although one for which there is something of a workaround. Here's the issue stated as a dilemma: Either episodic memory should be construed as involving a belief, or it shouldn't. If it should, what is epistemically evaluable is a memory belief, and that's just semantic memory (even if it is part of a larger whole that is an episodic memory); if it shouldn't, then there is nothing there to epistemically evaluate, at least if 'epistemic evaluation' is the sort of evaluation having to do with knowledge or justification.

The solution to this apparent dilemma is to define an episodic memory belief as a belief formed on the basis of a memory seeming that had been certified by a metacognitive process.[7] This characterisation of episodic memory belief allows us to make a clear distinction between semantic memory (which is not the immediate result of memory seeming)[8] and episodic memory, and yet gives episodic memory an epistemically evaluable propositional attitude and manages to slip between the horns of the aforementioned dilemma.

There remains, however, a serious issue. Recall that the model we are working with takes a memory seeming to be a representation. Standardly, if there is a representation that is the output of a process that ends in a belief, the content of the belief will be identical to the content of the representation. While undoubtedly an oversimplification, standard positions in the epistemology of perception imply that if one has a perceptual seeming that P (or more exactly 'that X is F'—e.g., that the book is red) and on that basis one comes to believe that P (or that X is F), the content of the representation and the content of the belief are the same.[9] I say this is an oversimplification because there is a lot more to standard perceptual content than what is captured in a single simple proposition. As we saw earlier, when I look out my office window and take in the view, I'm consciously aware of a lot more than I can pay attention to at once. In order for me to form a perceptual belief on the basis of my percept, I must pay attention to some aspect of my experience (either voluntarily or involuntarily). Once I notice, say, that the flag on my mailbox is down, I'll be in a position to form a belief with that content (it's plausible to think that there are metacognitive monitoring processes involved in perception too).

The characterisation of episodic memory (or memory seemings) with which we've been working construes it as quasi-sensory, as involving memorial analogues of sight, sound, smell, taste, touch, and introspective experiences. So, we can't equate the representation produced by the episodic simulation system with the propositional content of the resultant episodic memory belief. While the later chapters of *Mental Time Travel* don't stress this aspect of the product of the information producing process, Michaelian is explicit about it early on.

> Regardless of whether we locate the temporal aspect of episodic memory in content or in phenomenology, the key point for present purposes is that episodic remembering ... produces representations that are like perceptual representations in having sensory rather than propositional content. Episodic content need not be purely sensory ... But it consists at least in part of sensory content and sensory content is nonpropositional, in the

sense that it cannot be evaluated for truth and falsity in a binary manner. Unlike propositional contents delivered by semantic memory, which can be evaluated as simply true or false, the richer representations delivered by episodic memory can be *more or less* accurate—accurate in some respects and inaccurate in others.

(Michaelian 2016, p. 53, emphasis in original)

Because of the quasi-sensory (or as Michaelian puts it, 'sensory') nature of epi-sodic memories, their contents are richer than what is expressible by a single, relatively simple proposition.[10] Because their content is thick (and not in straightforward propositional form), they are often, as Michaelian says, 'more or less' accurate, rather than truth valuable.

The nature of the content of the representation that the information pro-ducer creates causes a problem for Michaelian's position. The following is a reproduction of a diagram of the two-level, metacognitive account of episodic memory belief formation (Michaelian 2016, p. 152).

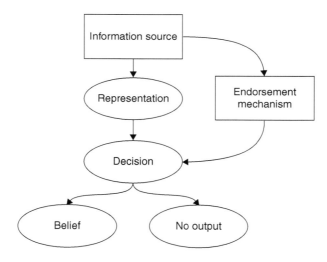

Figure 11.1   Reprinted from Michaelian (2016)

The difficulty is that the content of the belief is a proposition that is, at best, a part of the content (and likely a small part) of the representation produced by the information source. Let's reconsider my earlier example of my episodic memory of leading a Zoom discussion. My recollection of this meeting con-sists of myriad sounds and images. The session was an hour long; of course, most of it I can't freely recall (and likely much of it would be lost even if I were appropriately cued). But there is a hodgepodge of voices, faces, images of my computer screen, etc., that I recall when I recollect my meeting. According to Michaelian's model, my endorsement monitoring system will scan my quasi-sensory, multifaceted representation to see if the source is plausibly experience (rather than imagination) and if the process is memory. In this particular case, the automatic metacognitive process endorses my episodic memory of my Zoom meeting, and I accept the representation as at least mostly accurate.[11]

The problem is, how do we get from this endorsed, rich, quasi-sensory representation to a particular belief? Again, note that according to the diagram, if the decision is positive, a belief is formed. Yet there is nothing in Michaelian's model that functions to distil the plethora of information into a single propositional content. Of course, one way to avoid this difficulty is to maintain that the representation itself is propositional. But that isn't true to the psychological facts. It would also have the previously noted implausible implication that episodic memories are either true or false (not 'more or less accurate'), and that they would be true only if every conjunct in the large, single conjunctive proposition were true. So, what is needed is a step prior to belief formation in which the original representation gives rise to manageable propositional content.

This isn't to say that the decision bubble in Michaelian's diagram is inappropriately placed. Metacognitive monitoring of the quasi-sensory memory seeming is needed to validate the episode as deriving ultimately from experience and produced by the process of memory. But, again, the validation of the episode shouldn't be understood as commitment to its every aspect. What is needed, then, is a mechanism that takes the system from validation of the quasi-sensory representation to the forming of a belief that is based on some aspect of the representation. Naturally, there may be metacognitive monitoring at this level as well. That is, before one comes to believe that P on the basis of episodic memory R, there may be a subsystem that checks for reliability in much the same way the endorsement mechanism in Michaelian's model does.

It's important to see that not every belief formed on the basis of the same episodic representation R will have the same epistemic status. For example, suppose that I'm remembering having dinner with you a few weeks back. My memory includes the following: we ate at a local pub, that the room was dimly lit, that you ordered a vegetarian dish, and that you said you and your family had spent Christmas in Jamaica. Suppose that in fact the pub was better lit than I'm remembering (I'm getting interference from memories of a similar, but more dimly lit pub I frequent), that I had found it surprising that you ordered a vegetarian meal since you are generally carnivorous, and I know that I am particularly susceptible to gist memory. Now, as I am reflecting on our dinner together, I form the following episodic memory beliefs:

a.   We ate a meal together.
b.   You ordered a vegetarian dish.
c.   We ate at Smith's Pub.
d.   The room was dimly lit.
e.   You and your family spent Christmas in Jamaica.

Clearly, (a) is more justified than (c); while I might be confusing where we ate on this occasion with where we've eaten before, and so (c) might be wrong, the truth conditions for (a) are much broader and include the truth conditions for (c). Because your meal selection that evening was out of character, it was particularly noticeable, and the memory would have been well encoded, and hence the belief reliably formed. Given that my recollection of the light in the room is due to interference from memories of a different pub, this belief is not reliably formed. Finally, suppose that I know enough about human memory to know that we are much better at remembering the gist of what we are told rather than the details and that the conversation feels fuzzy to me. In such a case, my system 2 processing may be engaged (as a result of an endorsement mechanism), and instead of believing that your family was in Jamaica at Christmas, I instead come to believe that you spent the holidays in the Caribbean, with Jamaica being the most likely island.

Since all of these beliefs have their basis in the same episodic memory representation and yet their epistemic statuses are varied, the justification for the beliefs must come from something other than, or at least in addition to, the representation.

11.5 Two objects of epistemic evaluation

There are, then, two potential objects (and two levels) of epistemic evaluation for episodic memory. The first is the multifaceted, quasi-sensory representation after it has been certified by metacognitive processes. The second, and most obviously in keeping with the traditional concerns of epistemology, takes as its object of evaluation the belief that is formed by attention paid to an aspect (or aspects) of the episodic memory. Let's take these in reverse order, dealing with the easiest case first.

The most straightforward object of epistemic evaluation is the episodic memory belief formed on the basis of the quasi-sensory representation. Since the object here is a belief, and belief is the standard object of evaluation in epistemology, we are on relatively familiar ground. The reliabilist will think that the combination of processes that produce the propositional content from the quasi-sensory representation will be justification-conferring only if they are reliable. The reliability here is conditional in a threefold way: the original (typically perceptual) process must reliably reflect the event experienced; the processes that produce the episodic representation must reliably reflect the earlier experience or the event experienced, and the process that extracts the propositional content for the multifaceted, quasi-sensory representation must be reliable in the sense that the propositional content is imbedded in the representation.

Putting this altogether, we can say that S's episodic memory belief that P is *prima facie* justified iff:

1. The process that produces the belief from the quasi-sensory representation reliably extracts the particular propositional content from the representation;

2.   The combination of the information-producing and endorsement-monitoring systems reliably produces R (i.e., representations so formed are more or less accurate depictions of past experiences); and

3.   The original experience is a reliable depiction of (i.e., mostly accurately reflects) the facts of the original experienced event (typically, facts about the agent's immediate physical environment, perhaps together with conscious mental/emotional states at the time).[12]

While this account has the virtue of being of a piece with standard epistemic evaluation, one might think that the epistemologist can stop here only if she is guilty of a bait and switch. For the primary question that this chapter has been attempting to address is the epistemology of *episodic* memory. But the aforementioned account takes as its object *belief* formed on the basis of an episodic memory, and not the episodic memory itself. Is there a way to give an honest-to-goodness epistemology of episodic memory that offers a way of evaluating those memories themselves and not their doxastic progeny?

As expounded earlier, episodic memories are quasi-sensory representations with rich, multifarious, and largely non-propositional content. But representations that are non-propositional are not truth valuable; and states that are not truth valuable are (arguably) not candidates for epistemic evaluation. Why not? Because the targets of such evaluation are judged by the extent to which they tend to be successful at achieving the epistemic goal of truth acquisition and error avoidance. Therefore, they aren't directly truth valuable. Still, such states can be *more or less* accurate as accounts of past experiences. These representations are produced by the information producer but then monitored by the endorsement mechanism. While belief doesn't enter at this stage on the account I have suggested, there is an acceptance of the representation when it passes the endorsement stage. Thus, there is at least a proto-pro-attitude that might be a subject of epistemic scrutiny.

Does it make sense to call such a proto-pro attitude of a non-propositional representation 'justified'? As I mentioned earlier, that's not what is typically said of perceptual representations. But there is no reason to get hung up on terminology: we can always introduce a term of evaluation for these states and stipulate it as the term of positive epistemic status for a memory seeming. The more important question is what property or properties of memory seemings are relevant to their epistemic evaluation. For standard reliabilists, the answer will have to do with the extent to which the memory seeming accurately depicts the earlier experience. Notice that the relevant variety of reliability here is analogous to what Alvin Goldman has called 'conditional reliability' of the sort had by belief-dependent belief-forming processes (Goldman 1979). That is, what is required for representational positive epistemic status is that the (constructive) process that reproduces the original experience more or less accurately depicts the original experience; whether the original experience accurately depicts the experienced event in the subject's environment (i.e., the external world) is irrelevant to the reliability of the *memory* process.[13] However, if the idea is that we are evaluating the representation as a more or less accurate depiction of the event that was previously experienced by the subject, then it isn't enough that memory accurately reconstructs the original experience: That first experience has to be an accurate depiction of the event that is its intentional object.

This section of this book asks whether episodic memory can produce knowledge. So, suppose we cut to the chase and ask whether episodic representations (and the proto-pro-attitude that accompanies them) can constitute memory knowledge. Is this even a possibility?

Here's a reason to think that it isn't: It is mostly a truism amongst contemporary epistemologists that S knows that P entails that S believes P and P is true.[14] But episodic representation is non-propositional; so, it neither can be the content of a propositional attitude (e.g., belief) nor can be *true* (cf. Langland-Hassan 2015). Furthermore, there are several kinds of knowledge discussed in the literature: e.g., propositional knowledge, knowledge by acquaintance, and procedural knowledge. But none of these is akin to episodic memory knowledge, whatever precisely that would be.

All of these reasons are relevant, and their weight is significant. But still, we all know what it is to recall an event that (as we say) was seared into our memory; or even just a very recent event that was ordinary (like having dinner an hour ago). And when we remember them, they seem available to us again (even as we recognise that our recollection might not get every detail right). And it is natural to think that this kind of state is at least in the ballpark of knowledge; and it's only 'in the ballpark' not because it is less certain or secure than knowledge, but because it doesn't have the right formal structure—that is, it isn't propositional. But maybe the only reason we think of knowledge as necessarily propositional is because of our folk psychological categories. Is there a good philosophical or psychological reason for thinking that there can't be non-propositional knowledge?

I don't know the answer to that question. But I'll conclude with a bold suggestion: There is *episodic* memory knowledge that is not a form of *semantic* memory knowledge because it does not involve belief. Here is the idea.

S has non-doxastic episodic memory knowledge R of event E iff:

1. R is produced by processes that accurately depict S's original experience X,
2. X is an accurate depiction of event E (this entails E occurred), and
3. R has at least quasi-assertoric force for S (as it would if it were okayed by the endorsement mechanism).

This account of episodic memory knowledge raises many more questions than it answers. First, what is it for a representation to be 'accurate'? It isn't that it has to be true, since it is nonpropositional. The idea, roughly, is that there is an isomorphic mapping from details in R to the event that was originally experienced. Second, how accurate does the representation need to be to produce episodic memory knowledge? Must it be right in every detail? Or are there essential details that need to be accurate but inessential details that can be wrong while the subject still knows? Finally, what is the relationship between episodic memory knowledge and episodic memory belief? Obviously, even if an account along these lines is promising, a great many issues need much more development in order for it to deserve a place in one's epistemology of memory.

11.6 Is most justified memory belief Gettiered?

In his contribution to this section of this book (Chapter 12), Matthew Frise argues that the justified true memory beliefs of most people fail to count as knowledge because they are victims of Gettier situations.[15] Since Frise discusses Gettier cases in his chapter, I'll assume familiarity with them. The reason most subjects are Gettiered, according to Frise, is this:

> It's normal to have beliefs about the past from episodic memory. It's normal for these beliefs to rely on one's understanding of how episodic memory works. But it's not normal to understand how episodic memory really works. The typical subject takes for granted a folk theory in which episodic memory is archival. The beliefs from episodic memory that the subject has about the past rely on this falsehood.
>
> (Frise, Chapter 12)

Most people accept the archival theory of memory, which states that our episodic memories are like computer files of past experience; remembering is a matter of activating the preserved file. But, of course, episodic memory doesn't work like that.

Frise's diagnosis of what goes wrong in such cases is that the subject's justification depends on a falsehood that is essential for its justification. The account of justification that Frise accepts is starkly different from the reliabilist position taken in this chapter. On Frise's view, in order for an episodic memory to justify a belief, the memory must be part of the best available explanation of the truth of the belief. But this explanation, Frise claims, will include beliefs about how memory works. So, if my understanding of memory is the false archival view, then my best explanation for my episodic memory belief (that is, the best explanation available to me) will essentially include a falsehood. And on Frise's view of what goes wrong in Gettier cases, true beliefs, the justification for which essentially involve a falsehood, fail to count as knowledge. So, because the best explanation of the memory belief involves the false archival theory of memory, the subject who believes memory works that way has Gettiered justified true belief rather than knowledge.

Because we come at epistemological matters from such different perspectives, the objections I'm about to make will likely not move Frise. But it is easy enough for me to say where I think his argument goes awry; and it is right at the beginning. As quoted previously, Frise writes: 'It's normal to have beliefs about the past from episodic memory. It's normal for these beliefs to rely on one's understanding of how episodic memory works.' I see no reason to think that our memory beliefs 'rely on [our] understanding of how episodic memory works'. And it's not so much that I doubt that most people have a theory of memory (I'm agnostic about that). Rather, it's that our memory beliefs are virtually never dependent on whatever theory of memory we may have. We just aren't wired to go from memory-experience to beliefs-about-how-memory-works to episodic memory beliefs. When Maggie goes from recalling her job interview to her belief that the interviewer was pleasant, there is no intervening step that involves her theory of memory. Of course, those with significant knowledge about the psychology of memory may at times be unusually reflective if there is reason to think the circumstances of recall decrease reliability. But that will be the great exception. Frise's argument is that those who *don't* know how memory really works will be Gettiered because their beliefs 'rely' on a mistaken theory. But Frise has given us no reason to think that their views about how memory works play a causal role in forming their episodic memory beliefs.

Perhaps I'm misconstruing what it is that is supposed to rely on beliefs about how memory works. Although he says the *beliefs* rely on the theory, perhaps Frise is to be understood as saying that the *justification* of the beliefs relies on the subject's theory of memory (whether Frise also holds the first reading, he certainly holds the second). But this position has some rather counterintuitive implications. Here's one: Isaac Newton held the corpuscular theory of light, the idea that light is made up of tiny particles; seeing physical objects involves these particles striking our eyes. This theory of light is false; what he thought happens when we see physical objects is not what happens. So, let's suppose Newton looks at the object that bopped him on the head and comes to believe, 'That's an apple'. If what Frise has said is right, and people with the archival theory of memory are always Gettiered regarding their episodic memory beliefs, then Newton is Gettiered with respect to his justified true perceptual belief about the apple. And there is nothing special about this particular visual belief: if what Frise has said about Gettier cases is right, Newton has no knowledge of the physical world grounded in vision. Frise might accept this implication of his theory, but by my lights it serves as a reductio of what he says about memory knowledge, and perhaps also of the inference to the best available explanation account of epistemic justification.

11.7 Conclusion

Let me conclude with a few caveats. First, I've certainly not given an argument for reliabilism for either episodic memory belief or episodic memory knowledge. Rather, building on the work of Michaelian, I have outlined how a reliabilist might think about the epistemic status of both episodic memory and episodic memory belief. Second, although I haven't been explicit about it, background beliefs will often play a role in the production of both episodic memory representations and episodic memory beliefs. In cases where background beliefs are causally active in the appropriate way, there will likely be epistemic complications to the theories sketched in this chapter.

Finally, I've couched most of our discussion in terms of justified belief rather than knowledge (the only exception being the highly speculative account of non-doxastic episodic memory knowledge at the end of Section 11.4). Obviously, no justified *belief* counts as knowledge unless it is true. So, to get episodic memory belief knowledge from my account, one must add truth to the recipe. But, almost as obviously (and as Frise's discussion in Chapter 12 makes explicit), there can be justified true belief that fails to be knowledge (Gettier 1963). Hence, there will need to be a fourth condition (at least!) to get from what I've argued for in this essay to an account of episodic memory belief knowledge.

Acknowledgements

Thanks to the audience of the *Current Controversies in the Philosophy of Memory* conference, and especially to Matt Frise for helpful comments on an earlier draft.

Notes

1 Since the publication of Huemer (2001), the use of the word 'seemings' has taken on a particular meaning in epistemology (see also Tucker 2013). My use of the term here is intended to be independent of the way it is used in the literature on phenomenal conservatism.
2 Plantinga (1993, p. 105) points out that certain propositions on reflection have a kind of 'luminosity' that convinces us that our beliefs with that content are true.
3 Kourken Michaelian (2016, pp. 52–53) describes episodic memories as having 'sensory content'. If that description is meant to describe the causal origins of (most) episodic memory, then I take no issue with it. I prefer to call such content 'quasi-sensory' because I'm intending to describe the content *as it seems to the agent*, and not its causal origins. And while recalling what one has seen and heard is *something like* sensory experience (that is, the experience one has in vision and hearing), it is only something like it and not the real thing.
4 The idea that memories have this dual nature of being both about the past and about being the subject's own has been discussed in literature on autonoesis and chronesthesia. See Tulving (2001, 2002a).
5 For a helpful overview on 'mental time travel', see Tulving (2002b).
6 There are complications that we'll be ignoring: autonoesis and chronesthesia play an important part in making the subject take the representation to be a representation of her experience and an experience of the past.
7 I'm defining it this way for maximal clarity, although I don't mean to be committed to the details of Michaelian's account. The idea is that, on the assumption that his two-level/metacognitive description of the psychology of episodic memory is on the right track, we can think of episodic memory belief as the output of the system (when the output is belief). More generally, we might think of episodic memory belief as a belief that, at least in its current form, is the product of a current memory seeming.
8 'Immediate' here should be read both causally and temporally. For suppose I have a memory seeming that includes content P, my monitoring system gives it a thumbs up, and I form the belief that P—and suppose also this happened a year ago and I still have P but no longer the memory seeming. In this case, my belief that P is a semantic memory, not an episodic memory belief.

9 See Lyons (2016) for a discussion of the epistemology of perception.
10 As Michaelian notes, philosophers of perception do not speak with a single voice regarding the content of perceptual experience, and hence virtually anything said will be controversial. In this case, I say the content of an episodic memory can't be expressed by a 'simple, single' proposition because it could be that the content is expressible by a massive conjunction; such a position would be implausible, however, because it would make an episodic memory that was current save a single detail 'false' since conjunctions are true only if every conjunct is true. The primary claim here is that just as a visual percept may include the content 'The tree is green,' without thereby being exhausted by it, in the same way an episodic memory may include the content, 'The bird at the feeder was a cardinal' without its being the only content in the representation.
11 That's not to say that I'll have an idea which aspects are inaccurate. But knowing the serious fallibility of episodic memory, I'll figure that it is likely things are entirely right. This is something akin to the Paradox of the Preface. Except in this case rather than having a set of beliefs to which one is committed even while at the same time thinking of the set that it contains some falsehoods, it's more like having a picture that one thinks generally represents the world accurately, while at the same time thinking it likely that some detail is wrong.
12 Thanks to Matt Frise for noting the inadequacy of an earlier version of this condition in which I said that the original representation had to accurately depict the 'facts of the original experience' rather than the facts of the event that was experienced.
13 It should be noted that while Michaelian is a reliabilist, he would not accept this application of conditional reliability as a necessary condition of memory knowledge. On his view, memory aims at producing truth and not with accurately matching one's past experience. See Michaelian (2020) and Michaelian and Sant'Anna (2022).
14 I say 'mostly a truism' because it will be denied by Timothy Williamson and other 'knowledge-firsters'. See Williamson (2000).
15 Frise offers two arguments that there is little memory knowledge (at least among those who have relatively little knowledge of current memory research). I have the space here to reply only to his first argument.

References

Boyle, A. (2019). Learning from the past: Epistemic generativity and the function of episodic memory. *Journal of Consciousness Studies, 26*(5–6), 242–251.
Gettier, E. (1963). Is justified true belief knowledge? *Analysis, 23*(6), 121–123
Goldman, A. I. (1979). What is justified belief? In G. Pappas (Ed.), *Knowledge and Justification* (pp. 1–23). D. Reidel.
Huemer, M. (2001). *Skepticism and the Veil of Perception.* Rowman and Littlefield.
Hume, David (1739, 1978). *A Treatise of Human Nature* (L. A. Selby-Bigge, Ed.; 2nd ed., revised, P. H. Nidditch, Ed.). Clarendon Press.
Langland-Hassan, P. (2015). Imaginative attitudes. *Philosophy and Phenomenological Research 90*(3), 664–686.
Lyons, J. (2016). Epistemological problems of perception. In E. N. Zalta (Ed.), *Stanford Encyclopaedias of Philosophy.* https://plato.stanford.edu/entries/perception-episprob/.
Michaelian, K. (2016). *Mental Time Travel: Episodic Memory and Our Knowledge of the Personal Past.* MIT Press.
Michaelian, K. (2020). Confabulating as unreliable imagining: In defence of the simulationist account of unsuccessful remembering. *Topoi, 39*(1), 133–148.
Michaelian, K., & Sant'Anna, A. (2022). From authenticism to alethism: Against McCarroll on observer memory. *Phenomenology and the Cognitive Sciences.* https://doi.org/10.1007/s11097-021-09772-9

Plantinga, A. (1993). *Warrant and Proper Function.* Oxford University Press.

Tucker, C. (Ed.). (2013). *Seemings and Justification: New Essays on Dogmatism and Phenomenal Conservatism.* Oxford University Press.

Tulving, E. (2001). Origin of autonoesis in episodic memory. In H. L. Roediger III, J. S. Nairne, I. Neath, & A. M. Surprenant (Eds.), *Science Conference Series. The Nature of Remembering: Essays in Honor of Robert G. Crowder* (pp. 17–34). American Psychological Association.

Tulving, E. (2002a). Chronesthesia: Conscious awareness of subjective time. In D. T. Stuss & R. T. Knight (Eds.), *Principles of Frontal Lobe Function* (pp. 311–325). Oxford University Press.

Tulving, E. (2002b). Episodic memory: From mind to brain. *Annual Review of Psychology, 53,* 1–25.

Williamson, T. (2000). *Knowledge and Its Limits.* Oxford University Press.

12 You don't know what happened

Matthew Frise

12.1 Introduction

You know that rain comes from clouds and that fire requires fuel. This kind of knowledge is *propositional*. You know *that* something is so. What you know is, or has the structure of, a proposition. You've got a lot of this knowledge.

You remember a lot too. You remember that you have an important deadline next week. You remember feeling relieved when you met your last deadline. There's a subtle difference in the kind of thing you remember in each case, though. Remembering *that* you have an important deadline is similar to the knowledge I just described: The content of your remembering is a proposition. This remembering, or the memory system responsible for it, is often called 'semantic memory'. What you remember in this way is either true or false.

Remembering an instance in which you had a certain feeling is different. What you remember here isn't a proposition, but rather an event or your experience of a past event. This memory tends to be imagistic, and the event tends to be autobiographical. An event isn't true or false, though your recollection of it can be accurate or inaccurate. This remembering, or the memory system responsible for it, is often called 'episodic memory'.[1]

A lot of our knowing is because of our remembering. It would be natural to suppose our propositional knowing is fully explained by semantic memory in particular. After all, they have the same kind of content, namely, propositions. But it could be that we have propositional knowledge from episodic memory too. You might know that you felt relieved, not because you remember that you felt that way, but because you remember the event in which you felt that way. Remembering an event seems like strong evidence that the event occurred. Perhaps we know a lot by episodic memory.

I doubt it. In this chapter I develop two reasons for thinking episodic memory itself doesn't usually yield propositional knowledge of the past, even in the best of cases. Some philosophers (Fernández 2015; Frise n.d.) argue that certain *kinds* of episodic memory do not yield knowledge of the past. They claim, specifically, that episodic memory with a third-person rather than first-person perspective does not yield knowledge.[2] My claim here is broader, as it is about any kind of episodic memory, regardless of perspective.

DOI: 10.4324/9781003002277-19

If I am right, one notable consequence is that we might know much less than we had thought. We might have thought, after all, that episodic memory was responsible for a lot of our knowing. Another reason my claim matters is that it can shed light on whether the distinction between episodic and semantic memory matters in epistemology. Semantic memory might, to our surprise, have notably greater epistemic power than episodic memory.

Before I argue for my main claim, I will say more about the nature of knowledge. This way, we will be better positioned to see the limits that I claim episodic memory has. Knowing requires that several conditions are met. A failing to meet one or more of these conditions explains any failing to know. At least four conditions are necessary for a subject to know that a proposition is true: the subject *believes* the proposition; the proposition is *true*; believing the proposition is *justified* for the subject; and the subject's justification does not by mere accident arrive at true belief (the subject is *not Gettiered*).[3] The belief, truth, and justification requirements require little explanation. To know, you must think something is true, and it must be true, and you must have good enough reason to think it so. The fourth condition—the Gettier condition—is more opaque. To know, your reason for thinking something is true should have a proper connection to its truth. An example helps make this condition clearer.

Suppose you can't find your shoes. Through the window, you spot a pair of shoes outside, by the front door. They look like yours. So you believe they are. And so you believe your shoes are outside. But those aren't your shoes. They are your housemate's. She stepped in a deceptively deep puddle last night and left the shoes out to dry. But when she entered the house afterward, she tripped over your shoes. That was one stroke of bad luck too many. So she flung your shoes out the door before slamming it shut. You can't see them, but they're outside. You believe that your shoes are outside, and they are, and what you see through the window gives you good enough reason to believe your shoes are outside. But, in a way, it's just a coincidence that you believe both reasonably and correctly in this instance. Your belief is true, but not for the reason you think. So you don't *know* your shoes are outside. You are Gettiered.

Episodic memory typically helps us meet most conditions for knowledge. Episodic memory allows us to recall past events. During this recall, we tend to believe propositions about the past; we meet the belief condition for knowledge.[4] And we usually meet the truth condition too. Most of what we believe from episodic memory is accurate. And it might seem that we meet the justification and Gettier conditions. Recalling an event appears to give good enough reason for believing it occurred; and if it's true the event occurred, recalling seems properly related to its being true. I will argue we typically do not meet both of these conditions, however. We are usually Gettiered when accurately believing from episodic memory. And when we are not, we usually lack the justification that would enable our knowing. After supporting these arguments, I will evaluate Thomas Senor's (Chapter 11, this volume) claims about justification from episodic memory.

12.2 Getting Gettiered

Here I will give my first argument for the claim that we typically do not know the past by episodic memory itself. The argument is that we are typically Gettiered when justifiedly, accurately believing by way of episodic memory. And if that's so, we typically do not know by way of episodic memory; we are failing to meet a condition necessary for knowing, namely, that we are not Gettiered.

That there is a Gettier condition on knowledge is largely uncontroversial, so I will not defend it. The success of my argument here, then, mostly depends on the premise that episodic memory usually does not help us satisfy this condition.

We don't usually satisfy it, but not because when episodically recollecting we are typically in a silly case, like the one with the shoes in Section 12.1. It's not as if the following is normal. You recall yourself eating Puffy Snaps cereal at breakfast. You then justifiedly believe that you ate cereal for breakfast today, and that's what you indeed ate. So you justifiedly believe a truth here. But you're recalling a different morning. You had Puffy Snaps yesterday. Today you had Snuffy Pops. Episodic memory leads to the justified true belief that you had cereal for breakfast today, but the truth of that belief is poorly connected to your justification. You're Gettiered.

That is not why we rarely satisfy the fourth condition on knowledge by way of episodic memory. To see just why we don't satisfy it, we would do well to state this condition as carefully as possible. Unfortunately, no one has done that, and probably no one will. It's much easier to identify Gettier cases than it is to identify an informative condition that excludes them all. So, I will not state this condition in as much detail as would be ideal.

Still, some attempts at stating it are better than others. One promising attempt is Richard Feldman's. He (Feldman 2003, p. 36) thinks, 'The key thing in all Gettier-style cases is that, in some sense, the central belief "essentially depends on a falsehood"'. In the example with shoes, your belief that your shoes are outside depends on the falsehood that the shoes you see are yours. The dependence here is essential in that any reason you have for believing they are outside *relies* on the falsehood that the shoes you see are yours. You might not be aware that you rely on this falsehood. And you are not aware it is a falsehood. But you do not have, in Feldman's (2003, p. 36) words, 'a justificatory line that ignores the falsehood'. And that is why you are Gettiered. (When you do have a line that ignores the falsehood, you are not Gettiered, even if you also have a separate line that does depend on it. That's because the dependence here isn't *essential*. There's another line.)

If Feldman is right, we can state the Gettier condition on knowledge more precisely. If a subject knows a proposition, her justification for believing it does not essentially depend on any falsehood (Feldman 2003, p. 37). And even if Feldman is wrong, his condition is plausibly *sufficient* for being Gettiered. That is, it is plausible that *if* a subject's justification essentially depends upon a falsehood, she is Gettiered, and therefore does not know. This condition could be developed further—exactly what is essential dependence? But it is clear and plausible enough for our purposes.[5]

My controversial premise, again, is that our justified, accurate believing about the past by episodic memory is typically Gettiered. Given Feldman's view, my route to supporting my premise is clear. I must show that our justified, accurate believing about the past by episodic memory usually essentially depends on a falsehood. That is, the following is usual when a subject recalls an event, then forms a reasonable, accurate belief about it: the subject's reasonable believing here depends on something false. And the subject does not have an alternate line of support for the belief that excludes the falsehood.

What is the falsehood, and why suppose it's essential?

The falsehood has to do with how episodic memory works. It's that memory properly functions more or less like an archive. We have experiences of events, and memory keeps a copy of those experiences. The copy is faithful, and nothing tampers with it while in storage. When we remember an event, we are pulling the copy off a shelf and reviewing it. We glimpse just what's already there. Memory functions as it should when there is minimal interference at any point between the original experiencing of the event and the recollecting of it. There is little to no alteration in the depositing, storing, and accessing. Some types of changes are unfortunate but are within the parameters of a properly functioning memory. For example, we forget. Relatively unpopular items disappear from the shelves, degrade, or find themselves replaced by new deposits. But this is to be expected even in a well-maintained archive that runs long enough.[6]

Episodic memory is not in fact so archival. Before anything makes it to a shelf, memory does some screening—there's no need to keep everything, or to keep it all equally accessible. Often we do well enough to save just the contours of an event rather than its every word and strand of hair. And with a little editing, we can more efficiently hold on to what we haven't screened out; instead of storing copies of many relevantly similar experiences, we can store just a template for generating some of these copies. But the template doesn't generate uniformly. The context in which we draw on episodic memory affects the outcome. The circumstances in which we recollect often affect what we recollect.

This is just a brief caricature of how episodic memory works. The point is that episodic memory is normally generative rather than archival. It screens and edits. It synthesises new deposits with other experiences, past and imagined. Even during retrieval, information remains malleable.[7]

This would come as a surprise to a typical subject. It's normal to have beliefs about the past from episodic memory. It's normal for these beliefs to rely on one's understanding of how episodic memory works. But it's not normal to understand how episodic memory really works. The typical subject takes for granted a folk theory in which episodic memory is archival (see Simons & Chabris 2011). The beliefs from episodic memory that the subject has about the past rely on this falsehood.

Now I show the dependence on this falsehood is essential. That is, suppose a subject episodically recalls an experience of a past event. Typically, if this recall for her supports believing that p (where p is a proposition about the past), the support in part relies on the falsehood that memory is archival. My claim here, then, is that without this falsehood, episodic memory rarely supports believing p.

When episodic recall supports believing p, it's because the truth of p is part of the best explanation available to the subject for why she recalls p.[8] You recall an event in which you saw fireworks on the Fourth of July. Suppose this makes it reasonable for you to believe that you saw fireworks on the Fourth of July. How could that be? It's because your seeing fireworks then is part of the best explanation you have for why you would now recall seeing them then. You have other explanations available (for example, you wish you hadn't spent July 4 eating sugary cereal alone, and so you're confabulating an alternative past), but the best ones all include your actually seeing fireworks then.

Now, when the truth of p is *part* of the best explanation for recall, it is not the only part. Other parts involve how memory works. Other parts of the explanation include, for example, memory functioning in such a way that it is a good guide for believing. When recalling supports believing p, it's because the best explanation of the recalling involves both the truth of p as well as memory functioning in a way that puts us in touch with the past. Your recalling seeing fireworks on the Fourth of July supports your believing you saw them then. Part of the best explanation of your recalling seeing fireworks is that you saw them then *and* that memory puts you in touch with what you saw.

An explanation of your recall that omits how memory works does not make sense of how recall is relevant to the past. On this sort of explanation, recalling seeing fireworks says as little about the actual past as merely *imagining* seeing fireworks does.

The archival view sheds light on how episodic recall is relevant to the past. On this view, memory functions in a trustworthy way, one likely enough to put us in touch with what happened. Memory preserves a faithful record of what happened, and recall is a matter of reviewing the record. The archival view helps facts about past events explain our recalling those events in the present.

A typical subject does not have an explanation of the recall that omits the archival view but that includes facts about the past being a certain way. The typical subject does not have an alternative model of how memory works, on which memory puts us in touch with the past.

Of course, the subject could imagine such a model. Or the subject could learn about how episodic memory really works—how it is generative. In fact, episodic memory is generative in a way that still puts us in touch with the past. It's not an archive, but that is no flaw. Surprisingly enough, the way it alters what it receives, keeps, and delivers does not compromise the likely truth of what it delivers, or is disposed to deliver. It's still a good guide to the truth. If the subject has learned this, then for that subject, on the best explanations of episodically recalling the past being a certain way, the past is that way.

The typical subject has not learned this. The typical subject is unaware that memory is generative (and unaware that memory could still function generatively while guiding belief well). On all of the best explanations of her recall that the typical subject already has available, episodic memory is archival. So the following is true for the typical subject. Her support from episodic memory for believing about the past essentially depends on a falsehood, namely, the falsehood about how memory works.

I have shown, in other words, that the typical subject's justification from episodic memory alone essentially depends on a falsehood. But on Feldman's view, if a subject knows a proposition, her justification for believing it does not essentially depend on any falsehood. So I have shown that, given Feldman's view, the typical subject who accurately and justifiedly believes what episodic memory delivers is Gettiered. Episodic memory does not give her knowledge of the past.[9]

12.3 Gettiered or bust: A dilemma

Here I argue, for another reason, that episodic memory itself typically fails to provide knowledge of the past. The first reason mainly had to do with how episodic memory functions differently from what we had assumed, in an important way. The reason here, however, is not centrally about how memory functions. It's about how often episodic memory is correct. During recollection, episodic memory represents the past as being various ways. Sometimes it represents the past as it was, and other times it misrepresents the past. It might be that episodic memory is *usually* accurate. Still, I claim that it misrepresents *often*, and non-trivially.

This is not to say that episodic memory *usually* misrepresents. But it's at least not rare. Often it's predictable. To show it often misrepresents, it would be good to make clear just what sorts of things episodic memory represents, and then to make clear that it is often inaccurate. Unfortunately, it's not clear just what sorts of things episodic memory represents. When recalling an event in which I saw fireworks on the Fourth of July, does memory represent something in that event *as* fireworks? Or is that simply how I now interpret something in that memory? The content of episodic recollection merits greater investigation. I will not undertake that here.

As for whether episodic memory is often inaccurate, this is largely an empirical issue. And the empirical literature does support this (see, among many others, Schacter 2001; Schacter et al. 2011). (A little reflection does too. Since episodic memory is generative, it's unlikely that all it generates will be spot on.) It is not rare for imagination to alter the details of an episodically recalled event, or for imagination rather than experience to be the origin of a recalled event. It is also not rare for memory to incorporate information acquired after an event into our recollection of it, for memory to confabulate altogether new events or details of events, or for memory to present in recollection our interpretation of past experiences rather than experiences themselves.

I will not explore further how memory often misrepresents. What's important is that it does. And so, I claim, a dilemma emerges. Does a subject have evidence that memory misrepresents so often? Suppose the answer is yes, she has this evidence. I will argue that she therefore typically does not satisfy the *justification* condition for knowledge of the past from episodic memory. Suppose the answer is no, the subject does not have this evidence. I will argue that she therefore typically does not satisfy the *Gettier* condition for knowledge of the past from episodic memory. On either answer, a typical subject does not know the past by way of episodic memory. So she does not know it this way.

Let's start with the yes answer. We're supposing a subject has evidence that memory misrepresents often. I am not saying the subject thereby lacks *any* justification from episodic memory for believing propositions about the past. Episodic memory still typically does give justification of a sort. It gives *prima facie* justification. That is, it gives justification which, in the absence of reason to refrain from believing, justifies believing *overall*. And justification can vary in strength. One could have merely some justification for believing, all the way up to maximal justification. Episodic memory could still typically give very strong *prima facie* justification for believing propositions about the past. But evidence about how episodic memory misrepresents is *some* reason to refrain from believing. This evidence is a *partial defeater* for the justification from episodic memory. It reduces some but perhaps not all overall justification for believing.

I noted that knowledge requires justification. It is time to be more precise. I did not note that this justification must be overall and not merely *prima facie*. And I did not note how strong it must be. Philosophers tend to agree that it must be especially strong, if not Herculean. If that is right, then even a partial defeater can easily prevent knowledge. A partial defeater can turn *especially* strong overall justification into justification that is merely *very* strong overall. And that slight reduction is all it takes to fail to have the justification knowledge requires.

Evidence that episodic memory often misrepresents is a partial defeater. It is a partial defeater for just about any justification episodic memory provides for believing propositions about the past. The scope of the defeat is broad.

And this seems exceptional. There could be evidence that some other potential conduit to knowledge often mispresents. But it would not obviously be a partial defeater for just about any justification from that conduit. For example, we might have evidence that perception often misrepresents. Perhaps often, the world appears to be one way when it is in fact another. But perceptual misrepresentation is easier to flush out, even by further perception itself. If a subject has a misleading visual impression that the Mueller–Lyer lines are of unequal length, further visual experience easily brings the error to light; the subject can visually compare the lines to a ruler held up to them simultaneously. Perception reveals the error of its ways.

Episodic memory is not as well equipped to bring its own errors to light. It lends fewer rulers. Other memories or background information could help us discern whether memory is misrepresenting. But, given memory's generative nature, this misrepresenting could instead reshape the very information by which we might flush errors out. If I want to check by memory whether I really saw fireworks on the Fourth of July, I can try to remember what else happened that day. But I might end up reconstructing anything else I recall in a way that fits with my seeing fireworks then.

Episodic memory often misrepresents. And it is hard to tell just how often or gravely it misrepresents. A subject who learns that memory often misrepresents will have little sense of how extensive the misrepresentation is. Little is clearly safe. The subject has available explanations for why she recalls an event, explanations on which the event did not go quite that way. The subject has a partial defeater for almost any justification she has from episodic memory.

This defeater is ordinarily itself undefeated. The subject has some reason to doubt, and little reason to doubt the doubt. Usually, the subject will not have further evidence indicating that, in a given recollection, episodic memory is not in fact misrepresenting. Since this partial defeater is typically undefeated for the subject, her level of overall justification from episodic memory is not strong enough for knowledge. Even small reasons to doubt hinder knowing. It's not by episodic memory that she knows the past.

Now for the dilemma's second horn. I've suggested that memory often misrepresents. On this horn of the dilemma, the subject lacks evidence that this is so. The subject who lacks the evidence about how episodic memory often misrepresents may have overall justification from episodic memory that is strong enough for knowledge. But this subject, I claim, is typically Gettiered at best. That is, if the subject has justification (and true belief), it essentially depends on a falsehood. The falsehood is that normally functioning memory rarely or only trivially misrepresents.

I have already argued that this is indeed a falsehood. Now I must show that the typical subject's justification essentially depends on it. That is, she will not have an alternate line of justification that omits this falsehood. At first glance, what I am to show seems far-fetched. After all, the subject might easily have alternate lines of justification that swap out the falsehood for a truth, such as: normally functioning memory *usually* represents the past accurately; or, normally functioning memory is a good if imperfect guide for belief.

I grant that these are indeed truths. And I grant that they are parts of available lines of justification. That is, I grant the following. Take a typical subject who lacks the evidence about how memory often misrepresents. Suppose she episodically recalls an event in which p. She has a line of justification from episodic memory for believing p. And this line depends on only truths. Indeed, I grant that the line may even *essentially* depend on only truths.

However, this line of justification is lacking in an important regard. We have seen that knowledge requires not just justification, but overall justification that is quite high. A line of justification on which memory is merely *usually* accurate, or merely a *good* guide for belief, might be strong. But it is not knowledge-level. It is high, but not quite high enough. The subject's justification here might not essentially depend on a falsehood, but the subject's *knowledge-level* justification does. So the subject's knowledge-level justification leaves her Gettiered at best, and her other justification from episodic memory is not knowledge-level. So she does not know.

In Section 12.2, I argued that a typical subject who has justified true belief from episodic memory is Gettiered. Here I have presented a dilemma, the second horn of which argues the same. I note, however, that the subject is Gettiered in each argument for a different reason.[10] The subject's justification depends on a different falsehood. In the previous section, the falsehood centrally had to do with how memory normally or properly works. In the current dilemma, the falsehood has to do with memory's accuracy. How memory works, of course, can indicate whether it's often accurate. But we should not mistake facts about memory's functioning *to be* facts about its accuracy. The falsehoods that I claim the subject essentially depends on in each argument are distinct. Hence, we have distinct arguments for my claim that episodic memory ordinarily does not yield knowledge of the past.

Episodic memory misrepresents, and not rarely. A subject either has evidence of this or she doesn't. A subject with evidence of this typically has a defeater for her justification from episodic memory for believing propositions about the past. This subject does not know from episodic memory how the past was. A subject who lacks this evidence is typically Gettiered at best. Her knowledge-level justification from episodic memory depends essentially on something false. Either way, episodic memory usually does not provide knowledge of the past. By episodic memory, usually we don't know what happened.

12.4 Senor on the epistemology of episodic memory

My focus has been on whether we know much from episodic memory. I have discussed justification here only as it has pertained to my claims about knowledge. Propositional knowledge requires justification, something I have granted that episodic memory provides. I have argued, however, that when a subject has evidence about how episodic memory misrepresents, episodic memory does not provide overall justification strong enough for knowledge. But a closer look at justification from episodic memory is in order.

Thomas Senor (2022, Chapter 11, this volume) takes this look. He examines how episodic memory might provide justification at all. Episodic recollection has certain outputs. Senor reflects on how these outputs relate to what epistemologists evaluate—namely, doxastic attitudes, or the epistemic support we have for these attitudes. Senor calls for more adequate modelling of episodic memory in contemporary epistemology. He suggests a leading current model is incomplete at best, and he proposes some improvements. I will evaluate some of his main claims here. I note that Senor shows little alarm about whether it is possible to adequately model episodic memory. And Senor does not show concern about potential threats to our having justification or knowledge from episodic memory. Still, Senor's remarks appear at least consistent with my main claim that we typically don't know from episodic memory alone.

The model of episodic memory Senor critiques is Kourken Michaelian's (2016). Senor argues that Michaelian's model inadequately characterises the *output* of episodic memory processing. On this model, episodic recollection involves producing a representation. This representation is not automatically endorsed, but is first evaluated for likely accuracy. A metacognitive endorsement mechanism might endorse content at the conclusion of episodic memory processing. Michaelian's model interprets any endorsed content as belief. If this model is adequate, then some tasks of a complete epistemology of episodic memory become clear. Episodic memory generates a doxastic attitude. An epistemology here describes, among other things, what this causal process must be like for it to provide justification.

Senor finds this model lacking. It identifies endorsed content as belief. But for a few reasons, Senor thinks this is incorrect. For one, endorsed content from episodic recollection outstrips the content of any single belief. In endorsed content much more is represented than in the content of any one belief. The metacognitive endorsement mechanism may endorse a complex and detailed representation of an event, or of the subject's experience of that event, across many sense modalities. The subject is recalling what happened and how she heard and saw and felt what happened. But no single belief of hers captures all this nuance. Additionally, the relevant type of belief has content different in kind from what is endorsed in episodic recollection. Belief here has propositional content; a subject believes that *p*. But an endorsed representation from episodic recollection is of an event or of an experience of an event, and this is not propositional in form. It is unclear whether Senor thinks endorsed content and the content of belief always differ in these ways. They might not. Perhaps, for example, endorsed content only sometimes outstrips that of belief. But if there is any case in which the endorsing and believing are not identical in content, then the endorsing is not identical with the believing.

Senor seems to show Michaelian's model is incomplete at best. Presumably, eventually, episodic memory yields belief. But the model leaves epistemologists wondering: just how does episodic memory do this? In the absence of an answer to that question, the model does not allow a comprehensive epistemology of episodic memory.

Revising Michaelian's model in a way that avoids Senor's concerns might not be difficult. Senor might be right that endorsement isn't, or doesn't yield, just a single belief. But perhaps endorsement is, or results in, a multitude of beliefs, and these beliefs jointly exhaust the content of what's endorsed. This minimally revises Michaelian's model, and could sidestep the concern about endorsed content outstripping the content of belief. I don't think this revision will ultimately succeed, but Senor does not address it, and it handles one of his concerns.

In light of his objections, Senor proposes what we perhaps should understand to be a supplement to Michaelian's model. It further articulates how a belief that is based on the output of episodic memory processing is justified. Senor and Michaelian both accept process reliabilism, according to which the justification of a belief is a matter of the reliability of the process yielding it. Unsurprisingly,

Senor's supplement appears process reliabilist-friendly. It states three necessary and jointly sufficient conditions for the justification of belief from episodic memory. All three conditions centre on some kind of reliability:

S's episodic memory belief that P is *prima facie* justified iff:

1. The process that produces the belief from the quasi-sensory representation reliably extracts the particular propositional content from the representation;
2. The combination of the information-producing and endorsement-monitoring systems reliably produces [the representation] (i.e., representations so formed are more or less accurate depictions of past experiences); and
3. the original experience is a reliable depiction of (i.e., mostly accurately reflects) the facts of the original experienced event (typically, facts about the agent's immediate physical environment, perhaps together with conscious mental/emotional states at the time).

(Senor, Chapter 11, this volume)

The rough idea is this. Justified belief from episodic recollection will be based on content that is endorsed in the episodic memory processing. The belief, as noted, has propositional content, while the endorsed content is non-propositional. But the content types are related. A justified belief here results from a process that will 'reliably extract' propositional content from the non-propositional content. (Presumably, the content of the justified belief just is the reliably extracted content.) Additionally, what's endorsed needs to itself have been produced 'reliably'; the content endorsed in recollection is faithful to the remembering subject's past experience. Finally, the subject's original experience has a further kind of reliability: it was mostly accurate.[11]

Senor has helpfully found an apparent lacuna in the epistemology of memory, and his attempt to address it has many virtues. I'll limit my main remarks about his proposal to three brief points.

The first point has to do with how Senor's three conditions matter for the general epistemological view he endorses, process reliabilism. At first glance, reliabilism seems amenable to these conditions, since they too place reliability at the core of epistemic justification. But if Senor's proposals are correct—if he has identified three conditions necessary for justification from episodic memory—then traditional process reliabilism turns out to be *false*. That is my first point. Traditional process reliabilism states two sufficient conditions for justified belief, plus a claim that any justified belief meets one of those two conditions.[12] On neither sufficient condition must all or perhaps even any of Senor's three conditions be met. So if Senor's conditions are indeed necessary for justified belief from episodic memory, then traditional reliabilism states two false sufficient conditions for justification. His proposal departs from tradition.

One might reply that Senor's proposal simply improves on traditional process reliabilism. And that might be correct. But if it is correct, I note then that traditional process reliabilism turns out, all along, to have faced an unappreciated problem centring on episodic memory. It failed to account for how belief from episodic memory is justified. It implied there is justification in cases where there was none. This problem is why the traditional view needed improvement. And it is notable to discover flaws in such a celebrated view.

My next point is on the third of Senor's three conditions. That condition says justified belief from episodic memory must be about an event that the subject originally experienced mostly accurately. This condition has some unintuitive consequences. If there was no original experience—if the subject is misremembering and did not in fact experience the event—this third condition is not met. So there cannot be justified episodic memory belief in such a case, even when episodic memory is reliable, functioning well overall, providing good evidence, but simply not being true to past experience. Additionally, on Senor's third condition, there is no justified episodic memory belief in cases where the original experience was not mostly accurate. The original experience may have been part of a reliable belief formation process, and may have supplied good evidence, but was overall misleading. In some cases, the original experience even *originally* led to justified belief. But on Senor's third condition, the episodic memory belief sharing the content of the original justified belief cannot be justified. This would be because the original experience was not mostly accurate. Not only is this verdict on the episodic memory belief questionable, but so is the asymmetry.

My final point is on whether we must accept Senor's proposal. He (this volume) says he has 'outlined how a reliabilist might think about the epistemic status of both episodic memory and episodic memory belief'. Senor criticises Michaelian's model of episodic recollection, and his proposal is meant to overcome that specific model's flaws. That, I take, is the main consideration in favour of reliabilists accepting Senor's proposal. And if Senor's proposal indeed overcomes these flaws, it has something in its favour. Still, it doesn't follow that it has enough in its favour to recommend it, even to reliabilists. We have not heard whether there are promising models of episodic recollection other than Michaelian's, ones that do not share its alleged flaws. If there are any alternatives that are friendly to reliabilism, then there may be no need for reliabilists to accept Senor's proposal. Similarly, if there are other promising reliabilist-friendly fixes to Michaelian's model, then Senor's proposal has less to recommend it.

So we have not seen that reliabilists must accept the proposal. And we have not heard about the prospects of non-reliabilist supplements to Michaelian's model. I will briefly sketch one alternative to Senor's proposal. This alternative is simpler than Senor's and is acceptable to reliabilists and non-reliabilists. It is therefore at best unclear whether Senor's proposal has enough in its favour to recommend it. This is my final point.

Here is how endorsement in episodic memory may work in an epistemologically relevant way. Endorsement in episodic recollection is or results in something like *refining*—refining what a representation is evidence for. Prior to endorsement, the representation is evidence for little. This is because the representation is not labelled with an origin. It may originate from a past event, or from mere imagination. Endorsed content is content evaluated as likely enough to originate from a past event. Endorsement is, or creates, or indicates, evidence for the subject that a particular event occurred in the past. Endorsing content prima facie justifies the subject in believing that the past contains an event as represented by the endorsed content. Usually the content of no single belief will exhaust the endorsed content. But that's not a problem. Endorsement can simply justify the subject in believing many propositions. The subject might form some justified beliefs based on the endorsed representation, but probably does not form all she could.

This looks like a simple but adequate supplement to Michaelian's model of episodic memory processing. Senor's supplement looks more complex and might appeal only to reliabilists. For now, it's at best unclear whether we should accept his proposal.

12.5 Conclusion

I have raised some doubts about whether we should accept Senor's attempt to fill an apparent gap in the epistemology of episodic memory.

And for two reasons I have suggested that to know the past from episodic memory alone is unusual. But this is not as bad as it may seem. We can still know the past from other sources, even from other forms of memory. Perhaps semantic memory is not vulnerable to arguments paralleling those I have given in this chapter, and so semantic memory can typically provide knowledge of the past. Perhaps episodic memory, when joining hands with semantic memory, typically can too. And even if episodic memory does not itself provide knowledge, it can still provide strong justification for a broad range of beliefs about the past. And much of our justification from episodic memory is not fully defeated, if defeated at all.

And perhaps episodic memory does more. The kind of knowledge of the past I've said it rarely gives is propositional knowledge. Maybe episodic memory offers something else—non-propositional knowledge of the past. It is a task for tomorrow, however, to figure out just what that is, and how episodic memory yields it.

Acknowledgements

For helpful comments and conversation on a draft of this chapter, I am grateful to Earl Conee, Kevin McCain, Chris McCarroll, Kirk Michaelian, André Sant'Anna, Tom Senor, and an audience at the 2020 Current Controversies in Philosophy of Memory Online Conference.

Notes

1 See Tulving (1985) for influential discussion of the semantic and episodic memory distinction.
2 For criticism, see McCarroll (2017, 2018).

3 Gettier (1963) shows the first three conditions jointly are insufficient for knowledge.

4 It's less obvious whether we satisfy the belief condition for knowledge when not recalling. For discussion, see Frise (2018a).

5 Of course, Feldman's view is not the default, not even in the context of discussing knowledge from episodic memory. For alternative views in this context see, for example, Michaelian (2013). But no view is the default, and it helps to work with some view or other.

6 For more on forgetting, see Frise (2018b).

7 The literature on reconstruction in episodic memory swells. See De Brigard (2014), Michaelian (2011), and Schacter (2001), among others.

8 For amenable accounts of evidential support, see Conee and Feldman (2008), Frise (2018c), and McCain (2014).

9 My argument has to do with how having just a non-trivially false folk theory of episodic memory prevents knowledge from episodic memory alone. If this is right, it might suggest more generally that having just a non-trivially false folk theory of x prevents knowledge from x. And if that is right, we are probably Gettiered far more often that we had realised, since non-trivially false folk theories abound. It's worth exploring, then, whether the scope of knowledge is much smaller than we had supposed. Cf. Hetherington (2011, p. 81), who thinks that a subject whose perceptual belief is based on a folk theory of perception is Gettiered. Hetherington, however, denies that the subject thereby fails to know, and argues that knowing is compatible with being Gettiered. This denial is striking. If it is correct, then my argument in this section may not show that a typical subject who accurately and justifiedly believes what episodic memory delivers lacks knowledge. Rather, my argument may show such a subject is Gettiered. Evaluating Hetherington's denial, however, is beyond the scope of this chapter.

10 For a potential third but rarer route to being Gettiered by episodic memory, see Conee and Feldman (2004, pp. 71–72).

11 Although each condition in Senor's supplement involves reliability, each may involve a different kind, and perhaps none is identical to the kind of process reliabilists claim is essential to justification (for discussion of that kind of reliability, see Frise 2018d). It is unclear, then, which leading non-reliabilist views are incompatible with Senor's supplement.

12 See Goldman (1979) and Feldman (2003). For discussion of the two sufficient conditions in the context of memory, see Frise (2021).

References

Conee, E., & Feldman, R. (2004). *Evidentialism*. Oxford University Press.

Conee, E., & Feldman, R. (2008). Evidence. In Q. Smith (Ed.), *Epistemology: New Essays*. Oxford University Press.

De Brigard, F. (2014). Is memory for remembering? Recollection as a form of episodic hypothetical thinking. *Synthese, 191*(2), 1–31.

Feldman, R. (2003). *Epistemology*. Prentice Hall.

Fernández, J. (2015). What are the benefits of memory distortion? *Consciousness and Cognition, 33*, 536–547.

Frise, M. (2018a). Eliminating the problem of stored beliefs. *American Philosophical Quarterly, 55*(1), 63–79.

Frise, M. (2018b). Forgetting. In K. Michaelian, D. Debus, & D. Perrin (Eds.), *New Directions in the Philosophy of Memory* (pp. 223–240). Routledge.

Frise, M. (2018c). Metacognition as evidence for evidentialism. In K. McCain (Ed.), *Believing in Accordance with the Evidence: New Essays on Evidentialism* (pp. 91–107). Springer.

Frise, M. (2018d). The reliability problem for reliabilism. *Philosophical Studies, 175*(4), 923–945.

Frise, M. (2021). Reliabilism's memory loss. *The Philosophical Quarterly 71* (3), 565–585.

Frise, M. (n.d.). *Remembering trauma in epistemology.* Unpublished manuscript.

Gettier, E. (1963). Is justified true belief knowledge? *Analysis, 23,* 121–123.

Goldman, A. (1979). What is justified belief? In G. Pappas (Ed.), *Justification and Knowledge* (pp. 1–25). D. Reidel.

Hetherington, S. (2011). *How to Know: A Practicalist Conception of Knowledge.* Wiley-Blackwell.

McCain, K. (2014). *Evidentialism and Epistemic Justification.* Routledge.

McCarroll, C. J. (2017). Looking the past in the eye: Distortion in memory and the costs and benefits of recalling from an observer perspective. *Consciousness and Cognition, 49,* 322–332.

McCarroll, C. J. (2018). *Remembering From the Outside: Personal Memory and the Perspectival Mind.* Oxford University Press.

Michaelian, K. (2011). Generative memory. *Philosophical Psychology, 24*(3), 323–342.

Michaelian, K. (2013). The information effect: Constructive memory, testimony, and epistemic luck. *Synthese, 190*(12), 2429–2456.

Michaelian, K. (2016). *Mental Time Travel: Episodic Memory and Our Knowledge of the Personal Past.* MIT Press.

Schacter, D. L. (2001). *The Seven Sins of Memory: How the Mind Forgets and Remembers.* Mariner Books.

Schacter, D. L., Guerin, S. A., & St. Jacques, P. L. (2011). Memory distortion: An adaptive perspective. *Trends in Cognitive Sciences, 15*(10), 467–474.

Senor, T. (2022) (this volume). The epistemology of episodic memory. In A. Sant'Anna, C. J. McCarroll, & K. Michaelian (Eds.), *Current Controversies in Philosophy of Memory.* Routledge.

Simons, D. J., & Chabris, C. F. (2011). What people believe about how memory works: A representative survey of the U.S. population. *PLoS ONE, 6*(8), e22757.

Tulving, E. (1985) Memory and consciousness. *Canadian Psychology, 26,* 1–12.

Further Readings for Part VI

Bernecker, S. (2011). Memory knowledge. In S. Bernecker & D. Pritchard (Eds.), *The Routledge Companion to Epistemology* (pp. 326–334). Routledge.

A beginner-level introduction to the epistemology of memory.

Madison, B. J. C. (2017). Internalism and externalism. In S. Bernecker & K. Michaelian (Eds.), *The Routledge Handbook of Philosophy of Memory* (pp. 283–295). Routledge.

An overview of internalist and externalist approaches to memory knowledge.

Michaelian, K. (2016). *Mental Time Travel: Episodic Memory and Our Knowledge of the Personal Past.* MIT Press.

Argues for a reliabilist/metacognitive account of the epistemology of episodic memory.

Senor, T. D. (2019). *A Critical Introduction to the Epistemology of Memory.* Bloomsbury.

An advanced introduction to the epistemology of memory.

Shanton, K. (2011). Memory, knowledge and epistemic competence. *Review of Philosophy and Psychology*, *2*(1), 89–104.

Argues that memory does not meet externalist standards for knowledge.

Study Questions for Part VI

1) According to Senor, why can't episodic memories (or what he calls 'memory seemings') themselves be objects of epistemic evaluation? Does this mean that there can't be an epistemology of episodic memory?

2) What is the main problem that Senor sees in Michaelian's reliabilist approach? Do his amendments to Michaelian's theory succeed in dealing with this problem?

3) What are Frise's main arguments for the claim that episodic memory beliefs are typically Gettiered? Do these arguments succeed in establishing that episodic memory does not typically give us knowledge of the past?

4) Do 'ordinary' subjects hold the view that episodic memory is an archive? What is the relevance of this question to Frise's proposal?

5) How would a reliabilist who accepts Senor's account of the epistemology of episodic memory respond to the challenges raised by Frise?

Index

accuracy 23, 25–28, 30–32, 39, 48, 62, 67, 72–73, 83, 85, 110–111, 113–114, 116, 117, 119–120, 127–142, 150–160, 231, 234–235, 237–238, 244–256
acquaintance 238
actuality 21, 27, 29, 45–46, 48–49, 151–153, 160, 179–180, 230, 248
adaptivity 149, 151, 155, 167–169, 181
Addis, Donna Rose 19–20, 25, 33, 169–181
Allen, Timothy A. 191, 197–200
Alzheimer's disease 199
amnesia 129, 134, 136
animal memory 189–202, 206–219
archival model 64, 90, 109–110, 230–231, 239–240, 247–249
Aristotle 40, 89
attitude 33–34, 39–40, 48–52, 176
autonoesis 167, 206

behaviourism 65
belief 111, 112, 156, 158–159, 225–241, 244–256
Bennett, M. R. 65
Bernecker, Sven 25, 31, 69, 128, 132, 137, 139–141
Boyle, Alexandria 206, 208–209

causal holism 88–90
causalism, see causal theory of memory
causal theory of memory 19–34, 38–52, 63, 67–72, 76, 82–98, 109–121, 127–142, 162
causal theory of constructive memory 82–98; see also causal theory of memory
causation 62–65, 67–76, 150–151, 154–156, 193, 196, 207, 211, 214–219, 230; appropriate 20, 30–33, 38–41, 45, 48–49, 52, 67, 73, 85, 90, 94, 96, 98,

111, 113, 130–131, 133–135, 141; deviant 25, 30, 32; see also causal theory of memory
classical causal theory of memory, see causal theory of memory
Clayton, Nicola 190, 207–209, 213–214
cognitivism 89; see also connectionism
communication 158–161
computational theory of mind 86; see also connectionism
concept of memory 38–52
conceptual ethics 47
confabulation 26, 109–121, 127–142
connectionism 69–71, 82–98
consolidation 88
constructive episodic simulation hypothesis 157, 166–181
construction 19–34, 39–41, 48, 62, 66, 69, 82–98, 109–110, 112–113, 116, 136, 149, 154–155, 157, 160, 166–170, 173–174, 176–181, 207, 210–211, 213–219, 230–232, 237–238, 251
content 22–23, 26, 39–40, 48–49, 51, 62–76, 82–98, 110–114, 116, 120, 132, 153–156, 158, 160, 176, 206–207, 210–219, 229, 232–237, 244, 249, 253–256; hard problem of 68, 70–72, 74, 76
context-sensitivity 83–85, 87, 89–90, 98
continuism 19–34, 38–52
Craver, Carl 19, 21, 43–44, 50, 197
Csibra, Gergely 195, 208

Dalla Barba, Gianfranco 127–129, 132
De Brigard, Felipe 33, 75, 91, 109–110
default mode network 171–172
defeaters 250–252
Dickinson, Anthony 190, 207–209, 213–214

discontinuism, *see* continuism
Deutscher, Max 25–26, 30–31, 40, 67,
   83–84, 111–112, 130–131, 133
DRM effect 130, 141

embodied memory 83, 93–94
empiricism 64
enactivism 64–67, 75
encoding 22, 23, 28, 40, 75, 86, 88, 91, 95,
   111, 149, 154–155, 191, 211–213, 236
endorsement mechanism 121, 231–232,
   234–238, 253–256
engrams, *see* memory traces
episodic construction system 21, 24, 33,
   41–42, 45–46, 48, 131, 134, 136,
   142, 230
episodic counterfactual thought 21, 25,
   27–30, 41–42, 97, 152, 154, 156, 167,
   169, 175, 215, 230; *see also* mental time
   travel
episodic future thought 19–20, 25,
   27–30, 41–42, 66, 97, 109, 113–114,
   115, 128–129, 131–132, 134, 140–141,
   152, 154, 157–158, 166–181, 230; *see
   also* mental time travel
episodic hypothetical thought 109
episodic-like memory 191–192
epistemic authority 83, 150, 158–161
epistemic vigilance 159
event memory 192–193, 208–211
evolution 150, 160–161, 169, 181,
   200–202, 208, 231
explanationism 109–121, 128, 139–141
extended mind 71

false memory, *see* memory error
falsity, *see* accuracy
Feldman, Richard 246–249
fluency 31–32
Fodor, Jerry 89
forgetting 83, 89, 109, 121, 136, 231, 247
Fortin, Norbert J. 191, 197–200
Frise, Matthew 239–241
function: causal role 150, 167–170, 173,
   181; etiological 150–151, 167–170,
   181; of memory 62, 109–111, 149–161,
   166–181, 193, 195–196, 199, 208,
   247–249, 252, 255; proper 24–25, 41,
   113, 131, 135, 150, 230, 232, 247, 251

generationism, *see* preservationism
gettierization 111, 138–139, 239–240,
   244–256
Goldman, Alvin 237

Hacker, P. M. S. 65
Heil, John 65
hippocampus 72–73, 75, 87, 91, 115,
   167, 191, 193, 195, 197
Hirstein, William 137
Hoerl, Christoph 208
homoeostatic property cluster 192–193;
   see also natural kinds
Hutto, Daniel D. 92

imagery 33, 48, 210
imagination 19–34, 38–52, 66–76, 110,
   128, 151, 156, 166–181, 249;
   attitudinal 33, 47–51; constructive
   20–25, 28–30, 33, 47–52; imagistic 33,
   47–48
inaccuracy, *see* accuracy
information 63–64, 68–76, 86, 90–91
intentionality 40, 51
internality 113–114, 133–134

justification 110, 137, 233, 236, 239–240,
   244–256

Kandel, Eric 68
Keven, Nazım 189, 193, 196
knowledge 43, 110–111, 119, 138, 158,
   232–233, 238–240, 244–256

Langland-Hassan, Peter 47–51
Locke, John 89
"lost in the mall" 134–139, 141–142
luck 137–139, 141–142

Mahr, Johannes B. 166–167, 195, 208
Malanowski, Sara 193, 196–199,
   208–209, 213
Malcolm, Norman 65
malfunction 110, 114, 134–135; *see also*
   proper function
Martin, C. B. 25–26, 30–31, 40, 67,
   83–84, 111–112, 130–131, 133
McCarroll, Chrisopher Jude 32–34
McCormack, Teresa 208
memory: epistemic vs. empirical 43, 47,
   50; occurrent vs. dispositional 88–89
memory error 97, 109–121, 127–142,
   170, 175, 179–181, 231, 250–251; *see
   also* confabulation; misremembering;
   relearning
memory traces 19–34, 40–41, 48–49,
   61–76, 82–98, 109–113, 119–121, 155;
   distributed 27, 69–71, 76, 82–98, 112,
   174; minimal 72–76

memory seemings 228–229, 231, 233, 237
memory system 32, 62, 111, 113, 117, 119–121, 130, 135–136, 167, 194, 208, 211, 244
mental time travel 41–42, 66, 157, 206, 208–209, 230; *see also* episodic future thought; episodic counterfactual thought
metacognition 98, 137, 230–236, 253
Michaelian, Kourken 19, 21, 23–25, 33, 38, 41–42, 48, 69, 84–85, 109–110, 112–116, 227, 229–236, 240, 253–256
minimal trace theory, *see* trace minimalism
misinformation effect 113, 130
misremembering 114, 116, 130–134, 136–139, 141–142
mnemicity 42, 46
Moyal-Sharrock, Danielle 65
Munro, Daniel 49

narrative binding 193, 211, 214
natural kinds 189–202
navigation 169, 219
network: associationist 173–176; connectionist 70–71, 82–98, 112
normativity 39, 46, 51–52, 98, 137
nontransmissionism, *see* transmissionism

O'Brien, Gerard 69–71

particularity 40, 62, 67, 69, 72–73, 95–96, 110, 113, 151–155, 158, 161, 167, 174, 179–180, 212–213, 228, 256
pastness 151–155
perception 22–24, 31, 40, 72, 228–229, 233, 250
Perrin, Denis 19, 23, 38, 41, 70
personal past 21, 24–27, 29–30, 42, 45, 47, 61, 83, 89, 109, 127–128, 131–132, 135, 152, 172, 228, 230
phenomenology 38, 50, 152, 176, 228, 233
Plato 64
postcausalism 62, 75
predictive processing 72, 74–75
preservationism 64, 68, 110–113, 158, 160–161; *see also* transmissionism
previous awareness, *see* previous experience
previous experience 39, 45–46, 66, 153
procedural memory 61, 238
prompting 26, 111–112, 114, 117, 120

rats 191, 193, 199
reconsolidation, *see* consolidation
reconstruction, *see* construction
relearning 25, 27, 30, 83, 90, 94, 97, 111, 114, 116, 120, 130–136, 141
reliability 33, 41–42, 45–46, 48, 64, 67, 69, 72–74, 110–111, 113–116, 131–133, 137–139, 141, 154–155, 156, 158–159, 170, 230–232, 235–237, 240, 253–255
reliabilist epistemology 137–139, 232, 236–237, 239, 253–256
reliabilist theory of memory, *see* simulation theory of memory
representation 62–64, 67, 69–71, 73–76, 84–96; quasi-sensory 228–229, 234–237, 254
retrieval 26, 28–29, 40, 62, 75, 86–88, 90–92, 95–96, 110–112, 118, 130, 137–138, 149, 153–155, 157, 167, 173, 177–178, 189–190, 207, 211–212, 219, 231, 247
Robins, Sarah K. 27, 49–50, 61, 64, 69–70, 95, 112, 129–131, 133–134, 151–153, 157

Sant'Anna, André 32–34
Schirmer dos Santos, César 32–34
Schwartz, Arieh 150
scenario construction 74
scrub jays 190–191, 207–209, 213–214
semantic memory 61, 109, 155, 158, 179, 189, 191, 206, 213, 227, 232–234, 238, 244–245, 256
Senor, Thomas D. 245, 252–256
simulationism, *see* simulation theory of memory
simulation theory of memory 19, 23–24, 33–34, 38–52, 51, 65–66, 76, 109–110, 113–116, 120–121, 127–128, 131–133, 137–139, 141–142, 157–158, 161, 230–236; *see also* virtue theory of memory
source monitoring 113, 158–159
Sosa, Ernest 139
St. Augustine 64
storage 22, 23, 26, 28–29, 40–41, 48, 62, 65, 67–71, 74, 76, 86, 89–91, 109, 111–113, 130, 149, 155, 157, 167, 169, 173, 177, 189, 230–231, 247; superpositional 69–71, 84, 86, 88–91, 95
successful remembering 22–24, 26–27, 29–30, 33, 41, 49, 61–62, 89, 127–142

suggestibility 30, 112, 114, 117–118, 120, 134
Sutton, John 69–72, 112

terminology, *see* verbal dispute
testimony 27, 96–97; eyewitness 159–160, 180, 195
Theaetetus 64
theory of memory: causal, *see* causal theory of memory; constructive causal, *see* causal theory of constructive memory; minimal trace, *see* trace minimalism; simulation, *see* simulation theory of memory; virtue, *see* virtue theory of memory
time: metaphysics of 129; subjective 41
trace minimalism 63, 72–76; *see also* causal theory of memory
transmissionism 22, 63, 66, 75–76, 90–97; *see also* preservationism

truth, *see* accuracy
Tulving, Endel 149, 207, 230
type 1 vs. type 2 process 231–232

unsuccessful remembering, *see* successful remembering

Van Leeuwen, Neil 21
verbal dispute 39, 42, 44, 46, 50, 198–199, 201, 209
virtue epistemology 138
virtue theory of memory 114, 128, 139–142; *see also* simulation theory of memory

Werning, Markus 63, 72–75
what-where-when memory 190–191, 207
Wittgenstein, Ludwig 75
WWW memory, *see* what-where-when memory